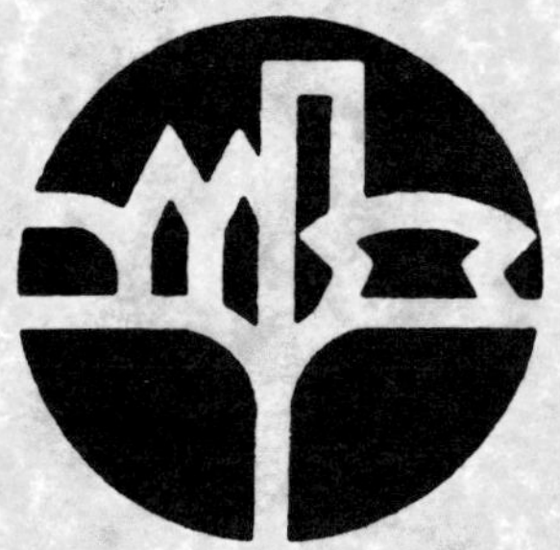

Salt Lake Area Chamber of Commerce

September 29, 1995

Dear ACCE Member:

On behalf of the Salt Lake Area Chamber of Commerce and Meridian International, welcome to ACCE's 1995 Annual Leadership Conference. We are honored that you have chosen to spend time with us here in Salt Lake City.

We are delighted to have you in our beautiful city. We are justifiably proud of its beauty, its history, its culture and its charm. We invite you to take full advantage of the many activities that Salt Lake City offers while you are here.

If we can be of service to you during your stay in Salt Lake City, please let us know. We would be happy to help in any way possible to make your visit unforgettable.

Please accept this beautiful book, *Utah, State of the Arts*, which was commissioned by the Chamber and published by Meridian International, as our gift to you. Utah is well-known as an oasis for the arts in the west. Many different art forms are represented in these pages. Please enjoy the book with our compliments.

Best wishes,

Fred S. Ball, CCE
President and CEO
Salt Lake Area Chamber of Commerce

UTAH
STATE
OF THE
ARTS

UTAH
STATE
OF THE
ARTS

WRITTEN BY
AN ASSEMBLY OF EXPERTS

DESIGNED BY
**THE WELLER
INSTITUTE FOR THE CURE
OF DESIGN**

PUBLISHED BY
**MERIDIAN
INTERNATIONAL, INC.**

Published by
Meridian International, Inc.
1720 Washington Boulevard
P.O. Box 10010
Ogden, UT 84409
801-394-9446

For Meridian International, Inc.—
Mike Hillis, President and CEO
Bart Barica, Vice President
 of Community Publications
Ellis Child, Vice President of Finance
Steve Furner, Vice President of Production
Douglas Hatch, Vice President of
 International Sales and Marketing
Caroll Shreeve, Vice President
 of Publishing
Thomas E. Berry
Margaret Shields Marti

For the Salt Lake Area
Chamber of Commerce—
Fred S. Ball, CCE and President
Verl Topham, Chair of
 Board of Governors
Alison Barnett

Trudy McMurrin, Editor

Book design by Don & Chikako Weller,
The Weller Institute for the Cure of
Design, Park City, UT

Cover photograph of Nancy Holt's
Sun Tunnels by Shayne Christiansen,
Logan, UT

Printed in the USA by Meridian
International, Ogden, UT

ISBN: 0-9635-893-2-6

Library of Congress Cataloging-in-
Publication Data

As Meridian International approaches its 50th year when Utah celebrates its centennial in 1996, it has been our privilege to capture in print the state of the fine arts in Utah. The satisfying results of intensive work on the part of many talented individuals during the past year has come to fruition in the beautiful hard-bound volume you hold in your hand—a tribute to Utah's artists and supporters and a promise of all the beauty that is yet to be.

Utah, State of the Arts refers to our legacy, but emphasizes the current scene from the traditional to the *avant-garde* in the performing, literary and visual arts. It is a taste only, but one that is full of the flavor of Utah. A flavor that has urged so many of us, like so many others from pioneer times to the present, to make Utah our home.

There was room in this book only to express the essence of each fine arts discipline, although we are fortunate that the sheer volume of what is going on in Utah is enough to create many books. To all of the artists, performers, authors and contributors, I add my personal thanks for the world-class results of a tremendous undertaking.

Meridian is proud to present *Utah, State of the Arts* for your reading enjoyment. We hope you'll share it with the enthusiasm with which it was created and from which it springs. It is not a summation of the arts, but a colorful glimpse—a glimpse that holds a little something for everyone of every age and persuasion who wants to explore the cultural frontier of our fine state.

Mike Hillis
President and CEO
Meridian International, Inc.

Collaborative labors of love and grit have accomplished a fresh assessment of the state of fine arts in Utah. The ambitious task of sampling Utah's visual, literary and performing arts has been nothing short of an electrifying experience. Because *Utah, State of the Arts* is a visual statement in and of itself, the Wellers and I worked closely on shaping the text to harmoniously fit the flow and rhythm of their book design. Final editing, additions and deletions were mine in creating a balanced whole.

Perhaps the most satisfying realization about *Utah, State of the Arts* is knowing that collectively we have only scraped the surface of the plethora of fine arts activity going on here. The wellspring touched upon flows with cultural opportunities for our own citizens and for visitors to Utah who are eager to experience them.

Caroll Shreeve
Vice President of Publishing
Meridian International, Inc.

The arts
of Utah
C O M I N G
of age
at last.

I have wanted to write this introduction for a long time. Indeed, for some twenty-five years have I been happily living and working in this place. So what is it? Without unduly prolonging the suspense, it is no doubt *Utah, State of the Arts* that I find so impressive and enchanting.

You scoff? Certainly you do. It is our way in Utah. To think positive thoughts about the cultural climate of Utah was for many years not really acceptable. Even today it is a dangerous activity to be pursued with great reserve and couched in terms of the peculiar Utah culture that is only now "coming of age" in certain ways.

The key question has always been: Why are most of us here in Utah? The answer is: We are here because we like it here. The lifestyle is basically what we want, and what we want is everything good about big cities, small towns and no towns—all at once. Utah gives us almost exactly that in many aspects of our lives, including the Arts.

It has been my belief that, almost from the beginning, this place has attracted, produced and included in its tiny population numerous very sophisticated artists with great talents, skills and ideas who have, one way or another earned livings; dreamed dreams and realized some of those dreams; exhibited their works and found both public and private buyers for them; been frustrated, but often also content; taught interested and interesting students; and, in general, found substantial and rather lively interest in their own varied thoughts and creations right here in Utah!

Our forebears knew that the creation and appreciation of the fine arts— painting, drawing, architecture and sculpture; and sometimes poetry, music, dancing and dramatic art—constitute the sum of what is timeless.

Perhaps eight or even nine hundred years ago, as great German and French Romanesque cathedrals rose in post-millennial celebration, ancient artists far to the west practiced a mysterious and monumental form of magic on live rock walls, this amidst some of the harshest and most beautiful country upon the face of the earth. Their images pecked or painted on stone, created remote integrations of design and nature so perfect in many instances as to provoke comparison today with the works of some of the most profound artists of known places and times.

Historians come around every so often to tell the rest of the people that they are part of an era, a period, a curve or cycle, or a paradigm (may the gods help us!); and that "it" has all happened before, sort of—and that sort of thing can be both shocking and boring all at once. That is why people always think a "dearth" happened before they came along.

The Arts of Utah. They are young and vital and they are just now coming of age—just as they always have.

Dr. Robert S. Olpin

Utah, State of the Arts is a symbol of the celebration of excellence in Utah's Fine Arts—today.

—The arts advisory committee for the Salt Lake Area Chamber of Commerce and Meridian International.

TABLE OF CONTENTS

"**ART** ... the use of skill and imagination in the production of things of beauty." That definition certainly describes this book. Many people have used skills or study to produce an exciting and useful volume of great beauty. **IN** the State of Utah, we are fortunate to bask in the handiwork and skills of very talented people. Art comes in many forms. It can be oil on canvas, words on paper, graceful motions to music, beautiful sounds from instruments, emotions on a stage that propel us to make-believe or reality, all transformed into something of beauty. As individualistic as art is for Utah artists and citizens, true art surrounds all of us in great abundance. **THE** Salt Lake Area Chamber of Commerce is proud to proclaim that, indeed, Utah is an oasis for the arts in the West. Art can give momentary retreat from a society raging with reason, frothing and foaming with discord and disharmony, rendered almost obscene by problems that confront us. Art can momentarily and magically transport us into worlds of beauty, contentment and tranquility and can make each of us a true humanist. **WE** are a community that has long embraced the arts. The profusion of Utah art which defines and enhances our lifestyle is created within a culture that nurtures, supports, celebrates and honors all art. It is through the generous giving of many Utah philanthropists that art and artists have flourished since the earliest days of Utah's history. Their humanitarian efforts allow each of us to revel in every art form and creative endeavor imaginable. **AS** a chamber of commerce we have not only supported but have also been creative partners in the arts. To recognize the individuals who have created and contributed so much to transform the world around us, the Salt Lake Area Chamber of Commerce initiated the annual Honors in the Arts awards in 1981. Fifty-seven artists and five area businesses have been honored over the years. They represent all disciplines of art, from painting, dance and music to filmmaking, crafts and literary works. **A** permanent collection of Honors in the Arts portraits, by Utah photographer Don Busath, graces the corridors of Abravanel Hall, and a duplicate exhibition is on permanent public display at the Chamber offices. **MANY** Honors in the Arts award recipients are featured in this book. With the abundance of new and invigorating art now being created in Utah by the artists highlighted in this text, it is certain that future Honors in the Arts recipients will come from the pages of *Utah, State of the Arts*. **UTAH** is a wonderful place! Much of what makes it so wonderful is displayed, illustrated and spoken of in this volume. We are indeed a **STATE OF THE ARTS**.

FRED S. BALL, CCE

President

Salt Lake Area Chamber of Commerce

This book is made possible through the generous donations of the following participants:

Founders

Bank One
Utah, N.A.

Bonneville
International
Corporation

Edutek
Corporation

First Interstate
Bank of
Utah, N.A.

First Security Bank,
Mortgage Loan
Division

First Security
Bank of Utah

First Security
Corporation

First Security
Insurance, Inc.

First Security
Investor
Services, Inc.

First Security
Leasing
Company

Holy Cross
Health Services
of Utah

Key Bank
of Utah

Lagoon

Novell, Inc.

Petro Supply
and Design

Questar
Corporation

Red Lion
Hotel

Salt Lake
Community
College

Sinclair
Oil Corporation
and Little
America Hotel
and Towers

Theratech, Inc.

Benefactors

Abbott Critical
Care Systems

Fidelity Investments

Fleming Companies, Inc.

Franklin Quest Company

Kemper Securities
Group, Inc.

Sweet Candy Company

Utah Power

Patrons

Christopherson Travel

Gump and Ayers
Real Estate, Inc.

Morton International

Quaker State Minit-Lube

R.C. Willey
Home Furnishings

Salt Lake City
Corporation

USPCI-A Subsidiary
of Union Pacific
Corporation

Utah Scientific, Inc.

ZCMI Corporate Office

Friends

Air Group Express, Inc.

Amalgamated
Sugar Company

American Express

Anderson and Watkins

Associated Title
Company

Big-D Construction

Blue Cross Blue
Shield of Utah

Celia Nash

Chapman Richards
and Associates

Deloitte and Touche

Deseret News

Eckhoff, Watson and
Preator Engineering

EIMCO Process
Equipment Company

Evans Group

Evans and Early

F.H.P. Health Care

Factor One
Funding Resources

Fast Signs
Carl Creer

GMX Corporation

Grant Thornton

Harris and Love, Inc.

Intermountain
Health Care

International Business
Machine

KPMG Peat Marwick

KUER FM 90

Mark Miller Toyota

MCI
Telecommunications
Corporation

NESCO Service
Company

Nielsen Valve and
Supply, Inc.

Northwest Pipeline
Corporation

Nu Skin International

P.S.I. Peripheral
Systems, Inc.

Parsons Behle & Latimer

Pepperidge Farm

Price Development
Company

Price Waterhouse

Raffi Daghlian

Ray, Quinney & Nebeker

Reed L. Hold, D.D.S.,
Steve H. Lazar D.M.D.

Reuel's Art and Frame

Rollins Hudig Hall
of Utah, Inc.

Rust Rare Coin

Salt Lake City Magazine

Salt Lake Convention
and Visitors Bureau

Scott Machinery
Company

Space Agency, Inc.

Stevens Wood, Inc.

Surety Life
Insurance Company

Syro Steel Company
Western Division

United Healthcare
of Utah

University Park
Hotel and Suites

US WEST
Communications, Inc.

Utah Jazz

Valentiner, Crane,
Brunjes, Onyon
Architects

Wheeler Machinery
Company

CONTRIBUTORS' BIOGRAPHIES

Carol Biddle: *Crafts, New Genres*
Biddle is the development coordinator for the Ogden Nature Center and former development coordinator for the Salt Lake Art Center. She is a board member of the Contemporary Arts Group and a juror for the Park City Arts Festival. She was vice-president and chairman of the development committee for Lallapalooza and has curated and installed exhibitions at the Chase Home Museum. Biddle holds an M.F.A. in arts administration from the University of Utah, a B.F.A. and B.A. from Indiana State University.

Herschel Bullen: *Jazz*
Bullen enjoys unusual dual careers in law and music. Self-taught as a musician, he began playing the saxophone at age eight and quickly became a local legend, playing professionally from the eighth grade on. He put himself through college and law school (B.S. and J.D., University of Utah) playing saxophone, clarinet and flute in local bands. While still a law student, Bullen spent about a year on the road with Woody Herman's band, also backing Tony Bennett and Dionne Warwick in Las Vegas shows. Bullen has played with pop and jazz artists Louis Bellson, Monk Montgomery, Gene Harris, Mel Torme, Natalie Cole, Bill Watrous and Doc Severinson. Additionally, he has worked the Telluride Jazz Festival, played with the Utah Symphony and taught clinics throughout the West.

He has recently recorded an album with a regional quartet under the working title of *Utah Jazz.*

Carol Edison: *Folk & Ethnic Arts*
As a folklorist for the Utah Arts Council since 1978, Edison has conducted fieldwork with traditional and ethnic artists throughout Utah and produced exhibits ranging from Native American crafts and traditional ethnic arts to the art forms that preserve Utah's Anglo-pioneer heritage. She has also produced numerous concerts, festivals and publications featuring Utah folk art and artists. Since 1986 she has directed public programs at the Chase Home Museum of Utah Folk Art. Edison has written and lectured widely about Utah folk art and is the author of *Cowboy Poetry from Utah: An Anthology.* She has also researched, written and lectured extensively on Utah gravestone art and is currently writing a book on that subject. Her most recent project, *Hecho en Utah (Made in Utah),* included an exhibit, concert series, radio broadcasts, seminar studio recordings and a bilingual booklet on the cultural history of Utah's Hispanic communities. A native of Utah, Edison holds an M.A. from the University of Utah.

Mary Francey: *Painting & Printmaking*
As a specialist in modern and contemporary art history and criticism, Francey serves as associate professor of art history and associate dean of the College of Fine Arts at the University of Utah. She recently curated the exhibitions and wrote catalogs for *Depression Printmakers as Workers: Re-defining Traditional Interpretations* and *American Women at Work.* She was a publisher's reviewer of the modern and contemporary section of the ninth edition of *Gardner's Art Through the Ages* and is a consultant with the Educational Testing Service of Princeton, N.J., to develop advanced placement classes in art history for secondary schools.

Robert K. Herman: *Architecture & Landscape Design*
Herman is vice-president of Sanders Herman Architects and principal-in-charge of design and planning. He is involved in the design of the Downtown Conference and Performing Arts Center in Ogden, the Ogden Regional Sports Complex and, recently, the Weber State University Alumni Center. Having a B.A. (summa cum laude) and M.A. from the University of Utah, Herman is president of the AIA of Northern Utah and an executive committee member of the Utah Society of the American Institute of Architects. He is past chair of the Ogden Arts Commission and is currently chair of the Weber State University Department of Visual Arts Advisory Board. In both 1991 and 1992 he was an invited juror for the University of Utah Graduate School of Architecture.

Edward Lueders: *Literary Arts*
During his twenty-six years at the University of Utah, Lueders, Professor of English Emeritus, served as chair of the Department of English, director of its creative writing program and editor of *Western Humanities Review.* Since retiring, he teaches writing on the summer faculty of the Bread Loaf School of English in Vermont. Instrumental in establishing the Poetry in the Schools movement throughout Utah during the 1960's, he has been a participant in its programs since. As an author, essayist, poet and reviewer, Lueders' writing has appeared in publications such as *The New Republic, Smithsonian, Poetry, The Southern Review, Theology Today* and *The Salt Lake Tribune.* Best known among his eleven books are *The Clam Lake Papers, The Wake of the General Bliss* and a collaboration with the Japanese poet Naoshi Koriyama, *The Poets of Contemporary Japan.*

Trudy A. McMurrin: *Editor*
McMurrin has edited and published scholarly books since 1965, the most recent of which include *Abravanel!* by Lowell M. Durham, Sr., *The Hogles* by Gerald McDonough, and *Medicine in the Beehive State, 1940-1990* with Dr. Henry Plenk. She edited the first eight volumes of *The Tanner Lectures on Human Values* and produced a fine-print edition of *A History of the Early Years* for the Tanner Lecture Trustees. Additionally, she edits the annual *Westminster Tanner-McMurrin Lectures on the History and Philosophy of Religion* and is currently completing a book about Paul Walton, the Utah exploration geologist who discovered the Wafra oil field in Saudi Arabia in 1949. McMurrin is the owner of Dancing Badger Enterprises, is active in professional writing associations and advises university and commercial publications.

Nancy Melich: *Theater Arts*
Melich is the theater critic and reporter for the *Salt Lake Tribune* and a correspondent for the *Wall Street Journal*. She has contributed her theater expertise at theater festivals and critic's conferences in the United States. She is a founding member of the Playwriters' Lab of the Sundance Institute. She spent a year at Stanford as a John S. Knight Fellow and currently serves as a member of the Executive Committee of the American Theater Critics Association. Melich was born and reared in the red rock country of Moab, Utah. Her claim to fame is having appeared as a child in the John Ford western *Rio Grande*, starring John Wayne and Maureen O'Hara.

Robert S. Olpin: *Opening essay*
Dean of the College of Fine Arts at the University of Utah where he also did his undergraduate study, Olpin is consulting curator of American art for the Utah Museum of Fine Arts. Olpin earned his M.A. and Ph.D. from Boston University, doing his research in 19th and early 20th century American art. He has edited and written numerous books and catalogs, the most recent of which are *The Arts at Land-Grant Institutions in the Nineties and Beyond* and the *Dictionary of Art*.

Steven W. Rosen: *Sculpture*
Rosen is director/chief curator of the Nora Eccles Harrison Museum of Art at Utah State University. Formerly, he was chief curator at the Columbus Museum of Art and an assistant professor of art and director/chief curator at Denison University. Rosen was principal investigator at Sirmium Excavation in Yugoslavia, a Smithsonian fellow in Sirmium-Bonona Excavations, administrator for the S.H. Kress-sponsored Ohio Consortium in art history and consulting director for the business collection at EXPO '70 in Montreal.

Dorothy Stowe: *Opera, Dance*
Stowe has been the dance and vocal music critic for Salt Lake City's *Deseret News* since 1978. Before that she reviewed for the *Hartford Times*. She is the Utah correspondent for *Opera News* and *Dance*, a freelance writer and frequent adjudicator. Trained as a singer, she holds a B.A. and M.A. in music from Brigham Young University.

Sharon Lee Swenson:
Film & Video
Swenson is assistant professor in the Department of Theater and Film at Brigham Young University where she administers the film program. She is a graduate of the University of Utah and is presently finishing her dissertation in film and video. Swenson has written for numerous academic projects, for *Utah Holiday*, network and *The Salt Lake Tribune*.

John Telford: *Photography*
For twenty-five years John Telford has garnered praise from national and international appreciators of his award-winning photography in both commercial and fine arts arenas. In 1979, his *Great Salt Lake Portfolio* with foreword by Wallace Stegner was published. Recently, *Coyote's Canyon* with text by Terry Tempest Williams and Telford's photos was enthusiastically received. Telford has been assistant professor of design, teaching photography at Brigham Young University for two years. Previously he was director of photographic services at the University of Utah. Telford's photography is available on books, calendars, posters and greeting cards.

Edgar J. Thompson:
Choral Music
Thompson, conductor of the University of Utah A Cappella Choir and chairman of the Department of Music, was appointed music director of the Utah Symphony Chorus in 1982. With a B.A. and M.A. in physics and mathematics from Brigham Young University, he earned an M.F.A. in music from California State University/Long Beach and a Ph.D. in choral music education at the University of Utah. Thompson has studied under choral directors Newell B. Weight, Bernell W. Hales, Frank Pooler, Eric Brickson and Norman Luboff. He has conducted honor choirs all over the United States.

Janet Travis: *Calligrapher*
Travis has earned a living as a freelance artist in Dallas, Texas, since 1972. She specializes in calligraphy and has taught workshops in eight major Texas cities. Though born in Baltimore, she has acquired a Texas drawl through many years of practice. She occasionally exhibits her paintings of original rambling thoughts on water, chaos and dreams.

Don & Cha Cha Weller:
Designers
The Weller Instittue for the Cure of Design, Inc., is a Park City firm serving graphic design clients nationwide. After 15 years in Los Angeles, the firm moved to Utah in 1984. Their work has often been honored, and among the awards are gold medals from the Society of Illustrators from both New York and Los Angeles. They have published three books: *Park City* and *Seashells and Sunsets* were both acclaimed by the American Institute of Graphic Arts, and *The Cutting Horse*, written and photographed by Don. He has illustrated numerous books, including *Phantom of the Opera* for children, plus hundreds of magazine articles.

Paul Wetzel: *Symphony & Chamber Music*
As a former classical music critic and now editorial writer for *The Salt Lake Tribune*, Wetzel has been intimately involved with the music community in Utah. A student of piano himself, he has followed Utah Symphony concerts and orchestra and choral events since his teens. Wetzel's enthusiasm for Utah's musical heritage and future spring from his family and community; his mother holds a music degree and his grandfather was a professional musician. His degree in journalism is from the University of Utah.

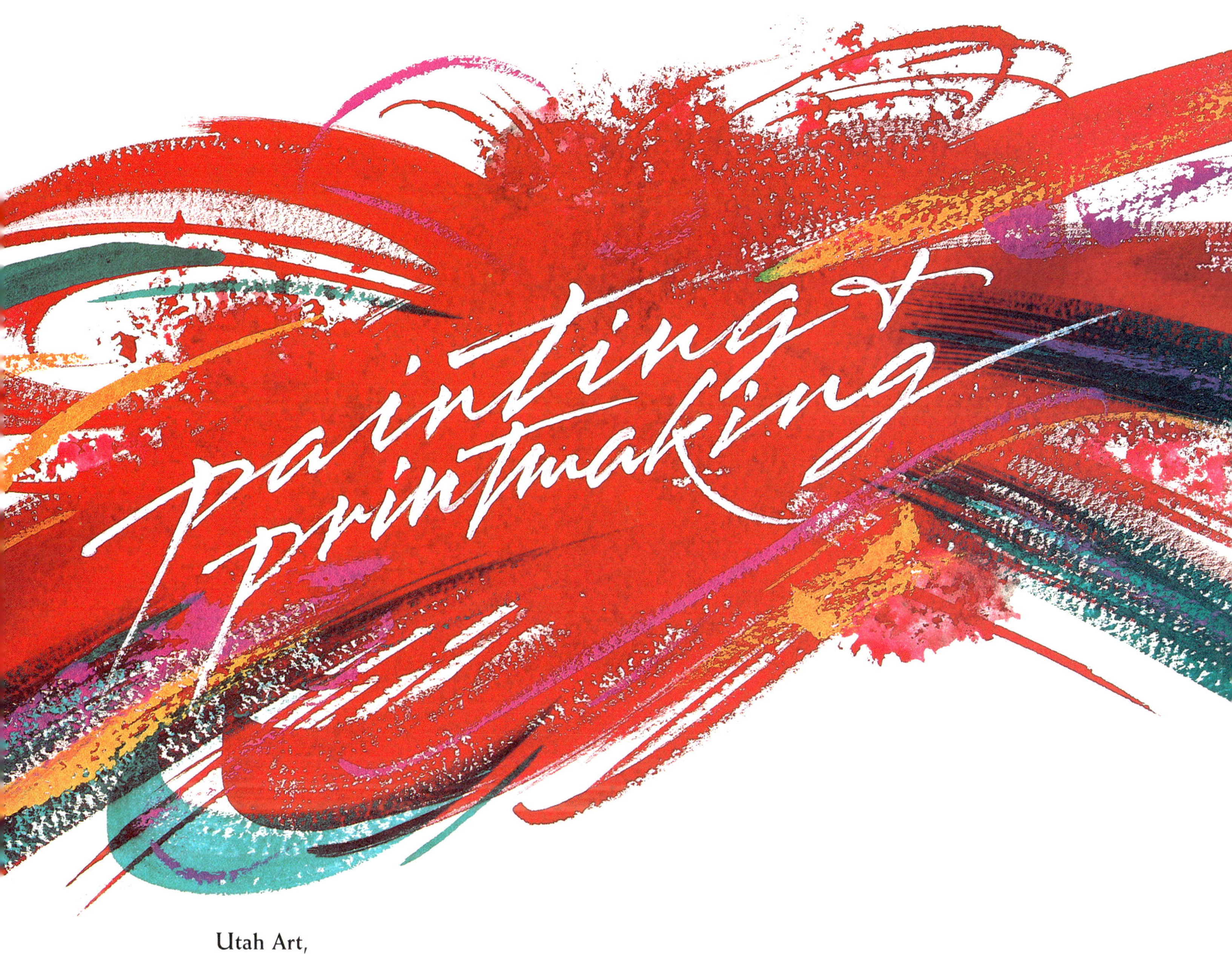

Utah Art, Toward A New Century

Mary Francey

Artists have always made, and always will make, valuable contributions to the quality of life in the communities in which they work; contemporary Utah artists are no exception. By investigating current processes that are intended to function outside galleries and museums, artists effect cultural change by constantly challenging and expanding our conventional definitions of art. Because new forms are not readily accepted, and because we actively resist change, contemporary art is nearly always controversial. Modern and contemporary art aggravates in that, for most of this century, it has

V. DOUGLAS SNOW

A native of Utah, V. Douglas Snow earned a Master of Fine Arts from the Cranbrook Academy of Art, after which he spent a year in Rome on a Fulbright grant. Although he deservedly is given most of the credit for introducing Late Modern movements to Utah, he asserts that he was, and is, "willing to take the risk of getting away from mainstream movements." Artists like Snow make significant contributions because they do not hesitate to take risks. In addition, Snow speaks of a transcendent feeling in his work that derives directly from the sweeping power and delicate infinity of the redrock country where he lives.

insistently denied us the representational pictorial image that affirms our own perception of the visible world. We want a window to the world we think we see and are uncomfortable when artists compel us to think about aspects of our society we would rather ignore or deny. Because they confront society with current social, environmental, and political issues, contemporary artists are important forces in the shaping of a cultural awareness that will lead us into the next century.

But artists are not social workers. They raise our social consciousness by emphasizing process over product. Product, the painting or sculpture that is intended to be a marketable commodity, is a relic of an earlier time. Today we value the concept illuminated for us by the artist who explores processes in which we are often involved as participants and contributors rather than spectators only.

Abstract Expressionism emerged from the complex social, psychological and political climate of the Post-War, Cold War period. It dominated the visual arts during the 1950's and sixties because the familiar forms of Early Modern European and American art did not adequately express the moral, social and political conditions of the time. Abstract Expressionism seemed to abruptly, and too abruptly, abandon the world of appearances, causing a puzzled public to wonder why art could no longer be simply a comfortable, recognizable represension of a familiar subject. The American viewing public wanted art to equate with moral excellence and the *uplifting* beauty of the American landscape. *Time's* acerbic art critic Robert Hughes asserted that, for the American audience, art was in nature, not in culture, which in most of the country was decidedly impoverished. American art and architecture could not compete with the European expressions rooted in a centuries-old classical tradition.

Post-World War II pictorial abstraction required yet another level of understanding. While it seemed to the public that *abstract art* required no training or experience, that any three-year-old child could do the same or better, a different message came from the world of *high art*. Critics and agents pompously declared that the incomprehensible images of Abstract Expressionism were *avant-garde*. Avant-garde, by definition, is not public art; its elitism excludes the majority of viewers, most of whom are intractably *rear guard*.

Curiously, given the state's firmly established and cherished resistance to change, Utah artists did not hesitate to replace earlier regionalist and social-realist pictorial efforts of the 1930's with current, innovative pictorial expressions.

Abstractions, expressive distortions and arbitrary color characterize the work of V. Douglas Snow of Torrey,

Utah. After his studies at the Cranbrook Academy of Art in Michigan and the Academy of Fine Arts in Rome, Snow imported a contemporary pictorial vision to Utah. Fortunately, although perhaps surprisingly, he received understanding and support from Alvin Gittins, the University of Utah's resident academician and portraitist. Although Gittins would not, could not and did not work in a non-representational style, he wholeheartedly defended artists who did and affirmed the rights of all artists to paint whatever subject, or non-subject, they chose.

The Gittins legacy lives on in Paul Davis' figures placed in implausible environments and Anton Rasmussen's powerful Utah landscapes that imply human presence. Susan Fleming, John Erickson, David Dornan, Diana Garff-Gardiner, Steve Fawson, Linda Barnes, Denis Phillips, Margaret Wadsworth-Morrison, Shauna Cook-Klinger, Carolyn Coalson and Frank Anthony (Tony) Smith, along with others too numerous to name here, must be included in any group claiming figurative pictorial roots.

Lee Deffebach aligned with the best and brightest of the second generation of the New York School. Developing a technique similar to that of Kenneth Noland, Morris Louis and Helen Frankenthaler, Deffebach applied paint in thin washes, staining the canvas with glowing tones that melted and mingled with each other to create lyrical improvisations that evidenced her distinctively Western American aesthetic. A June 1993 retrospective exhibition of

Deffebach's work summarized her remarkably consistent development from an abstract expressionist approach to today's strong visual statements that emerge from episodes and experiences in her life.

These and many other innovative contemporary artists were noticed and acclaimed in the prose of Utah's durable art critic George Dibble, whose column for the *The Salt Lake Tribune* first appeared in 1953 and continued weekly for nearly forty years. Dibble did substantially more than merely review artists' exhibitions. His critical judgments were based on a thorough understanding of aesthetic

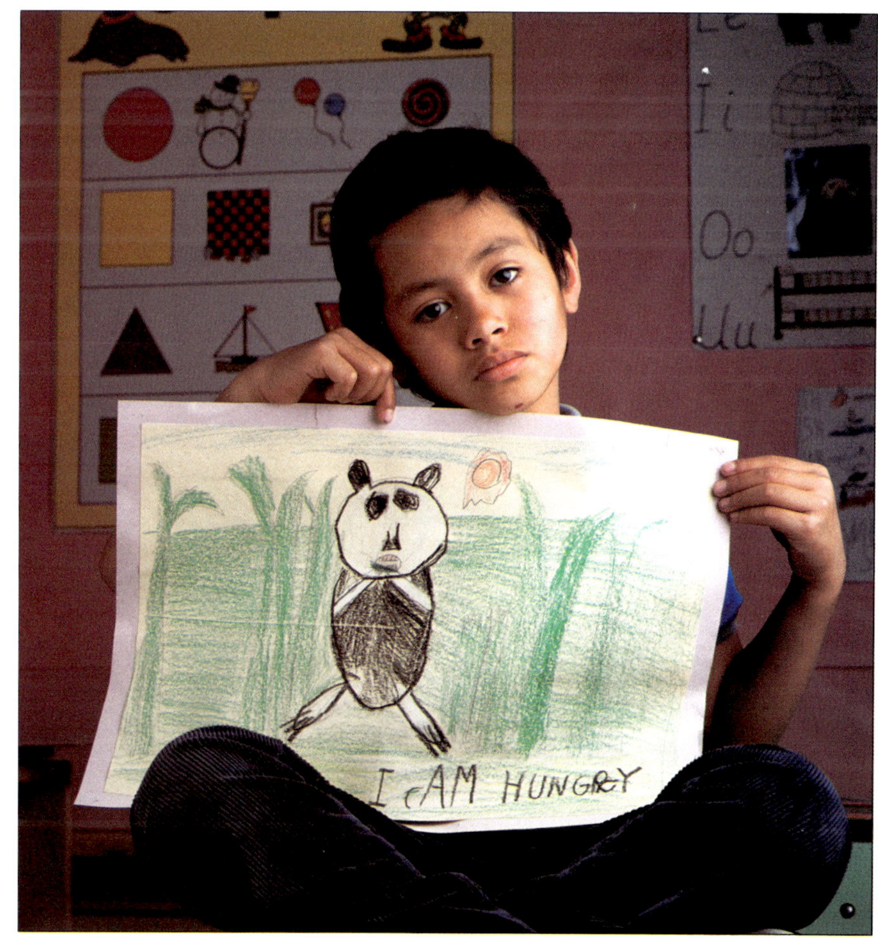

PAINTING BY ELDEN PEO / PHOTO BY STEPHEN SMITH

Printmakers,
muralists and
painters
contribute a
P R O F U S I O N
of contemporary
expression.

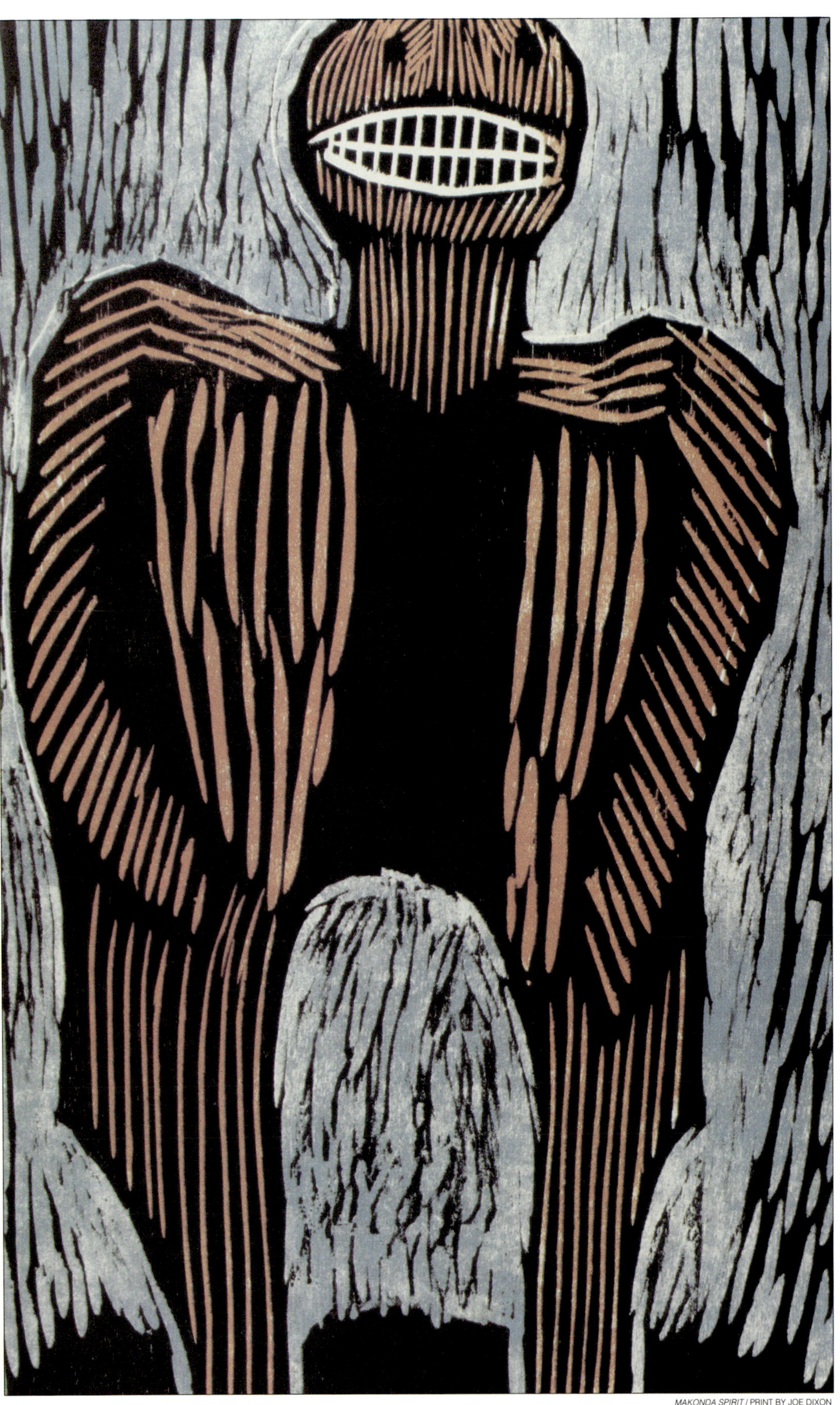

MAKONDA SPIRIT / PRINT BY JOE DIXON

philosophy and art history. He must be credited with focusing positive attention on changing directions in the visual arts by offering clarifications and reassuring explanations of the new generation of process-oriented artists. He deftly but gently interpreted the new visual language for the benefit of a reading and viewing public bewildered by the sudden profusion of non-literal expressions.

In Utah, as elsewhere in the country, the challenge for the American printmaker in the 1930's was in the search for unique and individual expressions relevant to current circumstances that could be apprehended and appreciated by the public. Much of the work was government sponsored and intended for placement in public buildings. Printmakers not only met the challenge, they were responsible for developing innovative procedures that led directly to radical and influential changes in print and paint vocabulary. Printmakers were enticed into the realm of color by color lithography and screen printing, both of which were explored in graphic arts workshops of the Federal Art Project located in each region of the country. Effects directly attributable to color processes developed by screen-print pioneers are seen in work by such major figures as Josef Albers, Andy Warhol and Robert Rauschenberg.

Anna Campbell Bliss, who worked with Albers at Yale, now combines screen-print methods with computer technology to create micro and macro views. Her grasp of contemporary technology brings her art into the new scientific world of dynamical systems and fractals. Bliss' mural *Windows*, permanently installed in the Data Processing Center in the State Office Building of the Utah State Capitol, is a contemporary document that connects Federal Art Project murals in public buildings with current definitions of public art.

More conventional print processes

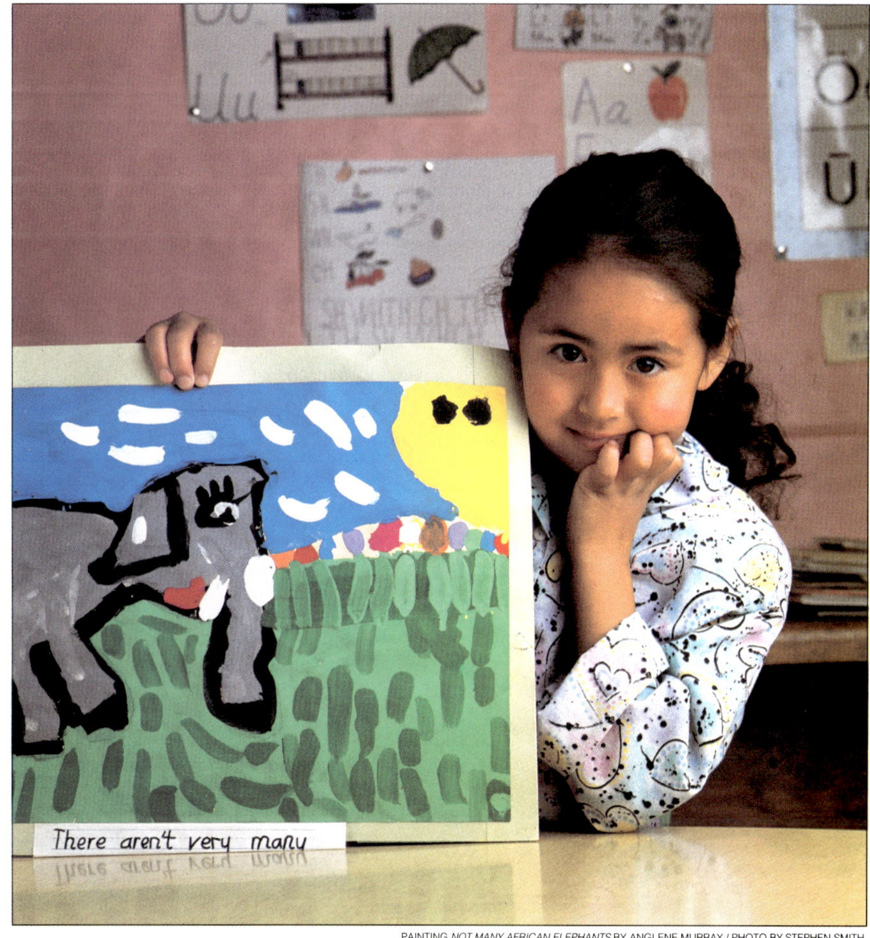

PAINTING *NOT MANY AFRICAN ELEPHANTS* BY ANGLENE MURRAY / PHOTO BY STEPHEN SMITH

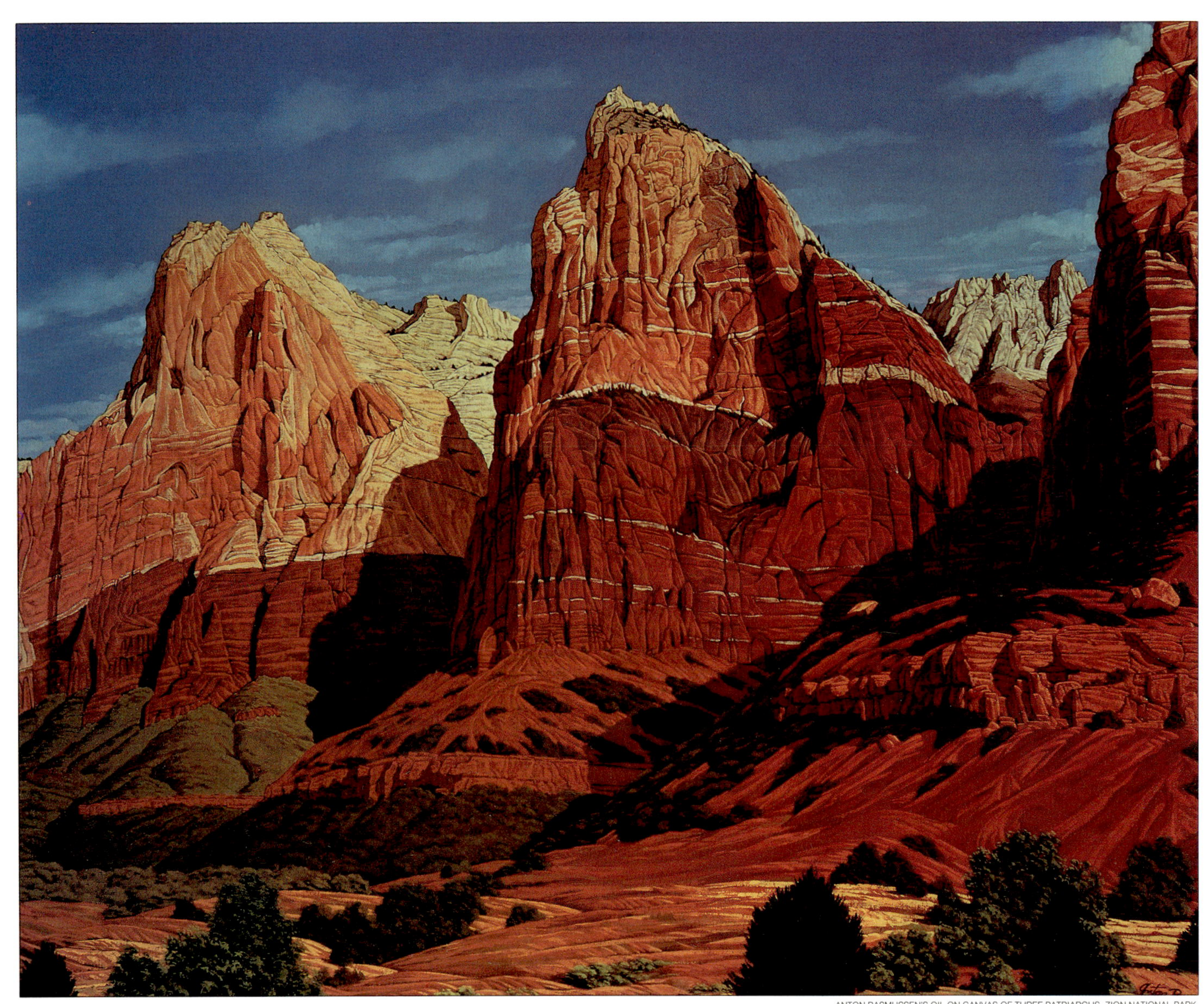

ANTON RASMUSSEN'S OIL ON CANVAS OF THREE PATRIARCHS, ZION NATIONAL PARK

Adult and child

P A I N T E R S

interpret the

Utah environment.

with contemporary purposes are the subjects of continual exploration and expansion by lithographers Robert Kleinschmidt (University of Utah) and Wayne Kimball (Brigham Young University). Kleinschmidt's eloquent, understated works suggest that we look around us more carefully; there is much of the world we fail to see. Kimball, on the other hand, creates complex fantastic worlds in small spaces.

The late Moishe Smith (Utah State University) experimented with intaglio and monoprint processes. The integrity of Smith's work derives from the artist's genuine sense of place. He was interested in all facets of the process, which demanded that he make choices at every stage of development.

Exploration of the processes necessary to their art has generated unique solutions that have earned these artists national and international reputations. For example, contemporary prints by these and others like Harry Taylor of Ogden, often incorporate photomechanically reproduced images, the addition of collage materials and the alteration of finished prints by drawing or painting. Printmaking in the hands of these artists and their colleagues contributed a dimension to the art of the 1960's without which American Pop could not have acquired its characteristic sophisticated edge. While Abstract Expressionism was painting about the process of painting, Pop was about mechanical reproductive processes.

Although Late Modern abstractions were hard for a general audience to accept, the expressions of the pluralistic 1970's and 1980's firmly repelled all known judgmental standards. Professionals and public alike had trouble deciphering the Postmodern art that everyone loved to hate. The Modern period ended sometime during the 1970's, and the realization dawned that our culture is not as homogenous as our

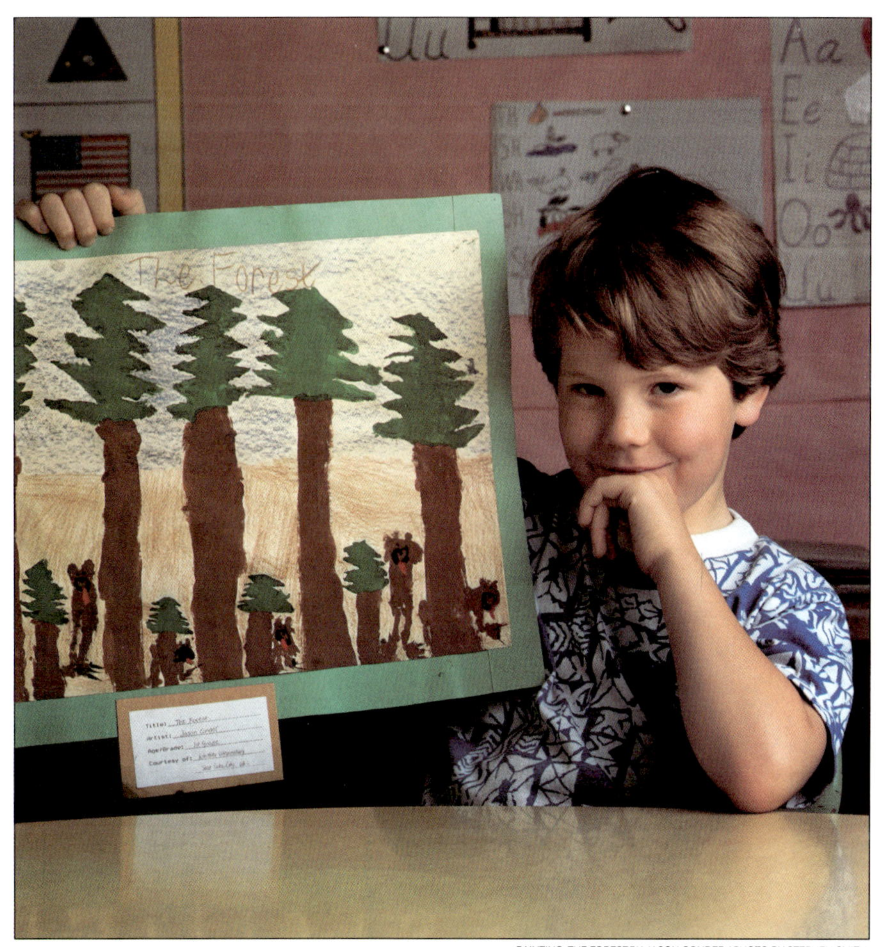

PAINTING *THE FOREST* BY JASON CONDER / PHOTO BY STEPHEN SMITH

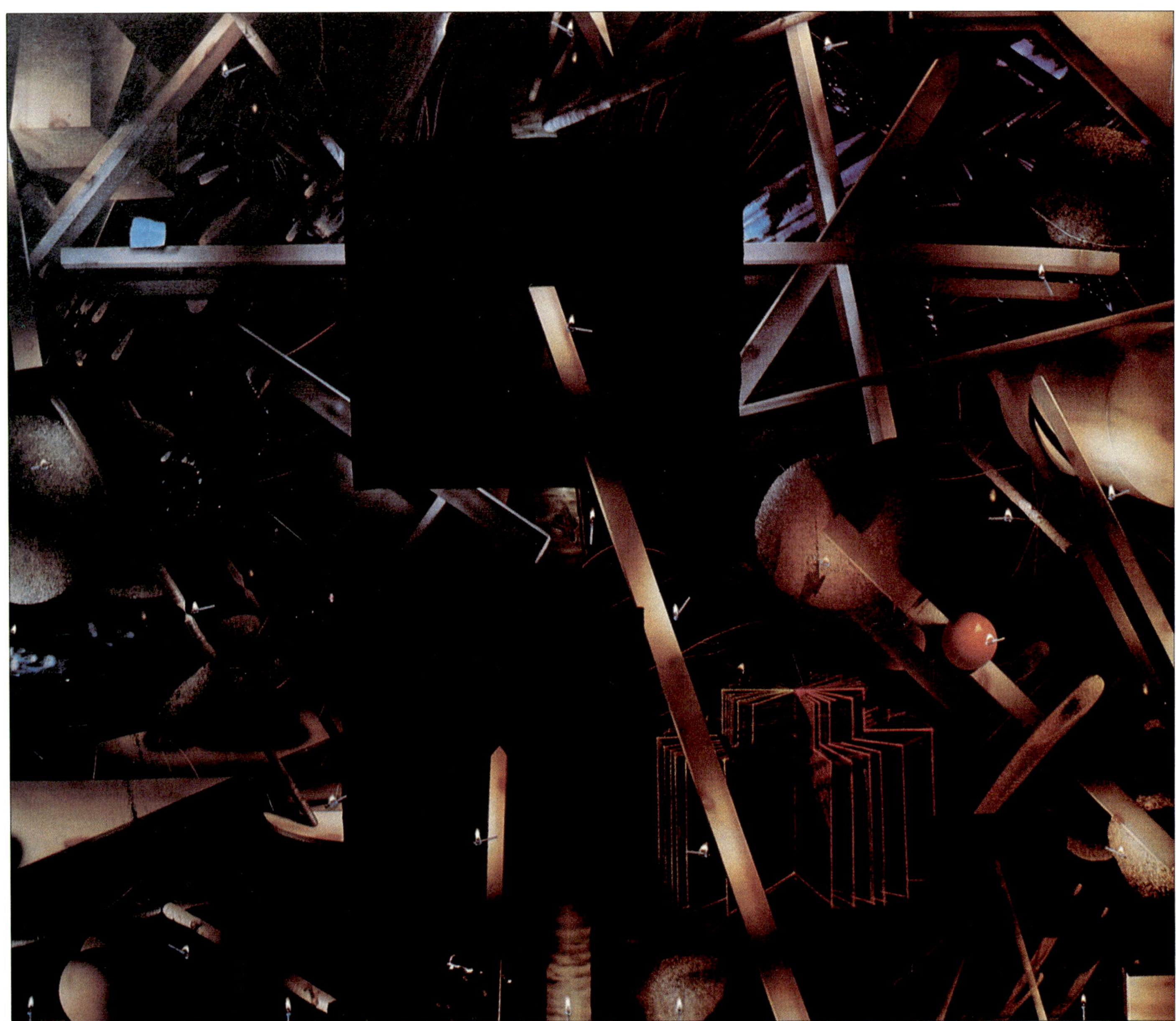

FRANK ANTHONY SMITH'S *NIGHT WRECK* ACRYLIC PAINTING ON CANVAS

FOLLOWING PAGE: HARRY TAYLOR'S *SHELLMAN* IS BOTH PRIMITIVE AND CONTEMPORARY

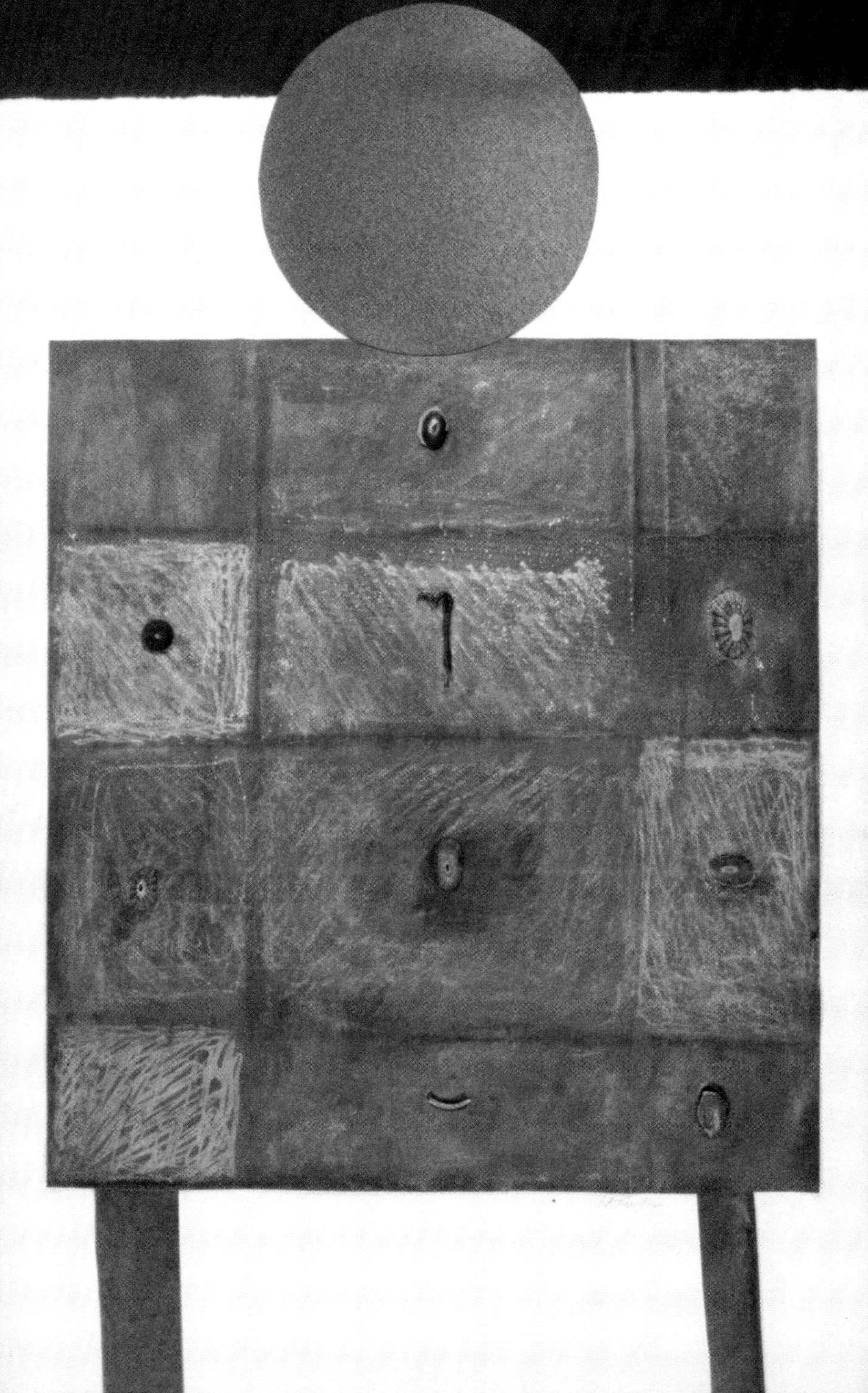

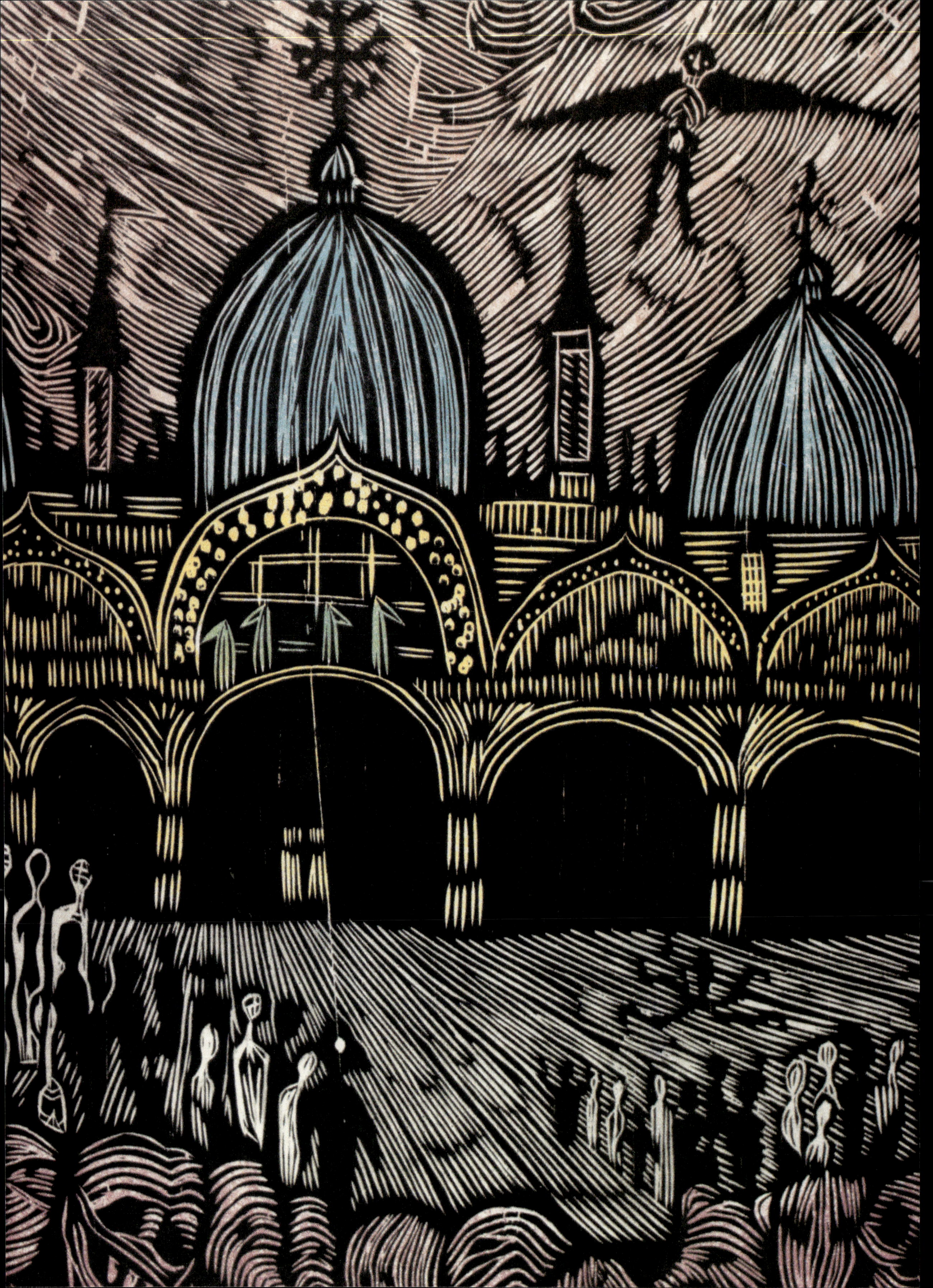

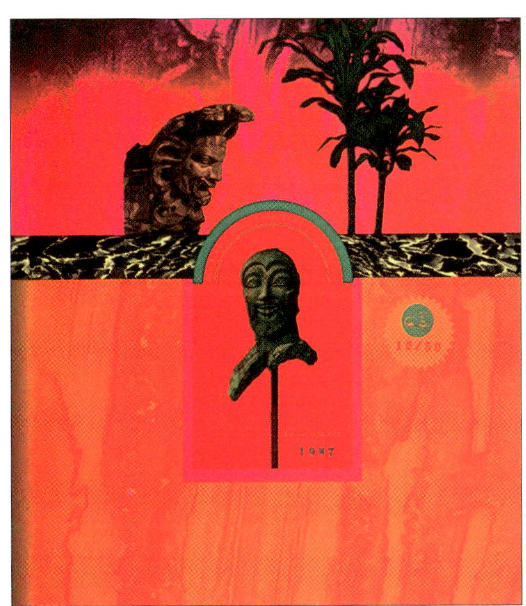

DISTANT RELATIVES AND SECRET, GUESSED / LITHOGRAPH BY WAYNE KIMBALL

Western attitudes led us to believe.

Traditionally, Western art and litera-ture have been limited to controlling reality with representational and narra-tive strategies which are inadequate and impoverished. Exclusion of women from history, and the history of art, is one example of this control of cultural reali-ty. Modern art was associated with the world of technological wonders; it was elite, isolationist and characterized by identifiable movements, each of which was headed by a heroic figure, almost always male. The obvious examples are Pablo Picasso, Henri Matisse, Marcel Duchamp and Jackson Pollock. In a hysterical compulsion to innovate, modernism was defined as "avant-garde," implying that it communicated only with a fortunate, informed few. In con-trast, the Postmodern seventies taught us about fragmentation, diversity, tolerance, pluralism, complexity and

feminism. Artists did not create new movements: Instead they scavenged from among the "ism's" of early modern for random elements that could be com-bined to make an art that is informative, irreverent and inclusive.

Today, *avant-garde* is a term becoming obsolete because it does not describe the range and diversity of contemporary art. No unique, ground-breaking movements on the scale of Analytical Cubism or Abstract Expressionism have surfaced in the last fifty years. Even 1960's Pop is acknowledged to have evolved logically from the doors opened by Abstract Expressionist artists. Today's artists are not interested in making pictures to hang on walls in galleries or museums. The new generation that emerged from the mercifully short, style-free, overly tolerant Postmodern period is made up of artists who do not sepa-rate art, or its making, from the life

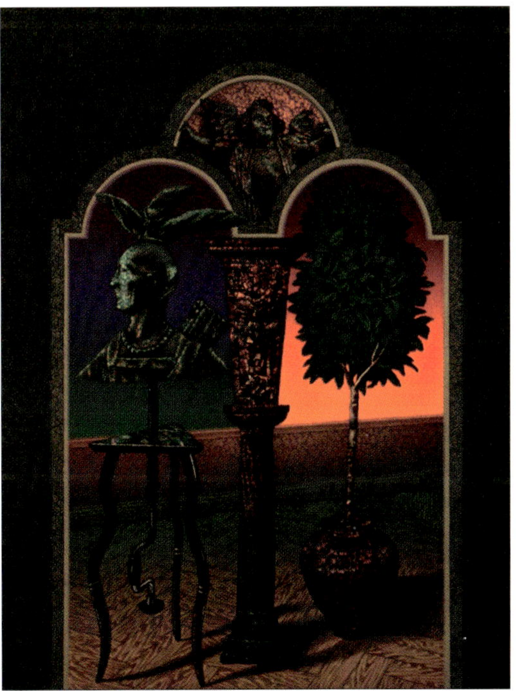

2ND ELDDIR WITHOUT THE (ERNST) NIGHTINGALE / LITHOGRAPH BY WAYNE KIMBALL

LEE DEFFEBACH

The high quality of contem-porary painting in Utah is best exemplified in Lee Deffebach's paintings. Her work has endured, matured and kept in touch with social changes in the years since she was identified as Utah's youngest Abstract Expressionist. Introspective and thoughtful, Deffebach quietly contemplates the nature of her compulsion to paint. She is, she says, pre-occupied with trying to know herself in order to effectively communicate with others. Children's art, she thinks, is made up of forms that emit life energy in a timeless, accessible language. "People are interested in what I know," Deffebach says, "but I am interested in what I don't know. I paint to find out why I paint."

PREVIOUS PAGE: WOODCUT CARNIVAL IN VENICE BY HARRY TAYLOR

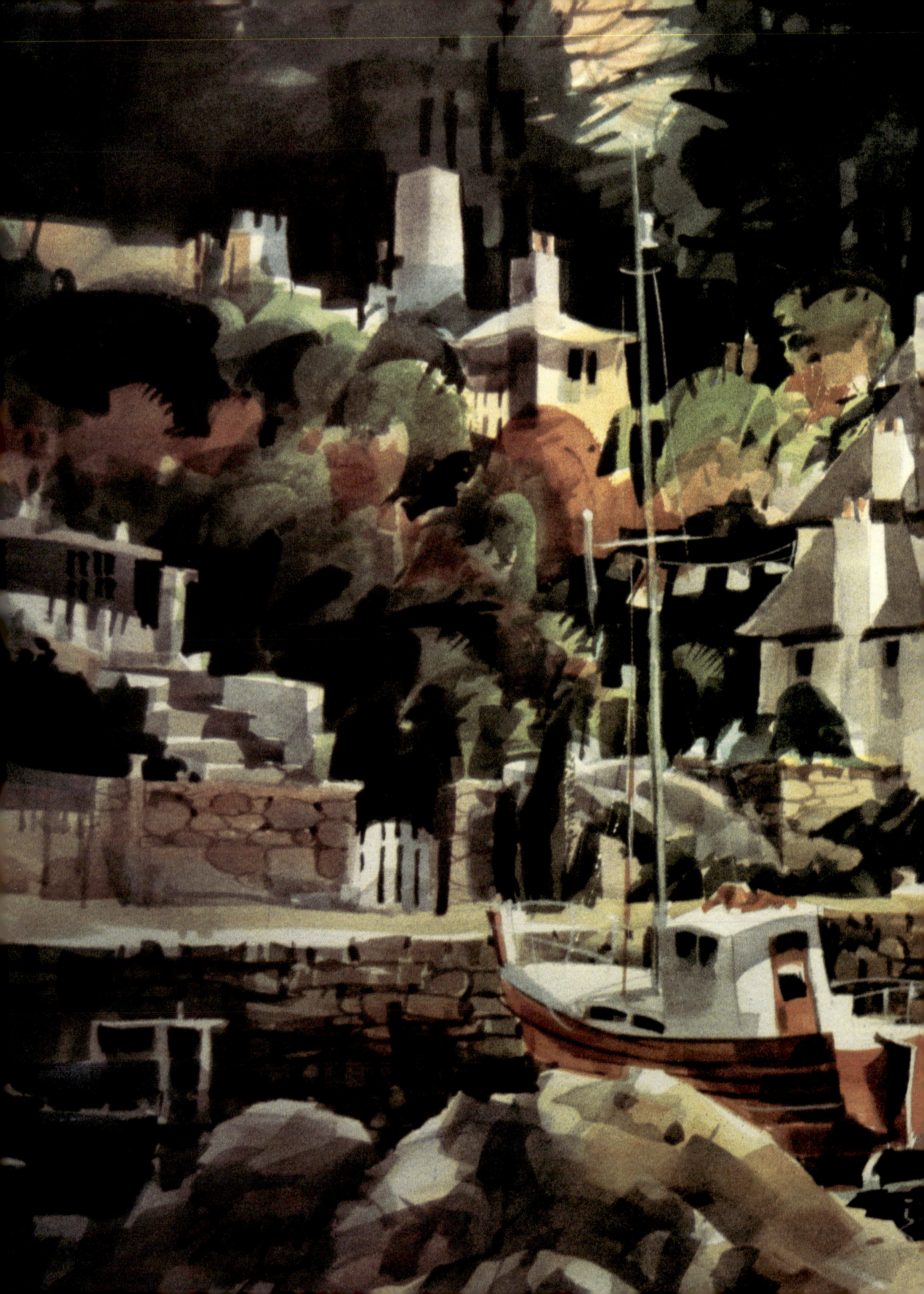

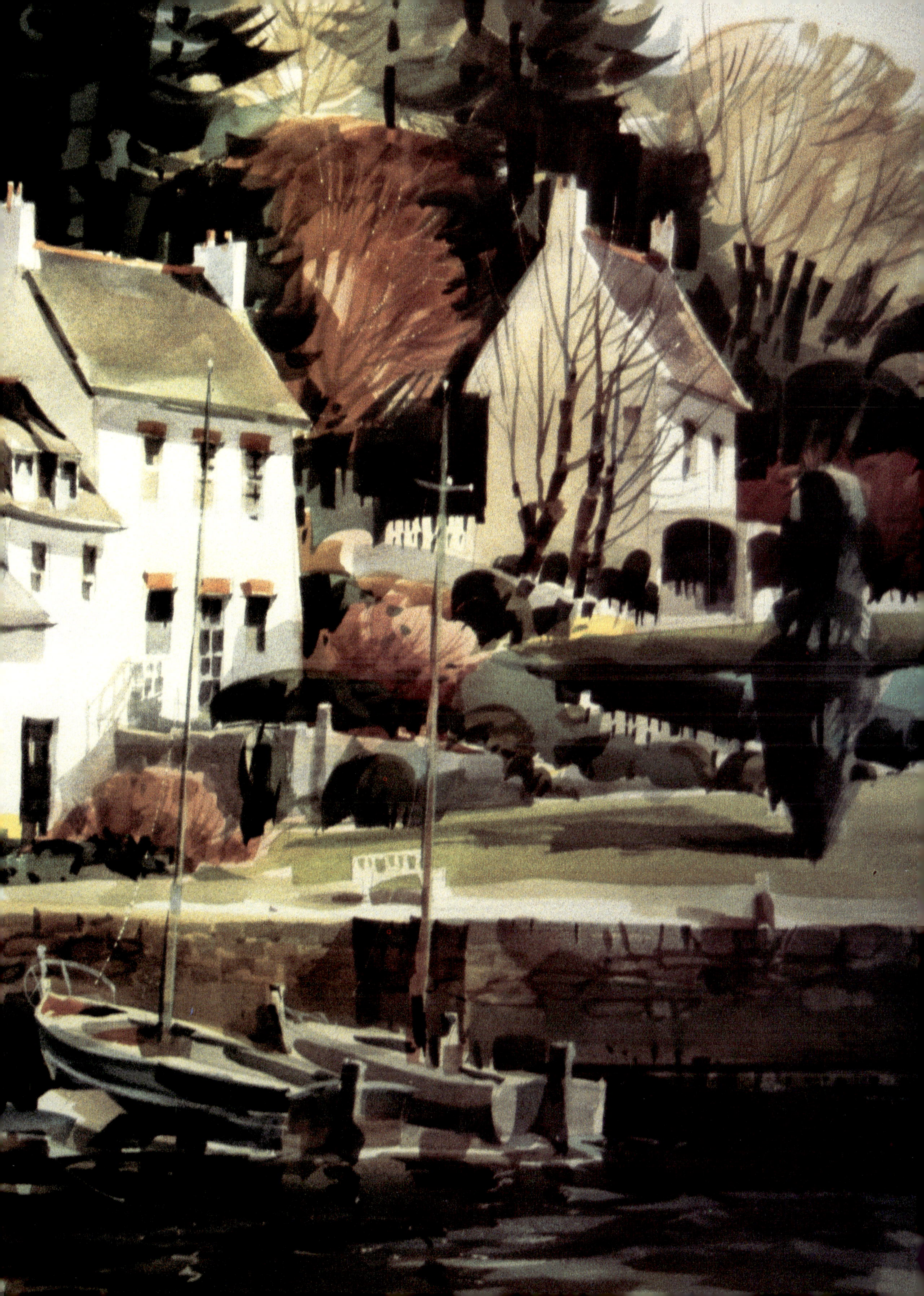

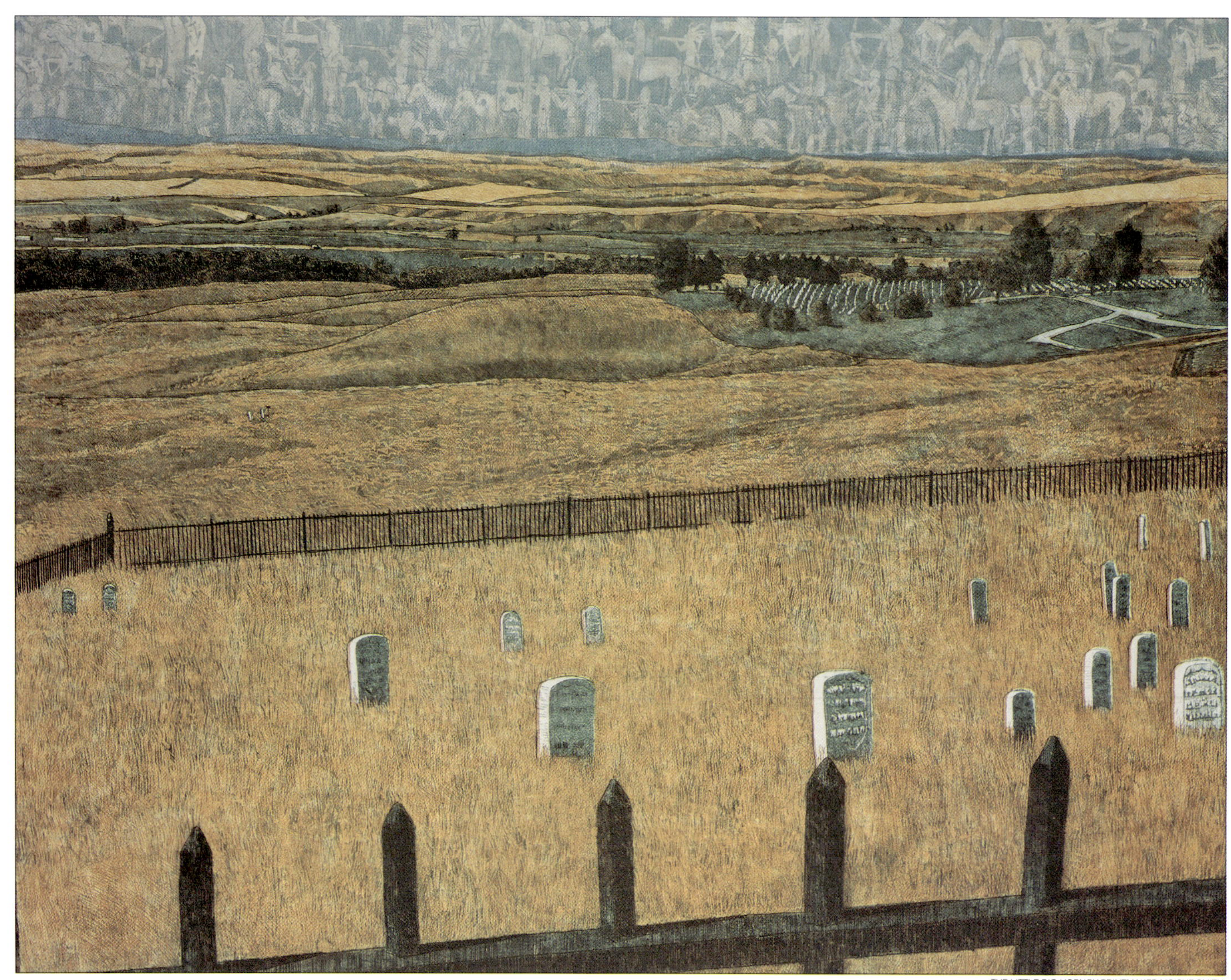

THE LITTLE BIG HORN BY PRINTMAKER MOISHE SMITH

Inspiration for
painters and printmakers
wells from the land,
N A T I V E
A M E R I C A N
art forms and
pioneer remnants.

PREVIOUS PAGE: WATERCOLOR HIGH TIDE AT POULE AVEN, FRANCE BY STEPHEN SONGER

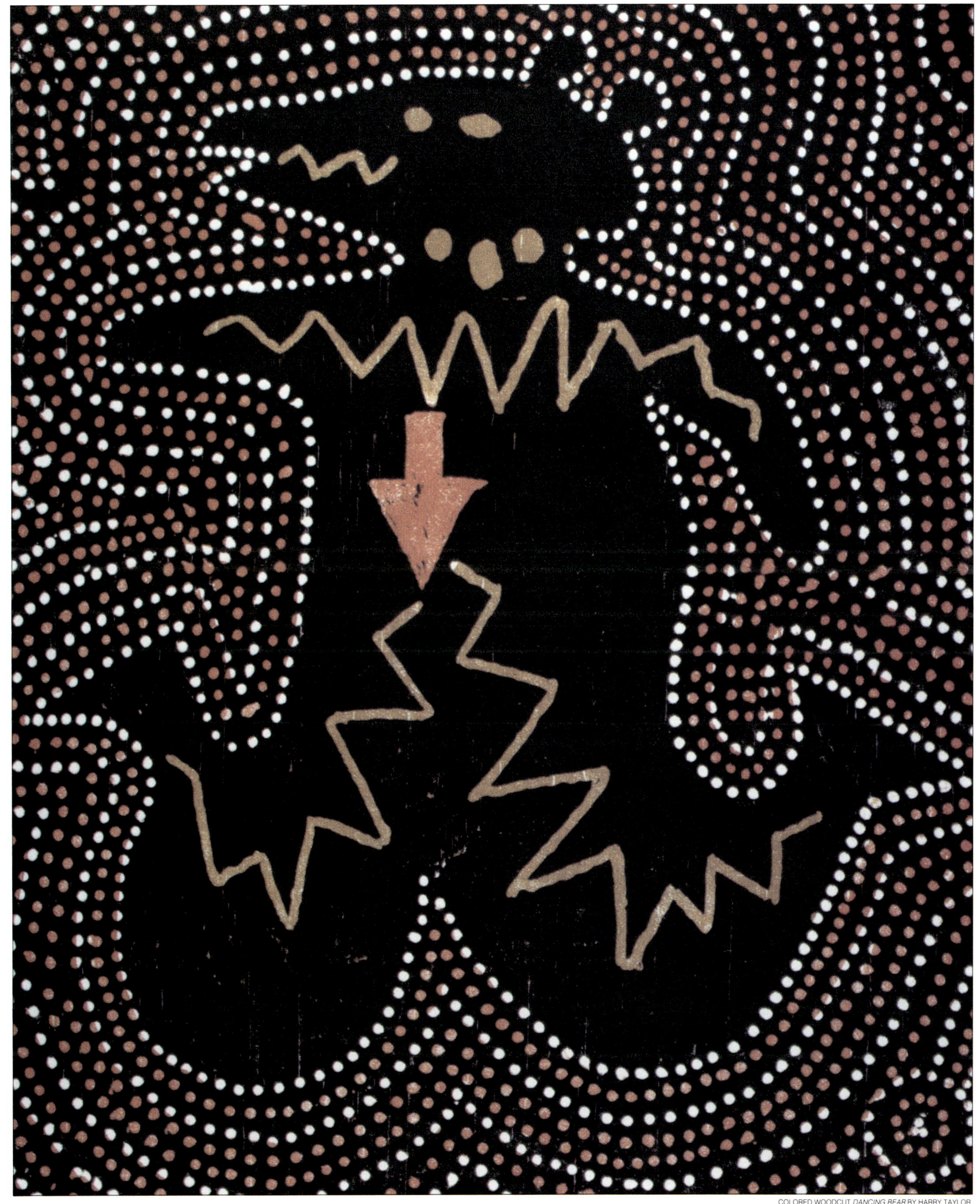

COLORED WOODCUT *DANCING BEAR* BY HARRY TAYLOR

Environmental and
human-condition
statements continue
to be fertile ground
for Utah
V I S U A L
artists.

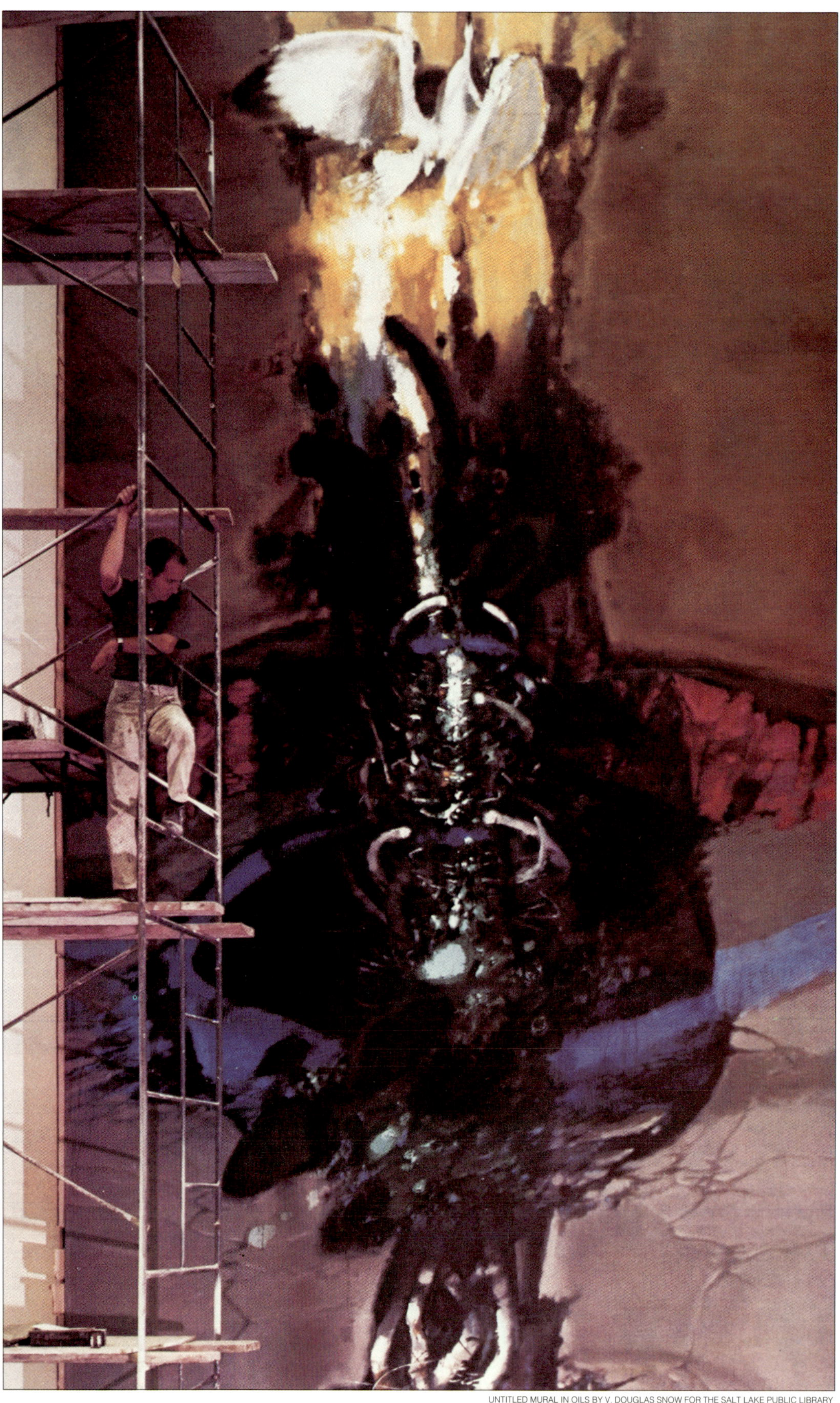

UNTITLED MURAL IN OILS BY V. DOUGLAS SNOW FOR THE SALT LAKE PUBLIC LIBRARY

of the community. They create imper-
manent works, often specific to a partic-
ular site, made of unlikely materials
appropriated and recycled, but rarely
purchased as *art supplies.*

Many of this generation,
including Antonia Hedrick,
are concerned with environ-
mental questions. Hedrick creates installations that are informed by her previous experience as a geologist working in
open pit mines. She combines materials
including, but not limited to, recycled
dress patterns, brief cases, geologists'
maps, and ore sampling jars. Her paintings are a summary of her experiences
and her search for a sense of place.

Place is also important to Mary Fish,
who creates installations that make eloquent environmental statements. Fish,
who lives in Sundance, Utah, recently
created a moving installation made up of
hundreds of white origami cranes combined with an endless audio recording
of the cries of this endangered species.

In contrast, Helene Fischer Elbein
explores various ways of representing
social issues. She recently probed the
general theme of inhumanity with an
arresting installation that recalled the
cruelty, horror and depersonalization of
the German Holocaust during the
Second World War. Her materials
included paving bricks stamped with
stenciled numbers and disembodied
hands cast in plaster.

Similarly, Susan Hyde Bland gently
probes controversial gender issues, often
with traditional feminine materials and
techniques, including sewing and

quilting. Her interest in how we view
and experience aging is represented in
an artist's book that chronicles events in
the life of a male centenarian, a former
ballet dancer and teacher.

Maureen O'Hara-Ure, one of Utah's
important artist-educators, translates
ideas into complex constructions that

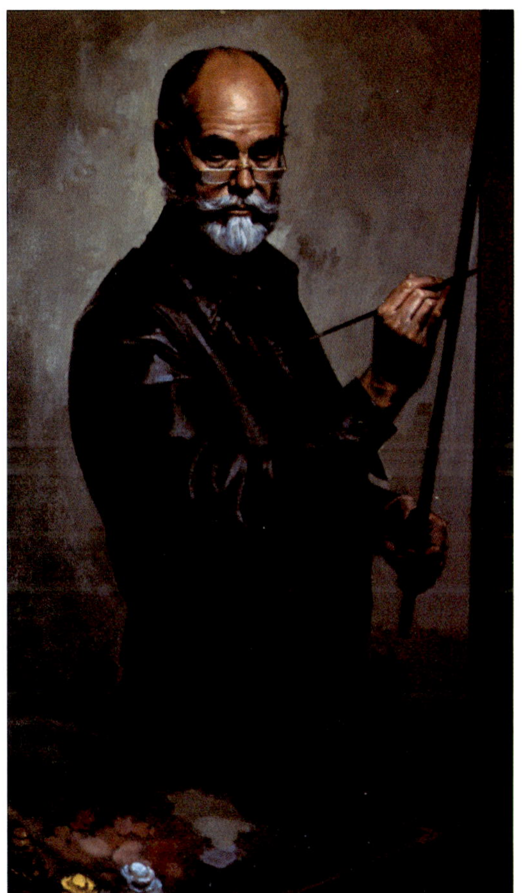

SELF PORTRAIT / ALVIN GITTINS

Self and
S   O   C   I   E   T   Y
are topics for
Utah painters.

defy classification but are rooted more
strongly in cultural ethos than a
singular aesthetic.

Bonnie Sucec's constructed paintings
communicate to all by virtue of a decep-
tively simple folk art vocabulary that
effectively disguises her sophisticated
observations of self and society.

FOLLOWING PAGE: *SIDEWALK ART, AN EARTH DAY CELEBRATION,* THE CHILDREN'S MUSEUM / PHOTO BY STEPHEN SMITH

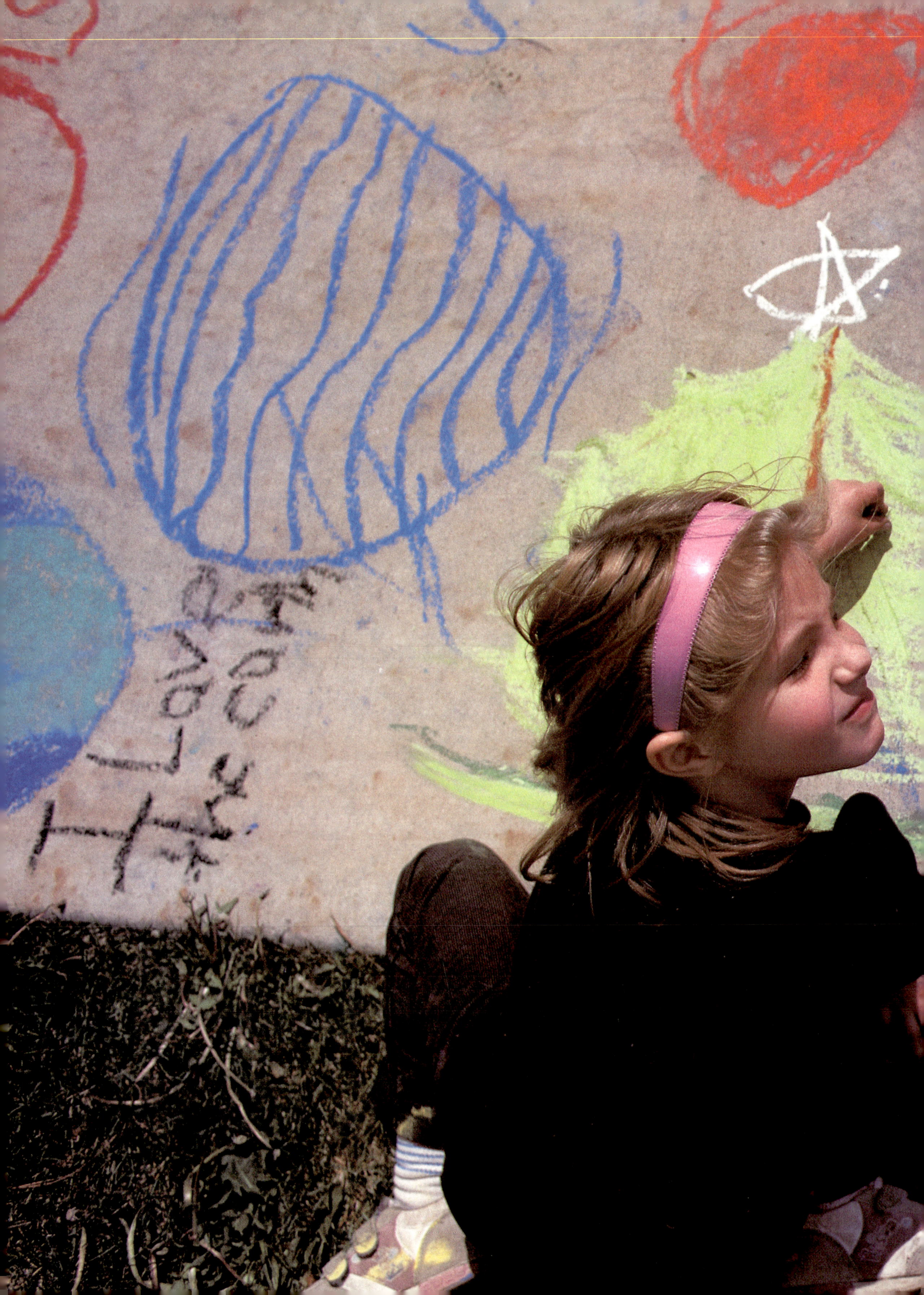

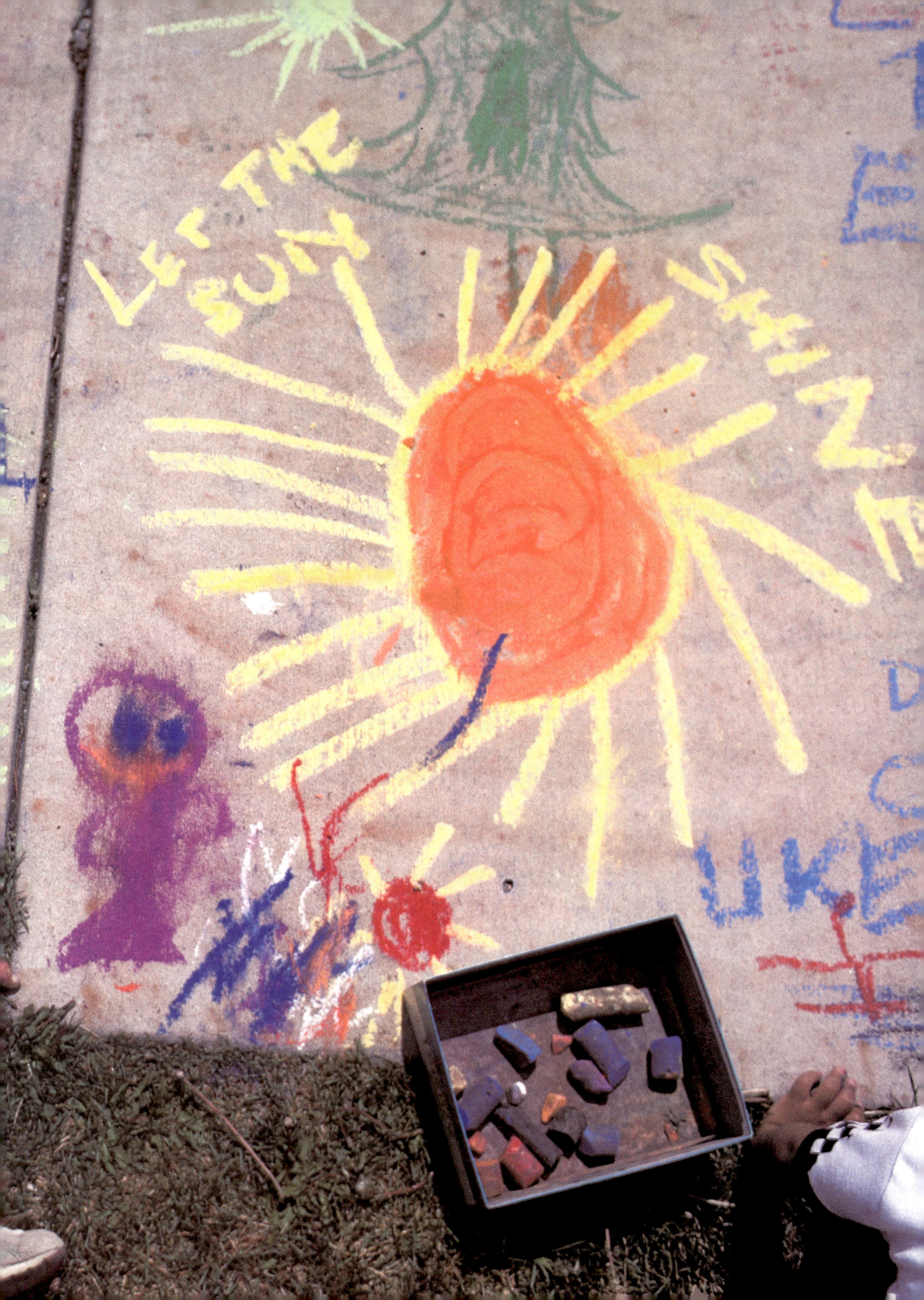

LET THE
SUN
SHINE

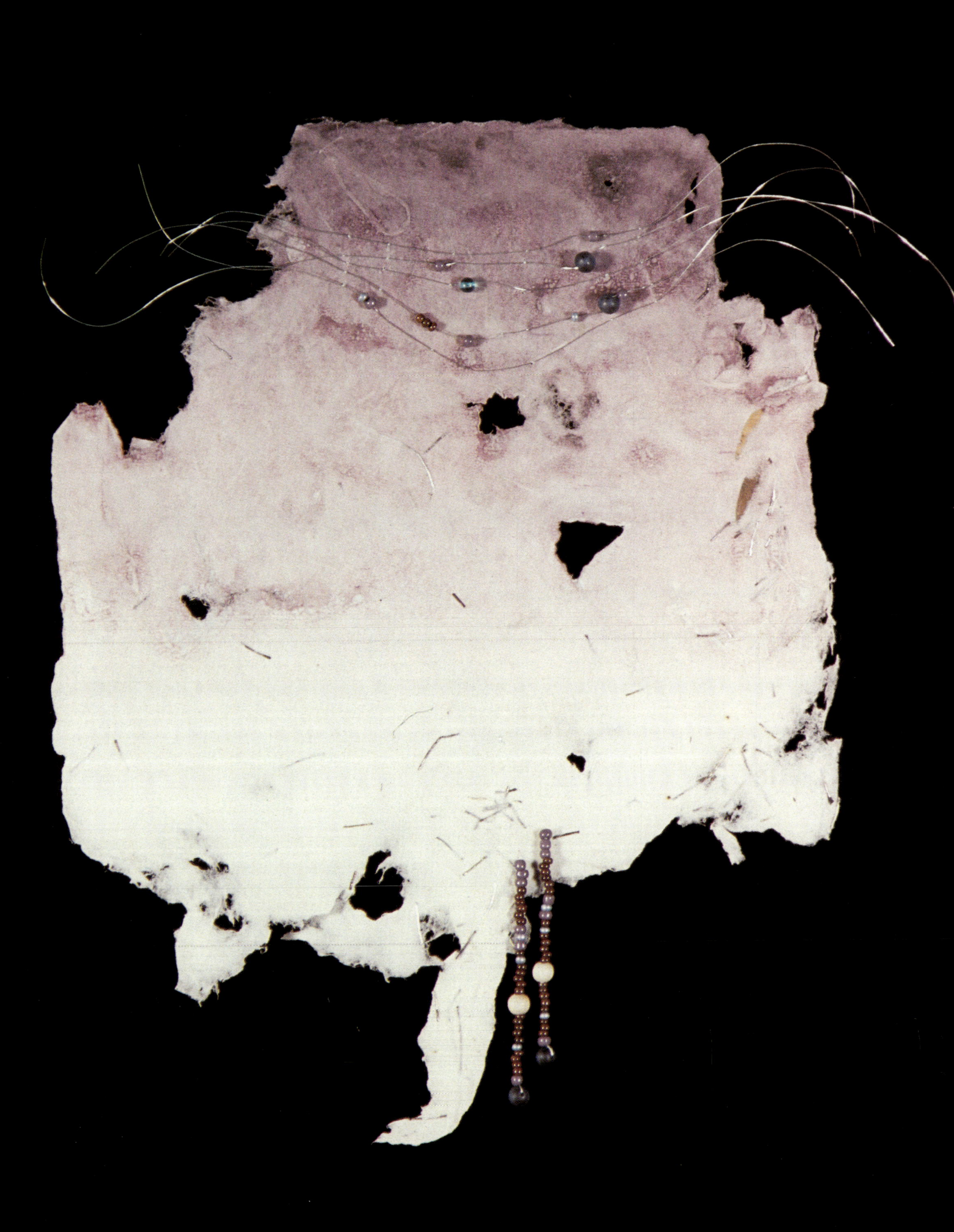

It is probably no coincidence that the artists mentioned in the previous paragraphs are all women. Women artists have pushed assertively into the realm of nontraditional art, developing a body of work that has grown out of a need to create a visual language of their own with which to express shared social and environmental concerns. Out of a sense of group, and because women are, traditionally if tiresomely, defined by structural anthropologists as closer to nature than they are to culture, these new artists do not shrink from the risks associated with the use of unorthodox materials or from processes that do not depend on studio experience alone.

The few mentioned here represent the larger group of contemporary Utah women artists who are responding to current issues in the most visual vocabulary. A recent exhibition, *Out of the Land: Utah Women Then and Now*, represented the wide range of work by women artists in Utah today and their concerns. As if to prove the social purposes of women's art, this exhibition generated controversy that sprang directly and logically from the conflict between local religious and moral attitudes and persistent alternative viewpoints. Thirty works selected from this exhibit were shown at the National Museum for Women in the Arts, Washington, D.C., an institution that itself has generated both internal and external controversy.

Community involvement is not limited to nontraditional artists, however. Roger (Sam) Wilson has painted a contemporary *Stations of the Cross* for the recently restored Cathedral of the Madeleine. Other painters/printmakers with strong community and teaching commitments include Susan Carroll, David Dornan, Nel Ivancich, Edie Roberson, Pat Eddington, Connie Borup, Tony Smith and Edwin Oberbeck. With designer-illustrators McRay Magleby, Arnold Friberg, Raymond Morales and Gail Watne, all of whom mix media and processes, these artists have achieved national recognition for the relevance of their work.

Contemporary artists in Utah are exploring values that will be central to society as we move toward a new century. We are unusually fortunate in the number and quality of Utah's artists and the scholars who industriously chronicle their work.

MOISHE SMITH

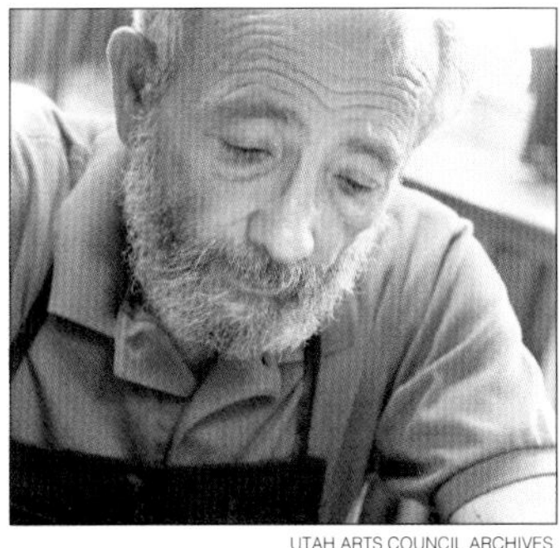

UTAH ARTS COUNCIL ARCHIVES

Printmaking, for the late Moishe Smith, represented a process that offered him an opportunity to investigate the countless nuances of the Cache Valley landscape in which he lived, taught and worked. Smith, who was born in Chicago, studied at the New School of Social Research (B.A. 1950) and the University of Iowa (M.F.A. 1953). Before coming to Utah, he taught at the universities of Wisconsin and Iowa and Ohio State University.

Life, teaching and art were inseparable for Smith, whose strong sense of place is immediately apparent in his prints. Process, for the printmaker, is vital to the final expression. For Smith, all facets of the printmaking process allowed him the "freedom and the possibility of creating a personal sense of the structure that art creates." He believed, he said, in "the primacy of laws, in personal, ethical responsibility and in the utmost necessity to respect the rights of all."

In 1993 Moishe Smith received the Governor's Award in the Arts.

PREVIOUS PAGE: CAST PAPER COMPOSITION *FRAGMENT* BY MARILYN MILLER

FOLLOWING PAGE: PAPER AND MIXED MEDIA *ROUGE ET NOIR* BY HARRY TAYLOR

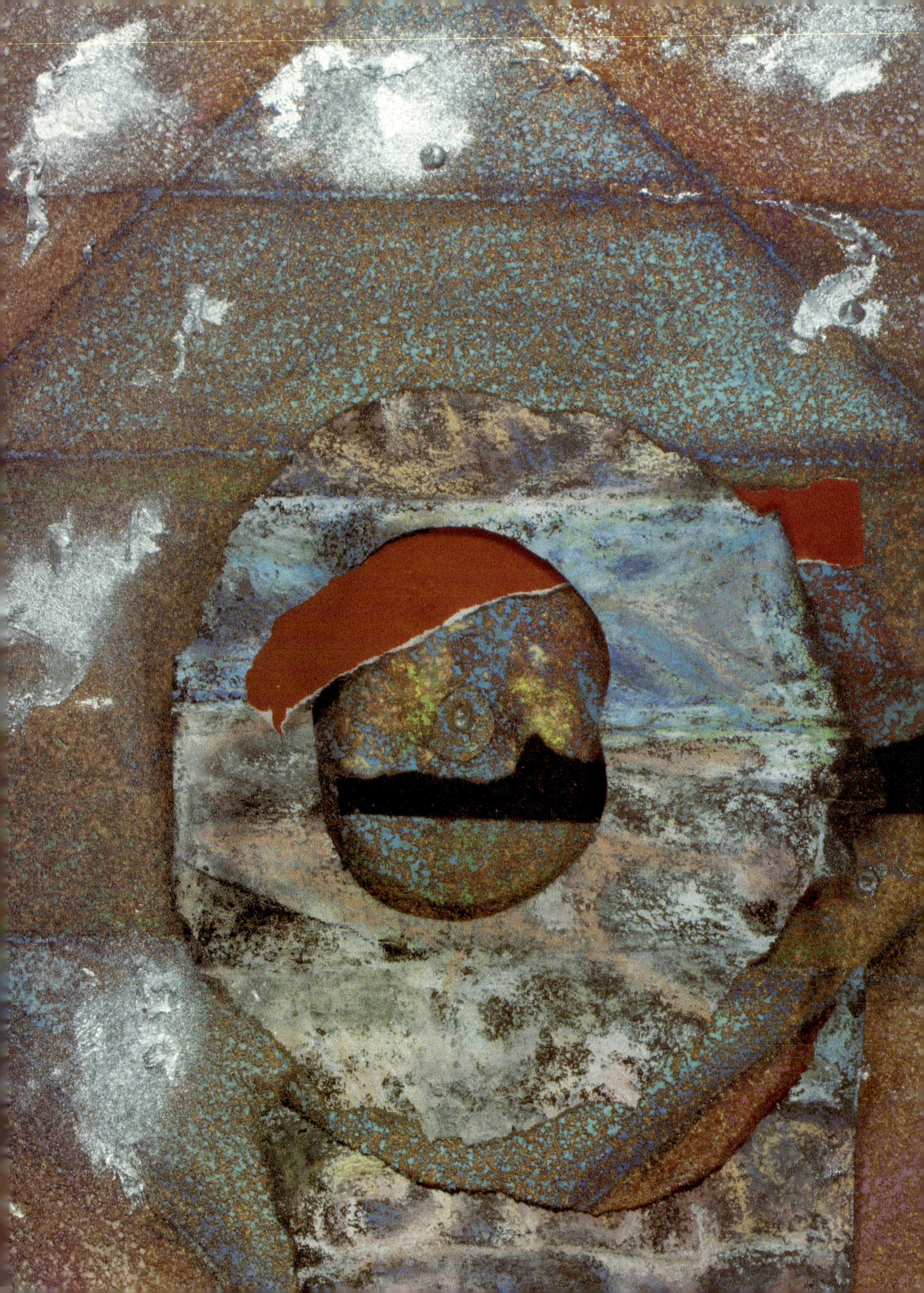

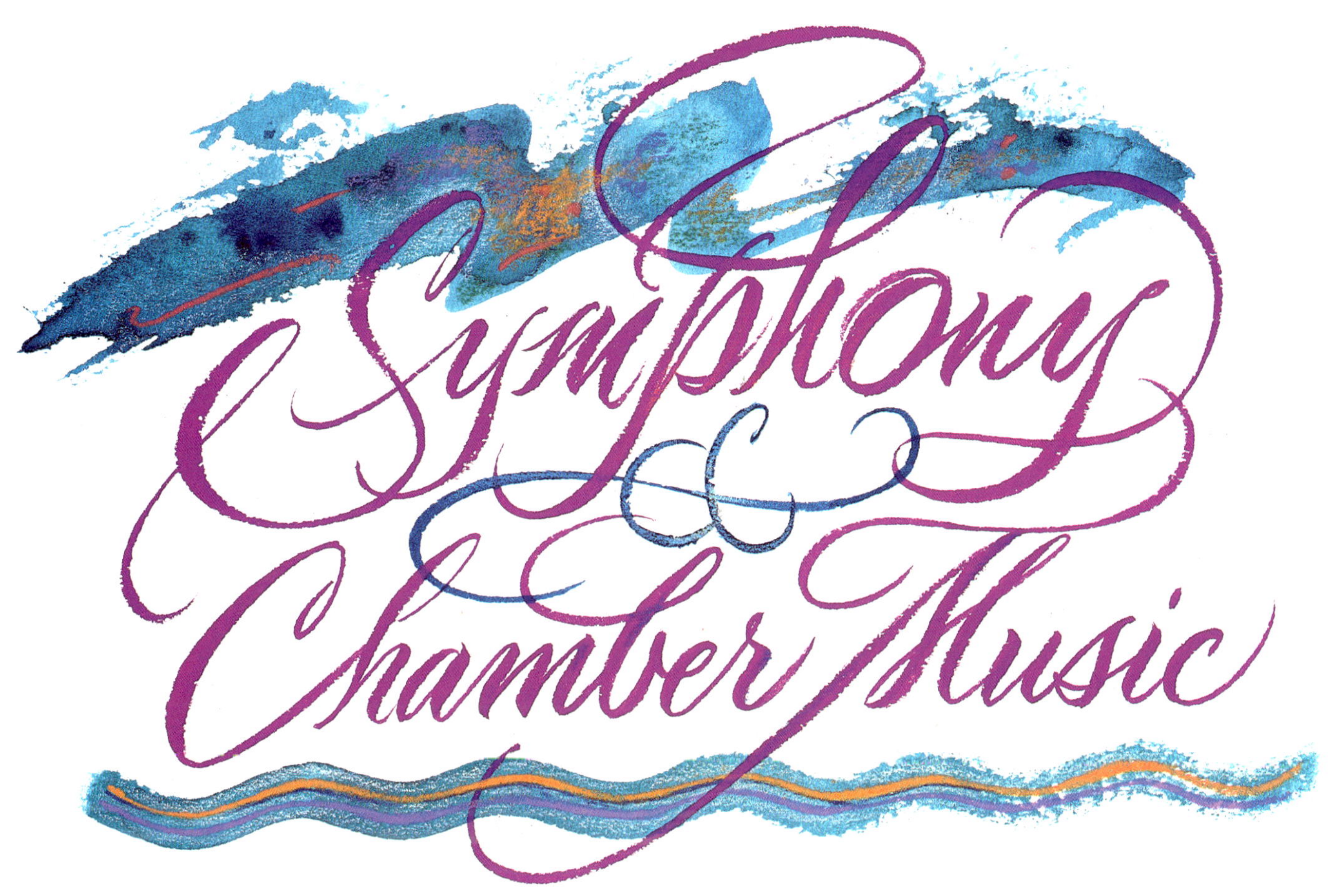

Great Basin Rhapsody

Paul Wetzel

UST ACROSS a downtown intersection from Temple Square rises Abravanel Hall, one of the finest contemporary concert halls in the United States and home of the Utah Symphony. Temple Square, the Mormon counterpart to Vatican City, is the historic and spiritual center of Salt Lake City. That proximity makes a significant geographical metaphor, because for five decades classical music in Utah has centered on the Utah Symphony just as surely as the state's spiritual life has centered on Temple Square.

In fact, for many years, those two cultural focal points were one. Prior to moving across the street to the newly constructed Abravanel Hall in 1979, the

MAURICE ABRAVANEL

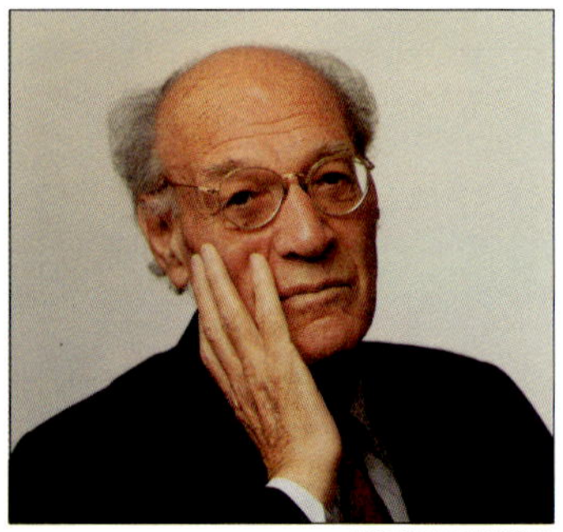

PHOTO BY DON BUSATH

When Maurice Abravanel took up the baton of the Utah Symphony in 1947, no one in Utah had heard of him, and no one outside Utah had heard of the Utah Symphony. During the thirty-two years that followed, Abravanel and his orchestra changed all that.

Abravanel was a man of the world: a Jew of Spanish heritage, born in Greece, raised in Switzerland. A student of Kurt Weill in Germany, where he launched his career, he was at home in Paris and New York as well as Salt Lake City.

Among the conductor's proudest achievements were the internationally acclaimed recordings he and his orchestra made, including the complete symphonies of Gustav Mahler. They won awards from the International Gustav Mahler Society of Vienna and the Bruckner Society. Other Abravanel recordings won the Prix du Disque and two Grammy nominations.

After his retirement from the Utah Symphony in 1979, Abravanel was named *artist for life* at Tanglewood, the renowned music school and summer home of the Boston Symphony. President Bush presented the maestro the National Medal of Arts in 1991.

Utah Symphony performed on Temple Square itself in the same Mormon Tabernacle from which America's most famous choir takes its name.

But while the Mormon Tabernacle Choir is a distinctly ecclesiastical institution with a mission in which art serves religion, the Utah Symphony always has been an independent, nonsectarian organization devoted to art alone. As such, the symphony enjoys the support of music lovers from throughout Utah and neighboring states, regardless of their religious affiliation. Few other Utah institutions, cultural or otherwise, can make the same claim to social universality.

Since the 1960's, the Utah Symphony has been recognized as one of the nation's two dozen major orchestras, and it has claimed national and even international attention through its tours and 125 recordings. Today, the heart of its winter season at Abravanel Hall is an eighteen-concert series of classical masterworks that runs from September through May. The orchestra presents standard symphonic works as well as concertos with guest artists who have ranged through the years from Rubinstein, Stern and Sills, through Dichter, Perlman and Norman. Two annual programs traditionally are devoted to choral-orchestral repertoire with the Utah Symphony Chorus.

In recent years, the orchestra has broadened its programming beyond the standard symphonic repertoire to include a four-concert series devoted to works for chamber orchestra, often from the Baroque period. The orchestra also offers a six-concert winter pops series, four family concerts, a cinema series in which the orchestra provides live accompaniment for classic silent films, four youth concerts and about five special productions annually. In addition to its youth series, the orchestra performs in about sixty Utah schools every year.

Outside Salt Lake City, the Utah Symphony presents winter series in three other Utah cities—Ogden, Provo and Logan—and it tours annually to other cities and towns in Utah, Nevada, Wyoming and Idaho.

In summer the orchestra plays pops and classical programs at the Deer Valley and Snowbird ski resorts in the Wasatch Mountains east of Salt Lake City, as well as in Abravanel Hall, and for three seasons has performed at the Big Sky Music Festival in Montana.

The Utah Symphony's current music director, Joseph Silverstein, enjoys a dual career as conductor and violin soloist, a role in which he is featured in recent Utah Symphony recordings of the violin concertos of Beethoven, Mendelssohn, Brahms, Tchaikovsky and Barber. Silverstein came to the Utah Symphony in 1983 from the Boston Symphony, where he had long been

JOSEPH SILVERSTEIN

regarded the dean of American orchestral concertmasters and where he also served as assistant conductor.

While the roots of the Utah Symphony run deep in Utah, the seeds of the orchestra itself were not planted until almost a century after the Mormon exodus to the Great Basin in 1847. There the Mormons founded Salt Lake City, and they brought a northern European musical tradition with them. Even as they struggled to survive through the early years of building their new Zion, the Mormons sang in choirs and played in brass bands. Undoubtedly a good deal of solo instrumental music existed as well.

Beginning in 1892 and continuing through 1925, movements to establish a permanent professional symphony orchestra in Utah's capital city rose and fell. Lack of financial support undid these early attempts, so it is ironic that the Great Depression would later give birth to the Utah Symphony. The Works Progress Administration created a precursor ensemble in 1936; it became the Utah State Symphony with joint WPA and state sponsorship in 1940.

From that beginning, the orchestra evolved quickly into an independent community institution. The Utah Symphony's early years were a patchwork of guest conductors coupled with artistic and financial successes and reversals, but, most importantly, the orchestra survived to engage an extraordinary music director, Maurice Abravanel, in 1947.

Over the next three decades, Maestro Abravanel built the Utah Symphony into an orchestra worthy of national and, to some degree, international recognition. In the process, conductor and orchestra traversed virtually the entire standard symphonic repertoire and introduced Utahns to scores of contemporary works. The orchestra made about one hundred commercial recordings and toured to other areas of the United States, to South America and to Europe.

The final monument to the Utah Symphony's thirty-two years under Abravanel was a building. In the early 1970's, the people of Utah began planning a permanent home for the Utah Symphony, and, as it turned out, the 2,804-seat auditorium which would become Symphony Hall was designed and built specifically for symphonic performances. It opened in 1979, six months after Abravanel's retirement from the concert stage, and was renamed for him in 1993.

Since its opening, the hall has not only showcased the Utah Symphony but has also played host to many of the nation's greatest orchestras, including those of Boston, Chicago, New York, Philadelphia and Cleveland, as well as the Vienna Philharmonic and the Concertgebouw of Amsterdam.

At the same time that the orchestra moved into Symphony Hall in 1979, it began a difficult period of leadership

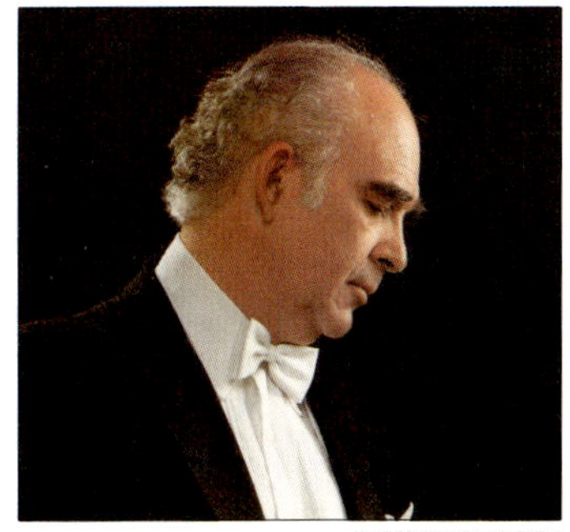

PHOTO BY DON BUSATH

In conversation Joseph Silverstein speaks of music with quiet authority, and for good reason. Few others have made orchestral music at the highest levels from such varied perspectives: as long-time concertmaster and assistant conductor of the Boston Symphony, as a sought-after concerto soloist, and, since 1983, as music director and conductor of the Utah Symphony. He's also a gifted teacher and chamber musician.

Born in Detroit, Silverstein was a student of Gingold, Zimbalist and Mischakoff at Philadelphia's Curtis Institute. He is known for his impeccable ear, and he has raised the technical standard of the Utah Symphony appreciably. Under his guidance, the orchestra shines particularly in works of Haydn and Mozart. He also brought a new dimension to Utah Symphony concerts as simultaneous conductor and violin soloist. Silverstein is a master of this difficult dual role, and he has worked the same magic as a guest with other major orchestras, including those of Minnesota, Atlanta, St. Louis and Leningrad.

FOLLOWING PAGE: SYMPHONY HALL, 1989 FILM FESTIVAL, SALT LAKE CITY, UTAH / PHOTO BY PATRICK CONE

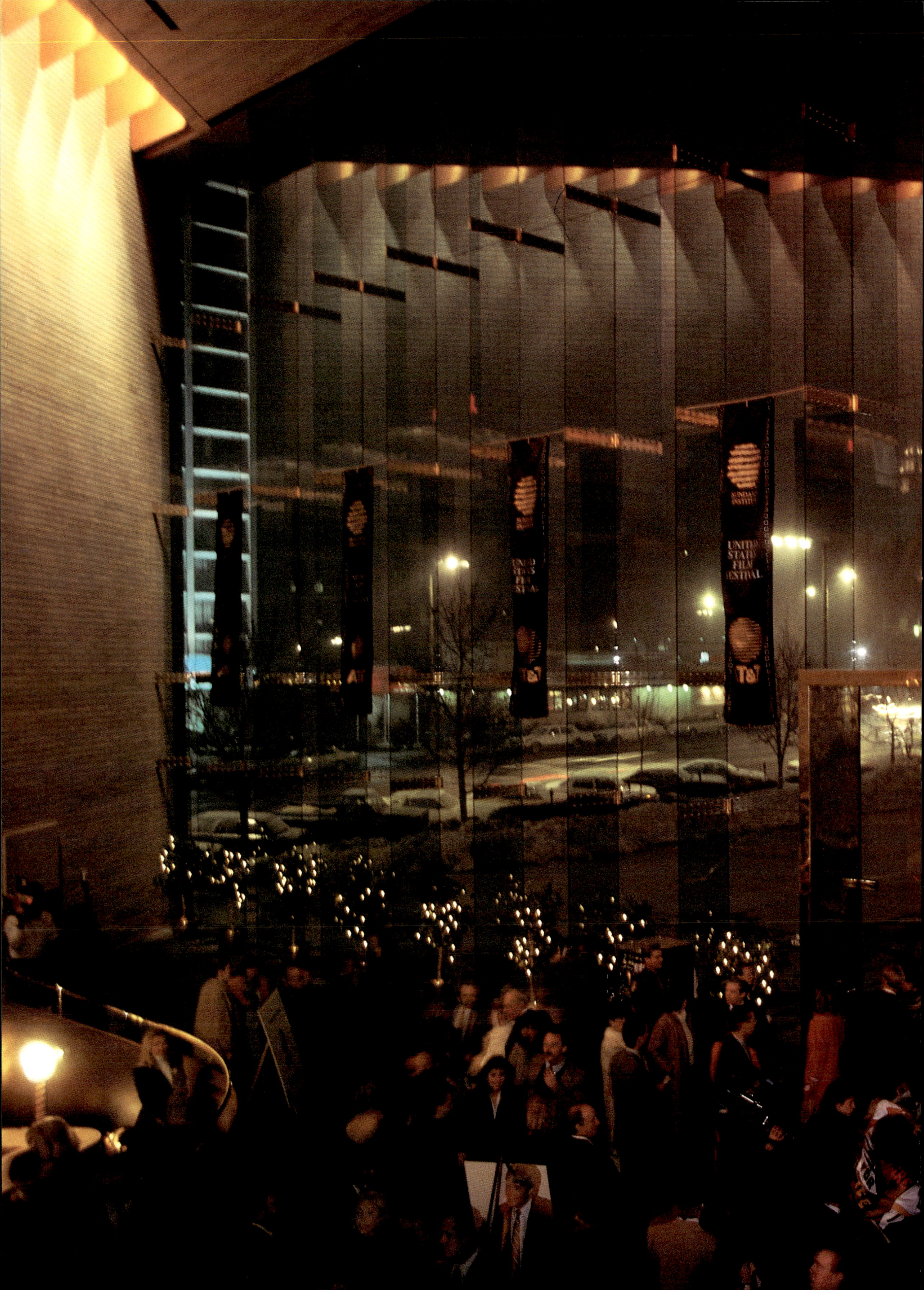

SUNDANCE INSTITUTE
UNITED STATES FILM FESTIVAL

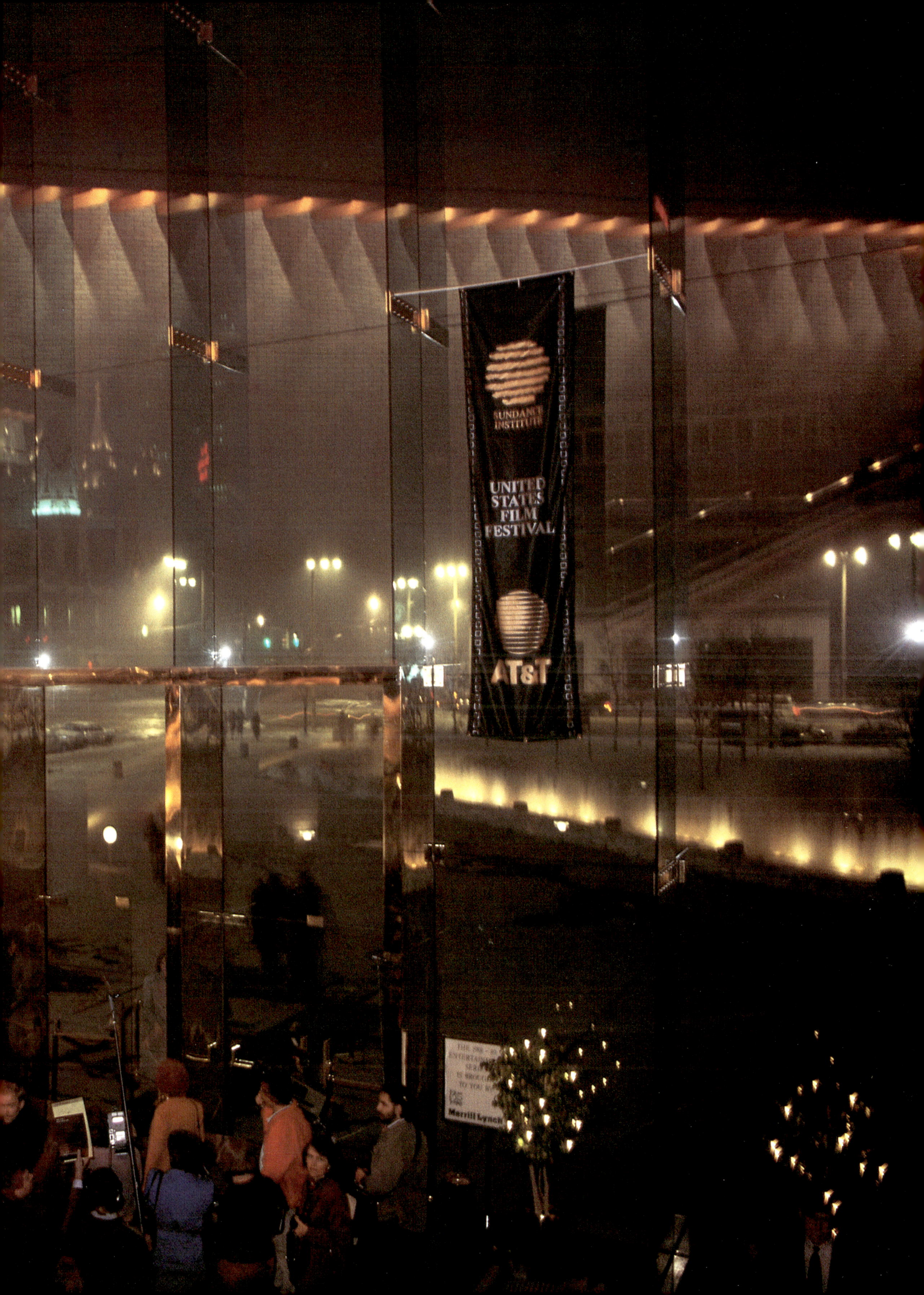

SUNDANCE
INSTITUTE
UNITED
STATES
FILM
FESTIVAL
AT&T

transition. Abravanel had retired after one of the longest tenures in American symphonic history. Varujan Kojian, a protégé of Zubin Mehta, was chosen as his successor, but the orchestra quickly became disillusioned with his leadership. Although he was a gifted musician, the depth of his knowledge was found lacking. Kojian's three-year contract was not renewed, and it fell to a new music director, Joseph Silverstein, to restore artistic stability and morale.

Like many other American orchestras, the Utah Symphony suffered financial setbacks in the late 1980's and early 1990's. Despite expanding both its audience and the diversity of its musical offerings, the orchestra developed chronic operating deficits as its annual budget surpassed $7 million. The situation became critical in the summer of 1993, after a plan to raise funds for arts organizations through an increase in the local sales tax failed in a public referendum.

On the eve of the 1993-94 season, the symphony's board of directors notified musicians that the concert schedule could be canceled if a solution to a projected budget shortfall of $1.2 million could not be found. The musicians agreed to a pay cut to salvage the season, and the board began planning an emergency drive to substantially increase the orchestra's $7 million endowment fund. As performances resumed, however, the orchestra's long-term financial prospects remained cloudy.

The Utah Symphony inevitably has influenced other musical institutions in the state, sometimes directly, sometimes obliquely. For instance, one of the symphony's greatest friends in the international music world was the respected Greek pianist Gina Bachauer, who facilitated the orchestra's first European tour with an invitation to the Athens Festival in 1966. As a result, her name has been memorialized by what may be Utah's most prestigious international musical event.

Paul Pollei, a Utah pianist and teacher, founded the Gina Bachauer International Piano Competition as a local contest at Brigham Young University in 1976, although it was not named in the late pianist's honor until two years later. Since that time, the competition's global reputation has grown rapidly. Today it brings about sixty aspiring professional pianists from some of the world's great conservatories to Salt Lake City and Abravanel Hall once every three years. The next competition will take place in June 1994.

While symphonic music in Utah is dominated by the Utah Symphony, it doesn't end there. The state is home to about two dozen community orchestras, approximately half of them clustered in Salt Lake County. These ensembles are the artistic outlet for people who wish to do more than just listen to orchestral music—they want to make it. The most venerable groups are the Wasatch Community Symphony and the Utah Valley Symphony. Others of prominence include the New American Symphony and Rocky Mountain Symphony, both of Ogden; the Salt Lake Symphony, Murray Symphony, and West Valley Symphony in Salt Lake County; and the Southwest Symphony and Chorale of St. George.

Some Utah children literally grow up in community orchestras. In Salt Lake County, the youthful All-City Children's Orchestra provides musicians of elementary school age with early orchestral experience. Performers in the venerable Utah Youth Symphony, another ensemble, are teenagers. Both orchestras are independent of the state's many school orchestras.

Chamber music did not command a wide audience in the United States until after World War II and in this Utah was no exception. However, during the post-War period, the Chamber Music Society of Salt Lake City has presented twenty-five years of distinguished concerts featuring many of the world's pre-eminent string quartets and trios, including the Juilliard Quartet and Beaux Arts Trio, the Amadeus, Guarneri, Cleveland and Emerson quartets. The series is presented in the Utah Museum of Fine Arts auditorium on the University of Utah campus.

The Chamber Music Society of Logan offers a winter season in that northern Utah community, while the Nova Chamber Music Series provides a forum for resident professional musicians in Salt Lake City. Often the performers are members of the Utah Symphony.

In summer the Park City International Music Festival presents six weeks of concerts in and around the picturesque former-mining-town-turned-ski-resort east of Salt Lake City. On the Salt Lake City side of the Wasatch Range, the Snowbird Institute's String Chamber Music Festival unveils a week of concerts each summer at the Snowbird Ski Resort in Little Cottonwood Canyon. For many years this gathering has been anchored by the Muir Quartet.

To the northeast, the Bear Lake Music Festival presented its second two-week summer season in 1993 in the quiet communities of Utah and Idaho that flank the lake. Both the Park City and Bear Lake gatherings offer concerts by festival orchestras as well. A new Utah Music Festival gave its inaugural summer season in 1993, primarily in Logan and Salt Lake City. Artist faculty

Ensembles,
orchestras and
festivals meet
the needs of a
D I V E R S E
Utah audience.

SYMPHONIC OPPORTUNITIES

Utah Symphony, Abravanel Hall, 123 W. South Temple, Salt Lake City, Utah 84101.

Wasatch Community Symphony, c/o 3070 Bluebell Drive, Salt Lake City, Utah 84124.

American West Symphony and Chorus, P.O. Box 1416, Salt Lake City, Utah 84091-1416.

Murray Symphony, P.O. Box 57704, Murray, Utah 84157.

West Valley Symphony, 3384 Hillsdale Drive, West Valley City, Utah 84119.

Salt Lake Symphony, 220 Morris Avenue, Salt Lake City, Utah 84115.

Utah Valley Symphony, c/o Beverly Dunford, 461 E. 2875 N., Provo, Utah 84604.

Rocky Mountain Symphony, Eccles Community Art Center, 2580 Jefferson Ave., Ogden, Utah 84401.

New American Symphony Orchestra, P.O. Box 1245, Layton, Utah 84041.

Southwest Symphony, P.O. Box 423, St. George, Utah 84771.

The Chamber Music Society of Salt Lake City, P.O. Box 58825, Salt Lake City, Utah 84158-0825.

The Chamber Music Society of Logan, P.O. Box 3620, Logan, Utah 84323-3620.

Park City International Music Festival, P.O. Box 354, Park City, Utah 84060.

Snowbird Institute String Chamber Music Festival, Snowbird, Utah 84092.

Bear Lake Music Festival, 904 Washington St., Montpelier, Idaho 83254.

Gina Bachauer International Piano Foundation, P.O. Box 11664, Salt Lake City, Utah 84147.

All-City Children's Orchestra, c/o Devon English Colby, 2348 Willow Hills Dr., Sandy, Utah 84093.

Utah Youth Symphony, c/o Lynn B. Larsen, 2032 E. Ridgehill Drive, Bountiful, Utah 84010.

for all of these festivals are drawn from orchestras and conservatories across the nation, though Utah musicians play prominent roles in the Park City and Bear Lake festivals as well.

During the traditional academic year, Utah's universities offer recitals and concerts by touring artists. Brigham Young University in Provo is particularly active in this regard, as are Weber State University in Ogden and Utah State University in Logan.

In 1947, when Maurice Abravanel was anticipating the move from New York to take over the Utah Symphony, he asked his mentor, the great conductor Bruno Walter, where Salt Lake City was located.

"Somewhere west of Denver," Walter replied.

It remained for Mr. Abravanel and his orchestra to put Utah on the musical map, and they succeeded beyond all expectations.

Today's musicians in Utah are building on that legacy, and they aren't looking back.

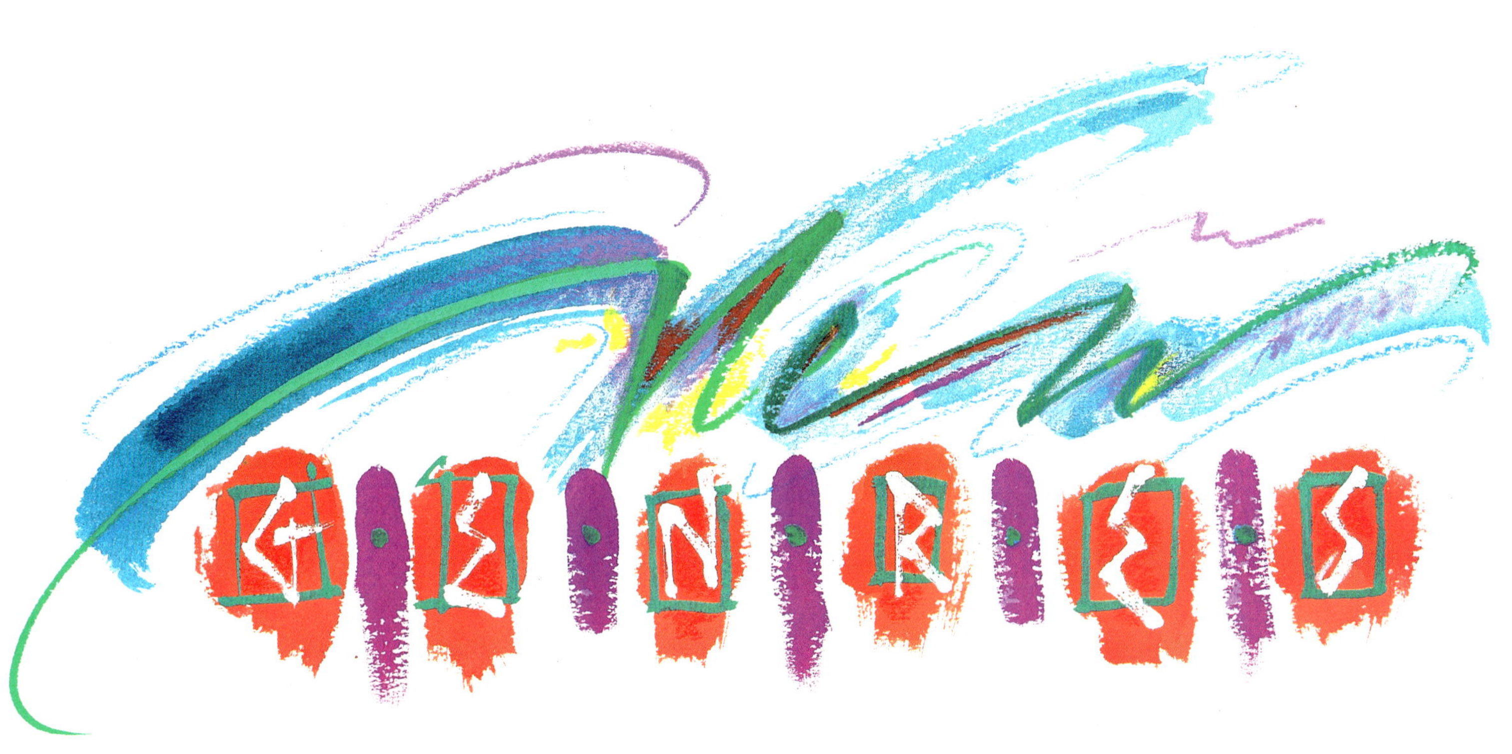

New Genres:
The
Orphans
of Discipline

Carol Biddle

FEW THINGS INTIMIDATE, confuse and anger people as much as contemporary art they do not understand. And of all contemporary art, the so-called *new genres* are often the most difficult to figure out.

It is not so much that "new genres" are truly *new* as that they are impossible to categorize neatly within historically defined disciplines. Artists presenting works called *installations*, *environmental art*, or *performance art* and artists working in visually based video and computer-aided art typically borrow freely from all disciplines—visual arts, architecture, dance, costume design, music, theater, opera—even from fields outside of art such as science and religion.

ANOTHER LANGUAGE

"It is an acknowledgment of the silent tornado inside."
—Beth Miklavcic

"Art is not a noun. It's a verb, an 'action' word. It's a long slow deep breath that one begins near birth and expends when one passes on. And if artists are doing their 'job' properly, that breath is expended into the mouth of a new generation."
—Jimmy Miklavcic

Another Language Performing Arts Company, "dance based,"mixes disciplines (visual arts, environmental sculpture, writing, dance, music, computer technology, video) to present challenging collaborative work.

Core-member dancers Chara Huckins, Marianne Benson, Jeannine Chan, Jane Gregory Payne and Spencer Powell are co-directed by Jimmy (computer scientist, performer, and electronic musician) and Beth (dancer and choreographer) Miklavcic. Their fresh body of performance work is neither self-conscious nor over-produced.

In Utah new-genre works are often presented during the Utah Arts Festival and at the Salt Lake City Arts Council's Finch Lane Gallery, Artspace, Art Access, Salt Lake Art Center, Bountiful/Davis Art Center, Brigham City Museum and similar facilities and at college and commercial galleries. However, artists are just as likely to present works in *alternative spaces*—outdoors in the desert, in the mountains or on the streets, or in warehouses, storefronts or cafés.

Two seminal and internationally known earthworks by American artists—Robert Smithson's *Spiral Jetty* in the Great Salt Lake and Nancy Holt's *Sun Tunnels* in the northwestern desert—are credited with putting Utah on the map in the history of environmental art. Created in the 1970's, the *Spiral Jetty* is now submerged by the flooded lake but on a calm day the spiral of rocks, shimmering with salt crystals, may be seen from the air.

Although the site is isolated, many Utahns make annual treks to the *Sun Tunnels* to observe sunrise during the solstices or equinoxes.

In 1987 Gayle Weyher organized the monumental project *Lost and Found,* a contemporary archaeological ruin. This multimedia collaborative installation with California artist David Furman and Utahn A. F. Caldiero explored the "ironies, paradoxes and possibilities of

living in a consumer culture and its transient and abundant remains." Funded by the National Endowment for the Arts, the project and corresponding catalog received national attention.

Utah photographer David Baddley uses the camera as just one tool in his conceptual artwork. He has presented performance art, photo and video installations (often as documentation of art events) and site/action earthworks, all of which may be accompanied by narrative text. Baddley explores the geography with a keen eye to human impact and asks his viewers to see land in a new way.

Darin Biniaz is known for site-specific works with pointed political and social commentary. A visit to the barren desert of Skull Valley exposes his environmental work entitled *No Choice: No Freedom,* a memorial to women who have died from illegal abortions. Other works include *No Home for the Brave,* a series of disquieting and larger-than-life portraits of homeless children, and *The Clean Air Is in the Box,* a Plexiglas cube filled with fresh mountain air and suspended above a busy Salt Lake City intersection.

Alison Ann Berkey recently burst into public view with human-scale papier mâché sculptures. A 1992 New Forms Regional Initiatives grant allowed her to produce a room-sized papier mâché

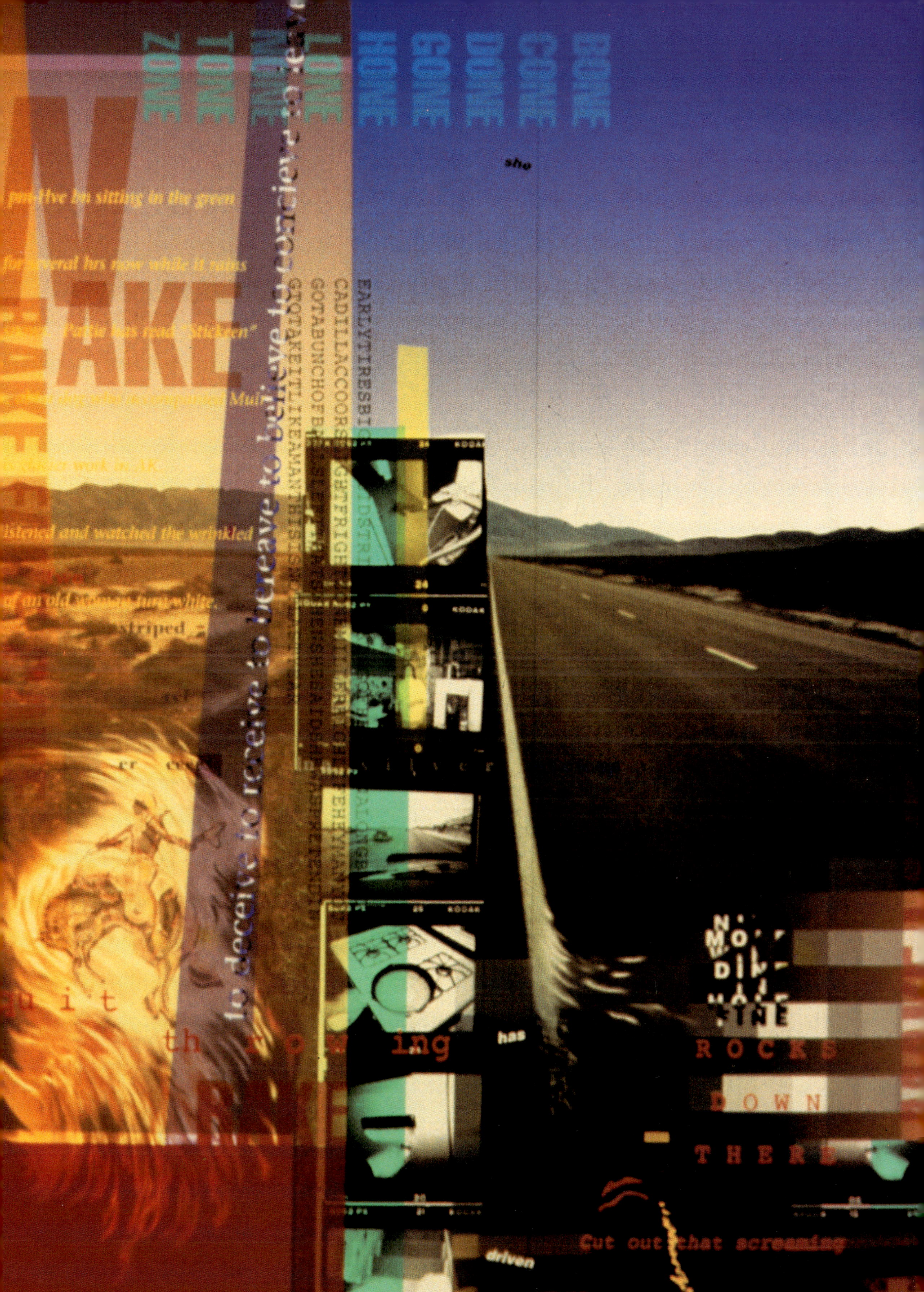
BONE
GONE
DONE
GONE
NONE
LONE
NONE
NONE
TONE
ZONE
WAKE
BAKE
she
positive Im sitting in the green
for several hrs now while it rains
to deceive to receive to bereave to conceive to
she who accompanied Muir
her work in AK.
listened and watched the wrinkled
of an old woman face white.
striped
EARLYTIRESBIG
CADILLACCOORS
GOTABUNCHOF
quit
th owing
has
silver
NO MORE
ROCKS
DOWN
THERE
driven
Cut out that screaming

UNCOMMON ART/COMMON GROUND

While new-genre works defy neat definition, they frequently bear certain common characteristics: They imply collaboration between creator and viewer, foster creativity through unstructured experimentation, and reinforce the interrelationship of art and life by taking art out of a sacred "museum" context. And while these *avant garde* works may initially confuse or intimidate the uninitiated, ultimately they may offer some of the freshest perspectives on contemporary culture and encourage us to question the very nature of art.

Mixed-media
assemblages offer
F   R   E   S   H
perspectives.

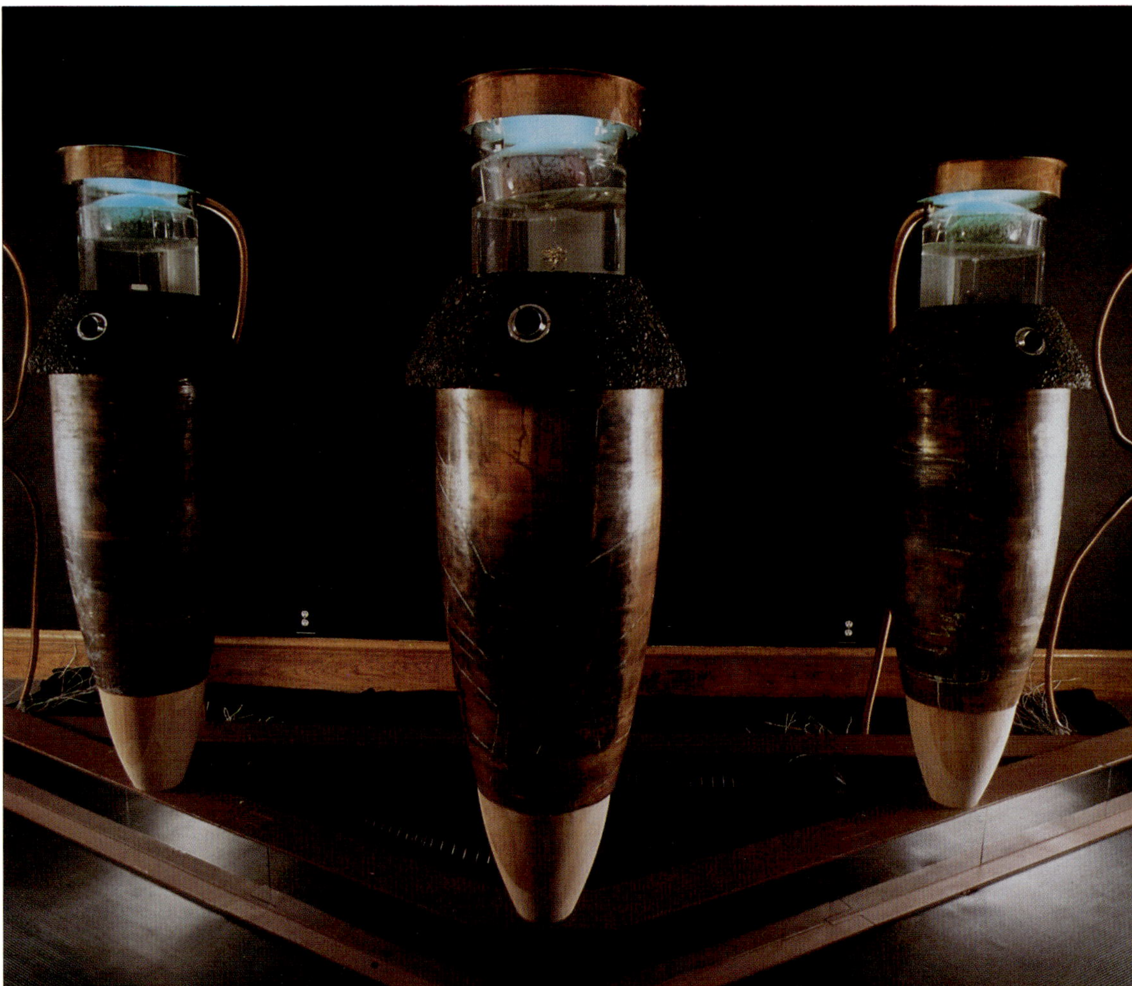

whiskey bottle which illustrated the effects of alcohol abuse. She also exhibits papier mâché sculptural portraits influenced by Mexican folk art.

Susan Hyde Bland's installations of photographs, narrative text and quilted, embroidered, appliquéd and embellished fabrics allow us an intimate peek into suspended moments in private lives. *100 Years 100 Pictures*, a room-sized three-dimensional "book," and *The Storytellers* remind us of the importance of memory, the value of human life at all stages and the richness of family history.

Helene Fischer Elbein's installations are dark reminders of what has gone wrong with society. Confronting issues such as racial and ethnic prejudice, waste management and our disposable society, Elbein simulates urban spaces with garbage cans, plaster casts of severed limbs and faces and bricks encoded with numbers or words.

An ongoing series by Mary Fish entitled *A Thousand Origami Cranes* expresses the fragility of species and nature. This hauntingly beautiful work combines a thousand hand-folded origami cranes with a multimedia presentation of projected images and audio

tapes of bird sounds. A recent installation, *She Mountain/Earth's Dress,* pays
homage to the Navajo women of Big
Mountain/ Black Mesa.

Frank McEntire assembles divining
instruments, discarded religious
objects and vessels used to store
sacred artifacts into installations and
personal altars that give new meaning to
Native American traditions, Hindu mys-
ticism, Asian religion, Jewish and
Catholic symbolism, Mormon beliefs
and other cross-cultural traditions.

McEntire—who has become something of a resident expert on local,
regional, and national artists working in
a *transformative* vein—states that this art
"challenges the values of post-
Modern society and its basic assump-
tions about the environment and the
human condition." In 1992 he organized *Dreams and Shields: Spiritual
Dimensions in Contemporary Art,* a major
survey of the work of more than forty
Western-region artists who mix art and
soul. The exhibition included a number
of mixed-media assemblages by Utah
artists John Evans, Lucy Fairchild,
Stephen Goldsmith, Carleen Jimenez,
Thomas Schulte and Thomas Tessman,
with performances by A. F. Caldiero.

Caldiero, who has received national
awards for poetry/art projects, incorporates traditional and experimental art,
performance, literature and sound with
studies into the nature and origin of language to present what he calls "trans-

environmental and language performance works" with rich images from
both sacred and secular life.

The past decade has seen a number
of other collaborative installations and
performances by both established and
emerging artists, including Susan Beck,
Maureen O'Hara-Ure, Bonnie Sucec,
Jen Shurtliff and Meredith Moench. The
recent exhibit *Natural Disasters* featured
painter/mixed media artist O'Hara-Ure
and poet Katharine Coles. *First Steps,* a
1991 installation—by Eric Robinson,
David S, Tony Weller, Shelley White,
Melodia Moore, Wendy Ajax, and
Larnie Fox (now living in California)—
combined performance with a kinetic
found-object installation.

*" . . . the brutal grandeur and ephemeral
charm of things that you won't see twice"*

—from "Performance: Live Art 1909 to the
Present," RoseLee Goldberg

A Company of Four combines
dynamic visuals, video, theater,
dance and sound to create surrealistic performances of disquieting beauty and mystery. Primary company members Gary Vlasic, Mark Lowdermilk and
Susan McGee-Lowdermilk tend to

FOLLOWING PAGE PHOTO: *THE BIRTHDAY PARTY* / PHOTO BY KENVIN LYMAN

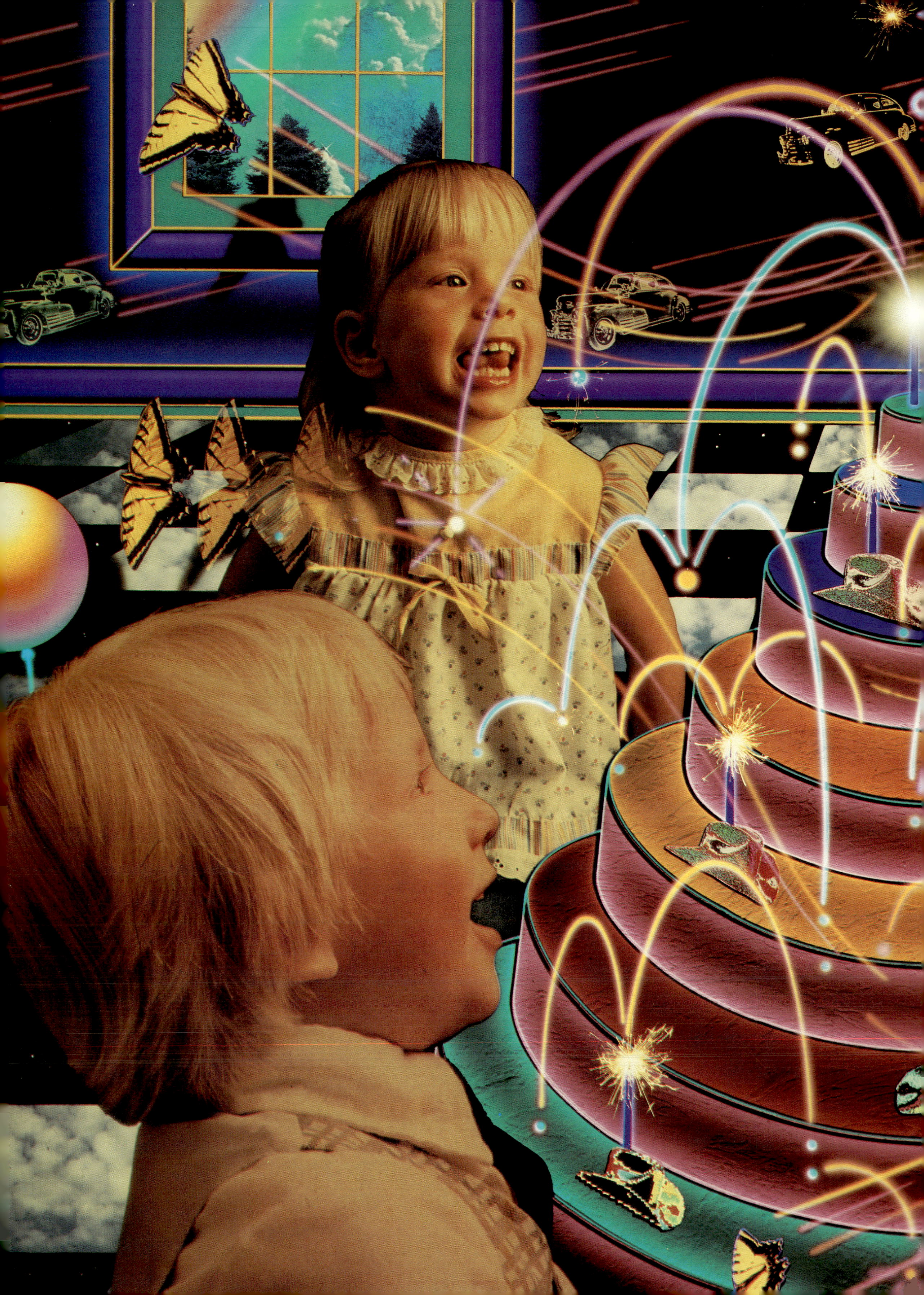

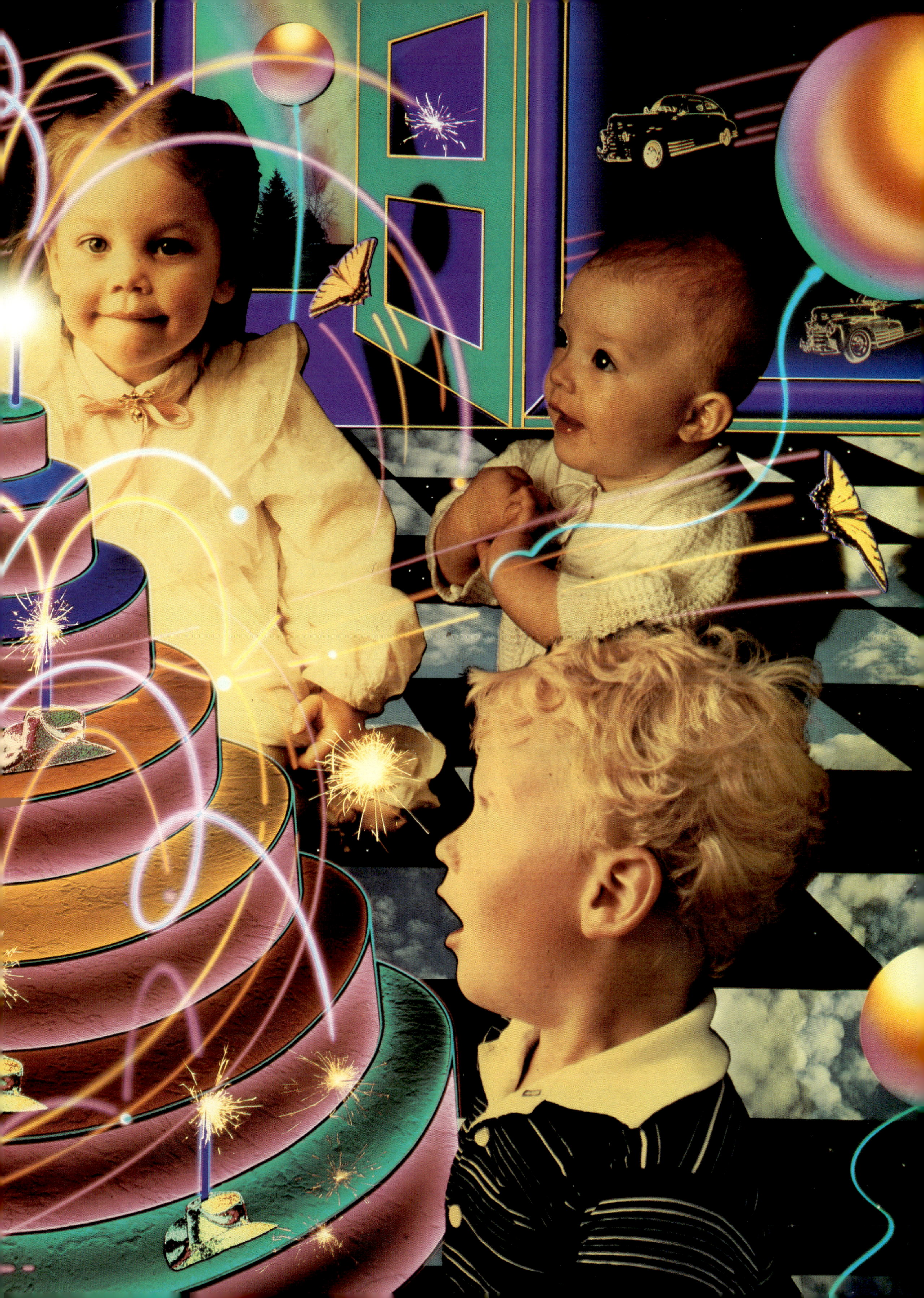

ANDREW KRASNOW

Andrew Krasnow has been inventing interactive mechanical sculptures and installations for more than a decade. Though he has perhaps only a baker's dozen actual works completed, each is a monumental accomplishment, and his commitment has brought its rewards. He has received several national awards, including a National Endowment for the Arts grant for a kinetic interactive installation called *Growth (Salt Lake Art Center, 1992)* and has exhibited at galleries such as PS 1 in New York City.

Merging a persona as artist/mad scientist, Krasnow is compelled to analyze machines—from the simple lever to the human brain—as extensions of man's desire for power and to incorporate them as a logical domain of art. *Core Texts of the Mind*—a series of five cones, each containing a human brain suspended in colored water and lit eerily from within the cone—explored one of the central conflicts of human existence: mind versus body, intellect versus emotion.

explore the complex side of our world—our environment, behavior, absurdities and irrationalities—with both biting humor and gentle wit. Essentially abstracted works, their pieces are often held together structurally and retain elements of narrative through the voice of a "barker," seemingly from the carnival underworld.

In addition to presentations by the Company of Four, Vlasic and McGee-Lowdermilk create individual works. Vlasic often collaborates with Crisanne Olsen or others on theatrical installations combining poetry, painting, mixed media constructions and performance. McGee-Lowdermilk recently received a grant from Dancing in the Streets, an international agency based in New York, for a May 1994 collaborative performance work in the empty Wasatch Plunge pool at the Children's Museum of Utah. Another work, *Mystére*, investigates the realm of personal choice and fashion.

Ceramist and performance artist Kelvin Yazzie received a New Forms grant in 1990 for a project in which he used found objects, his own hand-built pots and Native American music, costuming and dance to create his interpretation of a medicine wheel.

Curtis Benali, an emerging Navajo artist, has presented several performance works at Weber State University, including a Columbus Day art event, provoking an open dialogue regarding Native American issues and ceremonies.

In the past both the Utah Arts Festival and the Utah/U.S. Film and Video Festival (now the Sundance Film Festival) offered video art environments sponsored and organized by the Utah Media Arts Center—complete with the latest in visually based imagery, counterculture guerilla art, and low-tech/high-tech and interactive-tech computer animation.

These video environments featured well-known artists from all over the United States. Provocative works by Nam June Piak, Bill Viola and Utah native David Hayes were shown along with interactive work by artists like Skip Blumberg.

Although both festivals have eliminated the annual video components, the Utah Media Arts Center still periodically presents experimental multimedia screenings and multimedia exhibitions by Utah artists. *Blue Buddhas—Red Radar* (1990), for example, by video artist David Hayes, combined video, radar, altered kitchen appliances and origami birds.

One of the most interesting emerging artists is Karey Kay Walter, who teaches at the Visual Arts Institute and combines photography and video to create intense, flickering portraits.

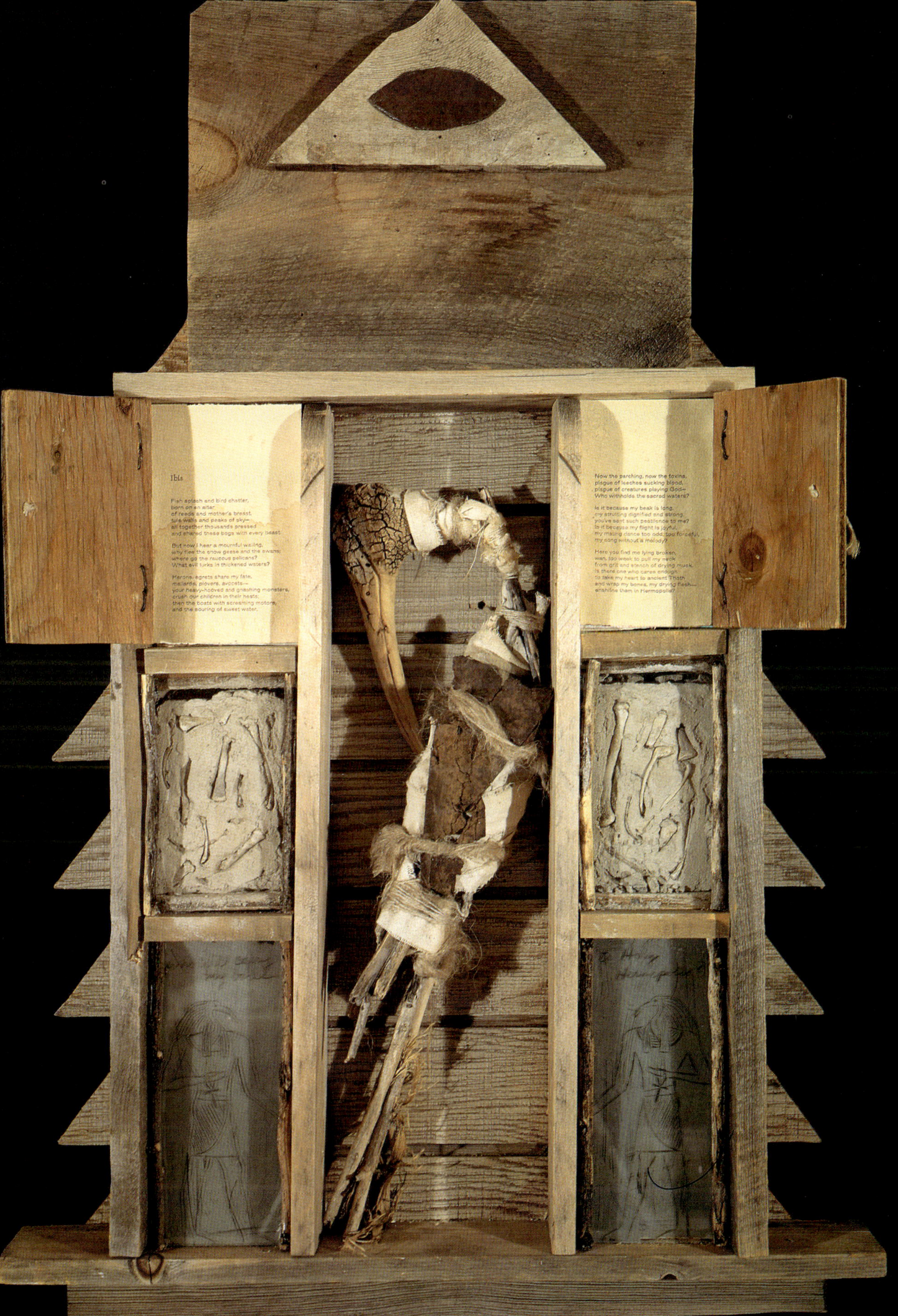

Ibis

Fish splash and bird chatter,
born on an altar
of reeds and mother's breast,
tule walls and peaks of sky—
all together thousands pressed
and shared these bogs with every beast.

But now I hear a mournful wailing,
why flee the snow geese and the swans,
where go the raucous pelicans?
What evil lurks in thickened waters?

Herons, egrets share my fate,
mallards, plovers, avocets—
your heavy-hooved and gnashing monsters,
crush our children in their nests;
then the boats with screaming motors,
and the souring of sweet water.

Now the parching, now the toxins,
plague of leeches sucking blood,
plague of creatures playing God—
Who withholds the sacred waters?

Is it because my beak is long,
my strutting dignified and strong,
you've sent such pestilence to me?
Is it because my flight is joyful,
my mating dance too odd, too forceful,
my song without a melody?

Here you find me lying broken,
wan, too weak to pull my neck
from grit and stench of drying muck.
Is there one who cares enough
to take my heart to ancient Thoth
and wrap my bones, my drying flesh—
enshrine them in Hermopolis?

The relatively short history of computer imaging is inextricably linked to Utah. A 1989 exhibit, *An Elegant Merging*, organized by Kenvin Lyman, traced the history of computer-assisted imagery in the United States as well as the University of Utah's seminal role in the development of virtually every significant new concept in computer graphics during the late 1960's and early seventies.

Lyman's own résumé reads like a definition of the "high-tech renaissance man." He is a composer and musician; a graphic, architectural, and engineering designer; and an artist working in neon, light, holography, computer graphics, optical imaging, painting, animation and performance. Commercial designs for national clients like AT&T, ABC Records, American Airlines, Datsun, Visa, Coca Cola, the Los Angeles Olympics and a host of music "greats" such as Stevie Wonder, Bo Diddley and The Grateful Dead are balanced by art projects with Ririe-Woodbury Dance Company, Salt Lake City Arts Council, Hansen Planetarium and a mural in the Baci Trattoria.

In 1992 Director Larry Douglass of the Brigham City Museum organized the first juried computer-aided art exhibit in Utah. This exhibit, which included artists from the Western United States, was featured in *Computer Graphics World* magazine. Computer-generated works by Mark Biddle, Jim Jacobs, Neal Slade, Richard Pogue, Wayne Chubin, Richard Haffar, Jim Rose, John Savage, Wayne R. Tyler and Steve Taft can frequently be seen in local galleries and exhibits.

A number of Utah artists working primarily in other media have created one-of-a-kind artists' books, among them Day Christensen, Doug Himes, Wayne Chubin, Stephen Goldsmith, Dorothy Greenland, Lucy Fairchild, Julie Stetzko-Taff and David S.

Sue Cotter approaches her one-of-a-kind conceptual books as experimental archaeological projects. Working with maps, landscape, nature and the human body, Cotter extracts shapes and stories which she calls "topographical mythology."

Blammoroots, a non-juried bound collection of original art and writing, initiates a dialogue among the participants. Organized by librarian and book artist Heidi Ferguson, the artists' journals are issued quarterly. In a similar process, a group of artists who call themselves *Hatu Teresed* (for Deseret Utah, backwards) sell their conceptual calendar at a price equal to the current year.

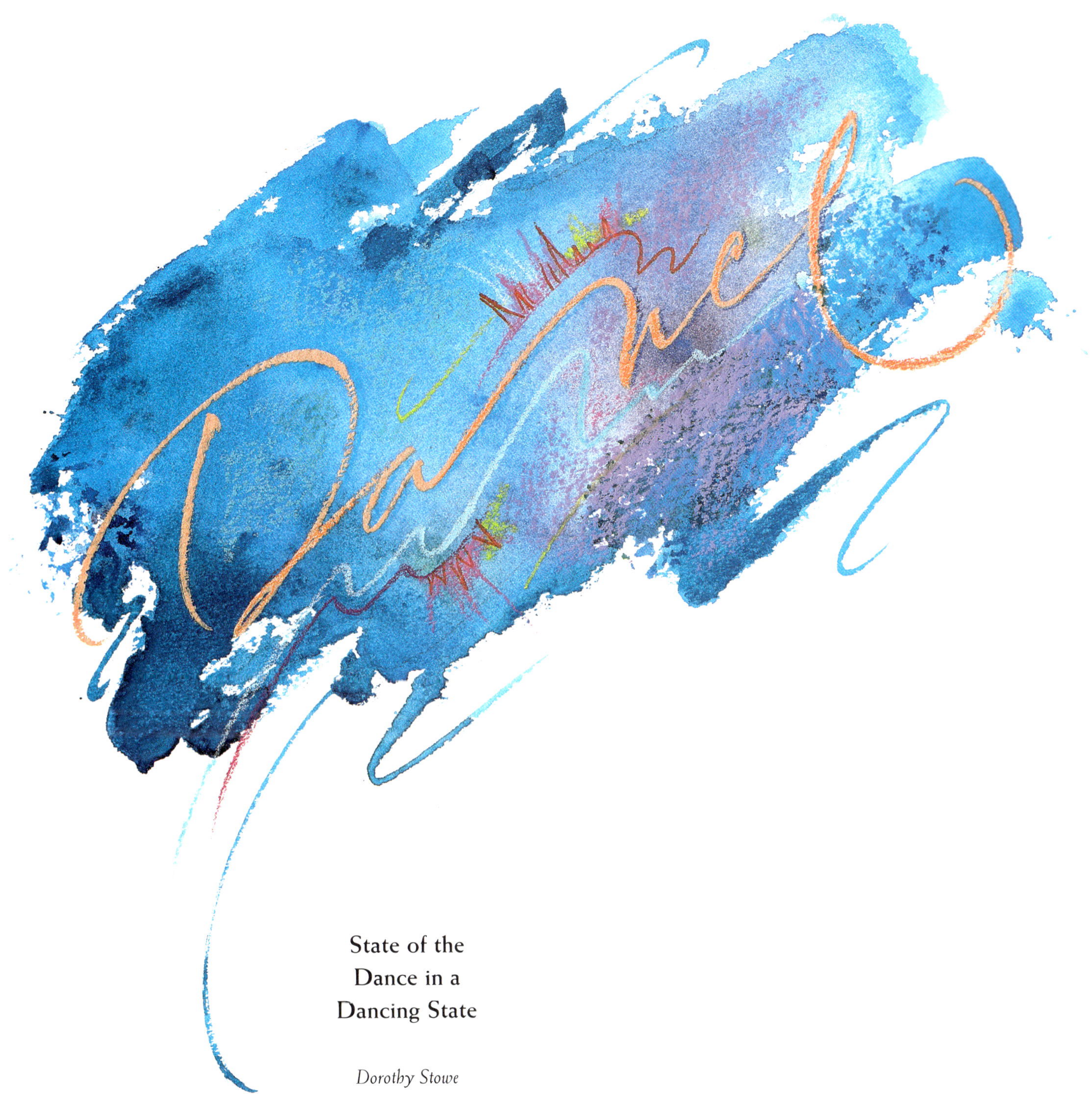

State of the
Dance in a
Dancing State

Dorothy Stowe

I T'S CHRISTMAS SEASON any year in Salt Lake City and your destination is Ballet West's *Nutcracker* where you will see Utah dance at its most ambient and Utah society at its abundant best.

As you step from the cold winter night into the ornate red-and-gold warmth of the Capitol Theatre lobby, profuse with greens and flowers, a wave of seasonal nostalgia engulfs you. An earnest high school choir proclaims peace-good-will from the balcony, while among the gala crowd, little girls with curly, beribboned hair and frilly dresses jump up and down in excitement.

LINDA C. SMITH

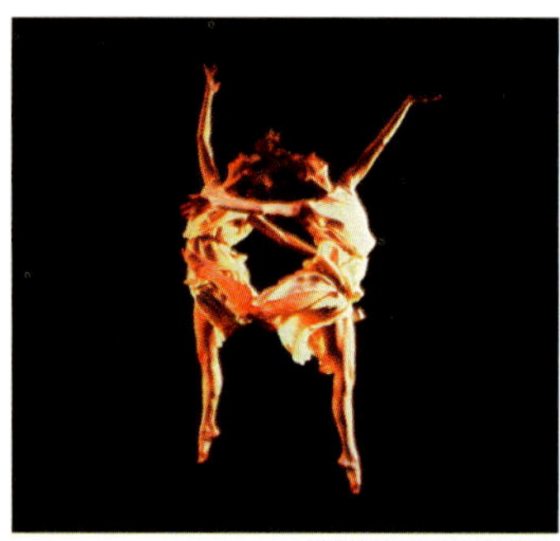

PHOTO BY JACK VARTOOGIAN

Salt Lake born and bred Linda Call Smith was a charter member of Virginia Tanner's Children's Dance Theatre and a founding member of Repertory Dance Theatre (1966). Now she's the only charter member remaining—a survivor of the first order, a leader who has held onto her dreams while confronting stern reality. Other Utah dance leaders have diversified themselves; she has poured her life's energies into one organization and magnified it.

Always a leader in RDT and sole artistic director since 1983, Smith has kept the company on course through good times and bad, working with nearly one hundred modern choreographers, major and minor, to collect and produce more than two hundred works. "I am a preservationist, a restorationist," she says. "And I feel closely tied to Utah and to this community where we do many school programs every year. It's important to reach the young in our culture."

In the darkened theater the orchestra strikes up Tchaikovsky, the Stahlbaums throw their party, Herr Drosselmeyer casts his spell, and Clara whisks away to the Sugar Plum Kingdom.

So it has been every year since 1955, when Willam Christensen, then head of ballet at the University of Utah, and Maurice Abravanel, conductor of the Utah Symphony, put their heads together over the first Utah *Nutcracker*— a project for which doomsayers predicted no good end. But Utah's *Nutcracker* has flourished, even appearing as a popular telecast on public television. Utahns return again and again for this magical transformation, with many sellouts in every run of twenty or so performances.

How long will *The Nutcracker* last? "As long as there are children," Christensen asserts.

And how long will dance endure in Utah: As long as there are descendants of the Mormon pioneers, who danced around their campfires after a hard day crossing the Plains and put up a Social Hall for dances and parties within five years of arriving in the Valley; as long as enthusiastic dancers and teachers come here to make development of dance in Utah their life's work, as dozens have done, creating one of the country's most nurturing and highly developed dance milieux.

Willam Christensen, a native of Brigham City, exemplifies this high level of expertise and dedication. He began his career dancing ballet in vaudeville, with his brothers Lew and Harold. After teaching in Portland, Oregon, he gravitated to San Francisco as ballet master of the San Francisco Opera Ballet, which in 1937 he reorganized as the San Francisco Ballet, now the nation's oldest ballet company. As artistic director there, in 1944 he choreographed the first-ever full-length *Nutcracker* in America.

In 1951 he accepted an invitation to form America's first ballet department in a fine arts college at the University of Utah. He first led the University Ballet, which evolved to the Utah Civic Ballet, then to Ballet West in 1966. As his patron, sponsor, and co-founder, Glenn Walker Wallace marshalled support from the town.

A resident of the Capitol Theatre since 1978, Ballet West gives four productions of eight performances each year, plus its extended *Nutcracker* run. With a frugal budget of $4.5 million, the company of thirty-eight dancers typically dances the great full-length ballets of the nineteenth century, including all Tchaikovsky works, as well as modern ballets by current choreographers.

Very successful as a regional and national company, Ballet West made a European tour in 1969, a New York City

FOLLOWING PAGE: SALT LAKE CONVENTION/VISITORS BUREAU PHOTO

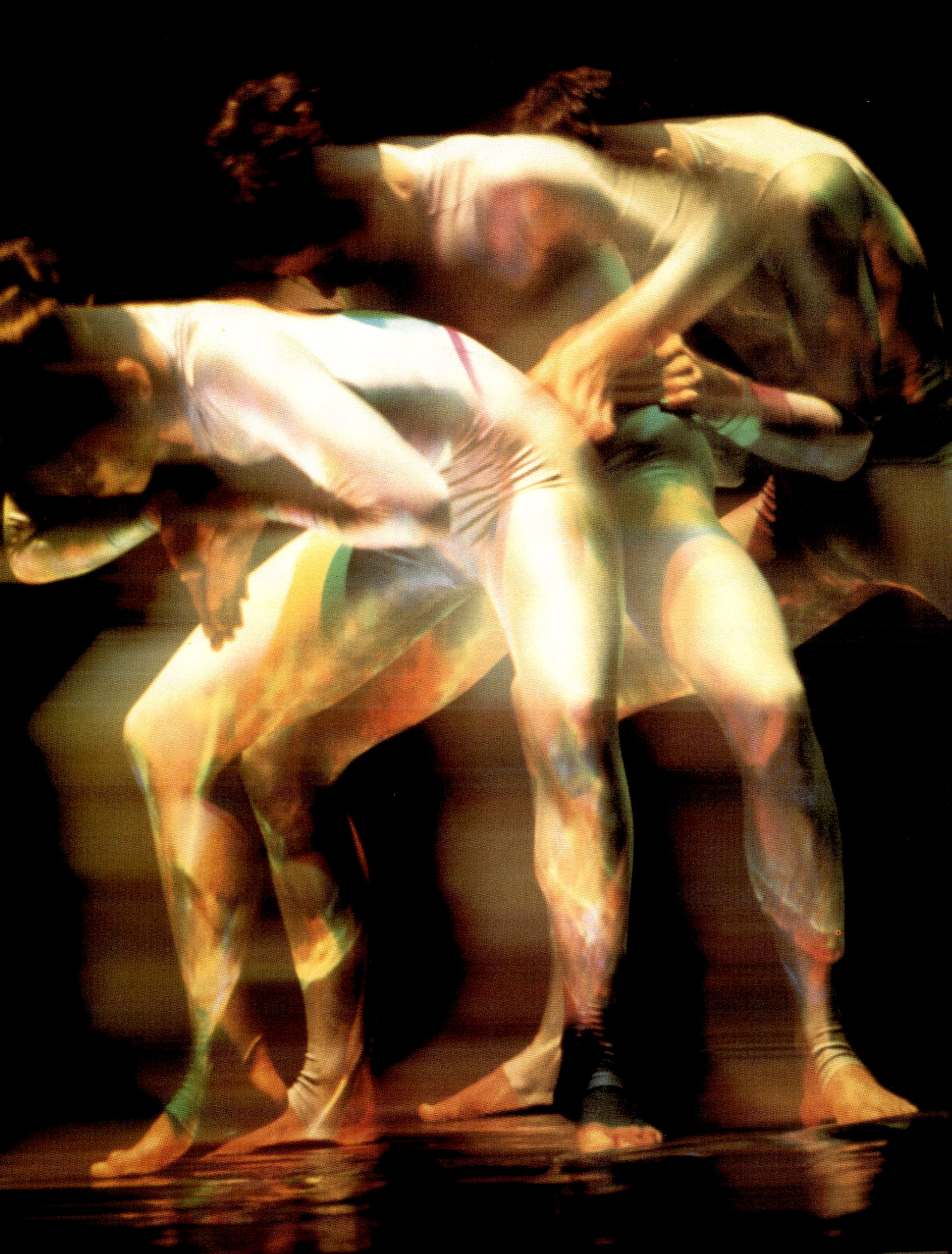

debut in 1980, and now tours often throughout the East, Midwest, and Southwest. The company has appeared at the John F. Kennedy Center in Washington, D.C., four times—in 1983, headlining with *Swan Lake;* in 1985 with *Abdallah,* a Bournonville revival that drew international acclaim; in 1986 with *Sleeping Beauty;* and in 1991 with Andre Prokovsky's *Anna Karenina.* In the summer of 1992 Ballet West was triumphant in Michael Smuin's *Romeo and Juliet* at Wolf Trap Farm, where it far outdrew Russia's Kirov Ballet.

Ballet West has had only three artistic directors during its twenty-seven years. Christensen was succeeded in 1976 by Bruce Marks, a former *premier danseur* with American Ballet Theater, who now heads the Boston Ballet. Since 1986 John Hart, C.B.E., who had danced and held administrative positions with Britain's Royal Ballet for many years, has added a perceptibly English influence to Ballet West's technique and repertory.

Under the long and deep influence of Mr. C., as Willam Christensen is affectionately known, ballet training in Utah has flourished, especially at the University of Utah, which offers one of the most respected student ballet programs in America, with nationally known faculty.

The university shelters the Ballet West Conservatory, headed by John Hart and Sharee Lane, where Mr. C., now ninety years old, still teaches. The Conservatory trains advanced students of secondary school age from the many good private studios up and down the Wasatch Front, many of which are headed by teachers who trained under Mr. C. Good ballet training is easy to find in Utah.

America's first

B   A   L   L   E   T

department

in a fine arts

college was in Utah.

The university's Utah Ballet (UB) is a scholarship company whose performance and touring is aimed at bridging the gap between amateur and professional status. Utah Ballet is directed by Hungarian-born and trained Attila Ficzere, formerly of the San Francisco Ballet. UB draws students from the conservatory and the nation and feeds Ballet West as well as other national professional companies.

Good amateur ballet companies include the Utah Regional Ballet (URB) and its school in American Fork led by Jacqueline Colledge. URB has excellent regional standing and its good full-length programs include a yearly *Nutcracker*.

Vivian Kosan-Bagnall, now teaching at Snow College in Ephraim, heads the Central Utah Ballet, and Sandra Emile, an eastern import, directs Cache Valley Ballet and its school. Both offer annual *Nutcrackers*. In Price, at the College of Eastern Utah, Carolyn Gwyther draws upon an enormous geographic area to train and lead Ballet Repertory Ensemble, a town-and-gown enterprise.

In 1992 the University of Utah celebrated one hundred years of dance on campus, dating from the arrival of Maud May Babcock, who first taught dance movement as an alternative to physical education classes and remained to become a beloved professor of drama.

Dedicated teachers expanded the dance program. In 1940 Elizabeth Hayes arrived at the university to begin fifty years of service, fulfilling almost every calling in dance education, performance, and administration. Hayes continues to teach as an emeritus professor.

Perhaps the university's most prized centennial possession is the beautiful

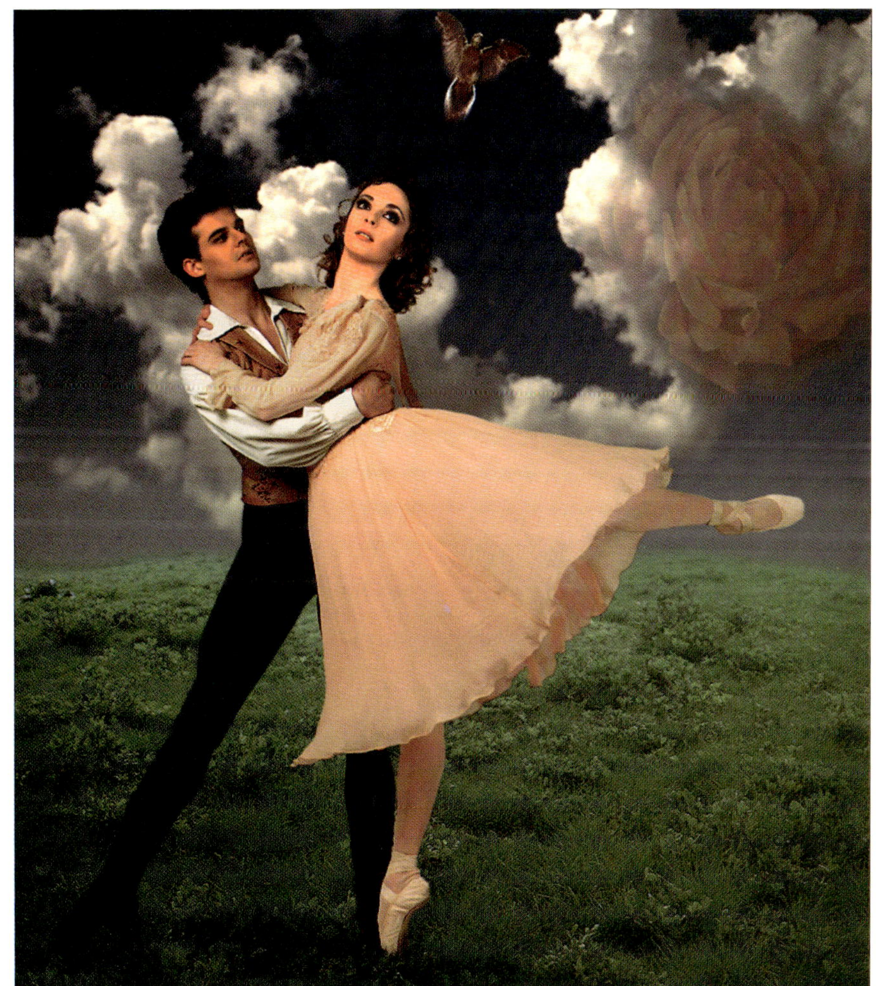

THE LADY OF THE CAMELLIAS / PHOTO O'VERY / COVEY

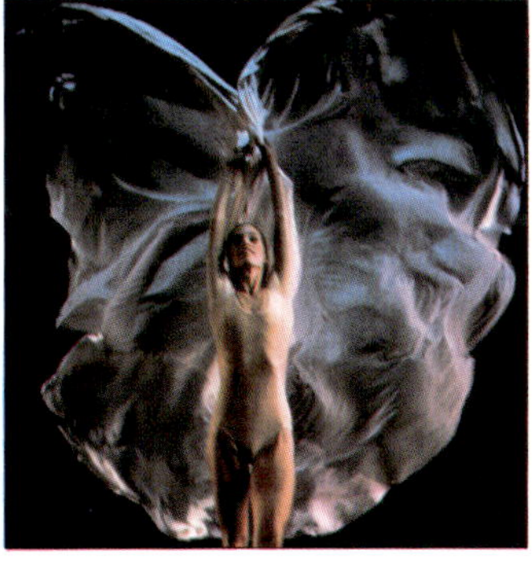

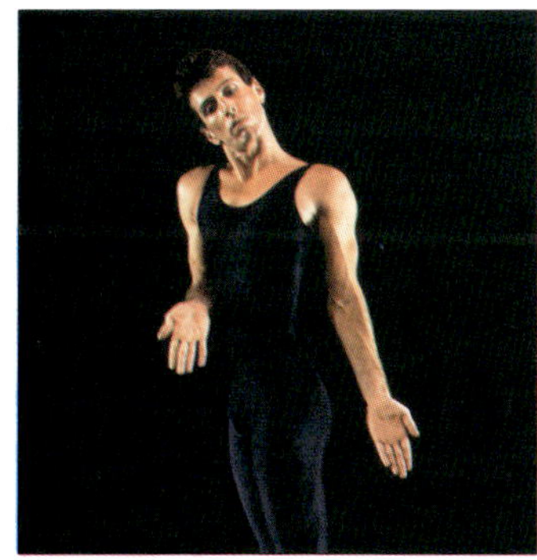

Alice Sheets Marriott Center for Dance, completed in 1989 with state funds and a gift of $2 million from the Marriott Foundation. This up-to-the-minute facility houses the Hayes/Christensen Theater, where many dance events take place.

Equal to ballet in importance and national prestige are Utah's modern dance training and companies, including the scholarship Performing Dance Company and two professional companies—Ririe-Woodbury Dance Company and the Repertory Dance Theatre (RDT)—both spawned at the University of Utah.

Joan Woodbury and Shirley Ririe were among the young teachers who surrounded Hayes and their exuberant talents led them through many combinations of dancers to finally coalesce as the spunky, wildly original Ririe-Woodbury Dance Company.

With influences from Alwin Nikolais, the six-member company thrives on choreographies off the beaten track and into the future by the co-directors and prominent guest choreographers. Their repertory is on the cutting edge, with much innovative use of multi-media and their own imaginative, often zany, resources.

Ririe-Woodbury, long famed nationally for work in schools, was at one time the most widely toured company in America under the National Endowment for the Arts' (NEA) dance touring program. Their children's program (now in its fifth inventive edition) is a spring favorite at the Capitol Theatre and with audiences nationwide, including appearances at Washington, D.C.'s Kennedy Center. Ririe-Woodbury gives two major concerts in the Capitol Theatre annually and tours extensively, often

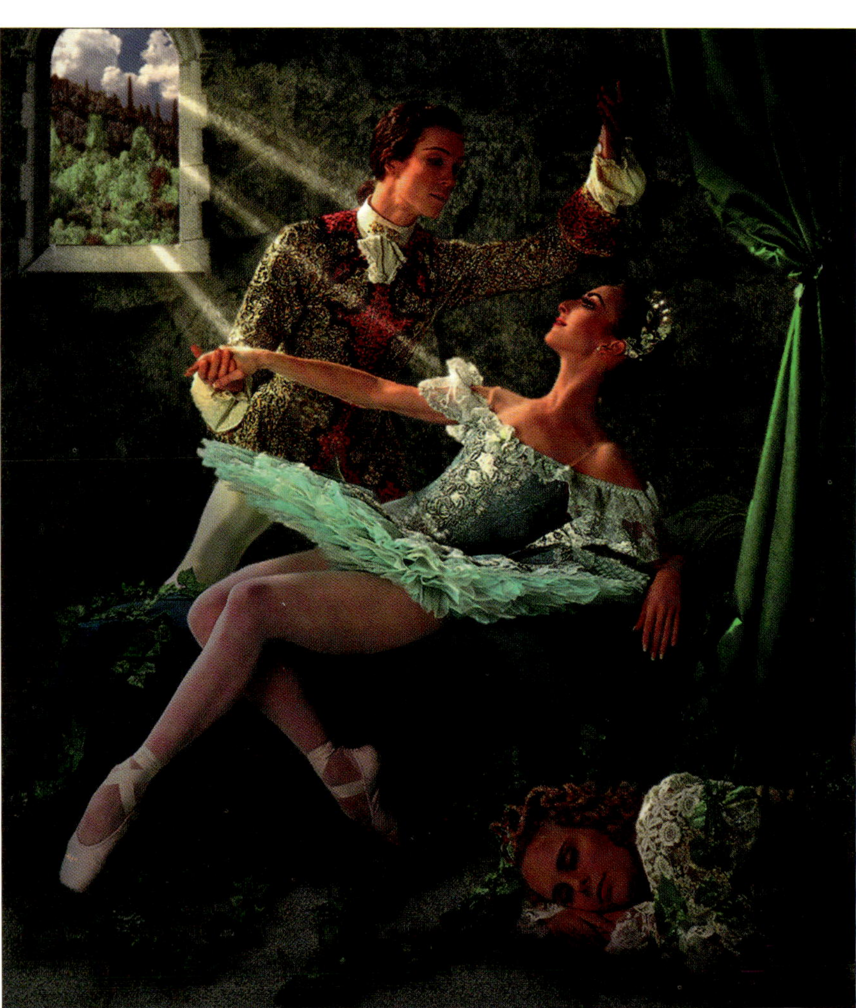

SLEEPING BEAUTY / PHOTO O'VERY / COVEY

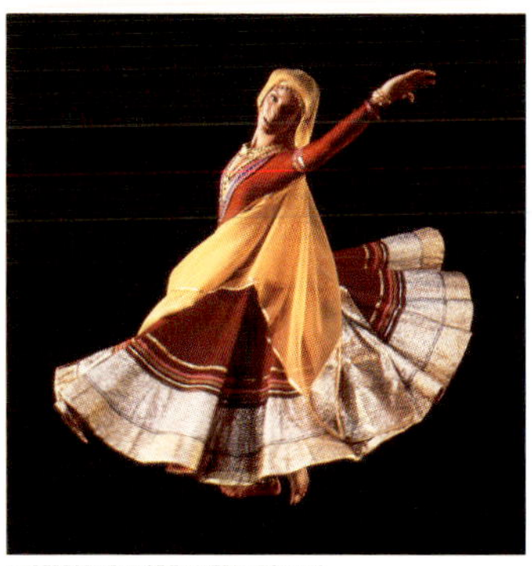

REPERTORY DANCE THEATRE ARCHIVES
PHOTO BY JACK VARTOOGIAN

spending a month in school and community residencies sponsored by such states as North Carolina, Kentucky and New Mexico.

During the 1940's a Utah original took "roots and wings" in Utah—Virginia Tanner, whose forte was the teaching and training of children. From Tanner's talents as choreographer, writer and educator evolved the Children's Dance Theatre, which she toured to national heights, right onto the cover of *Life* magazine.

Tanner died too young, in 1979, but her legacy remains in the delightful Children's Dance Theatre (CDT) now headed by Mary Ann Lee. Under Miss Virginia's inspiring motto, "Roots and Wings," the University of Utah's creative dance program teaches close to 800 Utah children, ages three to eighteen, at any given time—not only producing innovative children's ballets and movement, but training the whole child to valuable disciplines and the freedom experienced by those who get in touch with their own creativity. The company gives one major concert each spring, while the small CDT ensemble fulfills residencies in Utah schools and has toured nationally and internationally, often to prestigious children's dance conferences.

Not least of Tanner's accomplishments was her liaison with the Rockefeller Foundation, in the days when it heavily supported the arts. Ever-increasing Rockefeller grants brought top dance teachers and performers to Utah until Tanner's crowning success in securing a 1966 grant for

$370,000, under which the Repertory Dance Theatre was created.

The company flourishes still, usually with eight or nine dancers, under the artistic direction of Linda C. Smith, a charter member of both the Children's Dance Theatre and RDT. Smith holds high the company's charge to be a

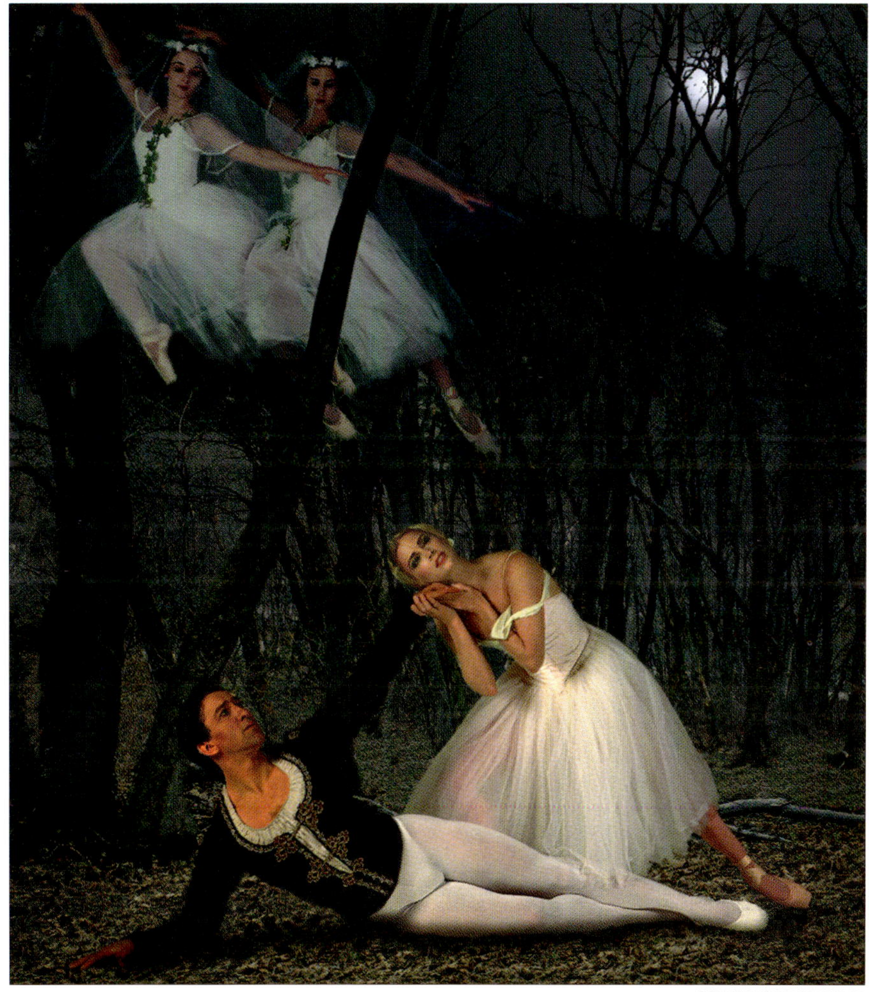

GISELLE / PHOTO O'VERY / COVEY

Utah is a

R E P O S I T O R Y

of ballet and modern

dance repertory.

WILLAM FARR CHRISTENSEN

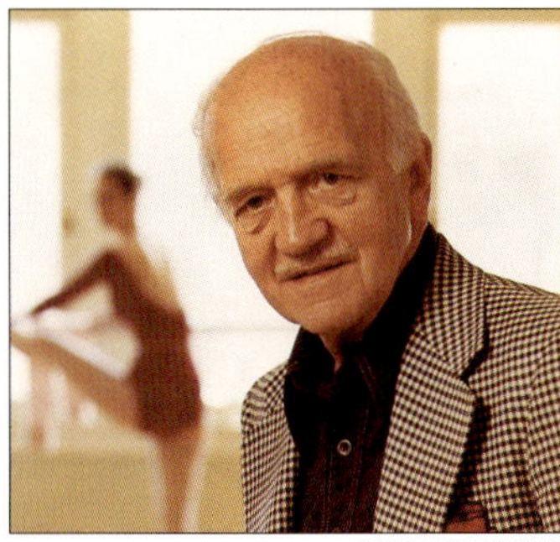

PHOTO BY DON BUSATH

From childhood in Brigham City to vaudeville hoofer to founder of two great Western ballet companies, Willam Farr Christensen has seen it all; as he enters his tenth decade, his heart still beats for ballet. "I know what to do better than ever before. My mind and imagination are good; I see what should be done and hope to do it as long as I can," he says.

With brothers Lew and Harold, he brought ballet to Main Street America. He founded the San Francisco Ballet, the country's oldest company, in 1937, staging America's first full-length *Coppelia* (1939), *Swan Lake* (1940) and *Nutcracker* (1944). At the U of U in 1951, he founded the first ballet department in a college of fine arts. His U of U dance company evolved into Utah Civic Ballet (1963) and Ballet West (1968) where he continued as artistic director until 1976.

Dancer, choreographer and teacher of danseurs, Mr. C's prominent students include Michael Smuin, Kent Stowell, Tom Ruud, Ray Bera, Bart Cook, Finis Jung, Ona White and Janet Reed.

repository of modern dance repertory. As such, RDT has danced more than two hundred works by at least one hundred noted choreographers. In two historic programs, RDT shows samplings of modern dance pioneers and the company dances a complete program of Doris Humphrey works. Of special merit has been RDT's recent ethnic program, *Separate Journeys*, a series of vignettes examining the influence of five Utah ethnic minorities.

Also a prominent company in the NEA's dance touring program, RDT has danced several seasons in Riverside Church in New York City, at Washington's Smithsonian Institution, and in almost every state in the Union. In 1992 RDT appeared for the first time abroad, triumphing at Vienna's Tanz Festival.

All of Salt Lake's professional companies have significant outreach programs in Utah schools where they demonstrate the possibilities of movement to enhance learning and develop creativity.

Ballet West has long had Utah Board of Education support, but in 1991 for the first time the Utah Legislature gave Ririe-Woodbury, RDT, and Children's Dance Theatre each a grant of $25,000 to expand their in-schools offering—gifts which provide the maximum inspiration for Utah school children through the thrifty expenditure of clever leaders.

Smith, Woodbury and Ririe have been, and remain, active in national dance panels and leadership positions as a holdover from the formative years of the NEA, when Utahns were ideally positioned by their pioneering programs to take national leadership. This position Utah has never had to relinquish.

Centers of good dance training exist elsewhere in the state. At Brigham Young University the Dancers' Company serves up original and interesting programs with many choreographies by co-artistic directors Caroline Prohosky and Marilyn Berrett. Ballet and children's programs also thrive there.

Modern dance flourishes year-round at Utah State University in Logan, where the Dance West summer school headed by Maggi Moar annually brings in visiting faculty. Weber State University in Ogden maintains an active modern dance program as well, with visiting artist/teachers.

In St. George, the Southwest Dance Theatre headed by Candy Fowler is not to be missed. No one has a better understanding of the principles that made Virginia Tanner great nor trains youthful dancers to greater innocence and charm.

Among Utah's unique features is the flourishing of high school dance clubs, led by professionally schooled teachers who do extraordinary work in training rank-and-file young students' creative instincts. Probably as much as any other one factor, this widespread early exposure accounts for much of Utah adults' interest in and dedication to dance.

Utah is also a center for folk and

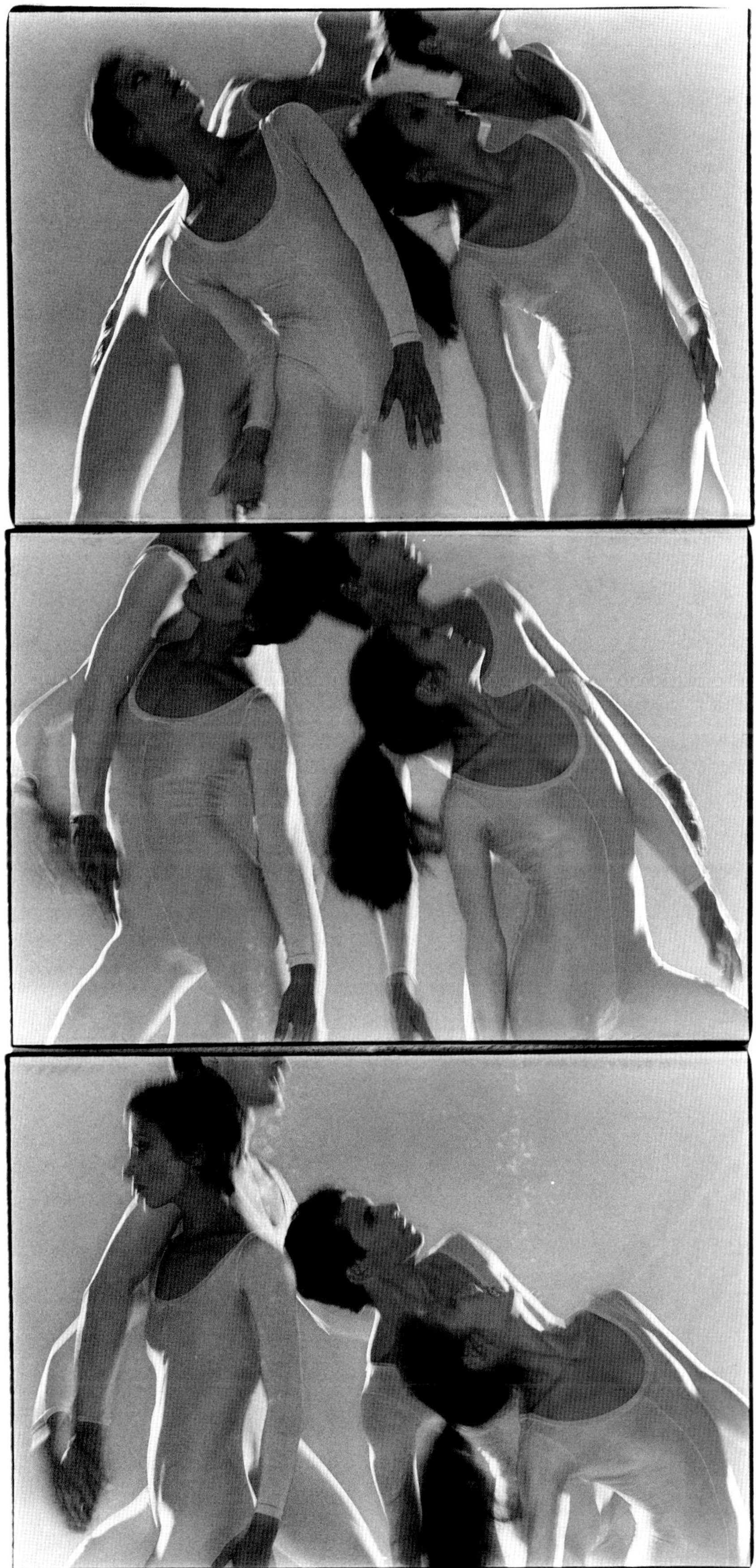

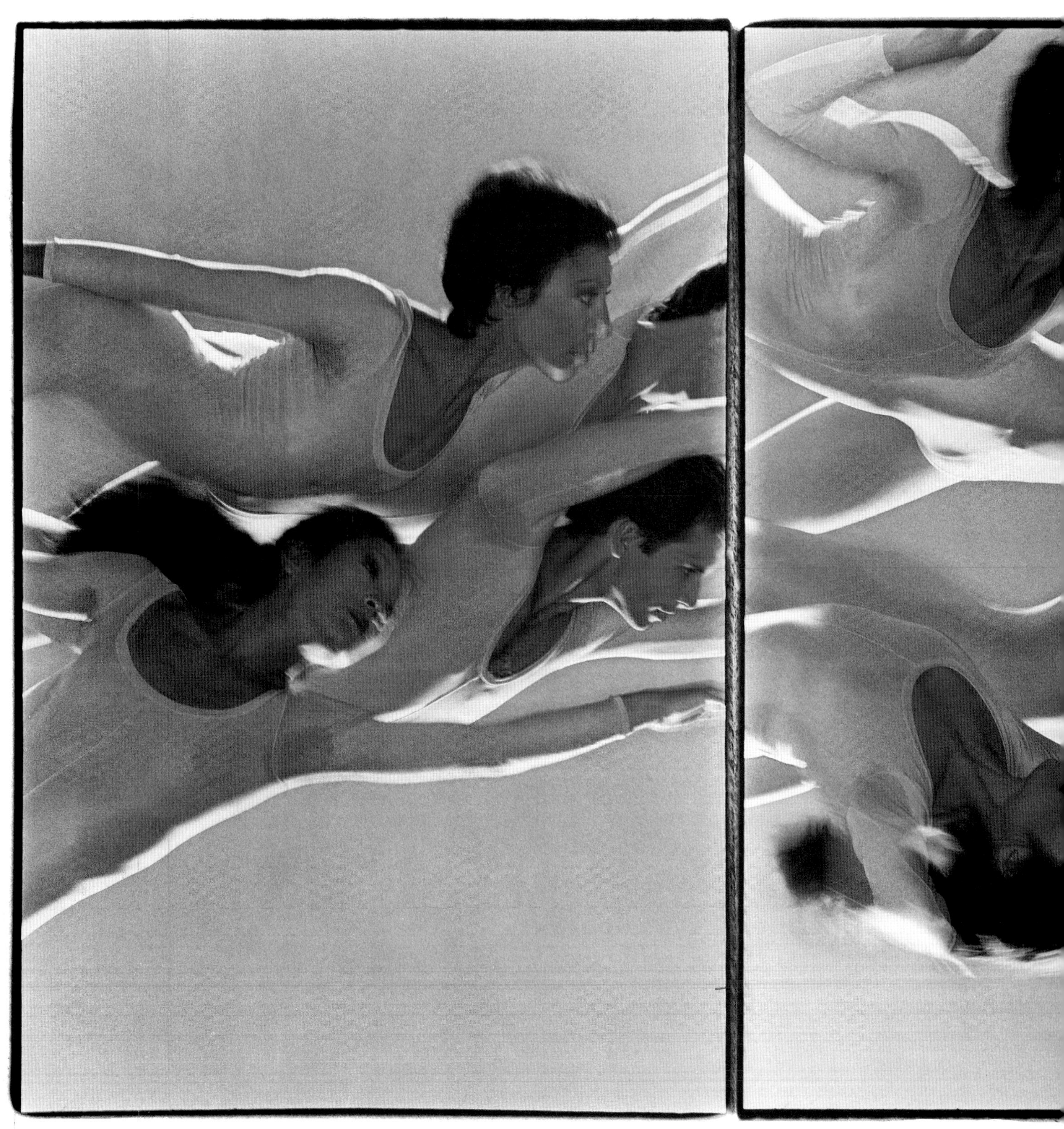

The essence of dance is

E M O T I O N A L

expression captured in

movement, sound and light.

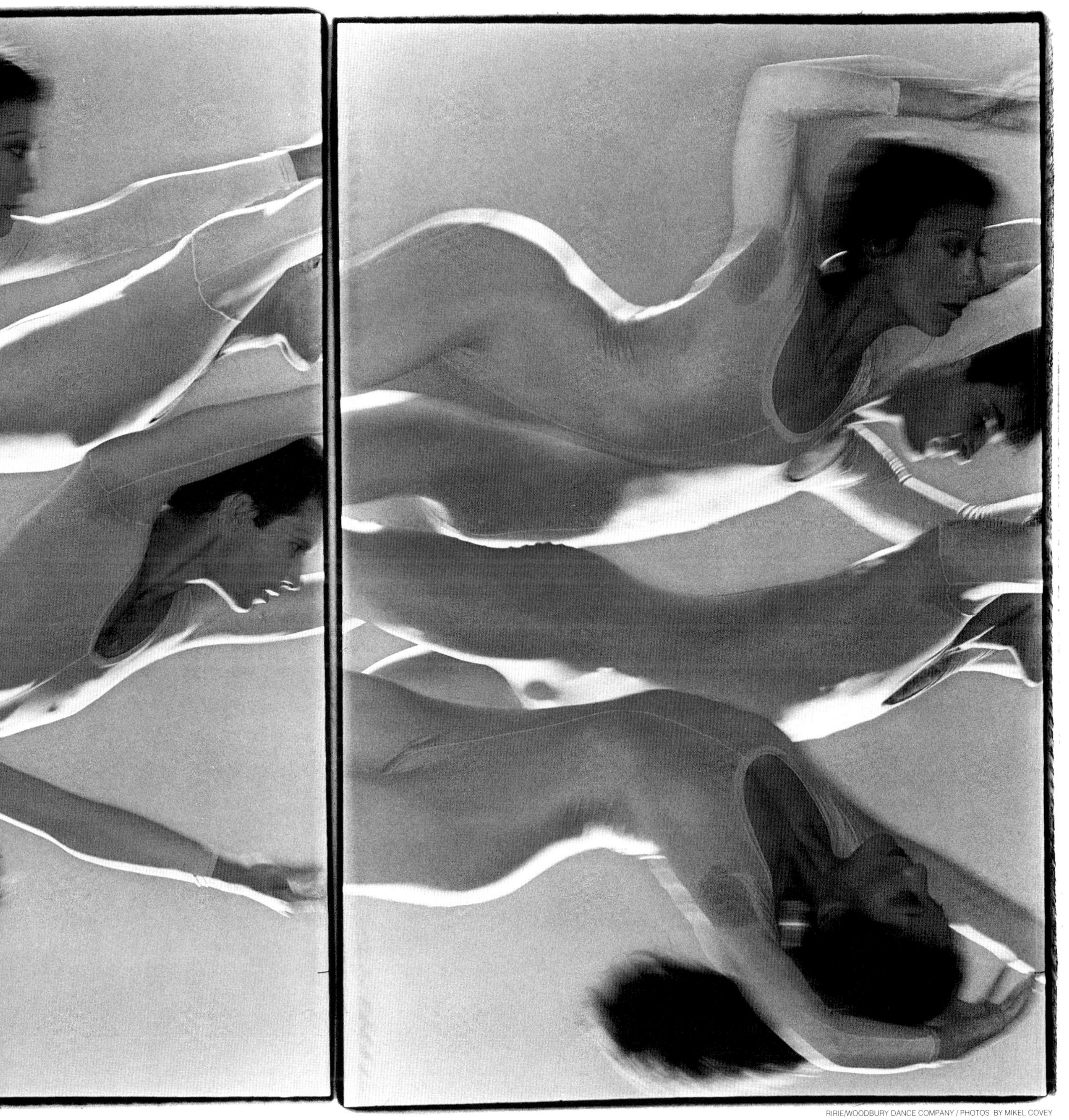

RIRIE/WOODBURY DANCE COMPANY / PHOTOS BY MIKEL COVEY

FOLLOWING PAGE PHOTOS RIRIE/WOODBURY DANCE COMPANY / PHOTOS MIKEL COVEY

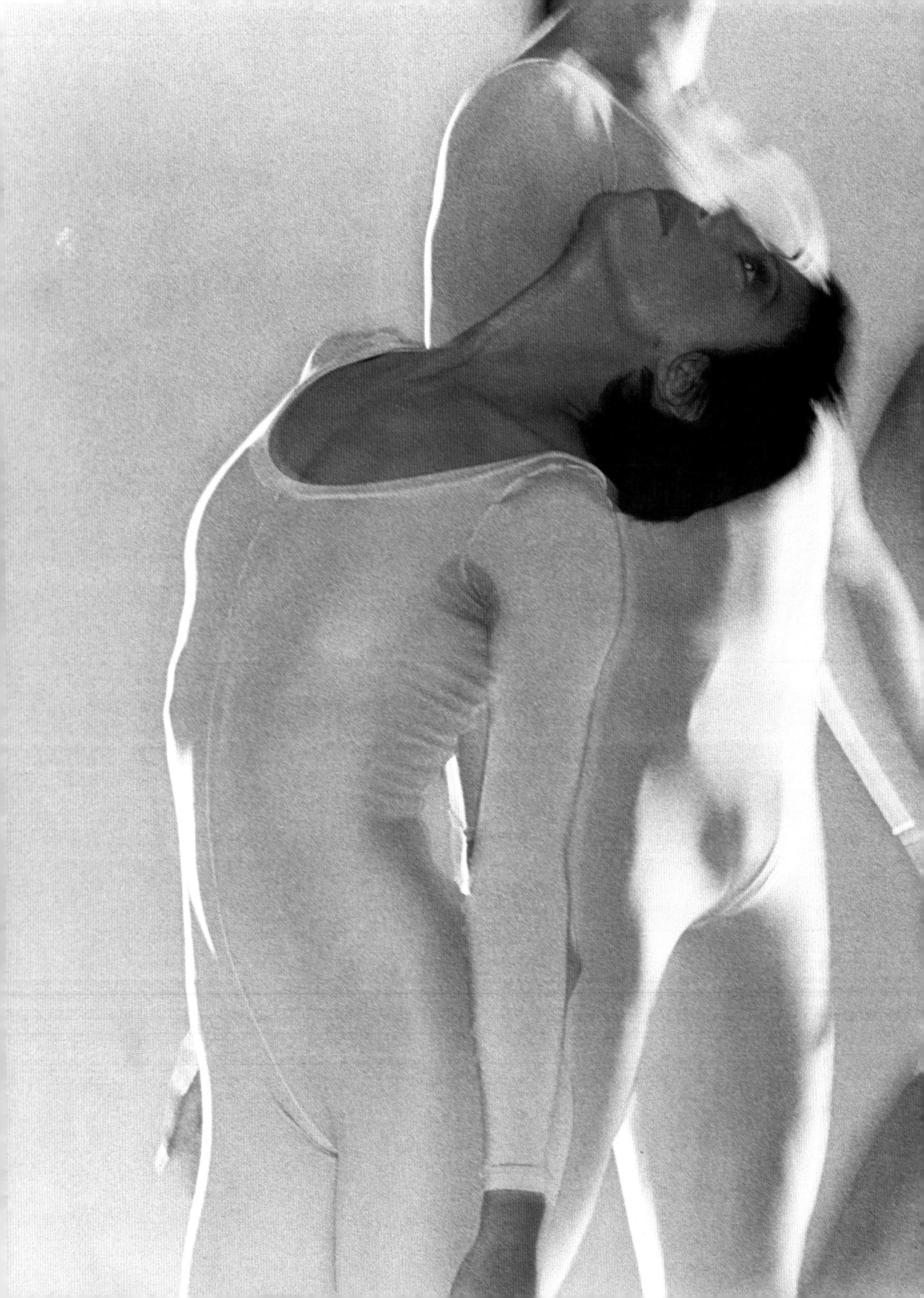

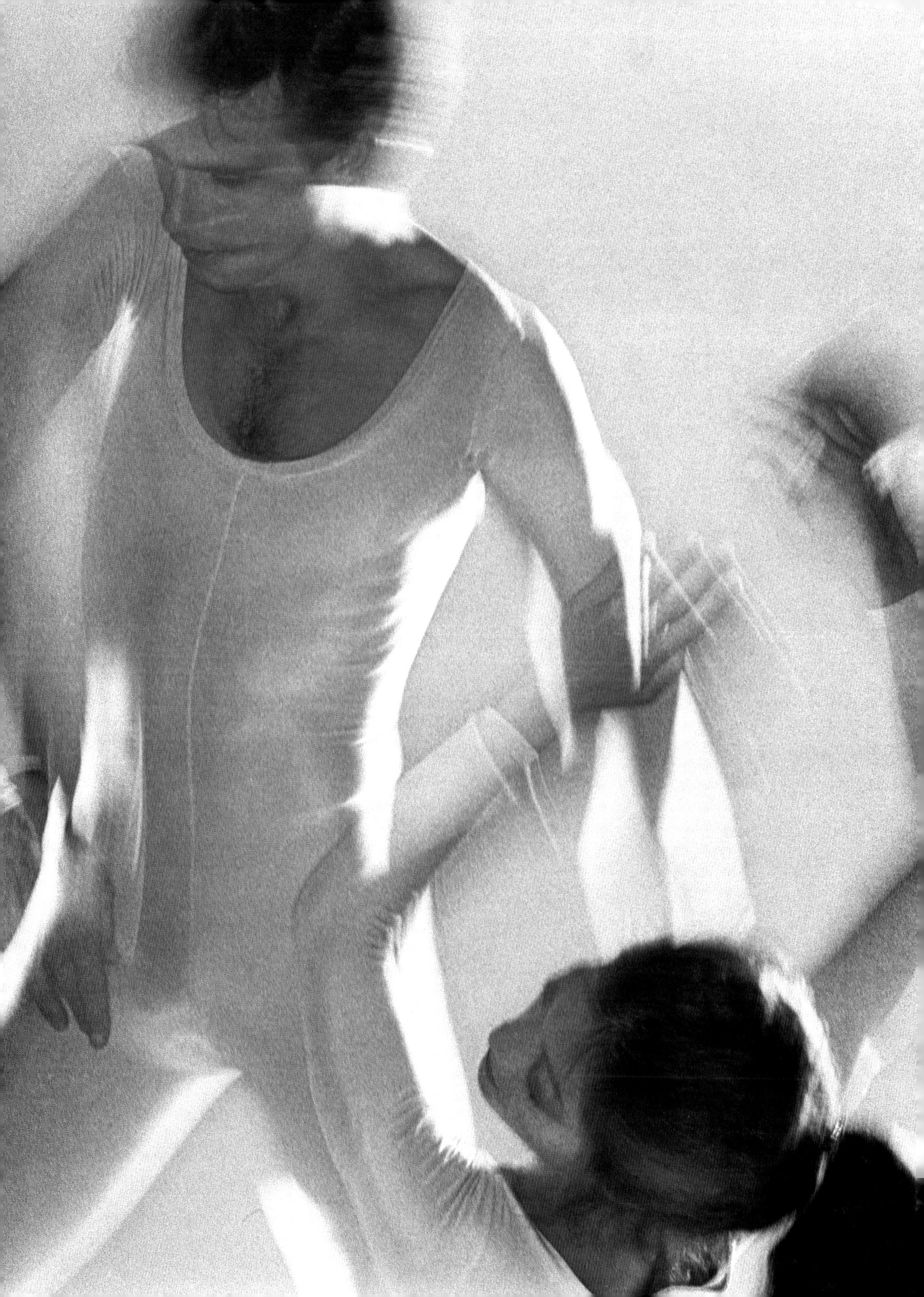

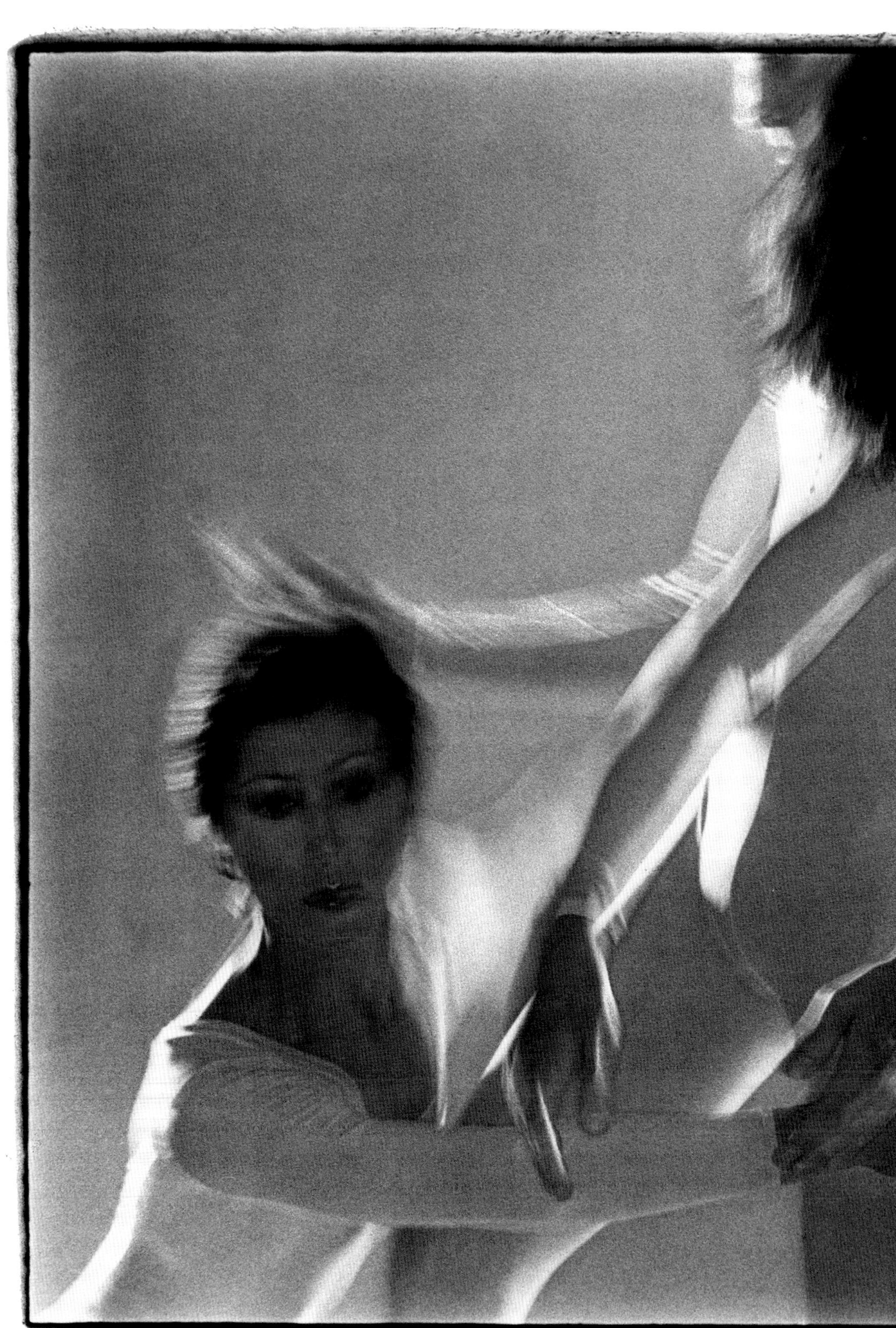

Great dancing

D R E A M S

are realized

through innovative

choreography

exported

through Utah's

international

touring companies.

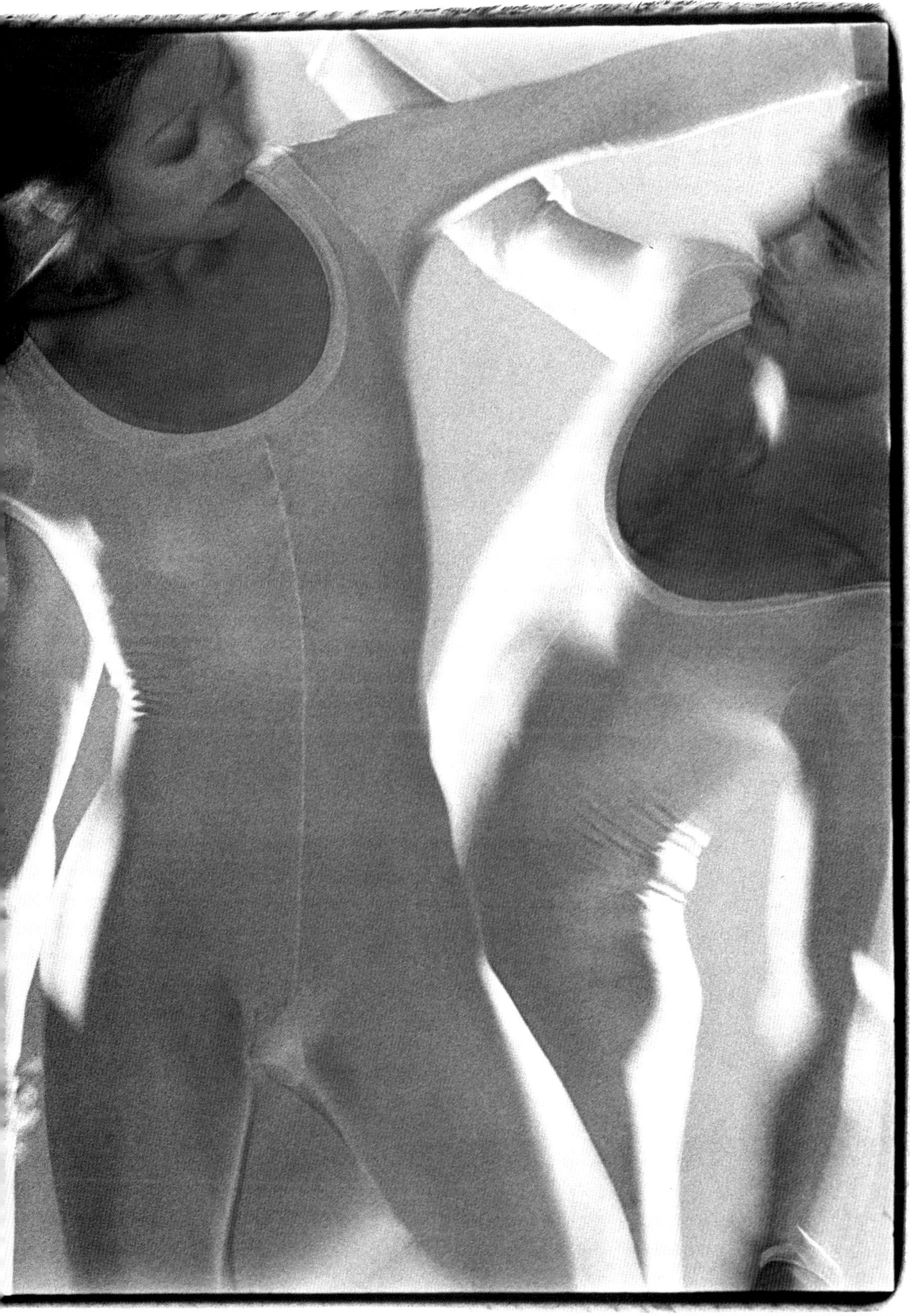

RIRIE/WOODBURY DANCE COMPANY / PHOTOS BY MIKEL COVEY

BENE ARNOLD

Texas born and California bred, Bene Arnold is a Utahn by preference and adoption. An elegant dancer in Willam Christensen's San Francisco Ballet, she was later ballet mistress there before coming to Utah, where she was Christensen's ballet mistress (1963-75) with Ballet West and the preceding Utah Civic Ballet. An expert teacher at the University of Utah, she has been artistic director of the ballet department's Utah Ballet and has taught dance to the deaf, even having a company of deaf dancers for a time. She's also highly prized as a dancer of character roles with Ballet West.

But Arnold is most identified with preparing Ballet West's *Nutcracker* children (as many as four complete casts), both at home and on tour. "Being with these children makes Christmas for me," she declares. The 1993 Utah Legislature gave Arnold a citation commending her work with Utah children.

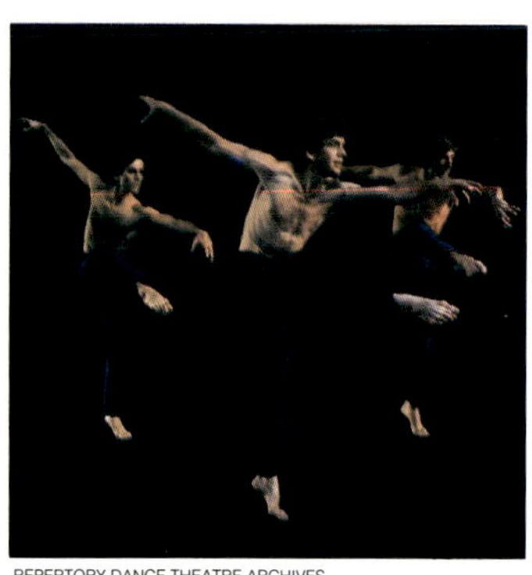

REPERTORY DANCE THEATRE ARCHIVES
PHOTO BY JACK VARTOOGIAN

ethnic dance, with international summer folk festivals in Springville, Bountiful and St. George that regularly draw as many as fifteen groups each from foreign countries.

Locally the Zivio Ethnic Arts Ensemble, with its authentic instruments, presents two concerts a year featuring song and dance of southeastern Europe. The troupe tours biennially to countries where its dances originate, such as Hungary, Romania, and Bulgaria, picking up choreography, costumes, and instruments along the way and savoring the special pleasures of people-to-people experiences.

Among the many groups from Brigham Young University (BYU) that tour worldwide is the BYU Folk Dancers Ensemble, a forty-eight-member troupe founded by Mary Bee Jensen. In Utah their major showcase is their annual Christmas Around the World. BYU's Lamanite Generation purveys the song and dance of Native American and Polynesian cultures. The BYU Ballroom Dance Company, headed by Lee Wakefield, regularly wins national and international titles for its precision dance routines and nourishes a statewide interest in the art.

Southern Utah University in Cedar City has availed itself of an incandescent presence in the person of Burch Mann and her American Folk Ballet (AFB). This Texas-born original toured her troupe widely out of Los Angeles for many years—in her own choreographies that brought to life Americana and the development of the American West. A great dream was realized in the summer of 1990, when the troupe danced by invitation in St. Petersburg's (Russia) White Nights Festival.

Mann and her daughter San Christopher lead the company, with Gwen Grimes and Roy Fitzell heading a good general dance program at Southern Utah University. Each summer the AFB dances in the Festival of the American West in Logan and also conducts a summer season at SUU at the time of the Utah Shakespearean Festival.

For square-dance and country and Western enthusiasts, there's dancing almost any night of the week in communities up and down the state. In 1991 Salt Lake City played host to 10,000 square dancers in national convention and, reportedly, they intend to come back again.

Up and down, far and wide throughout Utah exists the broadest spectrum of dance imaginable from children's clogging clubs to performances of the great Tchaikovsky ballet classics. Come, and you'll love it; stay, and you may come to take fierce pride in this century-old flowering of dance in the desert.

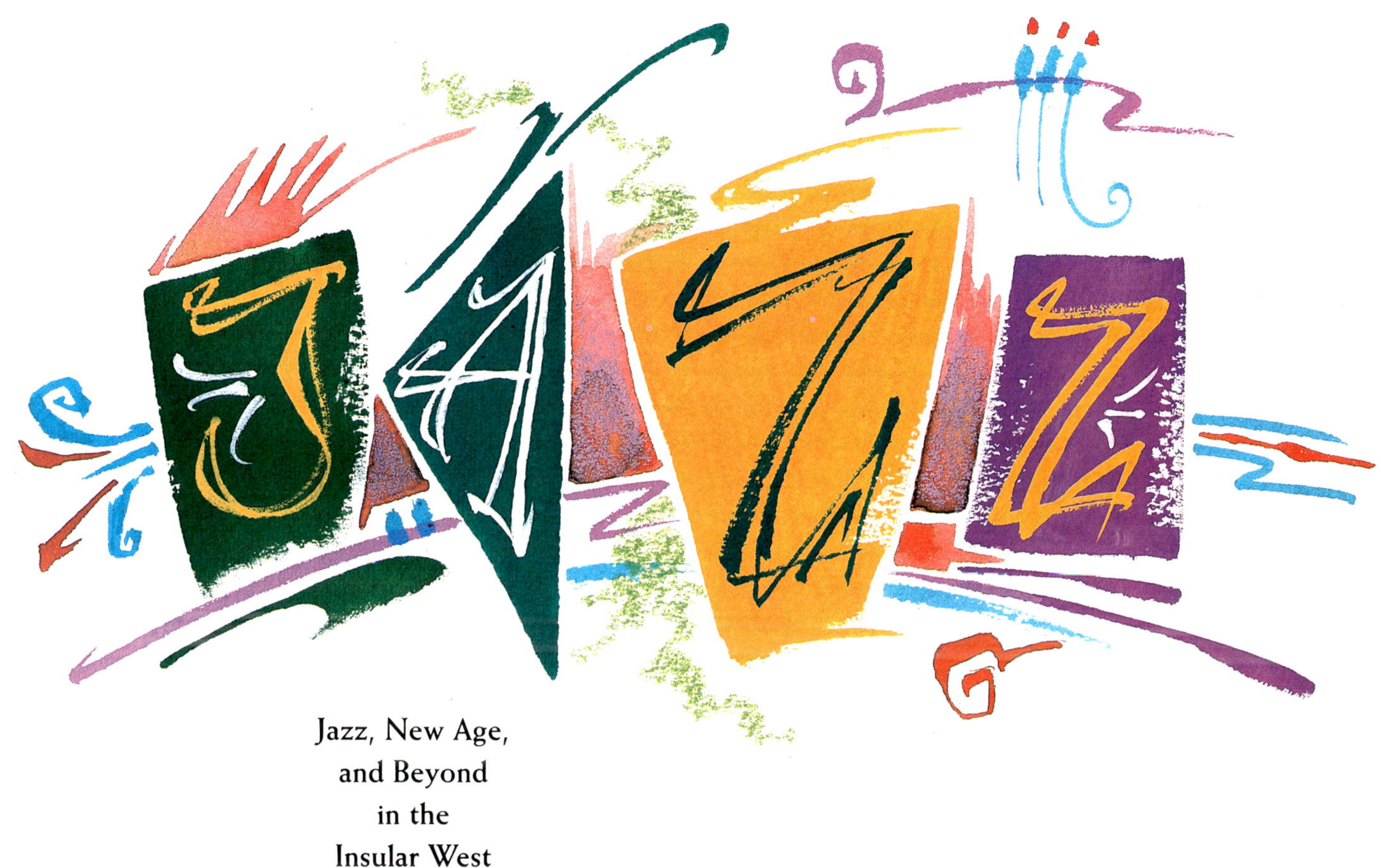

Jazz, New Age,
and Beyond
in the
Insular West

Herschel Bullen

I DON'T SEE WHY *our music can't be given the respect of European classical music. Beethoven's been dead all these years and they're still talking about him, teaching him and playing his music. Why ain't they talking about Bird or Trane or Monk or Duke or Count or Fletcher Henderson or Louis Armstrong like they're talking about Beethoven? . . .*

They've also got to accept that we do things differently. Our music isn't the same on Friday and Saturday night."

—*Miles Davis*

"The music of Richard Wagner is really much better than it sounds."

—*George Bernard Shaw, probably*

Jazz in Utah flourishes almost entirely on the basketball court. The bastard child of the union between European harmony and African polyrhythm does live, in one or another of its incarnations, but its presence like the esoteric artform itself can be so fleeting as to seem nonexistent.

So where does one go to sample the bittersweet fruits of the labors in bohemia's vineyards? Jazz may or may not have come up the river from New Orleans with the likes of Jelly Roll Morton (who claimed, with astonishingly scant opposition, to have invented it), but it most definitely did not come up, down or across the Virgin River or the Bear or the Weber. Jazz has long since ceased to be a rural art form, at least long before it rented the occasional flat in downtown Salt Lake City, and there are currently few ambassadors to the hinterlands.

But there *are* knowledgeable fans and loyal followers. The twelve-year-old Jazz Society of Utah (formerly the Salt Lake Jazz Society) is more than four hundred strong, according to 1993-94 Society president-band leader Mel Hall, with over a dozen solid corporate sponsors. The society supports a profusion of activities: a standing Monday night jam session; the Summer Canyon Jam at the Snowbird Pavilion (in conjunction with support from Local 104, Salt Lake Chapter, American Federation of Musicians), with featured artists such as Walt Fowler, Bobby Shew, Don Menza

and local groups of note, Jerry Floor's Big Band, pianist Dan Waldis and drummer Mark Chaney; a Jazz at the Library series spotlighting local ensembles; and a quarterly newsletter, the *Jazz Voice*, which reports local events and news and publishes articles by local artists plus album and book reviews. (A membership card commands a discount on chosen events as well.)

Dixieland fans will appreciate the Wasatch Mountain Dixieland Jazz Society. In its fourth year, the Society boasts two hundred-plus members from St. George to Logan and three successful Dixie festivals of continental proportions. Dozens of bands from across the country have wailed from morning to midnight, including Gene Kitrell's St. Louis Rivermen, Hot Frogs, the Uptown Lowdown Jazz Band. Others include Salt Lake's Riverboat Rhythm Kings and the redoubtable Salt Lake Goodtime Dixieland Jazz Band, featuring Reed LeCheminant, cornet, Jimmy Brown, clarinet, and trombonist Brian Priebe. Storyville in Utah took a hiatus in 1993, but prospects look good for another smashing festival in '94.

The most obvious live modern jazz performance venue is the private club. But the club scene is a will-o'-the-wisp. Clubs are notoriously fickle, making quicker changes than a Coltrane solo, and currently there are no real, dedicat-

Utah Jazz
Society's
M O N D A Y
J A M
has perked
for a decade.

ed jazz clubs in Utah. However, groups can sometimes be spotted at Cisero's or the Down Under in Park City, Green Street Social Club, D. B. Coopers, Club Cabana, the Marriott Hotel, Little America Hotel Lounge in Salt Lake, the Aerie at Snowbird or Alta Lodge. Of special note, the cloudless vocalizing of multitalented Dave Compton has graced the Salt Lake Hilton's Room at the Top piano bar with a little jazz and sundry divertissements for more than a decade.

The Zephyr, downtown Salt Lake's rock and rhythm showcase, interweaves jazz and fusion artists such as Larry Coryell, Maynard Ferguson, Al Dimeola, Wynton Marsalis, Christopher Hollyday and Lyle Mayes with spicy salsa bands like Poncho Sanchez, Tito Puente, Pete Escovedo, and Willie Colon. Staple rock and roll and fine rhythm and blues bands like Charlie Mussel-white and Robert Cray as well as a pot-pourri of Zydeco and worldbeat aggre-gations can also be heard. Also up and coming on the rhythm and blues scene is Salt Lake's Dead Goat Saloon which stages a killer Monday night jam session.

Humble folk-jazz shrine D. B. Coopers has presented jazz (amid a vari-ety of folk and acoustic entertainers) for more than twenty years and has hosted the Utah Jazz Society's Monday Jam for about a decade. Remember first hearing a local guy named Bobby McFerrin at D. B. Coopers? And every-one from Wynton Marsalis to Taj Mahal has wandered through looking for a copacetic place to hang.

Salt Lake City has a long, if not altogether venerable, history of smoky-club jazz. *Circa* fifties to seventies, places like the whiskey-drenched after-hours speakeasy Big Jim's Lounge featured at least a funky organ trio. Traveling (Jon Hendricks, Don Scalletta, Merle Saunders) and local (Millie Carter, Karen Hepworth-Hernandez, Mel Nowell, Jerry Johnson, Bill Crismon) musicians were always welcome at pianist Joe Katter's Latin Quarter which later became a purist joint, the Quarter Note. State Street's Radio City Lounge drew cosmopolitan Sunday night jam session crowds. Even the old Hotel Utah, thanks to impre-sario-pianist Larry Jacksticn, staged Dizzy Gillespie's quintet, the Thad Jones-Mel Lewis Big Band, George Shearing, and others.

Up north, time was when a jam ses-sion with great tenor saxophonist Joe McQueen and others could be found just about any time at Ogden's Porters and Waiters Club. No more—in fact, no more jam sessions just about anywhere. But McQueen (who garnered a Gover-nor's Award in the Arts in 1992) can still be coaxed out of retirement to rock the crowd as he did one summer night last year for *Three Generations of Jazz* at the Salt Lake Hilton. He was joined by fellow Ogdenite Lars Yorgason on bass, pianist Jackstien and friends. In the summer of 1993, he wowed the crowd in an outdoor Talent in the Park series concert in Ogden.

JAY LAWRENCE

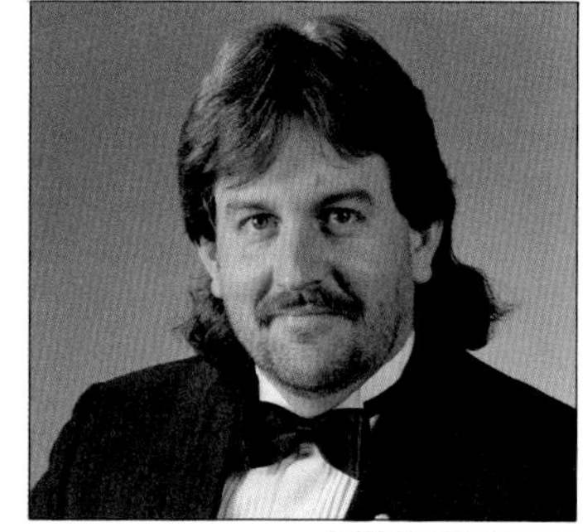

PHOTO COURTESY OF ARTIST

Former Reno/Las Vegas show drummer/percussionist (and Berklee College of Music-edu-cated) Jay Lawrence made his youthful reputation backing casino headliners and jazz artists James Moody, Art Pepper, Cat Anderson, Pete Christlieb, Don Alias, Plas Johnson and Carl Fontana. Former president of the Salt Lake Jazz Society, composer-arranger of his own uncompro-mising 1989 jazz-fusion cas-sette *Creative Endeavors*, leader-founder of the sizzling, popular, authentic fourteen-piece Latin jazz band Orquestra Pachanga, founder and drummer of the Underpaid Professors (University of Utah faculty jazz quartet) and respected private educator, Lawrence is also drum and jazz vibraphone instructor at the University of Utah.

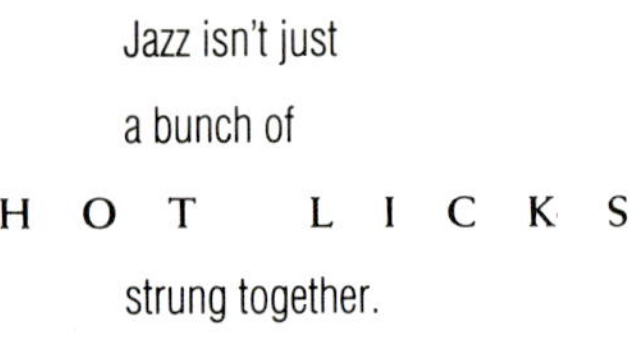

Jazz isn't just
a bunch of
HOT LICKS
strung together.

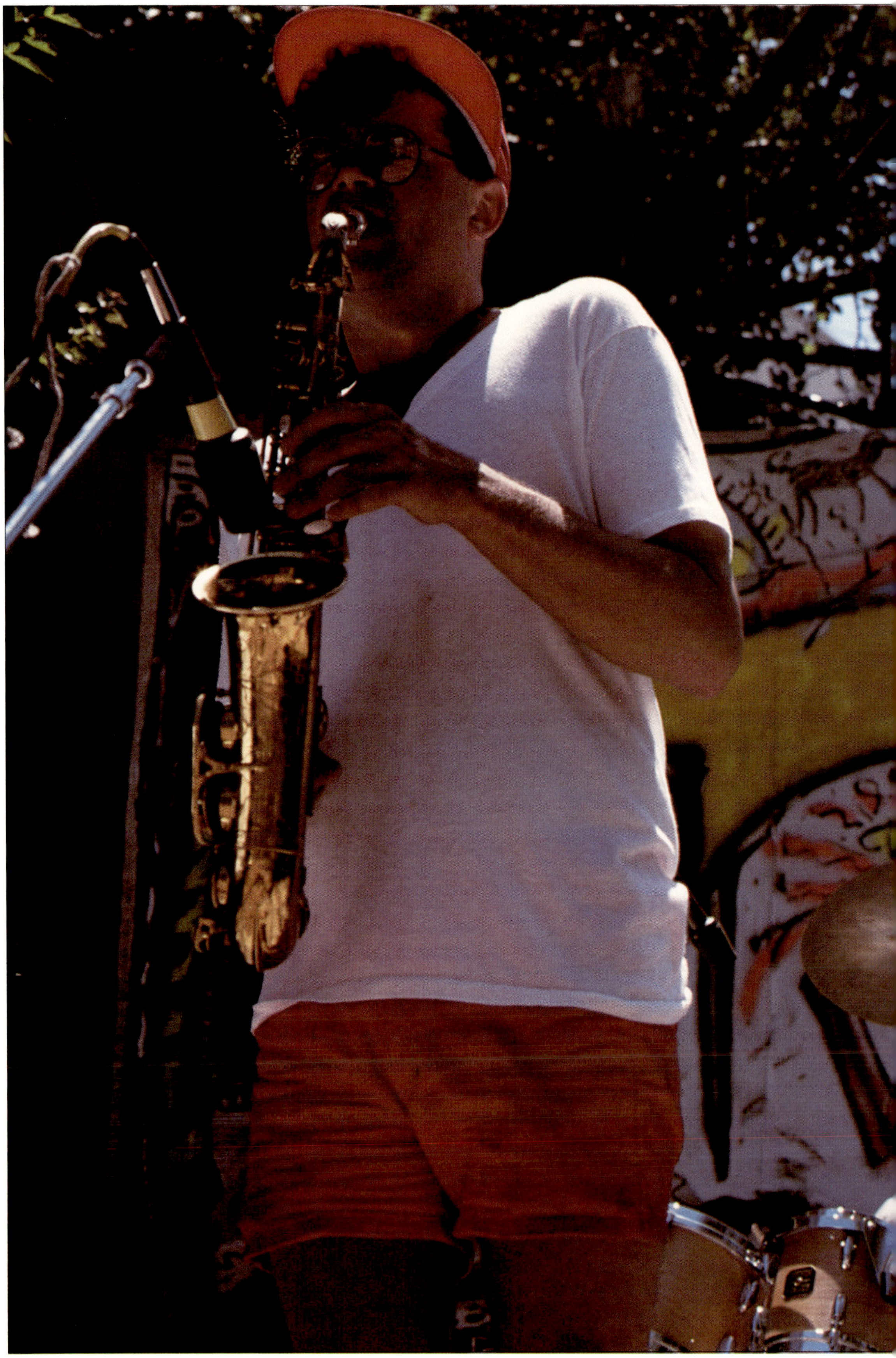

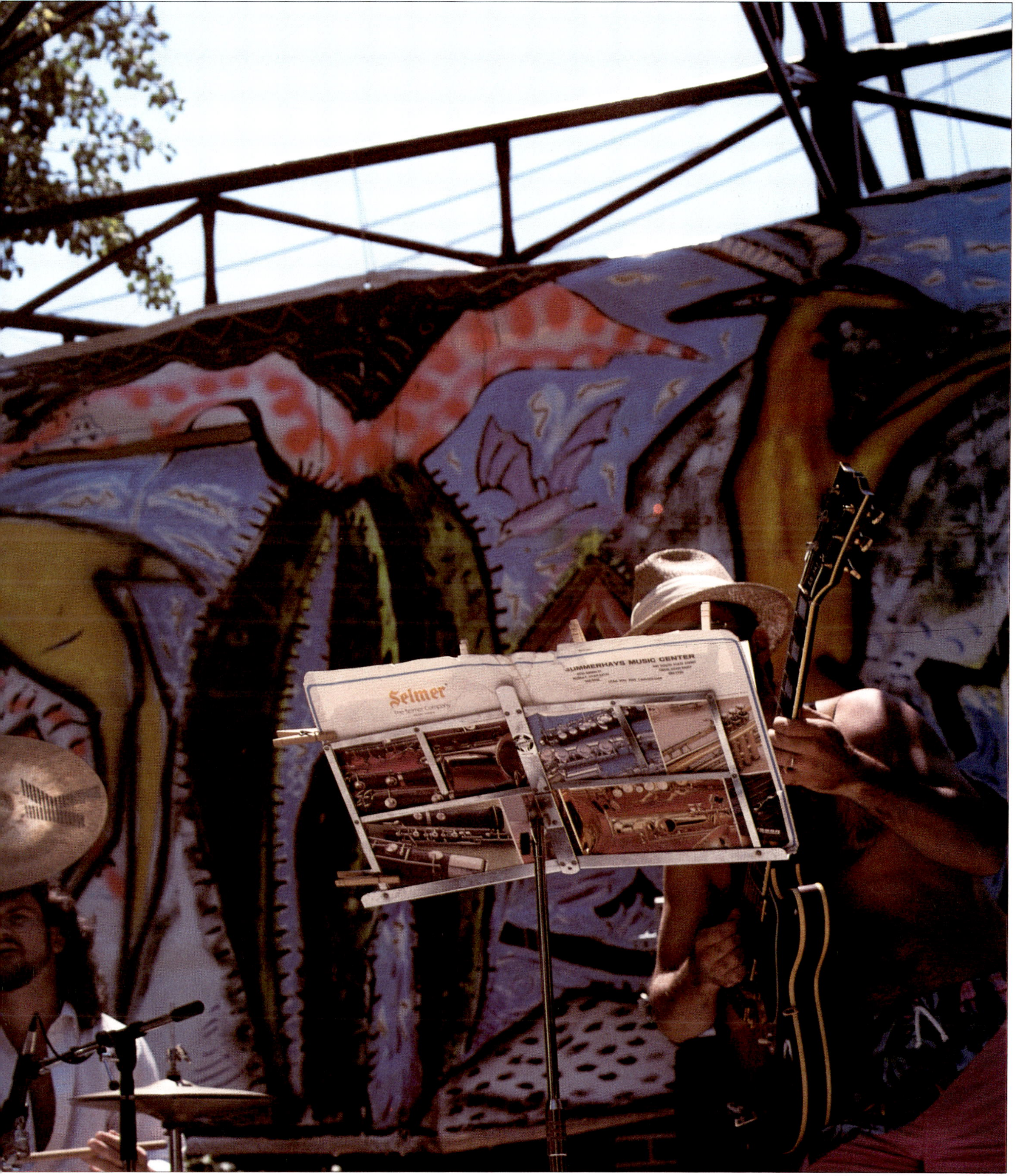

PHOTO BY PHIL MILLER

Back when acoustic was king (before Elvis), Utah was peppered with dance halls—Lagoon, the old Saltair Pavilion—enlivened by the top swing bands of the day. Mel Torme, Earl Bostic, even the venerated Duke Ellington played Ole's Terrace Room (later the Salt Lake Athletic Club). Trumpeter Doug Boll and the late clarinetist Bill Floor fronted popular local bands at the pre-World War II Roxy Theatre, Jerry Jones' Rainbow Rendezvous (which burned down in 1948), and the Coconut Grove, which became the Terrace Ballroom. The great traveling bands and artists Count

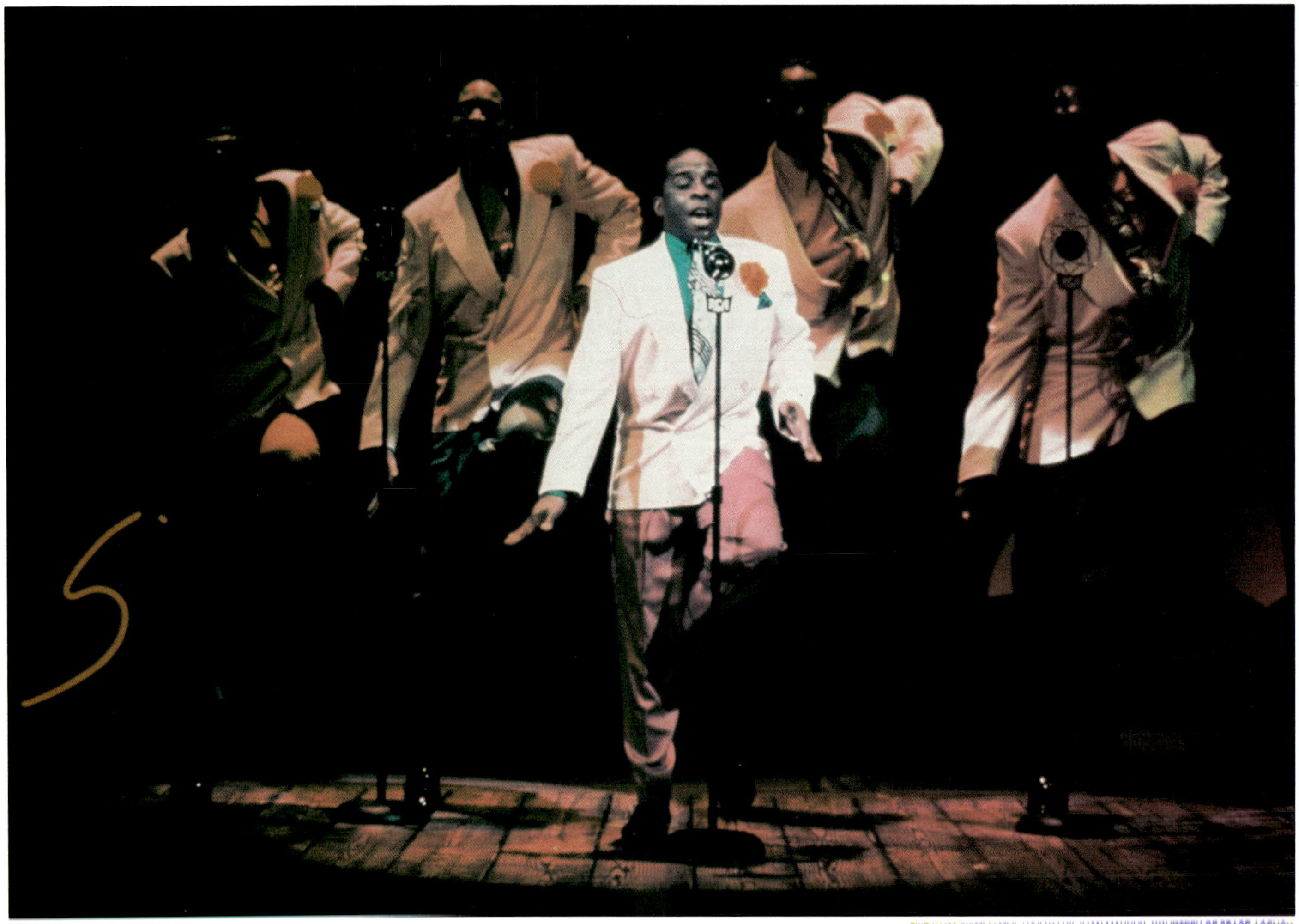
FIVE GUYS NAMED MOE / PHOTO BY JOAN MARCUS, COURTESY OF SPACE AGENCY

Basie, Stan Kenton, Dave Brubeck, Nat "King" Cole, the Modern Jazz Quartet, and even bebop trombonist J. J. Johnson, performed there during the fifties and sixties.

Swing still thrives in Utah. One of the finest nostalgia bands in the country, the Phoenix Jazz and Swing Band, continues to perform the arrangements of Shaw, Goodman, Kenton and Miller. With twenty-eight sidemen, this band works about once a month—pretty ambitious, considering a median age of around seventy, with a couple of guys over eighty. The band has recorded three cassettes, *Phoenix Jazz and Swing Band, Volumes I, II, and III*, "mostly for posterity," according to musical director Doug Boll. "We don't want to compete with other bands. We just want to enjoy ourselves."

Although the epicenter of the jazz-quake in Utah is definitely in the Salt Lake/Utah County area, tremors can be felt every summer at art festivals in Park City and Logan (with no small debt of gratitude to Professor Larry Smith of Utah State University) and even in Tooele. Way down south, Brianhead Ski Resort snaps its fingers every July Fourth with a bit of festival-style jazz. Salt Lake favorite Larry Jackstien, who has a new piano trio CD called *Cuban Fire & Classics by Richard Rogers* (on MacJack Productions), appears there regularly.

The Salt Lake Arts Festival always features great jazz talent, of course; locally renowned leader/contractor Joe

Muscolino, Amnesia, Tully Cathey, Linke Hebrew, Kelly Wallis, Dave Bennett and Warren Trulson, as well as nationally known Michael Brecker, Elaine Alias and Hermeto Pascual.

Utah's festival centerpiece, Space Agency's Snowbird Jazz and Blues Festival, is a world-class event in a spectacular mountain setting. Past years have headlined artists Albert King, Bobby Lyle and Albert Collins on Blues Night and Ramsey Lewis, Shirley Horn, Marian McPartland, Herbie Mann, Gene Harris and Ray Brown on Jazz Night. Space Agency Company, a national promoter of major non-rock shows and acts, has demonstrated a deep commitment to this highly creditable alpine jazz and blues extravaganza.

The first choral jazz festival was held at Ogden's Weber State University in the spring of 1993 with Steve Keen's Westminster College aggregation notable among entries from throughout the West. The festival was produced by Lars Yorgason, whose Lars Yorgason Singers warble all over the Wasatch Front *à la* Singers Unlimited, often with able assistance from revered Salt Lake veterans drummer Jan Hyde and pianist Craig Larsen.

A singular clarion blue note, Jazz Vespers at Salt Lake's First Unitarian Church, is in its fourth successful year. Pianist Vince Frates and guests, some

JERRY FLOOR

For more than twenty years, Jerry Floor, Salt Lake musician (clarinet, saxophone, flute) and CEO of Gump & Ayers real estate brokerage firm, has maintained a modern twenty-piece band with Utah's best jazz and ensemble performers, employing an extensive library penned by America's best contemporary composers. Never conceived to be more than just "kicks" for the musicians, Floor's band has nonetheless mounted several successful concerts featuring greats like Doc Severinson. Floor's current nonprofit project, Jazz Arts of the Mountainwest (JAM), will spotlight a jazz orchestra with a regular season and promote live music, especially in Utah's educational institutions.

RAY SMITH

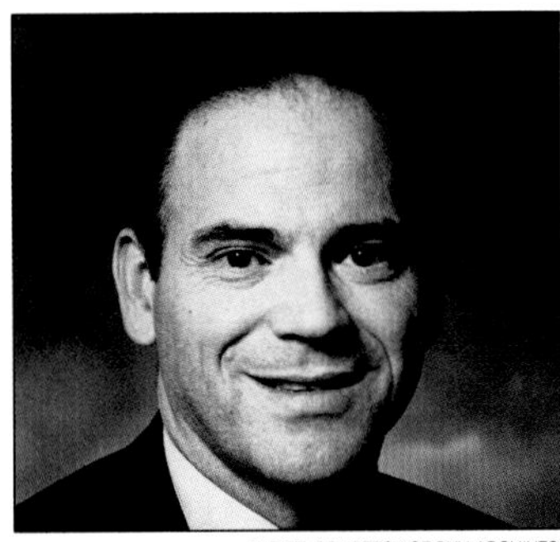

PHOTO COURTESY OF BYU ARCHIVES

Brigham Young University's resident jazzman, educator (director of jazz studies and professor of saxophone), and jazz-classical performer (oboe, flute, clarinet, bassoon and saxophone), Dr. Charles Raymond "Ray" Smith, frequently concertizes with Sam Cardon, Michael Dowdle and Kurt Bestor. His breathtaking alto and soprano saxophones can be heard on nationally acclaimed Utah CD recordings, Lex DeAzevedo's *Mountains* and *Moab*, Kurt Bestor's *Airus Christmas II*, and Lisa Rey's *Noel Nouveau*. Winner of the Woody Herman Award for Musical Excellence, teacher and adjudicater at festivals and clinics, Smith also directed BYU's big band, Synthesis, in the Soviet Union in 1990 and Scandinavia in 1992.

times Mike "Saxman" Johnson or bassist Jim Stout, perform in the quintessential jazz tradition without being "liturgical"— in a fashion unique for Utah. Pastor Tom Goldsmith provides an ideal setting for top-flight local jazz and inspirational services throughout the winter season.

Likewise, Lloyd Miller's noon "deli-jazz" concerts at the University of Utah student union have provided an ideal vehicle for local professionals to stretch out.

The institutions of higher learning provide both a performance and an educational foundation for jazz on the Wasatch Front. The University of Utah has consistently presented great national artists like Michael Brecker, Branford Marsalis, Spyro Gyra and, in an earlier era, Count Basie, Louie Armstrong, Dave Brubeck and George Shearing. Beginning in 1971 with Stan Kenton, Brigham Young University (BYU) has fostered great jazz with Randy and Michael Brecker, Jon Faddis, George Cables, Bill Watrous, Gary Burton and many others.

The University of Utah's rag-tag jazz program of the seventies has been absorbed into the overall music program which currently vaunts a good dozen bachelor candidates earning degrees in "performance with a jazz emphasis." Noted composer-trombonist Henry A. Wolking teaches jazz improvisation, theory and scoring. Scott Hagan, assistant director of bands, leads the big band. Guitar is king—as where isn't it?

Guitar professor Keven Johansen leads a guitar ensemble that mopped up the 1993 Moscow (Idaho, of course!) Jazz Festival student competition. Utah performers have consistently carried the torch to victory in the regional competitions in Moscow.

Sean Halley, the year before, took three *Outstanding* awards: Collegiate Guitar, Instrumental Soloist and Jazz Group, while a student at Utah State.

BYU boasts three big bands, including its locally popular Synthesis and sports a justifiably popular faculty jazz quartet. Trumpet-flugelhorn virtuoso Bob Taylor (a computer programmer by day) teaches improvisation, sax master Ray Smith teaches jazz history, Salt Lake lawyer-pianist Craig Larsen teaches jazz piano and professor Ron Brough plays and teaches drums. This is a performing group which can and should be heard.

In broadcast music, the University of Utah's public affiliate station KUER-FM maintains the mainstream. Mannerly DJ Wes Bowen declaims KUER's continuing commitment to quality jazz air play. With good reason. "People in this town . . ." Wes mused one afternoon, ". . . well, when Charlie Byrd, or the MJQ or Andre Previn or Shelley Manne used to come—they were knocked out by the warmth of Salt Lake audiences." To appropriate some of his apt and witty airwave vernacular, Bowen, and adept confrere Steve Williams, "tear off chunks" of the "pure stuff." Amen.

The synth-driven polar extreme of the bundle of styles loosely called *New Age* is a meditative, often rhythmless, otherworldly soundscape called *space music*. The shifting sands of programming at Radio Free Utah, Salt Lake's first-rate community radio station KRCL-FM, preclude foretelling a firm dispensation, but traditionally the astrological signs have pointed to Sunday evenings—"Nexus," "Hearts of Space"— and holidays as resonant times for the spiritually evolved to bliss out to the galaxies. Also, check out "Musical Star Streams" on KBZN-FM Sunday mornings. As with all art, less inspired offerings of *space music* are humdrum at best, while the finest of the *oeuvre* can be genuinely transporting.

Of course most folks in these environs favor a jazz hybrid known to programmers as "contemporary jazz," a more commercial (purists insist watered-down) version, or jazz-lite, like Spyro Gyra or Kenny G., perhaps best exemplified by the homogenized FM offerings pleasantly emanating from the aforementioned Wasatch Front station KBZN (the BREEZE). Utah recording artists can be heard there with astonishing frequency.

In fact, the Utah recording firmament is positively luminescent with local stars' contemporary, New Age (which, alas, can't be defined any more than can jazz, which can't) and jazz-fusion successes—nothing heady, hard, or esoteric, but no dilute, slick supermarket McJazz, either.

Sam Cardon is one of a generous handful of world-class artists located in Utah who is writing, recording and occasionally performing contemporary jazz. The pianist-composer-arranger's top-selling Airus CD, *Impulse*, followed by the very popular *Serious Leisure*, which hit number two on the national radio charts, are delightful examples of the genre.

In a more New Age vein, Kurt Bestor is making serious waves. His 1989 *Airus Christmas* was the number-one seller in the Intermountain area, and his subsequent releases, *Seasons* (1990) and *Airus Christmas II* (1991), have become standard works. Likewise, guitarist Michael Dowdle's *The Touch* (1990) and *From the Hip* (1992) on Airus received both critical and popular accolades. With Cardon's, these were some of the first local productions to achieve national recognition and commercial success.

Randy Thornton, spokesperson for the Airus label, predicts the market will be shifting, de-emphasizing New Age and going more to contemporary jazz: "less Yanni, more Kenny G." Will Airus do more jazz? "We did great when we concentrated on New Age and jazz-lite," says Thornton. "When we ventured into pop—not so good." So if Airus can clear the studio of orchestras and film moguls (sister company L. A. East does a couple of dozen film scores a year there), maybe more jazz.

Meanwhile, Sam Cardon and Kurt Bestor, with some financial assistance, have opened their own state-of-the-art digital-analog 24-track Pinnacle Studio in Orem, where they are toiling in the contemporary vineyards producing jazz-inspired and New Age elixirs.

Not the least of the studio moguls is former Californian Lex DeAzevedo. A composer-arranger-pianist-synthesizer wizard reminiscent of Hollywood's Dave Grusin, DeAzevedo opened Studio One in Sandy about five years ago and has been doing his own film scores and stellar recording projects ever since.

DeAzevedo distinguishes himself not only by forays into the recorded annals of contempo-jazz and fusion-New Age, but also because, like Grusin, he occasionally consents to be the centerpiece of a dynamic concert ensemble. His popular first CD, *Mountains* (on his Aubergine label), one of the hottest releases of 1992, is destined to become a contemporary fusion classic for DeAzevedo's fresh writing and piano-synthesizer work. His 1993 Aubergine release *Moab* displays more of Utah's finest professionals—the ubiquitous Michael Dowdle, Ray Smith and fine guitarist Rich Dixon. The result is carefree, cool, contemporary.

In spite of such fine commercial endeavors and the growing understanding and appreciation of a wider audience, jazz remains, at its essence, a challenging and enigmatic music. If its practitioners are true to their muse, taking chances and straining at the conventions, it can be quite inaccessible, as, say, a string quartet by Alban Berg or Béla Bartók. Demanding almost as much from the listener as the performer, moody and often inconsistent, it is not destined to entertain the masses in the manner of rock or pop performances by the likes of Madonna or Michael Bolton.

But contrary to what the casual observer might conclude, jazz does have a fully developed language, a vocabulary and grammar, albeit with countless dialects. It ain't just a bunch of "hot licks" strung together. And fortunately a growing number of outstanding local performers speak the language fluently.

So, upon closer inspection, although Utah jazz is not going to provide any real competition for Los Angeles or New York—except on the basketball court—the artists, audience and potential cannot be denied. Here, as everywhere, like disco and rap, fads come and go. But in the words of Professor Wolking, "What endures is jazz and blues." Like Mozart and Beethoven, eh, Henry?

Crafts: A Legacy
of Tradition
and a Search
for New Forms

Carol Biddle

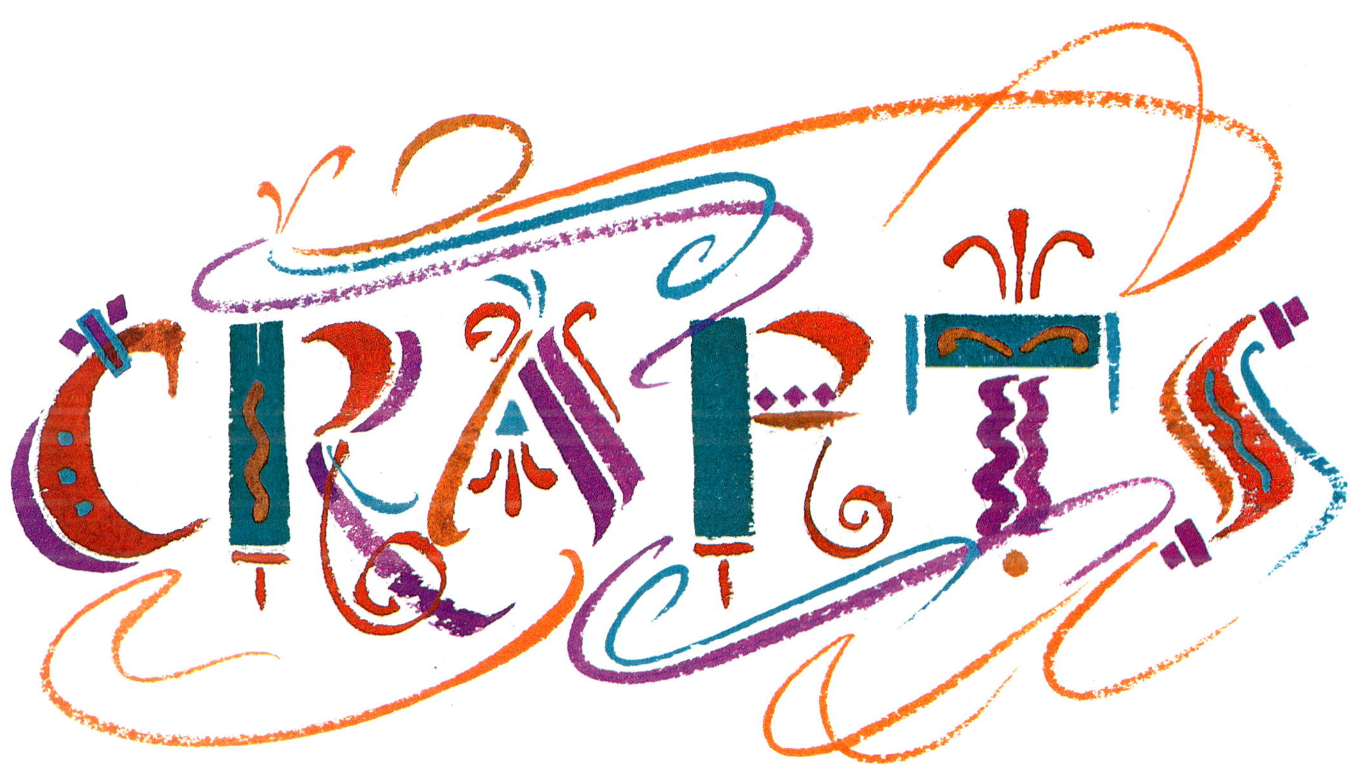

A good life is found only where the creative spirit abounds, when people are free to experiment and create new ideas within themselves …

—*Aileen Osborn Webb, 1892-1979, founder and patron of the American Craft Council*

THE WORD "CRAFTS" evokes traditional images: quality, honesty of expression, truth in materials, a certain practicality of form. Today the field of crafts includes beautiful objects whose forms originate in function. Yet it also includes new forms—works which

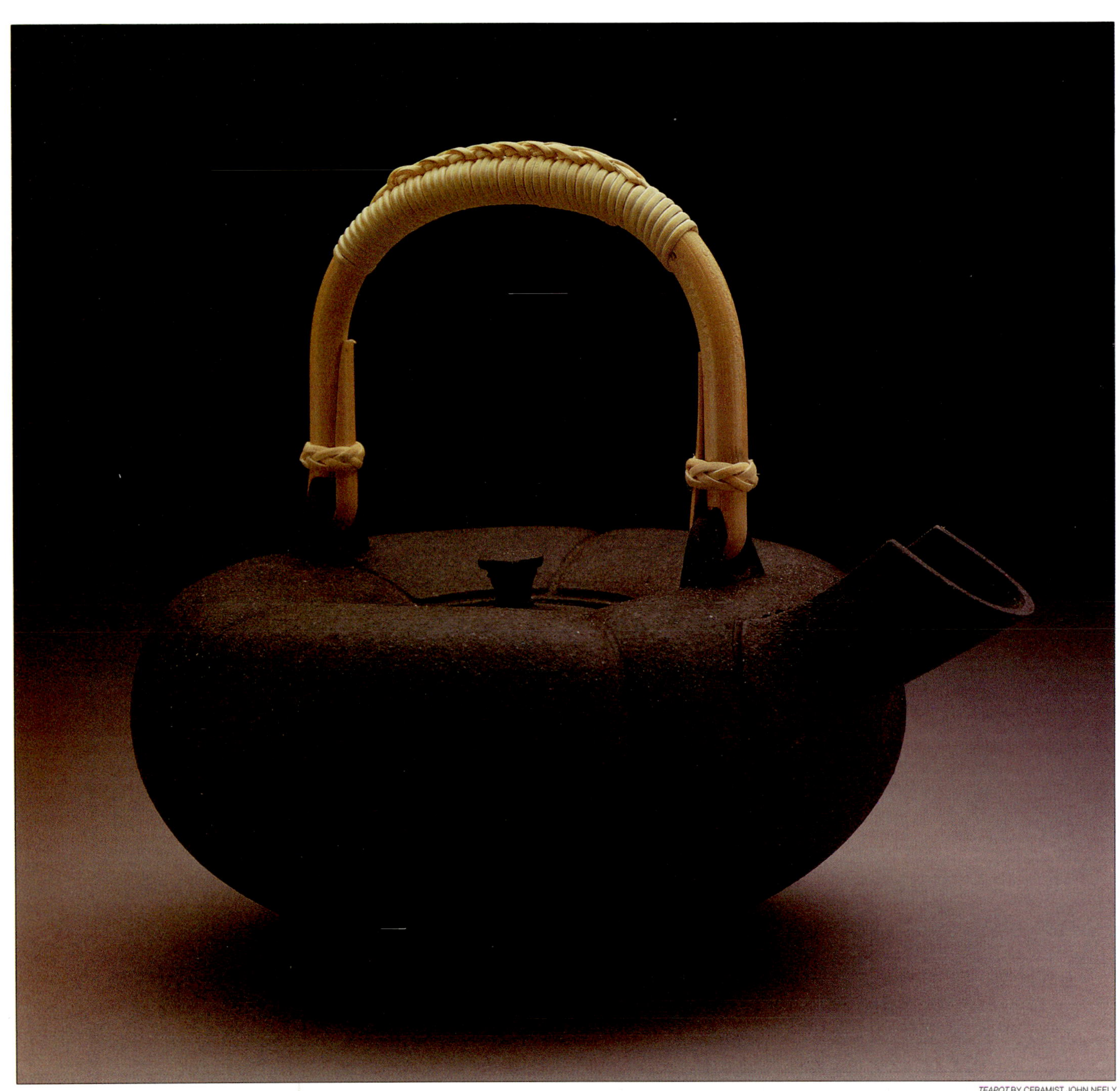

TEAPOT BY CERAMIST JOHN NEELY

The beautiful

pot is the

Q U I E T

one.

may trace their origins to traditional craft forms, either through material, technique, or style, but which deviate dramatically from craft's traditional function. Utah—as part of the legendary West—has a wealth of artists who create traditional works which reflect our unique geographical, social and historical environment. Craft artists in Utah also reflect, and sometimes lead, national and international trends toward conceptual innovation.

Among weavers, Sharon Alderman stands out as a sensitive colorist, flawless technician, arts writer, lecturer and teacher. Her wall pieces—painstakingly woven from cotton sewing thread—and her fabric to wear, upholstery and other interior fabrics emit a subtle energy as geometric shapes defined by hue dance and tease the eye.

Using folded paper for initial studies, John Hess employs a double-weave technique to duplicate the scored-fold lines of the paper in the fabric for his wall hangings. The fabric is then pinched, pleated and fanned to become "kinetically charged, implying a transformative movement."

Roberta Glidden uses a variety of techniques in creating silk paintings, kimonos, jackets, vests and scarves, all distinguished by delicately balanced colors and seasonless design. Surface images range from portraits to landscape, plant forms to abstract designs reminiscent of 1940's and fifties "retro-Modern" patterns.

Martha Klein Haley constructs both conceptual garments covered with writing based on political ideas, memories and personal stories and functional "art to wear," inspired by Japanese shibori and African tie-dye. Working with seemingly fragile silks, Haley crushes, scrunches, or pleats the fabric, permanently setting the texture with heat. From the resulting material, she hand-crafts lined vests, kimonos, bolero-style jackets and other garments.

Haley's work was recently included in an exhibit, *Bound by Tradition*, in which she and artists Jen Shurtliff, Kathleen Deneris and Danna Jacques used fiber arts to explore traditional societal roles defined by gender. Shurtliff fuses fabric, quilting and painting into fiber illustrations of the domestic, marital and moral situations of women. Her quilt *Bound by Tradition* provided the title for the show and is now traveling throughout the United States with an exhibit organized by the San Diego Museum of Art.

JOHN NEELY

John Neely is known nationally and internationally for his pioneering work in exploring the flashes of color that can occur with wood firing, salt firing and reduction firing (or—more appropriately—cooling). Although he constructs a wide variety of forms, it is his exquisitely crafted teapots which draw the greatest recognition from Utah's public.

Neely, who teaches at USU, spent years as a potter in Japan and is fluent in both the Japanese language and the cultural legacy of clay. Evidence of his commitment to the Japanese aesthetic and philosophy lies in his choice of process. Wood firing is one of the oldest and most complex of firing processes, as much an ethic as a technique. It is time-consuming at every step—in constructing (and reconstructing) the kiln, in learning the subtleties of clay and the vagaries of chemistry. Neely's pots—refined and elegant—define economy of form, achieving a level of art that transcends material and process.

Rebecca LeCavalier and Sandra Ence Paul create classic handwoven and hand-dyed natural fiber wearables as well as abstract wall pieces, while Kay Robinson and Jean Marshall sew, quilt and embroider wearable art based on ethnic and historical clothing styles.

Charlotte Warr-Anderson, one of Utah's premier quilters, has won numerous national and state awards. Her quilt *Spacious Skies* took second prize in *Expressions of Liberty: The Great American Quilt Festival*, organized and toured nationally by the Museum of American Folk Art in New York City; it is now in the museum's collection of contemporary quilts.

Mary Ann Hutto-Jacobs uses traditional basket weaving techniques as a point of departure to create elegant sculptures. Forming amphora, urn, or cylindrical shapes, Hutto-Jacobs explores the full range of possibilities of "vesseldom"—to protect, divide, embrace, exclude, or entrap space; as metaphor for human existence; as veneer and soul. Not satisfied with the natural surface alone, she applies everything from gold leaf to velvet flocking, wood putty to acrylic paint.

Felt wall hangings by Maggie Harrison bear the look of something long loved, like a child's cherished blanket. Harrison often collaborates with her husband, Steve. The resulting work resembles the irregular shapes of animal skins and evokes Western landscape or Native American imagery.

Dolls tell stories and, for those who approach them intimately, the stories they tell are our own. Bonnie Sucec, a well-known painter and mixed-media artist, creates dolls evocative of the modern-day myths that flavor our lives. Sucec's work blends an "imagist" influence with Mexican folk art and personal narrative. She is a skilled storyteller, and all of her works reflect something about both the artist and the viewer.

Susie McGee-Lowdermilk, a mixed-media and multidiscipline artist, makes whimsical dolls, pillows, opera bags and clothing. She occasionally collaborates with Jody Plant on painted, sewn and appliqued collages as well. Exotic and Victorian in feel, her dolls combine unusual contemporary and antique fabrics, jewelry, buttons and lace with

FLOWER PAINTING ON SILK BY ROBERTA GLIDDON

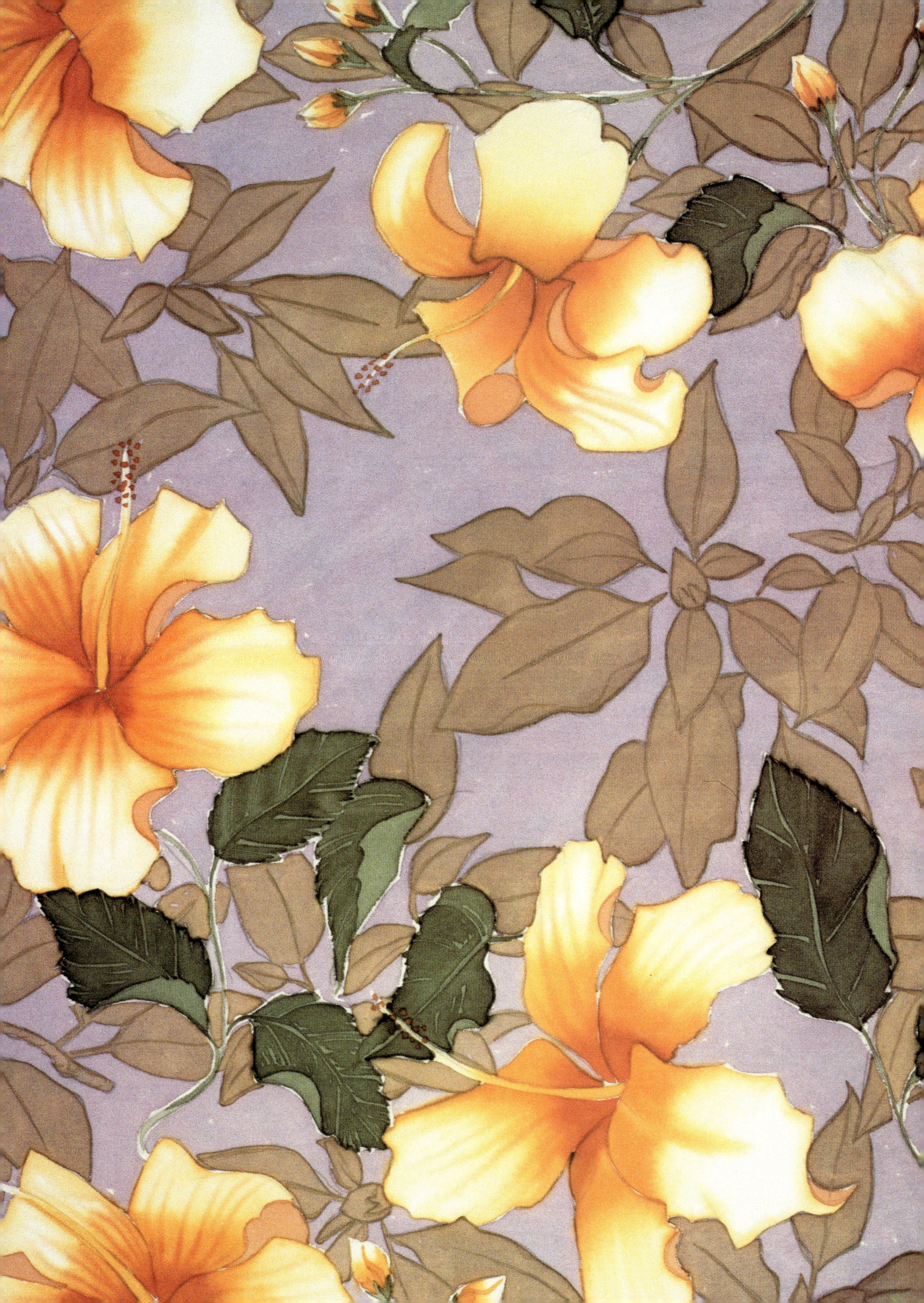

PETER PAUL PRIER

Luthiers are makers of stringed instruments and Utah's luthiers painstakingly craft some of the best instruments in the world. A visit to a luthier's shop reveals a room filled with warm curves, richly gleaming surfaces and resonant hues.

Though there are numerous luthiers throughout the state, it is perhaps through the efforts of Peter Paul Prier that Utah has become known as an international center for stringed instruments. German-born Prier—an alternately "charming" (my word) and "difficult" (his word) taskmaster—learned the art of violin making at the prestigious school in Mittenwald, Germany. After moving to Utah, he established the Violin Making School of America in 1972—the first such school in the United States.

Each year more than forty applicants from all over the world apply for only five to six openings. A dormitory connected to the school allows students to "eat, sleep and dream instruments." In its more than twenty years of operation, the school has graduated ninety-one students, many of whom have returned to their native countries or states to establish their own luthier shops.

hand-painted polyform heads and limbs.

Carole Alden Doubek has a fertile imagination . . . or perhaps she just knows amphibians and reptiles. Her delightful soft sculptures—painted, stuffed, beaded, embroidered, jeweled— attest to her knowledge and love of all creatures of the Earth.

Bri Matheson's mixed-media boxes tell stories as rich and satisfying as writing by Norman Maclean or a song by Greg Brown. Matheson is never far from fly-fishing—and he has built a career on the ubiquitous trout. The core of his work consists of papier mâché sculptures based on native Western freshwater fish which take form as anything from whimsical jewelry to large, free-floating mobiles. With a well-developed sense of place, he also crafts boxes in the Joseph Cornell tradition, blending nostalgia and irony with symbols from the local culture.

Inspired by the spirit of Utah's ancient rock art, Winston Gamble, Roger Fuller and Randy Fulbright design elegant wearables in silver and gold to celebrate the myths, legends and symbolism of primitive cultures. Frances Garrett creates fluid shapes with twisting ribbons and entwining filament. Patricia Harader's designs are influenced

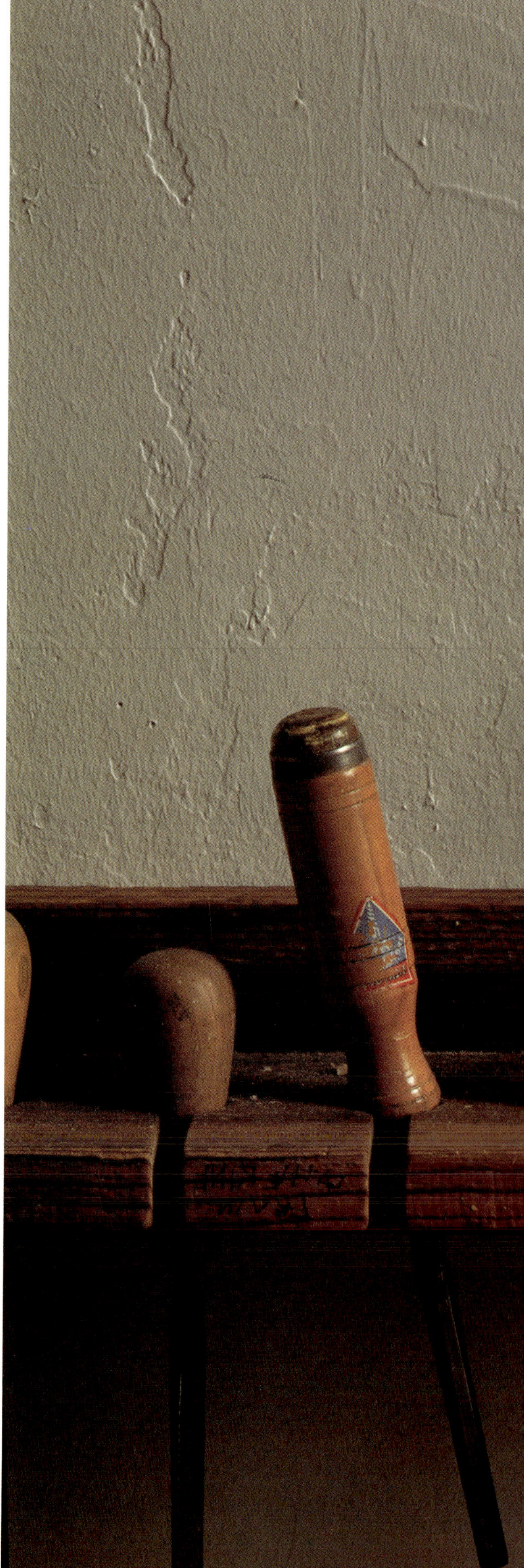

VIOLIN MAKING SCHOOL OF AMERICA, SALT LAKE CITY / PHOTO BY STEPHEN SMITH

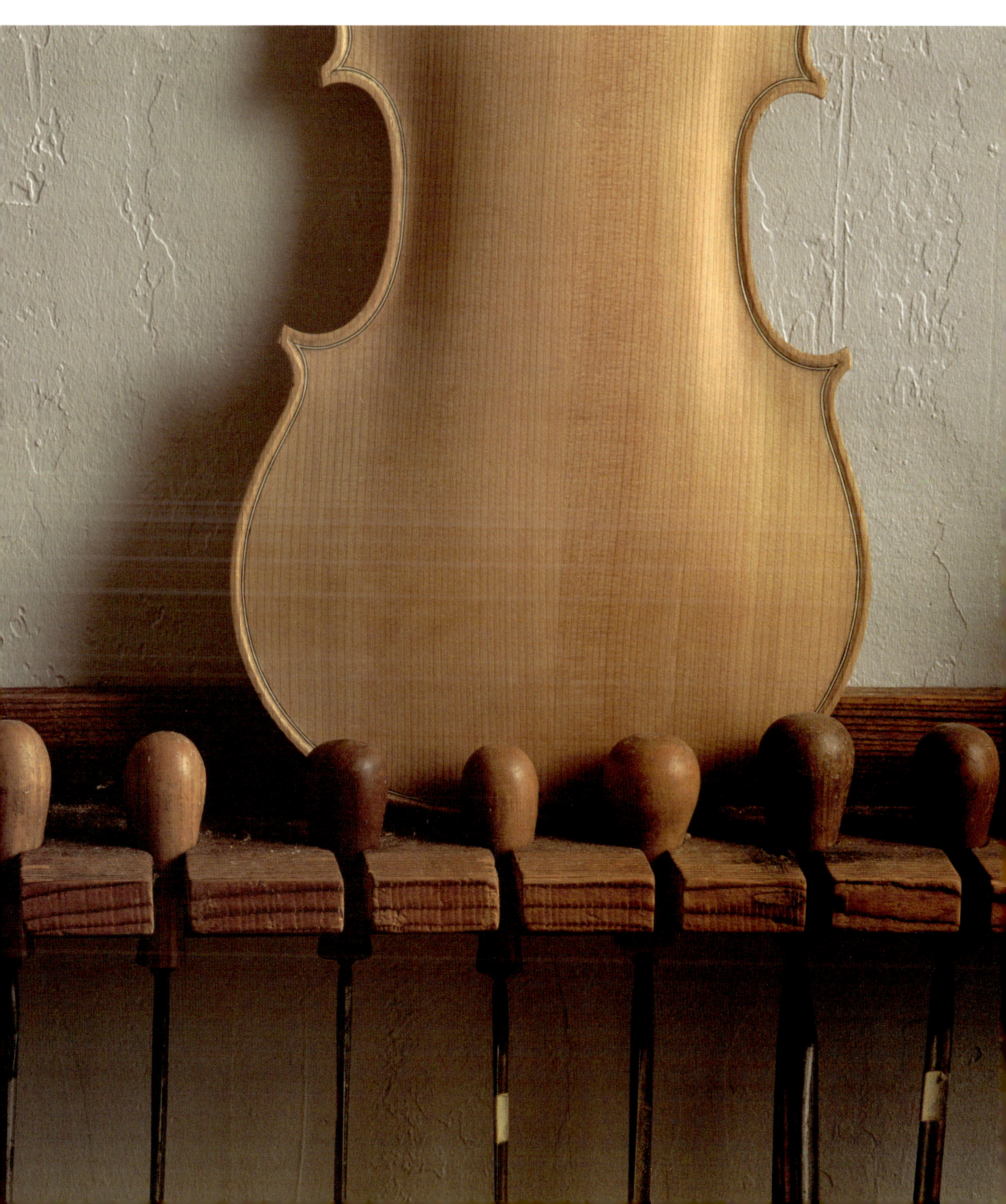

DOROTHY BEARNSON

Dorothy Bearnson began her love affair with clay as a child and later studied with German artist Marguerite Wildenhain, Japanese artist Shoji Hamada and Kyllikki Salmanhaara of Finland with funding from a Fulbright grant. A pioneer in pottery techniques, Bearnson has also been instrumental in craft organizations: She founded the University of Utah ceramics program in 1948; organized Utah Designer Craftsmen in 1960; was actively involved with the American Crafts Council and National Council of Education in the Ceramic Arts (NCECA); and has received numerous grants, including a fellowship from the National Endowment for the Arts.

Bearnson's work is typically included in national exhibits of seminal ceramic artists and documented in classic textbooks on the history of contemporary ceramics. Her highest recognition to date came in April 1991, when she received an honorary membership in NCECA, the most prestigious honor in the field, bestowed on fewer than fifty artists to date.

by Art Deco, oriental art and nature.

Kristie Krumbach combines beads with silver, copper, or other metals, forming delicately wrought animals in miniature landscapes. Bears, elk, fish, cows, horses, pigs, telephone poles and cacti are suspended in the environment of her work.

Carla Jimison uses an ancient Egyptian and Greek "glass-can" technique with polyform, a thoroughly modern material, rolling various colors into tiny patterns of cats, fish skeletons, spirals, stars and industrious bees.

The philosophy of potter Joe Bennion is summed up in his statement, "The best pots are quiet ones." Working with salt-firing and wood-firing techniques, Bennion throws quiet, humble, functional pots which express a meditative beauty, marked by a search for balance and order. He has exhibited, lectured and presented workshops all over the world and is a frequent contributor to national ceramics magazines.

Weber State University professor David Cox has served on the board of American Craft Enterprises and received a National Endowment for the Arts Craft Fellowship Grant. Cox is known for both his anthropomorphic sculptures and production pottery. Whether gently

erotic, tongue-in-cheek, or pointedly ribald, his sculptures display a unique perspective on the politics of sex. Each piece in his entire line of production pottery is painstakingly designed to work with all the others, so that even a highly mixed collection maintains a pleasing continuity.

Lee Dillon creates classic forms such as tea or rice bowls, teapots and platters with understated elegance and sumptuous glazes, such as delicate celadon and rich *sang de boeuf* (a deep, luscious red).

Christopher Gittins combines hand-built and wheel-thrown clay to construct sculpture loosely based on vessel forms. By pushing the dialogue between positive and negative shapes, his enclosed double-wall constructions create the impression that each piece is part of an implied whole.

Ceramist Susan Harris, artist-in-residence for the Alliance for the Varied Arts, currently serves as the exhibition chair for the National Council for Education in the Ceramic Arts (NCECA). Harris uses reduction firing techniques, eschewing glazes which can mask the surface design, and the exteriors of her embossed, latticed, combed, carved and scraped pots contrast sharply with the smooth, luster-glazed interiors.

Her pots often have mythological creatures (frogs, alligators and birds) perched astride them, inspired by cultural artifacts such as ancient Chinese ritual vessels.

Trained in ceramics, glass blowing and jewelry, David R. Pendell teaches ceramics at the University of Utah and has served on the American Crafts Council and NCECA. Pendell layers his bright colors through under- and over-glazing, firing each piece as many as a dozen times. His decorative wall panels intertwine opposites in texture, color and pattern. Pendell is also known for his fantastic versions of functional pottery, such as enormous teapots. Combining humor and parody, his work reflects the new tradition in clay, a tradition which respects the skill of craft while searching for innovation in art.

John and Diane Shaw collaborate to varying degrees on all their work. Using white porcelaneous clay, they assemble textures and casts of objects like everyday tools, fruits and vegetables into impressions of their lives. John states that one goal is simply to "express what you know about yourself . . . to try to have a dialogue with the things in your life."

Starting with titanium sheet metal, ceramist and jeweler Steve Hansen corrugates, bends and pierces the surface, then dips the entire piece in clay slip, firing a work up to a dozen times. Tom Bettin's sculptures integrate Native American visual and spiritual concepts with contemporary social themes.

Enormous coiled terra cotta pots by Tom Gale are burnished by hand prior to firing, resulting in silky unglazed surfaces. Anne Quigley is one of only a few artists working with colored inlaid and marbled clay called *neriage*. Betsy Quintana presents terra cotta amphora vessels, influenced by ancient Mediterranean cultures, blended with contemporary images. Stan Roberts creates exquisite raku vessels and jewelry in smoky hues tinged with metallic flashes. Catherine Kuzminski, Victoria Hixon and Kathy M. Royster hand-build distinctive vessels and sculptures decorated with funky images of cats, fish, shells, or bones.

An increasing number of artists are using polyform, a synthetic oven-baked clay loosely related to ceramics, as a fine art and craft medium. Alan R. deHaan molds polyform into funny little constructions, many of which explore humanity's obsession with food.

In addition to restorations and reproductions of period works, Willy Littig creates powerful contemporary works, generally preferring to use line and texture as color or a small amount of colored glass for contrast. During

Clay—one can have a love A F F A I R with it.

the past year, Littig and his team made 120,000 glass tiles for the fountain and two monumental stained glass domes on the tenth floor of the remodeled Hotel Utah, now the Joseph Smith Memorial Building.

Other glass artists include Dan Cummings (who specializes in etching and sand blasting), Jenkyn Powell (traditional, painted and fired glass), and Julie Tanner (stained glass panels for cabinets, mirrors, hanging pieces and table pieces with lighting). Somewhere between glass and furniture is the work of artist Stacey Sharp who creates etched plate glass screen.

In 1990, Artspace director and artist Stephen Goldsmith was curator with museum director Steven W. Rosen of a survey of the work of thirteen of Utah's finest furniture designers and makers for the Nora Eccles Harrison Museum of Art. Called *A Dozen and One Utah Furniture Makers*, the exhibit featured the contemporary work of Jim Banta, Robert Bliss, Jeffrey Karl Cobabe, Andrew H. Glantz, Stephen Goldsmith, Michael Iannone, Glenn D. Leonard, Kaethe Radomski, O. Rhees Ririe, Earl V. Sevy, Ruth Sundberg, John Sundberg and Tom Tessman. From traditional, Native American-inspired inlaid wood

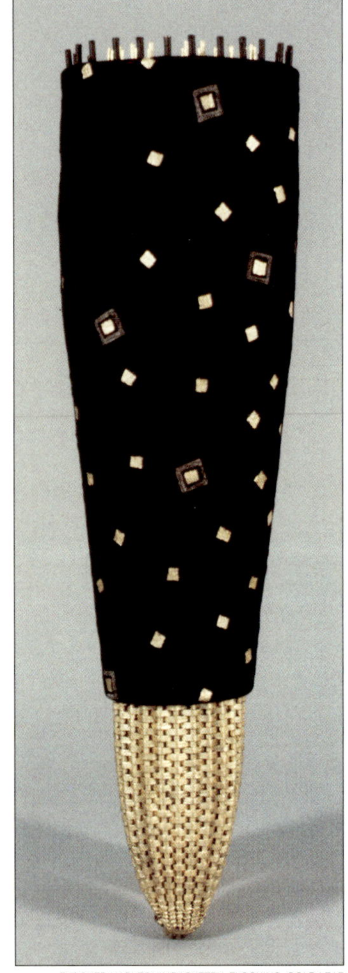
FLOCKED HARLEQUIN BASKETRY, FLOCKING, GOLD LEAF BY MARY ANN HUTTO-JACOBS

tables to post-Modern tables of granite and glass to conceptual sculpture based on functional forms, the work represented a broad range of furniture possibilities.

Tom Tessman and Steve Goldsmith create both utilitarian and *conceptual* furniture—work evocative of function, but only in concept. Goldsmith mixes wood with concrete, glass, metal, fabric, found objects and other materials to form ritualistic and somehow familiar pieces. A "renaissance man" trained in art, architecture, sociology, and comparative religion, Tessman creates furniture of steam-bent and carved wood as well as acclaimed liturgical works such as

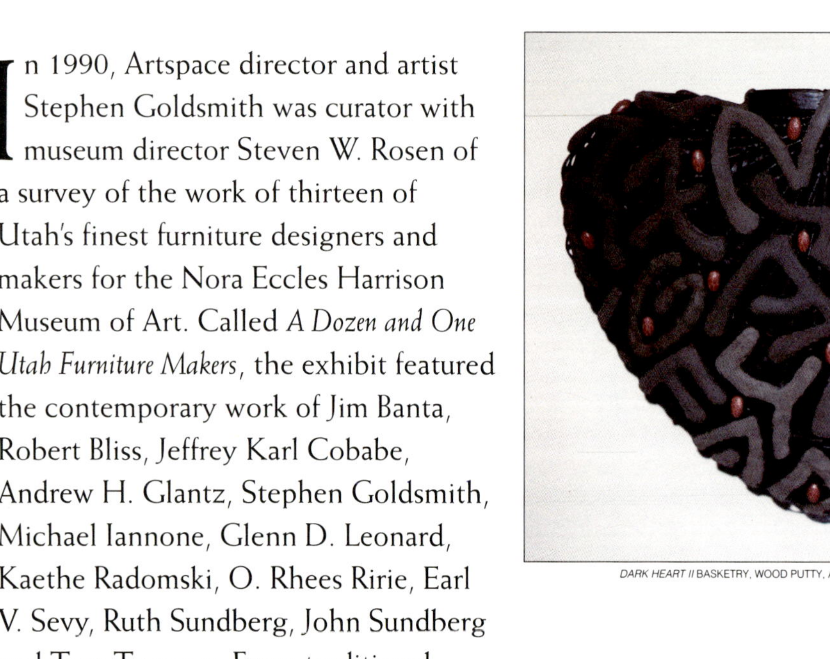
DARK HEART II BASKETRY, WOOD PUTTY, ACRYLIC / BY MARY ANN HUTTO-JACOBS

baptismal fonts, crosses and scepters for local churches in wood, stone, metals and minerals. Retired dean of architecture at the University of Utah Robert L. Bliss makes minimalist "knock-down" furniture in wood, metal, leather, plastic and fabric—chairs and tables fold or disassemble for storing or moving.

Rhees Ririe, Kaethe Radomski, Glenn Leonard and Jeffrey Cobabe characteristically mix dark and light woods and varied grains. Ririe's breathtaking *Lady's Writing Table and Chair* is a study in contrasts—black grainless ebony and blond, swirling bird's-eye maple. Radomski is noted for her sinuous highboys with drawers that snake through space like boxes tilting on the verge of disaster.

Andrew H. Glantz's furniture, aesthetically pleasing, practical and comfortable, is the result of carefully thought-out ergonomic design. Glantz is also a generous advocate for other artists; he has curated several exhibits of contemporary furniture for local galleries and museums, such as *Sitting Pretty* for the Salt Lake City Arts Council's Finch Lane Gallery.

Janet and Clinton Call combined degrees in wood sculpture and metalsmithing to start their own furniture business, creating from a variety of woods, metals and plastic laminate.

In pursuit of an American style, Geoffrey Fitzwilliam initiated a self-guided study of furniture construction and style. Coming to Utah originally to study violin making, he has now built a career in furniture and has produced many Frank Lloyd Wright reproduction pieces.

Finally, the glitz and kitsch of Lucy Fairchild surface in recycled and painted furniture. Searching out second-hand household goods, Fairchild gives them a new life. Coffee tables, chairs and dressers are reincarnated with funky, candy-colored pastels and a playground reality.

Written in bold letters on the blackboard in the ceramics studio at the Alliance for the Varied Arts in Logan are the words *"The best things in life are not always things."* Ceramist Susan Harris says she needs those words to remind her of what's important and to help pace herself. Yet, looking at Utah crafts, one is tempted to disagree. Life, when filled with creative things, is very good indeed.

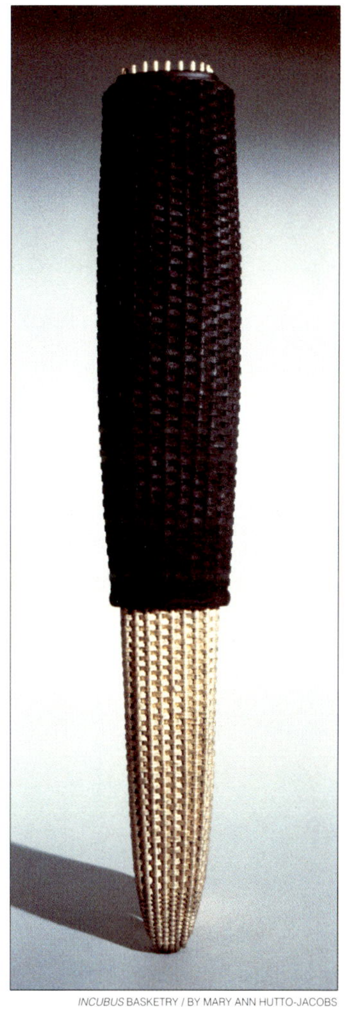

INCUBUS BASKETRY / BY MARY ANN HUTTO-JACOBS

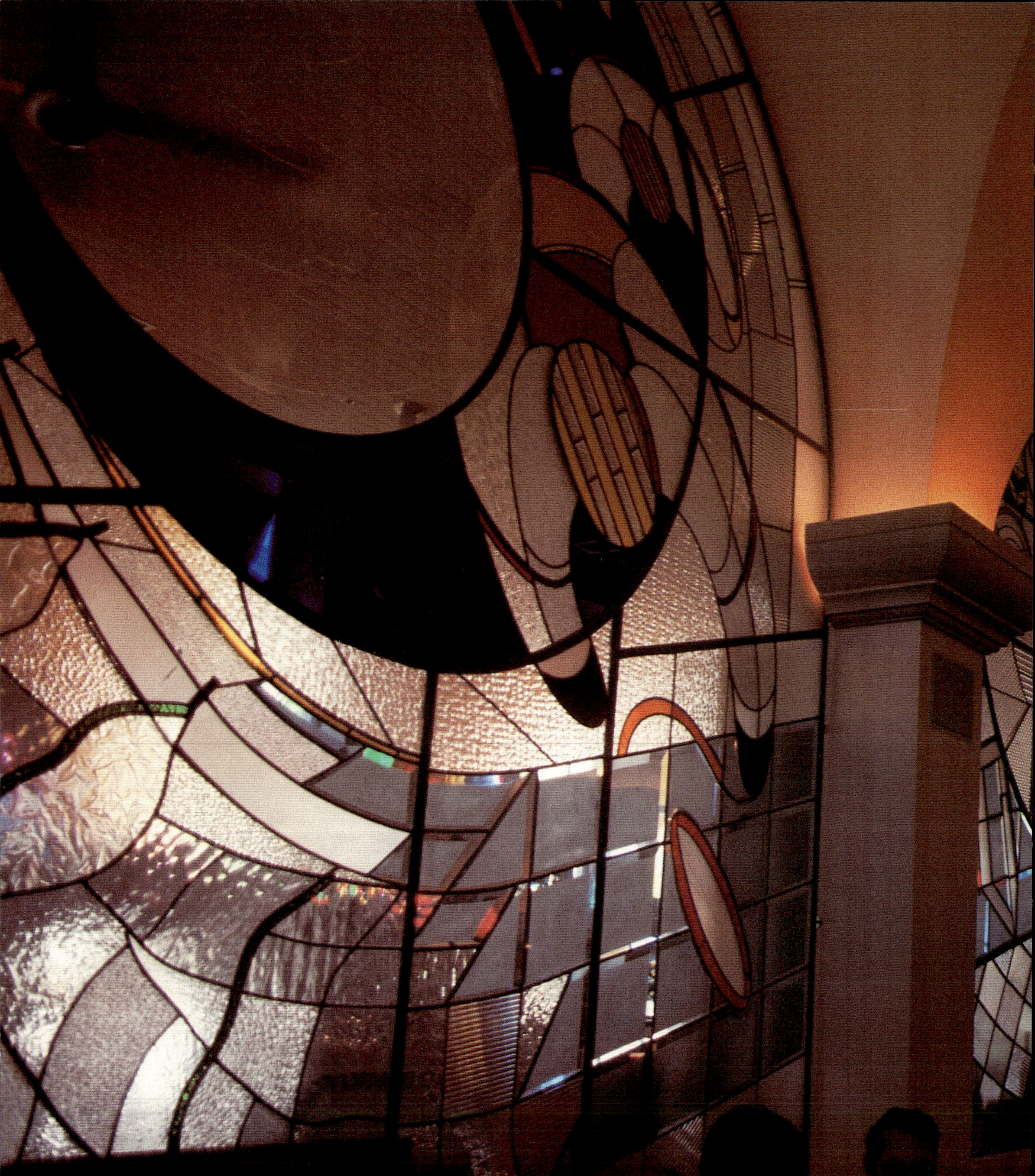

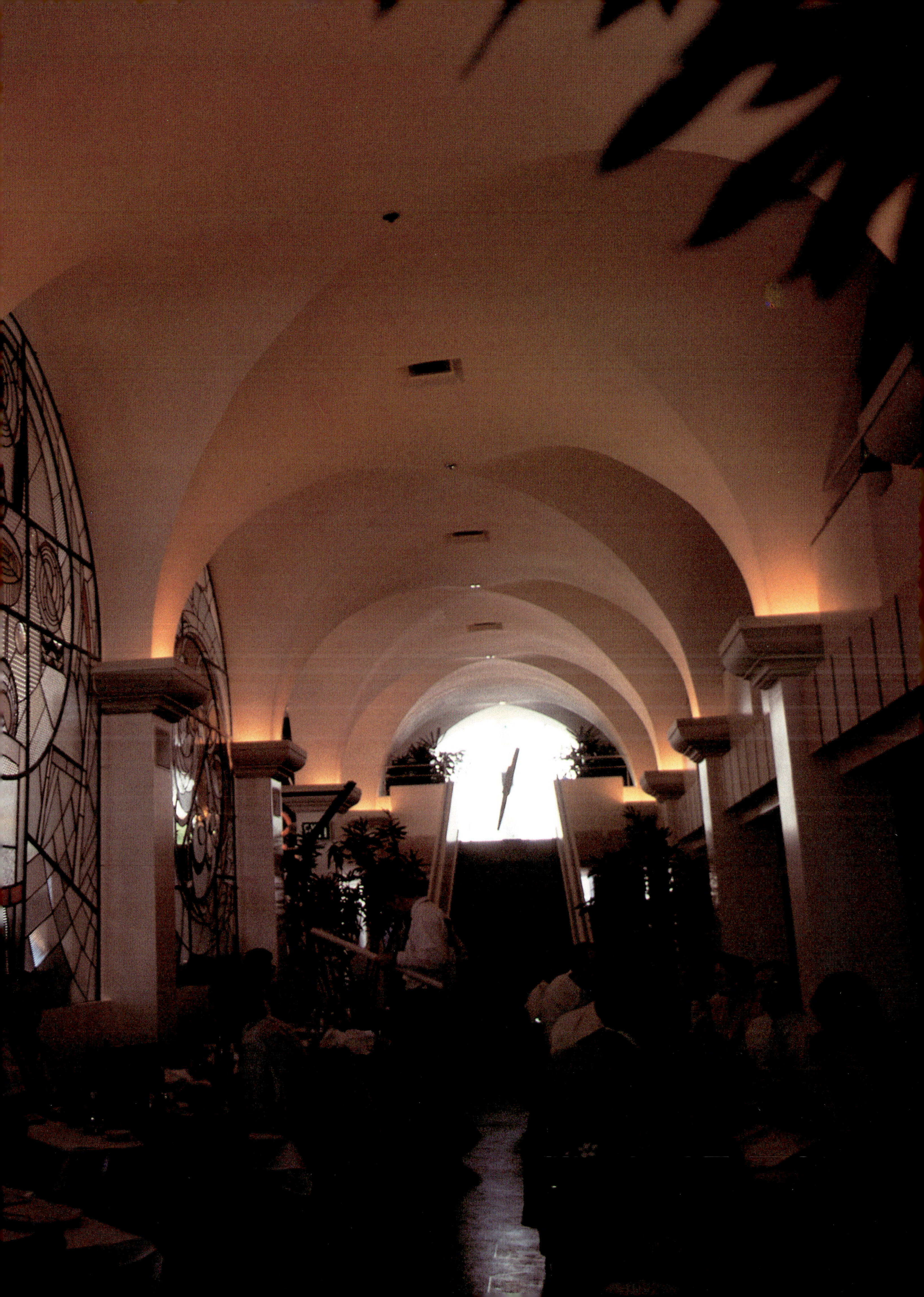

CRAFTS OPPORTUNITIES

The Utah Arts Council Visual Arts Program now sponsors a biennial crafts exhibit as part of its rotating series of statewide competitions and, in conjunction with Utah Designer Craftsmen, is in the process of publishing a craft artists directory. The Arts Council is also a good source for current addresses and phone numbers of craft artists, guilds or organizations. The Salt Lake Art Center offers regular classes in ceramics as well as exhibits in textiles, fiber, quilts, furniture, jewelry and glass and an annual holiday exhibit of hand-crafted nutcrackers. Their Triangle gift shop features many Utah craft artists.

The Utah Museum of Fine Arts on the University of Utah campus has developed notable collections of contemporary American ceramics and Navajo weavings. Traditional crafts from world cultures are represented in its historical collections.

Salt Lake City Arts Council and Utah Designer Craftsmen together offer a holiday crafts sale in the Finch Lane Gallery. The Living Traditions Festival in late May, sponsored by the City Arts Council, offers traditional and contemporary crafts which celebrate the ethnic diversity of the area.

Artspace Artist Association on Pierpont Avenue in Salt Lake City provides a unique studio and living environment for artists. The association participates in monthly gallery strolls and artists are available for consultation by appointment on a regular basis. Art Access/VSA Utah, also on Pierpont, is "an arts council representing the disability community's" *Very Special Arts* program. Included are artist residencies, festivals, classes, theater programs, exhibits, a preschool course and a visual arts gallery.

The Chase Home in Liberty Park, managed by the Folk Arts Program of the Utah Arts Council, was remodeled with many permanent works by Utah craft artists.

Traditional quilt exhibits are extremely popular in Utah, with annual exhibits at the Springville Museum of Art and the Utah State Fair and periodic shows at the Kimball Art Center (Park City), Eccles Community Art Center (Ogden), Pioneer Craft House (Salt Lake City), and Bountiful/Davis Art Center.

The Cathedral of the Madeleine in Salt Lake City, originally built by some of the best craftsmen in America, now boasts magnificent restoration work by some of the best stained glass, mural, woodwork and fiber artists in Utah and the nation. Local business and government building planners have begun to incorporate craft arts into their sites (among other media) as integral aspects of the environmental design. The new Gallivan Utah Center Plaza and Pierpont Avenue, for example, boast indoor and outdoor installations by John Shaw, Diane Shaw, Jim Jacobs, James McBeth, Stephen Goldsmith, Silvia Lis Davis, Jan Striefel and Willy Littig.

Utah festivals, including the Utah Arts Festival in Salt Lake City, the Park City Arts Festival and myriad community festivals, provide excellent sources for discovering emerging craft artists. The Ogden Arts Commission is involved with several fests in Ogden.

Readers may contact the Salt Lake Gallery Association for a complete listing of commercial and nonprofit galleries in Salt Lake. The Phillips Gallery offers a wide selection of contemporary crafts, artists' books and books on art. It holds an annual small packages exhibit and sale during the holiday season. The Greystone Gallery in Logan features craftspeople from Utah and the Western region with an eclectic mix of funky costume jewelry, wearables, glass, wood and ceramics. Also in Logan, the Alliance for the Varied Arts has a new exhibition space and a well-stocked gift shop The Kimball Art Center in Park City has one of the largest craft gift shops in the state and the Eccles Community Art Center in Ogden offers a charming and plentiful selection. Artist-owned Utah Designer Craftsmen Gallery opened in 1985 and is one of the best sources for unique crafts representing some of the finest artists in Utah.

**The State
of
the Place**

Robert Kimball Herman

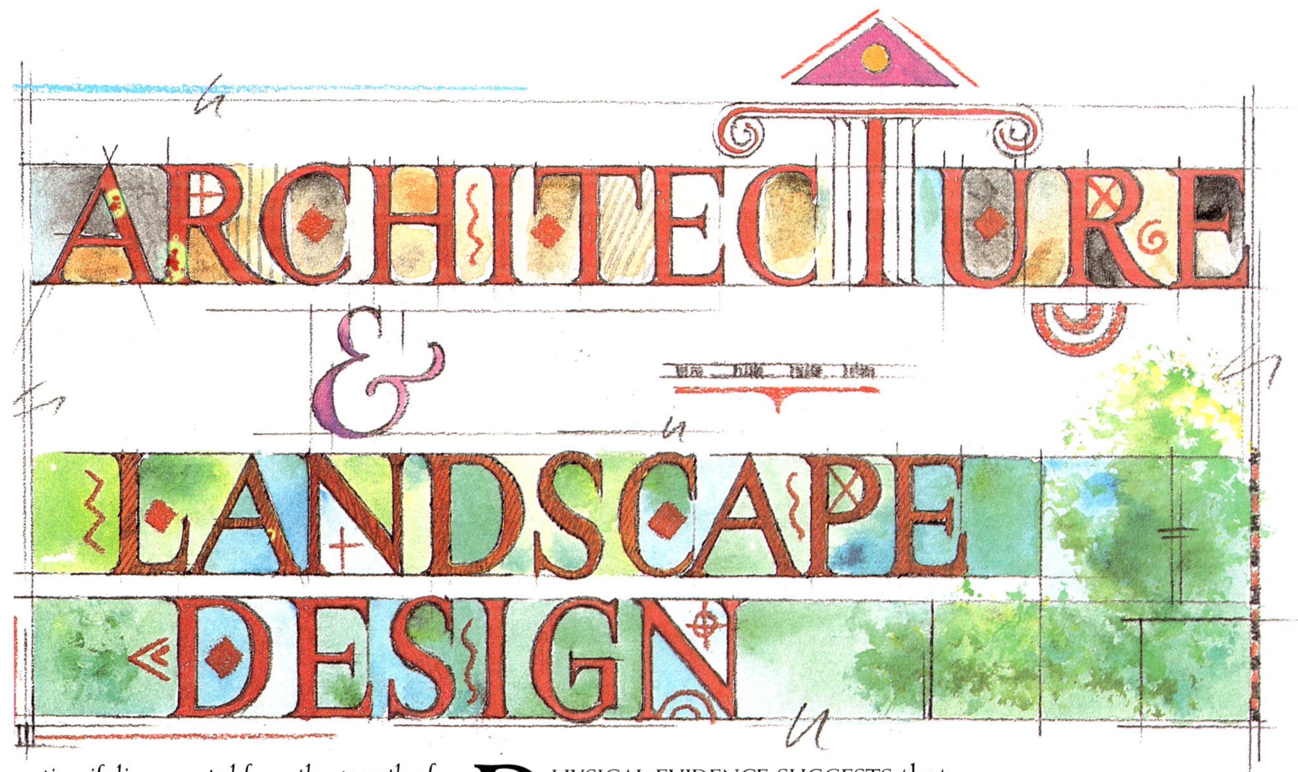

*Invention if disconnected from the growth of
architecture upon itself, is always sterile,
abstract, insubstantial.*

—*Aldo Rossi, 1972*

Nothing comes from nothing.

—*Lucretius, 50 BC*

PHYSICAL EVIDENCE SUGGESTS that
for at least eight millennia
humans have consorted with
Utah's vital forces to fashion shelter,
garden and artifact from the physiology
of the mountain desert. From the 1850's
on—the point when Mormon colonists
staked out their castrum-like settlements
and established Utah's ongoing link to

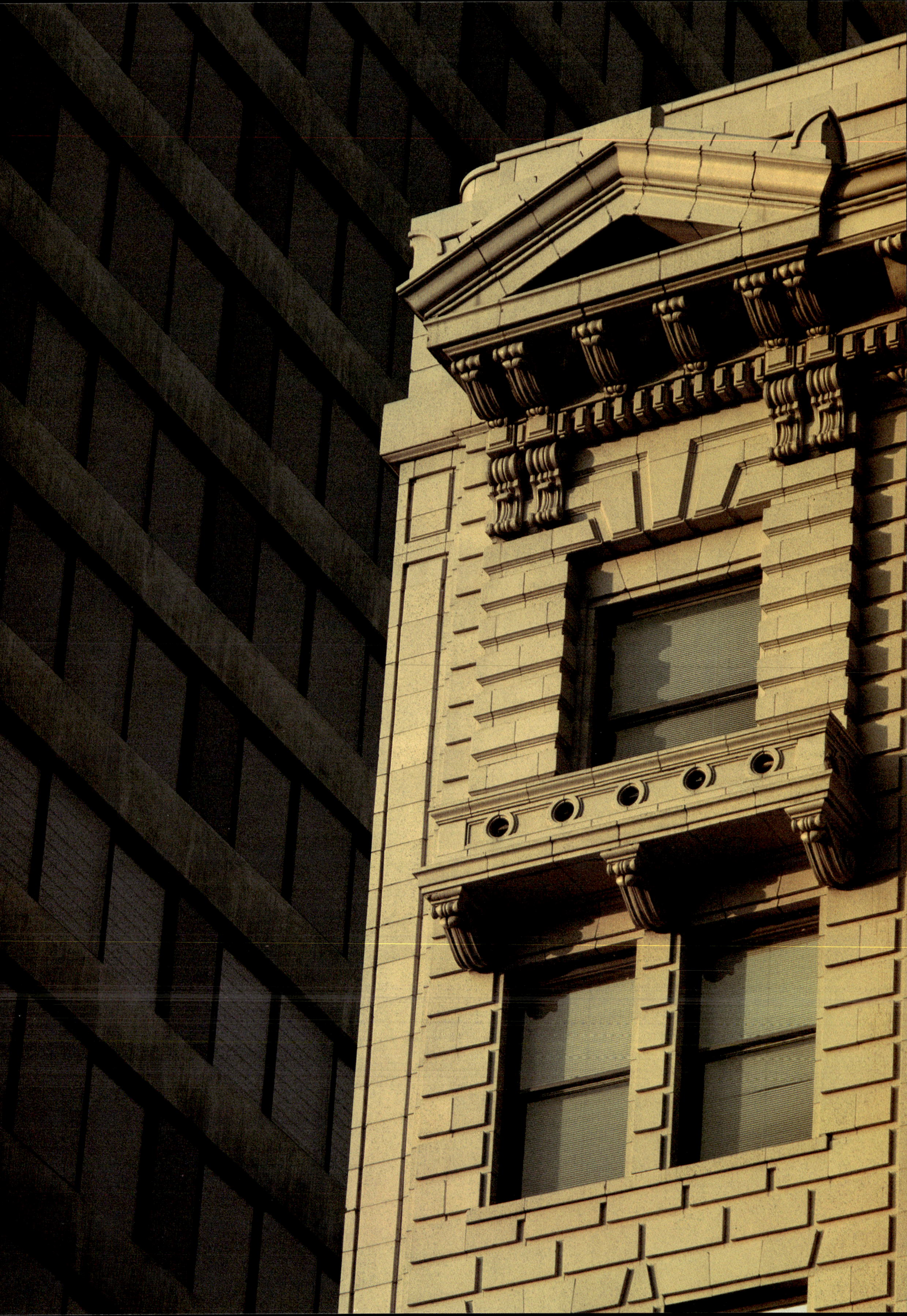

the traditions of European art and American economics—Utah's architecture in all its forms has evolved into a stylistic melange of buildings set squarely within the rigorous order of Utah's towns and cities. These manipulated environments have revealed through the years a process by which every generation of builders, in its turn, has reinterpreted its relationship with this place (Utah) by reconciling through architecture the duality of wilderness and civilization, of the heart and the head.

There are places I remember in my life, though some have changed . . .

—*Lennon and McCartney*

Utah's urban areas (which include not only the communities that comprise the so-called Wasatch Front but also boom towns like St. George, Park City, Cedar City, or Moab) suddenly appear in the vastness of the Wild West like man-made archipelagos along a wave of mountain fault-blocks and crenellated mesas, tethered to world-outside by 727s, interstates, and the ganglia of tele-anything. Utah has ceased—perhaps inevitably—to be the aggregate of the discrete pioneer towns that were the poignant manifestation of the communal yearning for civitas. But in the process, it is being consumed by the post-World War II settlement patterns that inform nearly all American cities and towns conceived under the liberating effect of democratic capitalism and modern technology— sprawling, dispersive urban patterns that deny in many ways the authentic forces of civilized living and Utah's natural environment.

Fortunately, many of Utah's architects, planners, designers and artists, in collaboration with a new generation of visionary business, civic and cultural leaders, are attempting to grasp an understanding of the complex and fundamental systemic relationships that make cities sustainable both as outposts of human habitat and as demonstrations of the unique and place-defining qualities of the new West. These declarations of interdependency include strategies to analyze form-giving natural systems (like rivers or mountains), transit (rather than freeway) oriented development, integrated (rather than artificially stratified) multi-use development, contextual (rather than universal) design, as well as comprehensive urban agendas directed specifically at community fabric and texture. From this new and still-forming regional paradigm, a startling variety of solutions are emerging to address Utah's special cultural and ecological needs.

Over the years, Utah cities have explored the speculative distant ground afforded by such urban plans as Salt Lake's Second Century Plan, which

Every generation of **B U I L D E R S** has reinterpreted this place.

There is
a structural
EVOLUTION
to each city's
central business
district.

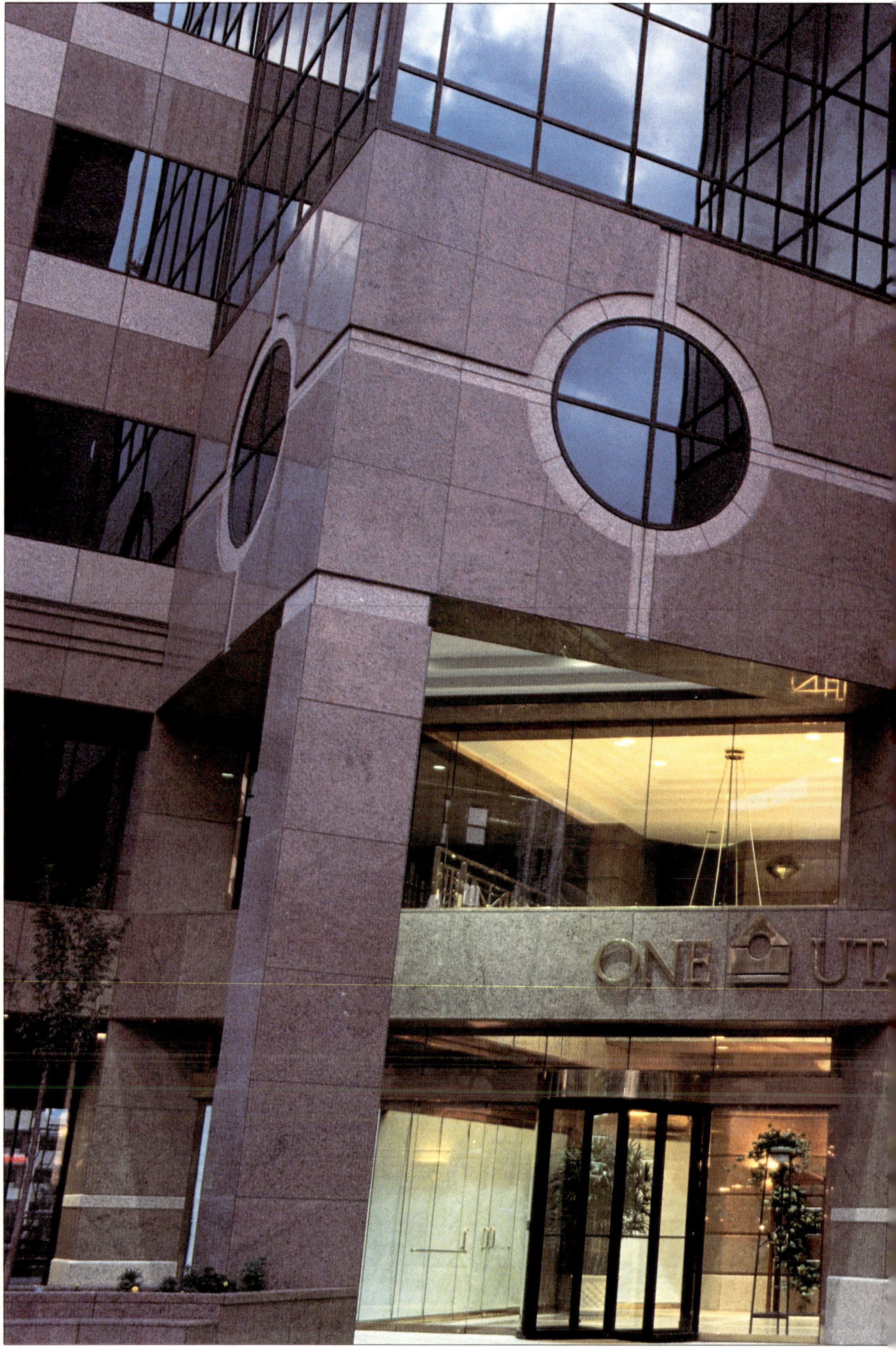

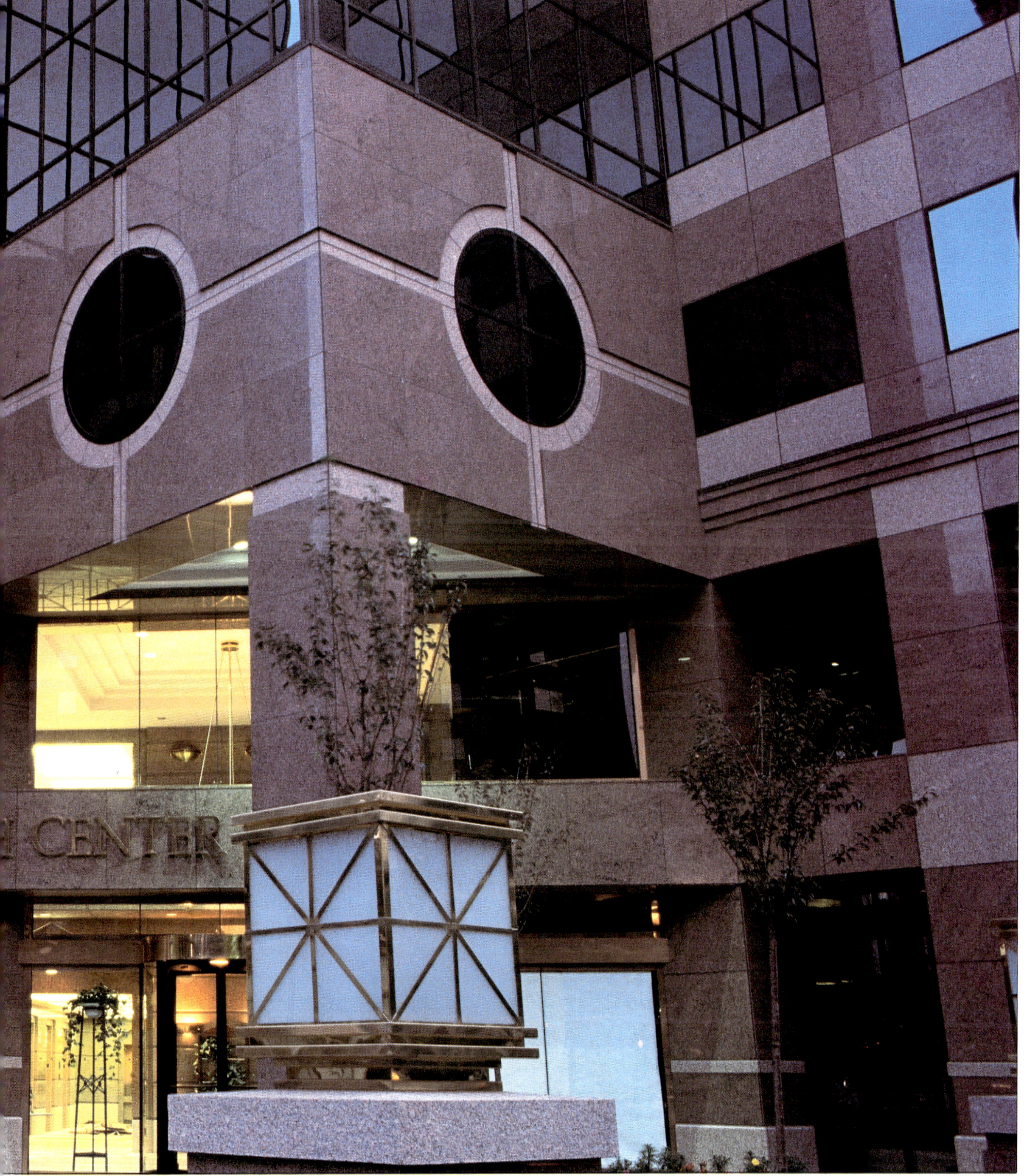

ONE UTAH CENTER, DOWNTOWN SALT LAKE CITY / PHOTO BY STEPHEN SMITH

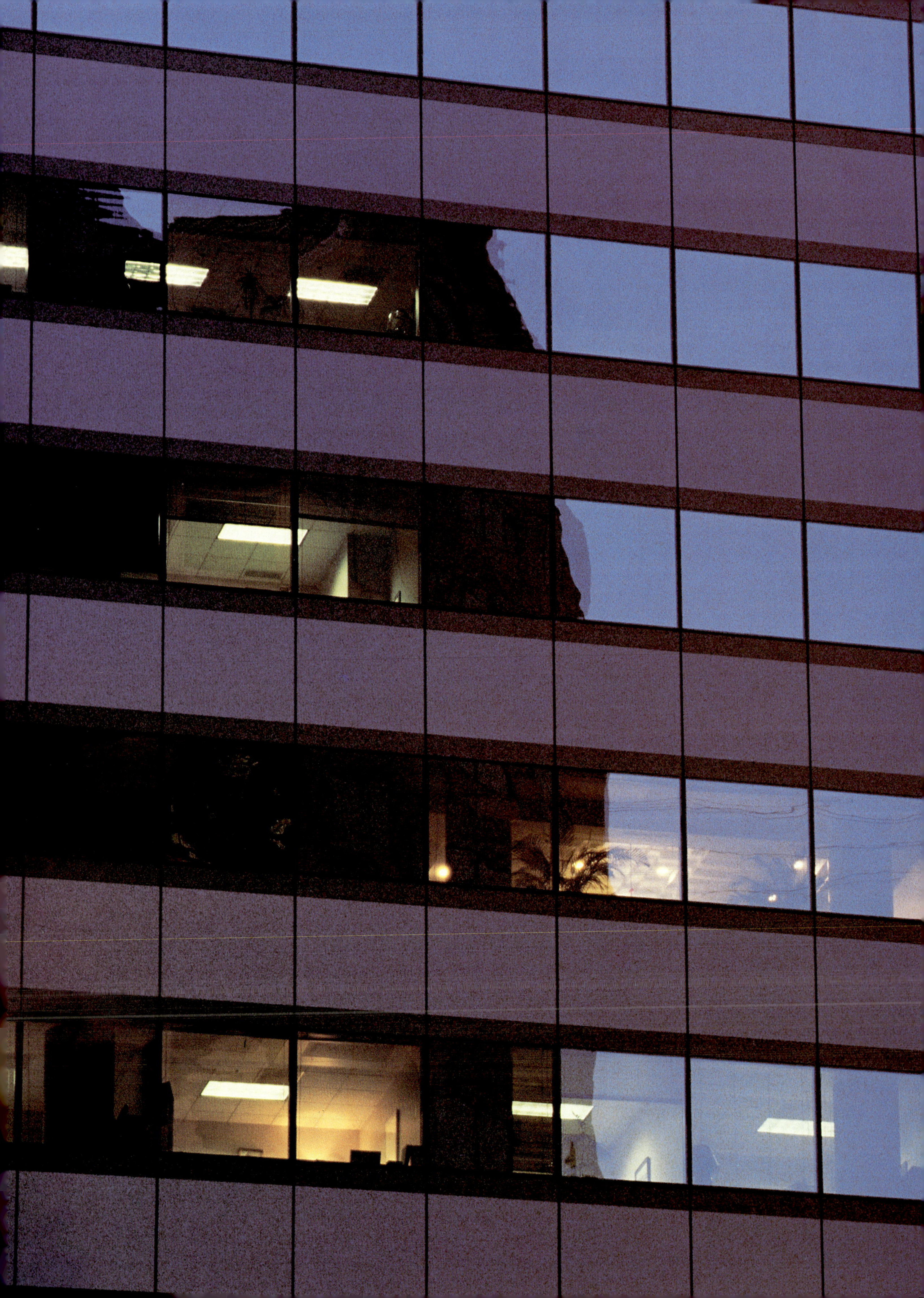

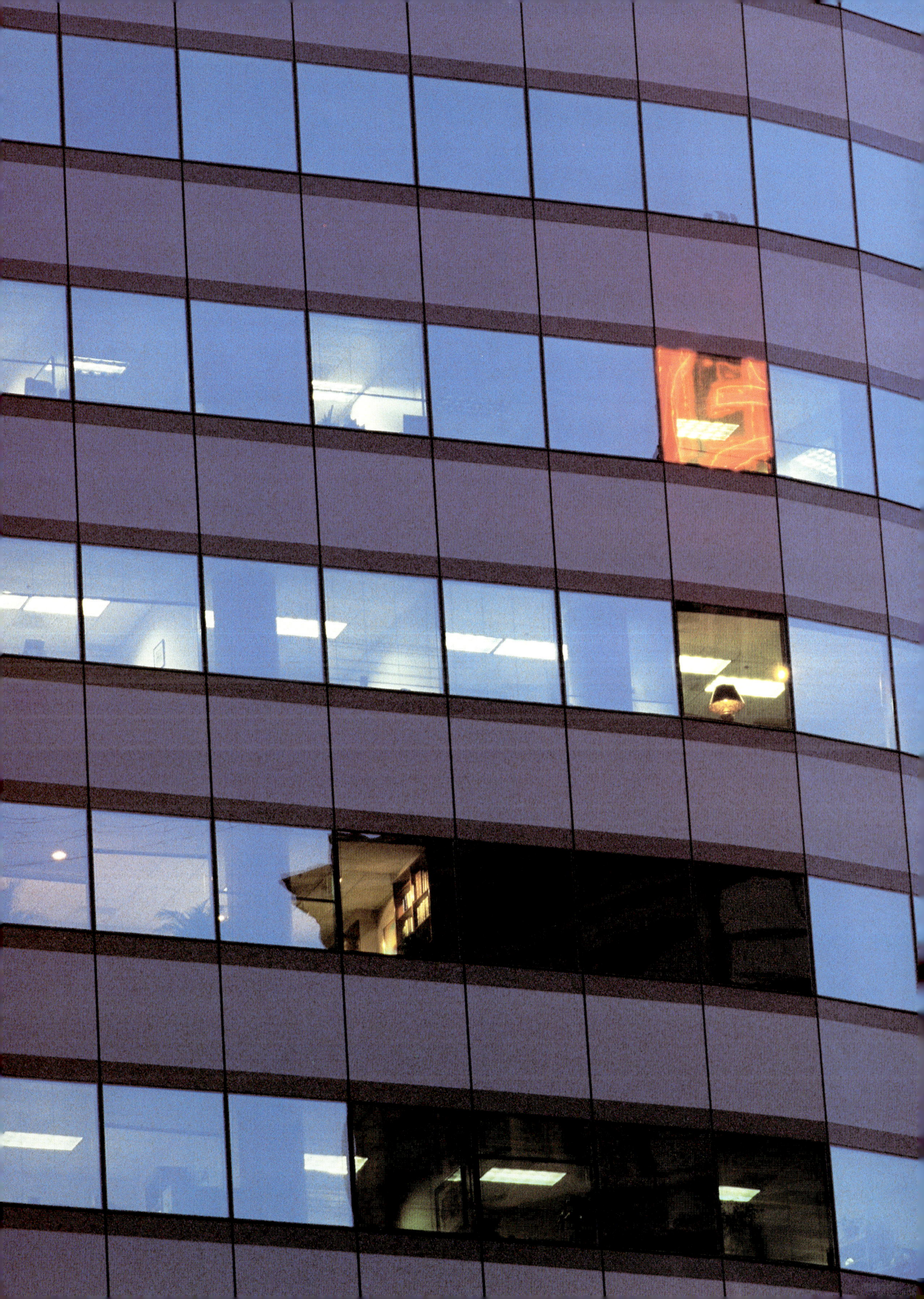

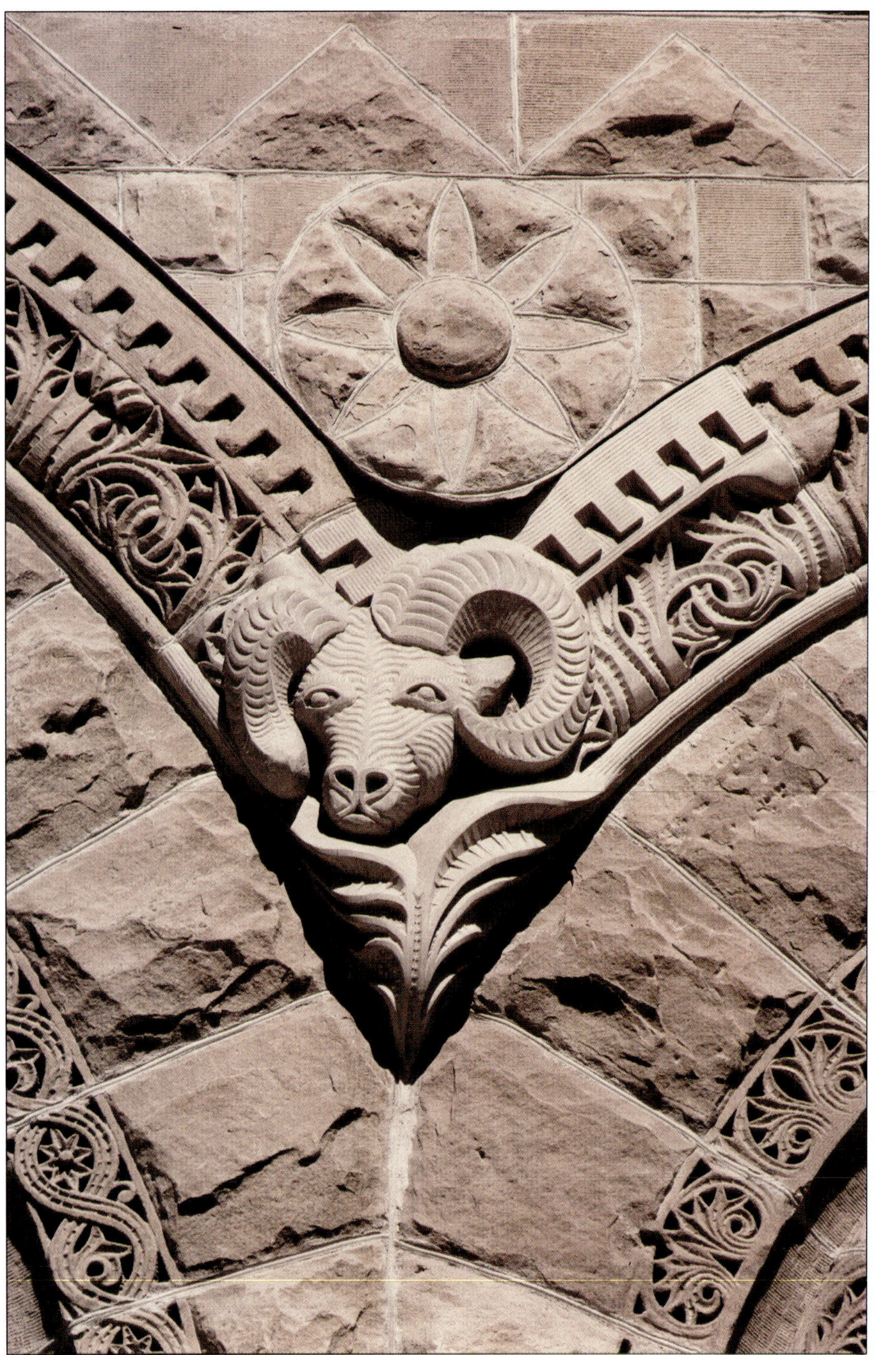

STONE RAM, SALT LAKE CITY AND COUNTY BUILDING, SALT LAKE CITY / PHOTO BY PATRICK CONE

fostered the development of the Salt Palace (ca. #1970), downtown retail malls and the Bicentennial Art Center. Recently both Salt Lake and Ogden have revisited their guidelines through prestigious regional urban design assistance teams (R/UDATs) of the American Institute of Architects (AIA), which have delineated comprehensive diagrams for the use of discrete intervention by municipalities and private enterprise to catalyze a structured evolution of each city's central business district. Incorporating planning proposals that will guide district creation, boundary definition, housing and cultural facility development, and image enhancement, the assistance teams, according to AIA Utah Director Elizabeth Hallstrom, have helped to unify the urban vision of these cities and precipitated numerous projects that support the traditional social structures of these communities.

In just the last decade, Salt Lake City has developed the Delta Center; restored the splendid Cathedral of the Madeleine and the Romanesque City and County Building; renovated the Inn at Temple Square, the Peery Hotel, and the New York Building; and created the nascent Artspace and design district along Pierpont Avenue. In progress are a nearly $70 million expansion of the Salt Palace and a 12,000-seat baseball stadium (designed by stadia masters Hell-muth, Obata and Kassabaum in the manner of the Baltimore Orioles' neo-traditional Camden Yards).

The recently completed Block 57, now Gallivan Utah Center, represents an ambitious amalgam of constructs, land-forms, artwork and activity forums that will become, under the urban convention of the open agora, both the downtown's backyard and its circus maximus. Within this framework, nearly half a million dollars' worth of various art media, linked by their shared interpretation of the Utah landscape, have been orchestrated by architect John Pace and include works by James McBeth, Kazuo Matsubayashi and Jim Jacobs, among others. Although time will reveal the importance of this project as a local model of urban land use and—more significantly—as a place for people, the controversial gestation of the Block 57 plan has provoked much-needed and unexpectedly bracing dialogue on a range of urban design issues regarding massing, edge definition, historic preservation, public art, design guidelines, and prescriptive architectural detailing.

Like Salt Lake, Ogden has made investments in the Union Station civic center, the burgeoning 25th Street Historic District and the Downtown Conference and Performing Arts Center, which includes the restoration of the beautiful Egyptian Theatre to accommodate groups like Utah Musical Theatre. Other communities in the state

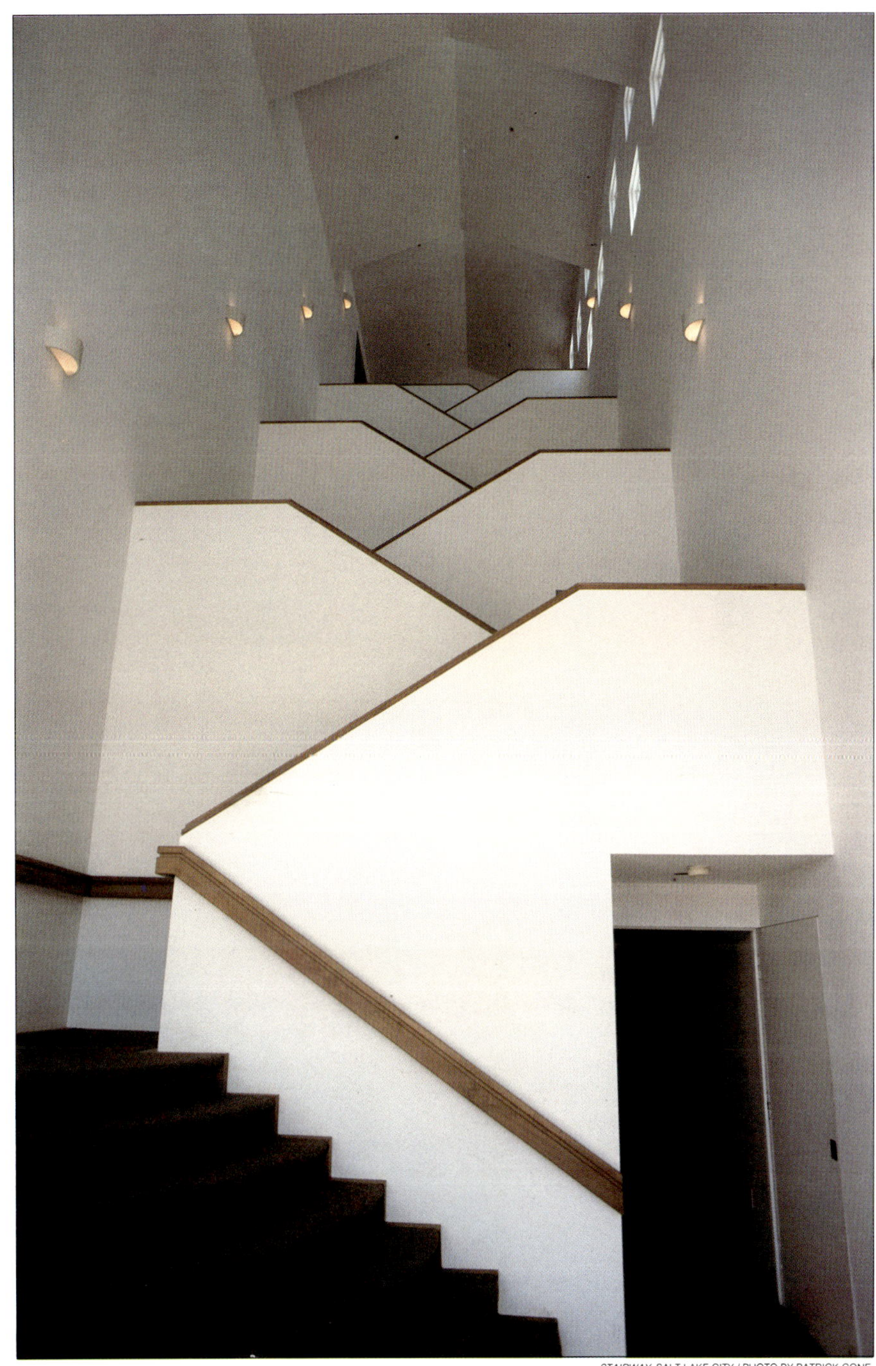

STAIRWAY, SALT LAKE CITY / PHOTO BY PATRICK CONE

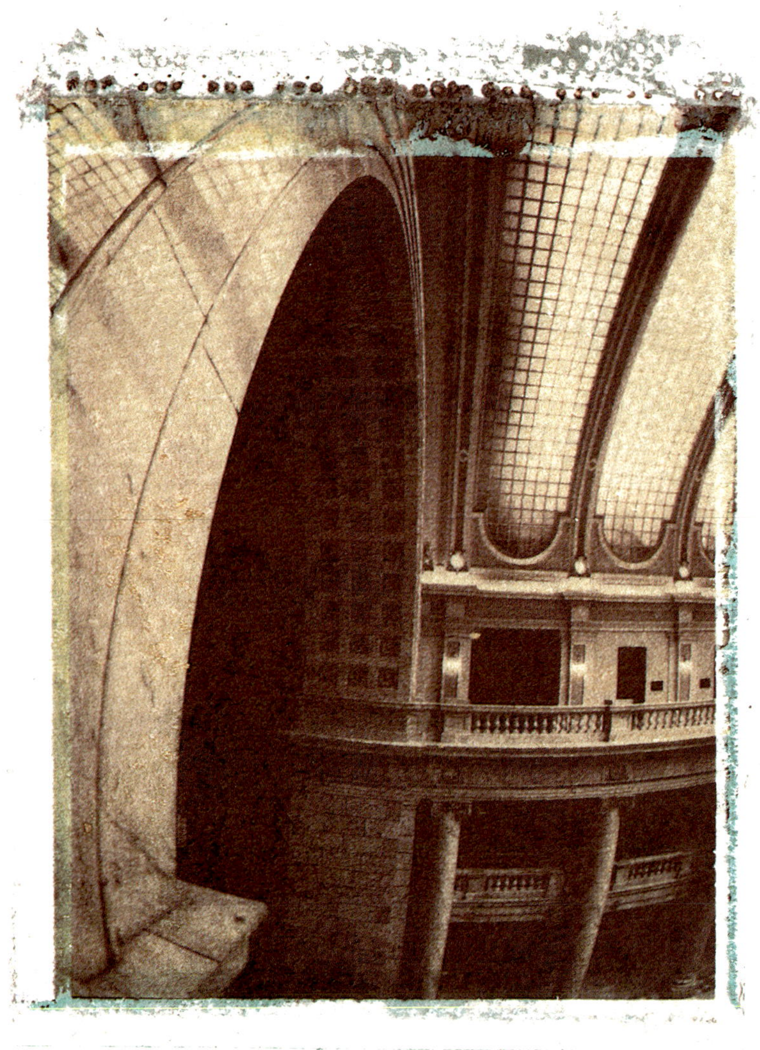

UTAH STATE CAPITOL, SALT LAKE CITY / PHOTO TRANSFER BY MICHAEL ROBERTS

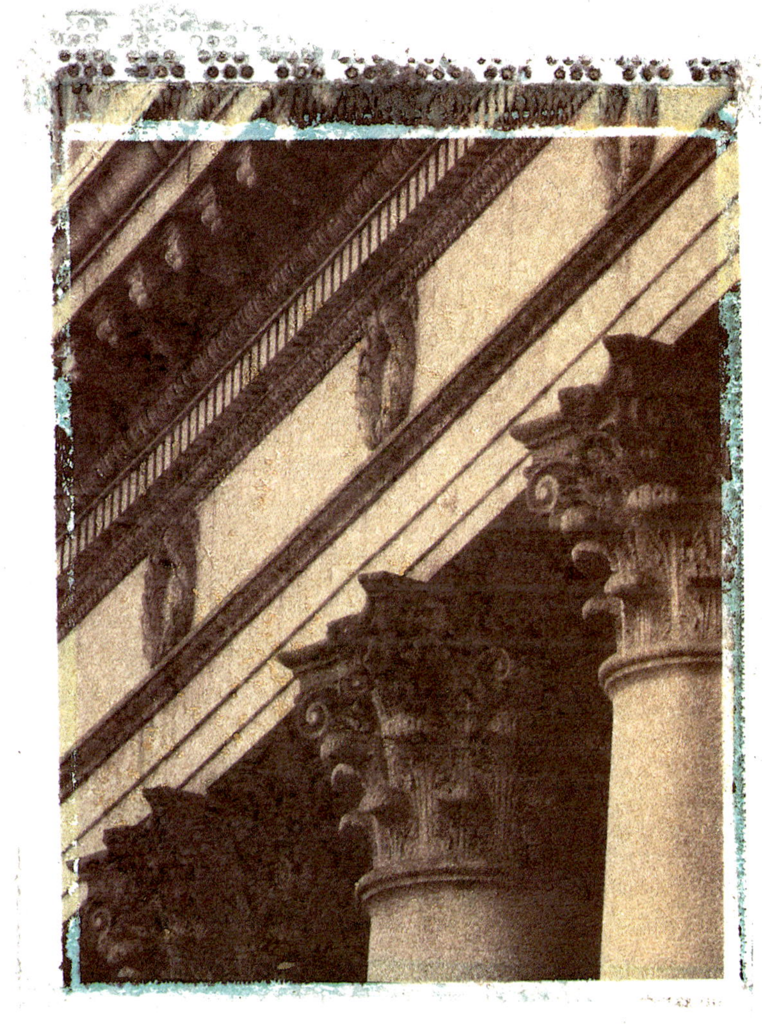

COLUMN AND CORNICE STUDY / PHOTO TRANSFER BY MICHAEL ROBERTS

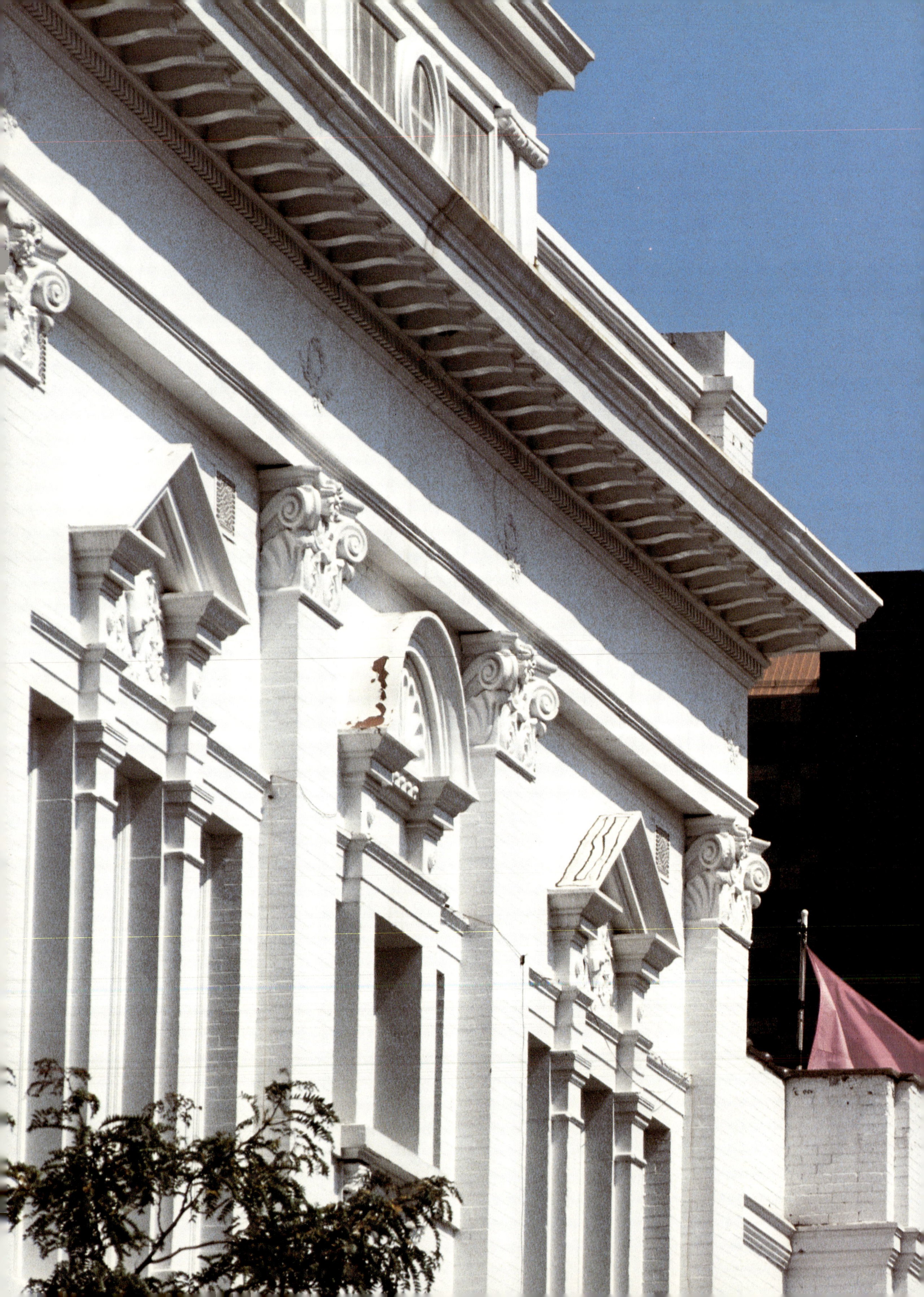

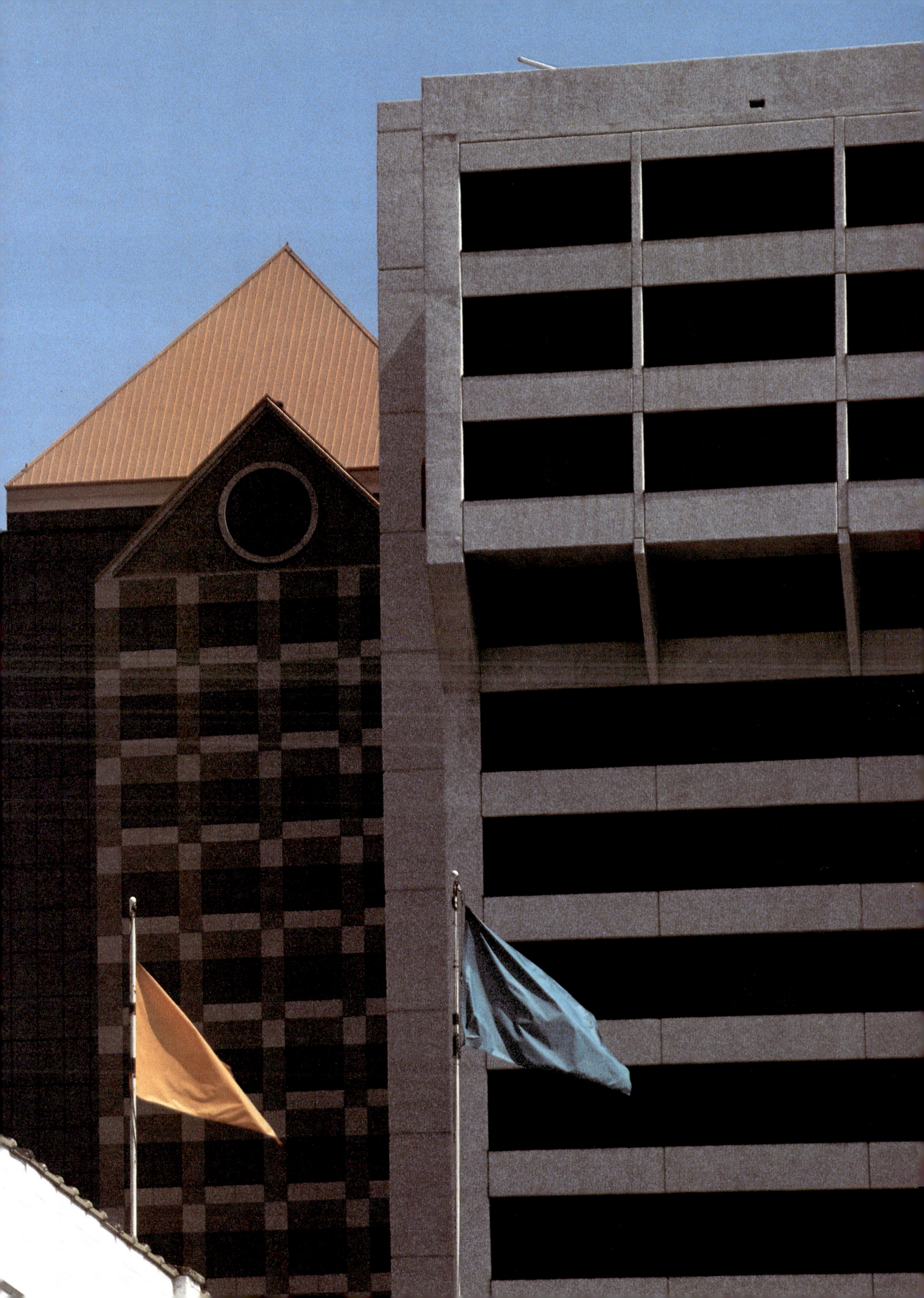

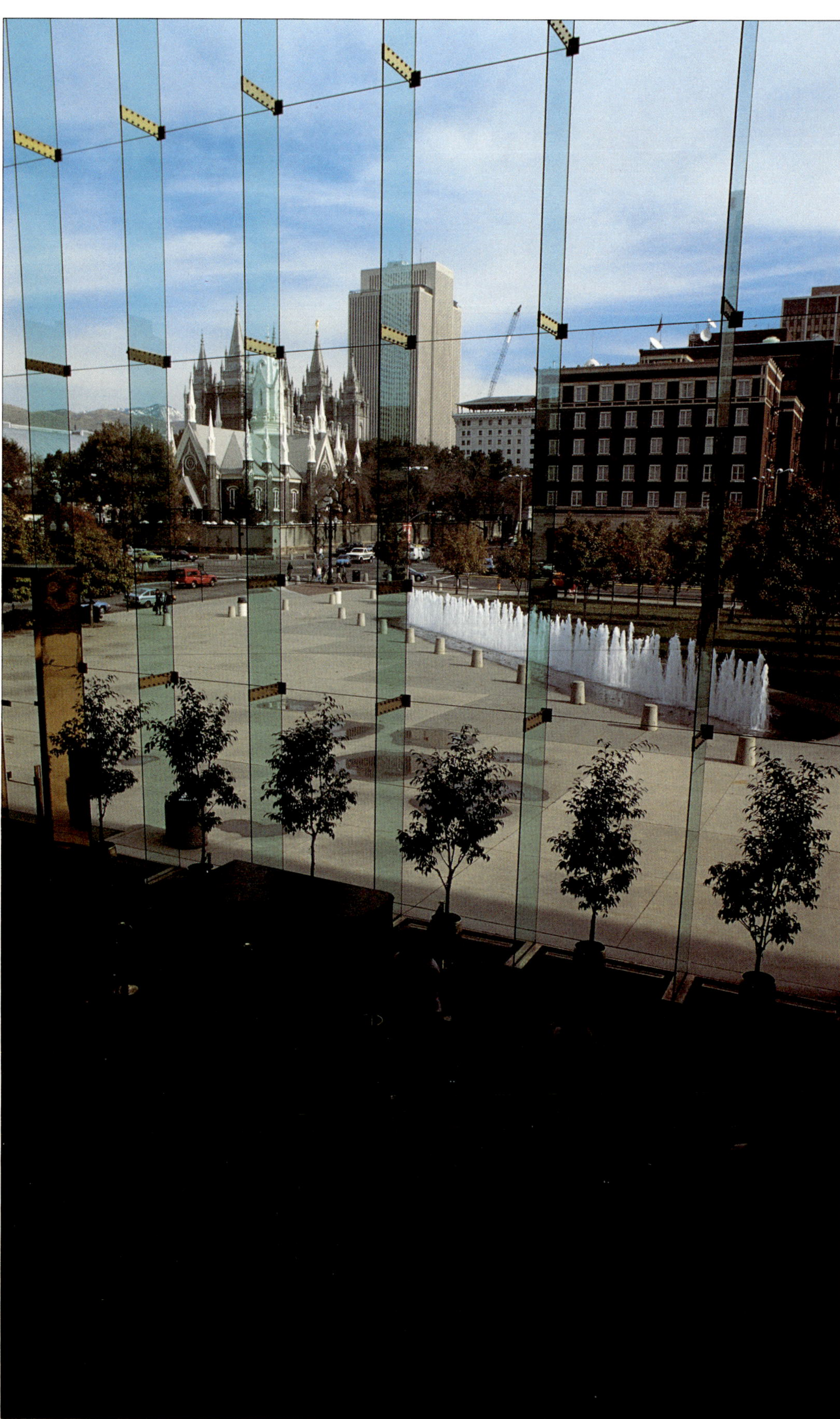

Urban landscape
planning involves
the integration of
the natural
ENVIRONMENT
within the city.

DOWNTOWN SALT LAKE REFLECTION FROM ABRAVANEL HALL / PHOTO BY PATRICK CONE

ROBERT BLISS, F.A.I.A.

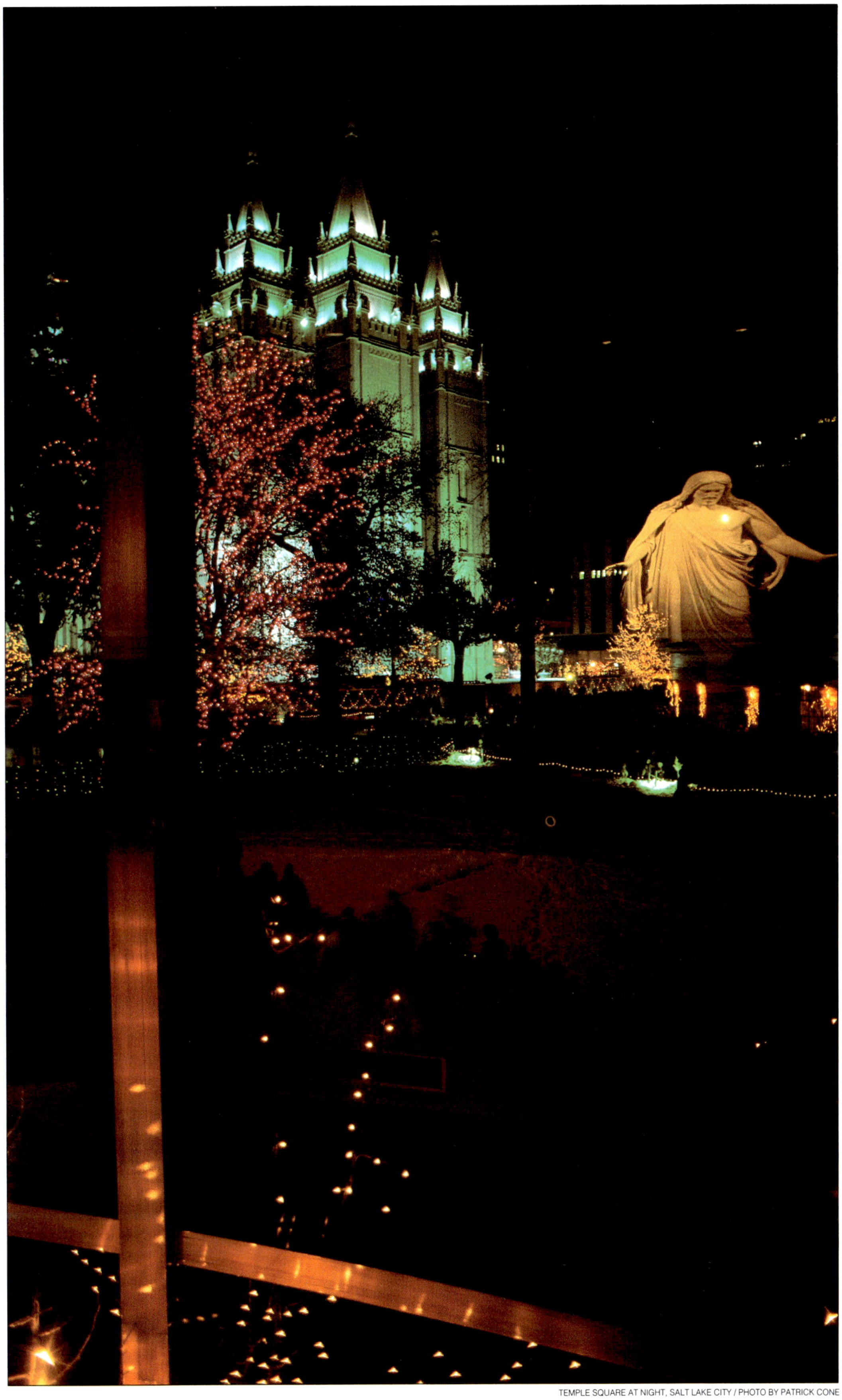

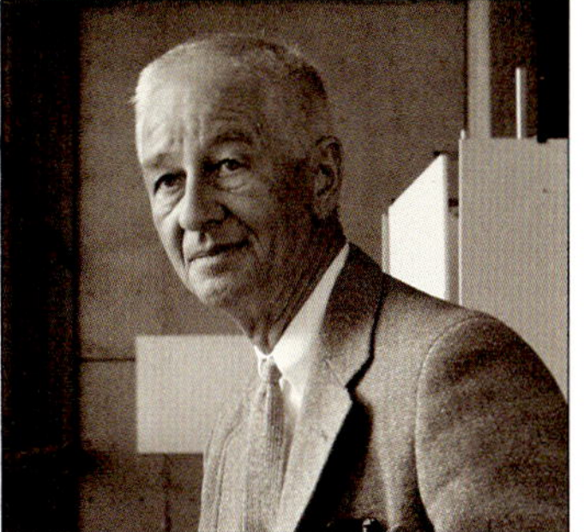
PHOTO BY DON BUSATH

With his patrician looks, Bob Bliss makes an elegant and quiet statement wherever he appears in his ongoing efforts toward producing a better built-environment for Utah. His professional journey (which took him to MIT, where he schooled in architecture, and then to the University of Minnesota, where he taught) landed him at the University of Utah School of Architecture where he served as dean from 1969 until 1988. Married to his some-time collaborator and full-time designer, Anna Campbell Bliss, he has devoted years to preparing students of all ages and professional standing for the arduous (and occasionally delightful) practice of environmental design. His dedication to excellence and to the advancement of the architectural profession has been recognized by the Western Mountain Region of the American Institute of Architects with the Silver Medal—its highest honor.

TEMPLE SQUARE AT NIGHT, SALT LAKE CITY / PHOTO BY PATRICK CONE

ASSIST, INC.

Behind a suitably plain store-front on 4th South in Salt Lake City resides Assist, one of the first community design centers in the United States. The brainchild of Robert Bliss, Marty Brixen, Jim Christopher and Carl Inouye, working on behalf of the Utah Chapter of the American Institute of Architects and the University of Utah School of Architecture, Assist was created in 1969 to provide quality design to members of the community on a *free basis* similar to legal clinics that were emerging at the same time.

are producing exciting developments like Logan's Capitol Theatre, Provo's Brigham Young Academy project, Cedar City's Randall Theatre—anchor to the Utah Shakespearean Festival master-plan—and St. George's Dixie Center.

We mark our progress by how much we leave behind.

—Mark Strand, from the "River of Words,"
Block 57 interim landscape improvements

While these projects represent a heartening commitment to the renascence of urban institutions, equally exciting is the aesthetic and material response by Utah's designers that is mining the expressive potential of the region's unique historical legacy and natural landscape. Through architecture, pioneers and native Utahns always strived to create a surrogate of some personal but invariably cosmic order through both the

pragmatic and aesthetic cultivation of Utah's geology. Perhaps for the first time in decades, Utah designers—like their progenitors—are effecting truly place-defining work that can celebrate their peculiar relationship with the land.

This attitude has helped to restore the binding cultural roles of natural systems like the Ogden and Jordan rivers and to shape large-scale projects like Interstate 215's nine-mile-long xeric planting scheme, which demonstrates the beauty of foreground vistas that harmonize in coloration and texture with the Great Basin backdrop. The surrealistic aspect of the Great Salt Lake and western desert provided the inspiration for two world-famous pieces of environmental art: Robert Smithson's earthen *Spiral Jetty* (partially submerged by the Great Salt Lake) and Nancy Holt's desert *Sun Tunnels* near Lucin, which at once frame the physical dynamics of entropy and the cosmos and magnify humanity's connectedness to this larger environment.

The Ogden Arts Commission has proposed a fascinating community planning concept that would establish a comprehensive framework for urban landscape. Conceived by the urban design group Citywest, which authored the celebrated Phoenix Art Plan, its most intriguing feature is its integration of the natural environment within the

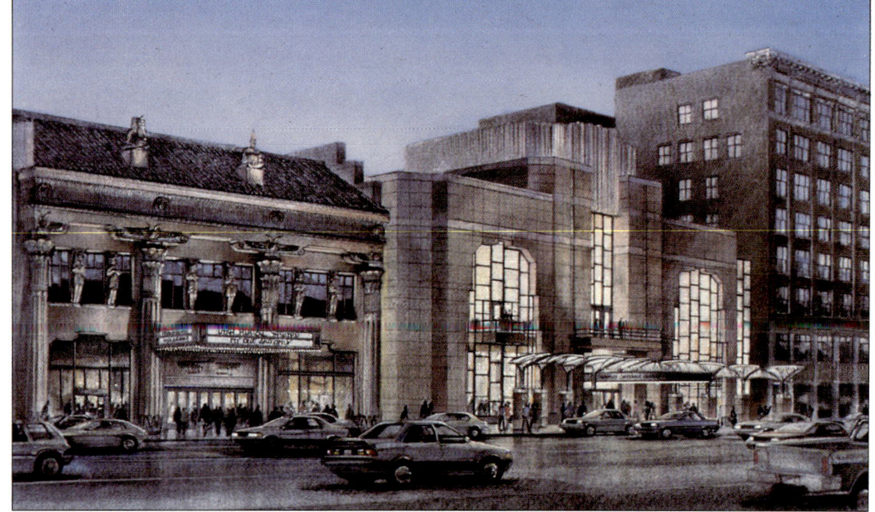

DOWNTOWN CONFERENCE AND PERFORMING ARTS CENTER, OGDEN, UTAH/ RENDERER, STAN DOCTOR

city employing a kind of feng-shui (Oriental art of building placement for good fortune) to create a more balanced urban ecology for Weber County.

Inquiries into the transitory nature of space are reflected in the *interim* landscape improvements on the southern portion of Block 57, in Salt Lake, which incorporate building detritus created in the continuous act of creation, destruction and re-creation of our cities. Here scavenged timbers are reordered by landscape architect Jan Striefel and sculptor Stephen Goldsmith into debauched Shinto shrines connected by sinuous paths, *native plantings,* musician/composer Ricklen Nobis' *sound-cilia* (prerecorded noises or sounds with attractive properties), and poet Mark Strand's "River of Words."

Water taken in moderation cannot hurt anybody . . .

—Mark Twain

Water has formed the theme for much of this new earth art, and among the most fascinating and pleasurable projects are those that incorporate water in ways that acknowledge its unique value in the desert climate of Utah. These new-style water works range from the handsome minimalism of the Tanner Fountain at Salt Lake's Primary Children's Medical Center, which exploits limestone pieces that—depending on one's point of view—are the building's construction residue or its raw material; to Liberty Park's Seven

Canyons fountain, funded by O. C. Tanner and the City of Salt Lake and designed by Stephen Goldsmith, Boyd Blackner, Elizabeth Blackner and John Swain. Disposed like an amphitheater that mirrors the Salt Lake Valley topography, this absurdly wonderful piece creates a composite image of playground and didactic artifact that describes the cultivation of water as it emerges from the seven surrounding canyons and is then transformed by the grids and gutters of public works before being expelled into the Great Salt Lake.

We can only construct a building if we know how to live in it.

—Martin Heidegger

As part of their struggle with the meaning of regionalism, a few designers have been experimenting with different expressions and technologies in hopes of finding anew a specific and appropriate response to a building's context. Burke Cartwright and Kenton Peters' design for the Poison Spider bike shop in Moab employs straw-bale construction—a pioneer technology for expedient but highly effective insulation. The common-sense but daring approach of this design also allows for relatively uncommon low-technology systems for the heating and cooling of a building located in the desert climate of southern Utah.

Since then, its mission has expanded to help local non-profit agencies like the Utah AIDS Foundation, New Hope multicultural center and Odyssey House. It also provides, according to Assist director Roger Borgenicht, "a community seat at the development table" providing a vital perspective to the dialogue on long-range community planning, urban design, transportation, housing and the needs of underserved populations in eight Wasatch Front communities. After twenty-five years, Assist has lost none of its energy in promoting and producing a more humanely designed Wasatch Front—efforts that have earned the respect of the design professionals who donate their services to Assist, and the appreciation of the people and organizations who are the beneficiaries of its unique vision.

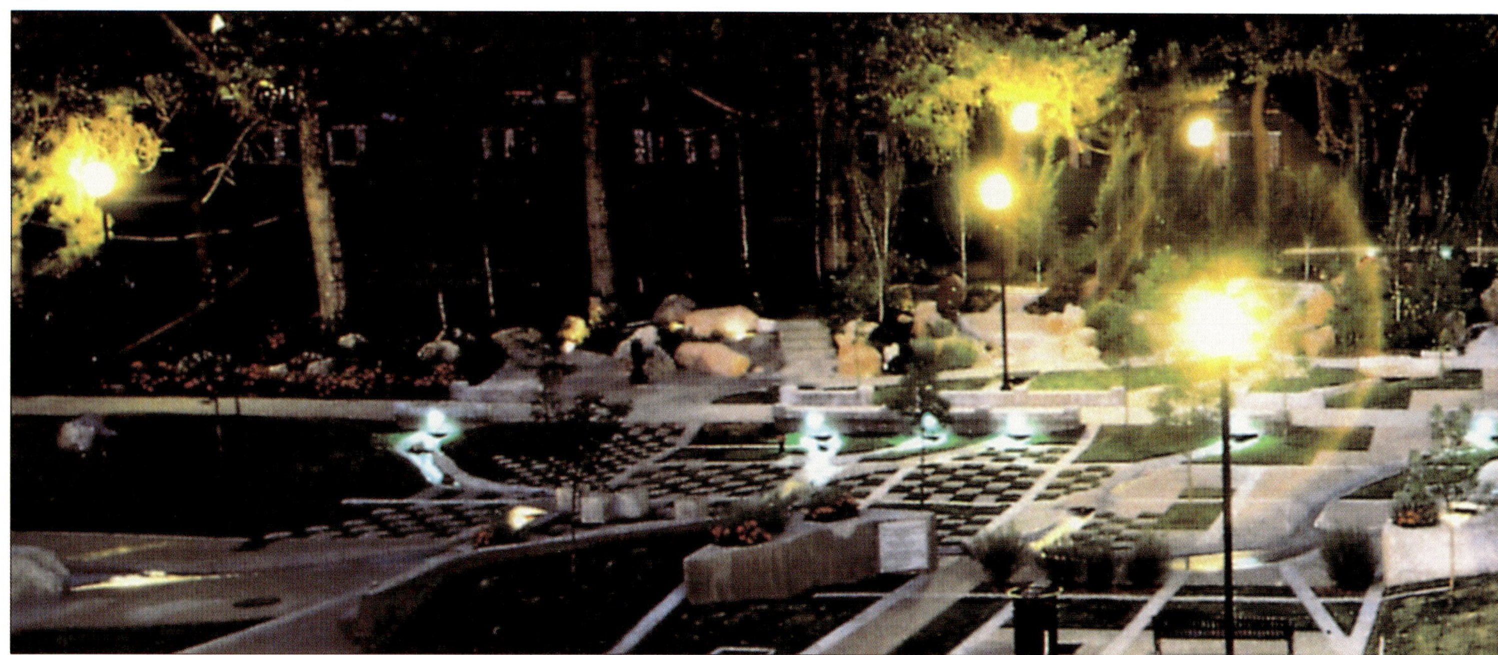

W A T E R
has formed
a theme for
much of this
new earth art.

On a much larger scale, Snow-bird resort, located within a delicate cleft of the Wasatch Mountains, is a stunning object lesson on the multi-disciplinary approach to land-use, programming and design. Two decades old, this *community* remains a seminal work beyond mere environmental mitigation, executed by a consortium of Utah architects (Brixen and Christopher, FFKR and Enteleki, among others) in an atypically unsentimental manner (compared with Park City) of modern Brutalism as hard edged as the granite peaks around it.

Contrast Snowbird to the Deer Valley lodges whose very conventionality supplies their substance. Designed by San Francisco architects Esherick, Homsey, Dodge and Davis, the doyens of Bay Area regionalism, Silver Lake and Snow Park lodges are knowing interpretations of vernacular mountain construction cum Ralph Lauren that respect the natural forces of wind and snow and the building traditions for dealing with each of them.

What is torn, torn must remain.
—Ludwig Wittgenstein, architect

Utah is moving to blur the line between art, craft and the built-environment that was drawn by architectural moralists Wittgenstein and Adolph Loos when they sought to separate art from the inviolate planes of modern architecture some eighty years ago.

It is only recently that the public arts of Utah have moved out of the museums and away from the wastelands of lobbies and plazas to be synthesized in a corporate conception of environ-

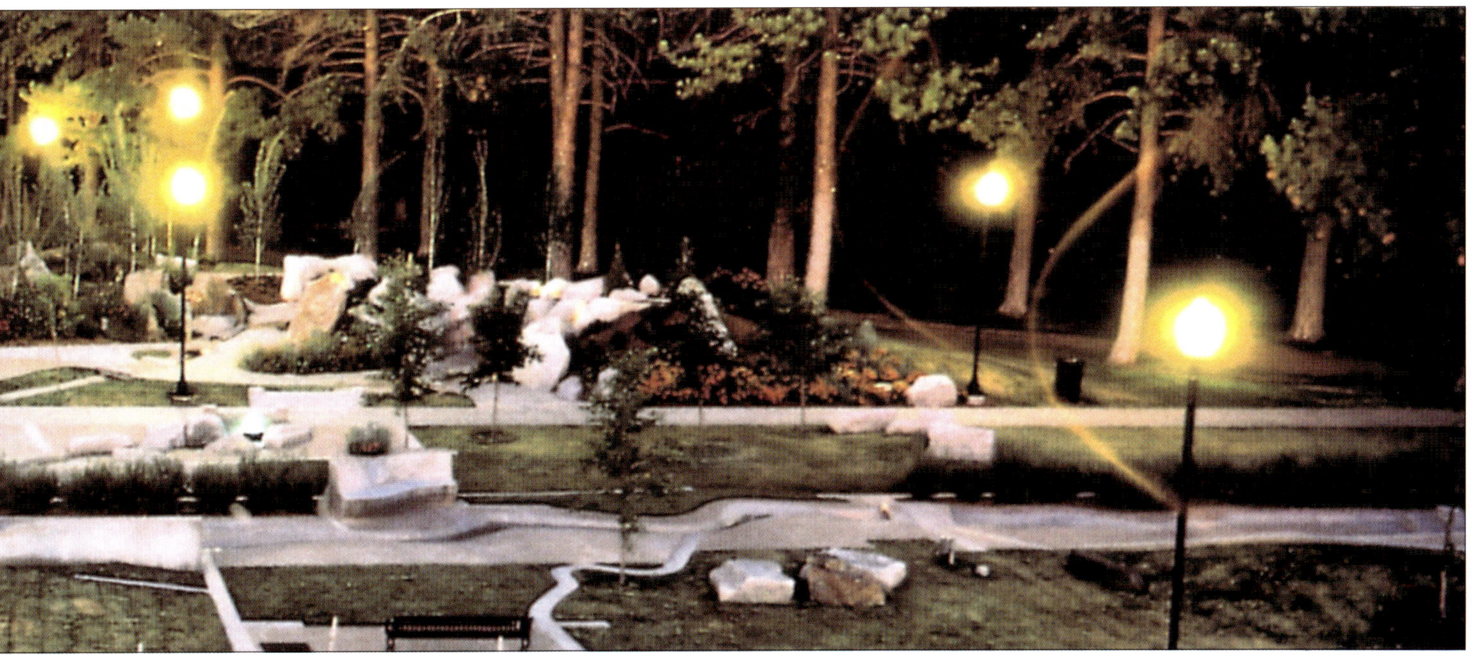

mental art and architecture. Artists, architects, planners and landscape architects are intrigued by the possibilities present in this multidisciplinary and highly collaborative approach to design that reinforces the interactive tension between art and architecture. Enriched public space is the outcome.

The art is coming from everywhere. The largest government-supported efforts are the Salt Lake City and state 1% for Art programs, which afford one percent of a building's construction budget for the production and installation of art created specifically for that site. Projects of the monumental sort include the Delta Center (a public/private partnership) and, of course, Block 57 (a Salt Lake Redevelopment Agency project), which made headlines for months. Smaller projects, often sponsored by private entities, are contributing unexpected and delightful detail to the urban fabric, like Janet Shapero's modern petroglyph at the Triad Center, which was supported by the Art in Public Places program of the Utah Arts Festival. And it seems that, although it has been a while since Utah has practiced the specialized work of site-specific and collaborative art projects, the public for the most part likes the results.

Each project or program has its own opportunities and problems. One dilemma, according to Salt Lake Arts Council director Nancy Boskoff, has been the city's two-stage funding mechanism (the artist fees are funded concurrent with the approval of construction funds, but well after the completion of the building design). This fact, maintains Boskoff, "has obviously undermined any true and effective collaboration between architect and artist."

In spite of this handicap (and, in no small measure, because of its rather limited project budgets), Salt Lake has established a brave pattern of experimentation which has resulted in highly inventive art pieces that have caught the public's attention, if not always its acceptance.

The state's significantly larger funding capability has made possible more than thirty site-specific works. Although the sheer size of the program and the artist selection procedure has led to the commissioning of mostly discrete pieces, David Holz of the Utah Arts Council has worked, since the program's inception in 1987, toward effecting more opportunities for outright collaborations and unified treatments of the manipulated environment.

The list of artists and designers whose work has interpreted Utah's cultural and natural condition includes the likes of Angelo Caravaglia, Richard Johnston, David Phillips, Dale Eldredge, David Sucec, Jeff Juhlin, Silvia Davis, Tom Tessman, Neil Hadlock, Darl Thomas, Willy Littig and William Disbro, among others. The list continues to grow, as does the density and texture of the place.

A place is nothing, not even space, unless at its heart a figure stands.

—Amy Lowell Briedch, Srce, Coeur, Ajert, Groi, Corazon, Heart, Hyung Jae Ae, Çertzo . . .

Tom Tessman, inscriptions on the Pierpont Walkway

Utah is at a kind of brink that, like any frontier, holds the promise of what is beyond. Utah is already a place of spare beauty that possesses (we know now) a limited carrying capacity for the enviable and fragile quality of life Utahns take for granted. Utah has admittedly produced but has not irrevocably bound itself to its share of insubstantial *inventions* that are related primarily by infrastructure and not by any cultural, aesthetic and ecological fabric. Robert Hermanson, professor of architecture at the University of Utah, maintains that "the notion of architecture as a collection of mere building-objects is dead and buried, to be replaced by an understanding of architecture as a system for the creation of holistic environments." These environments must necessarily exploit the full practical and artistic sensibilities of architects, landscape architects, environmental artists, developers, *et al.*

The people of Utah are starting the hard but exciting work of interpreting, *ex novo* and, yet again, the continually unfolding relationship between humanity and the common ground. It is—perhaps—the primal urge of pioneers to do so. The talents and conscientiousness of Utah's many fine architects, artists and designers, in the collective service of a society that prizes its cultural and natural assets, must warrant optimism. After all, only nothing comes from nothing.

Architecture
is a
system for the
C R E A T I O N
of holistic
environments.

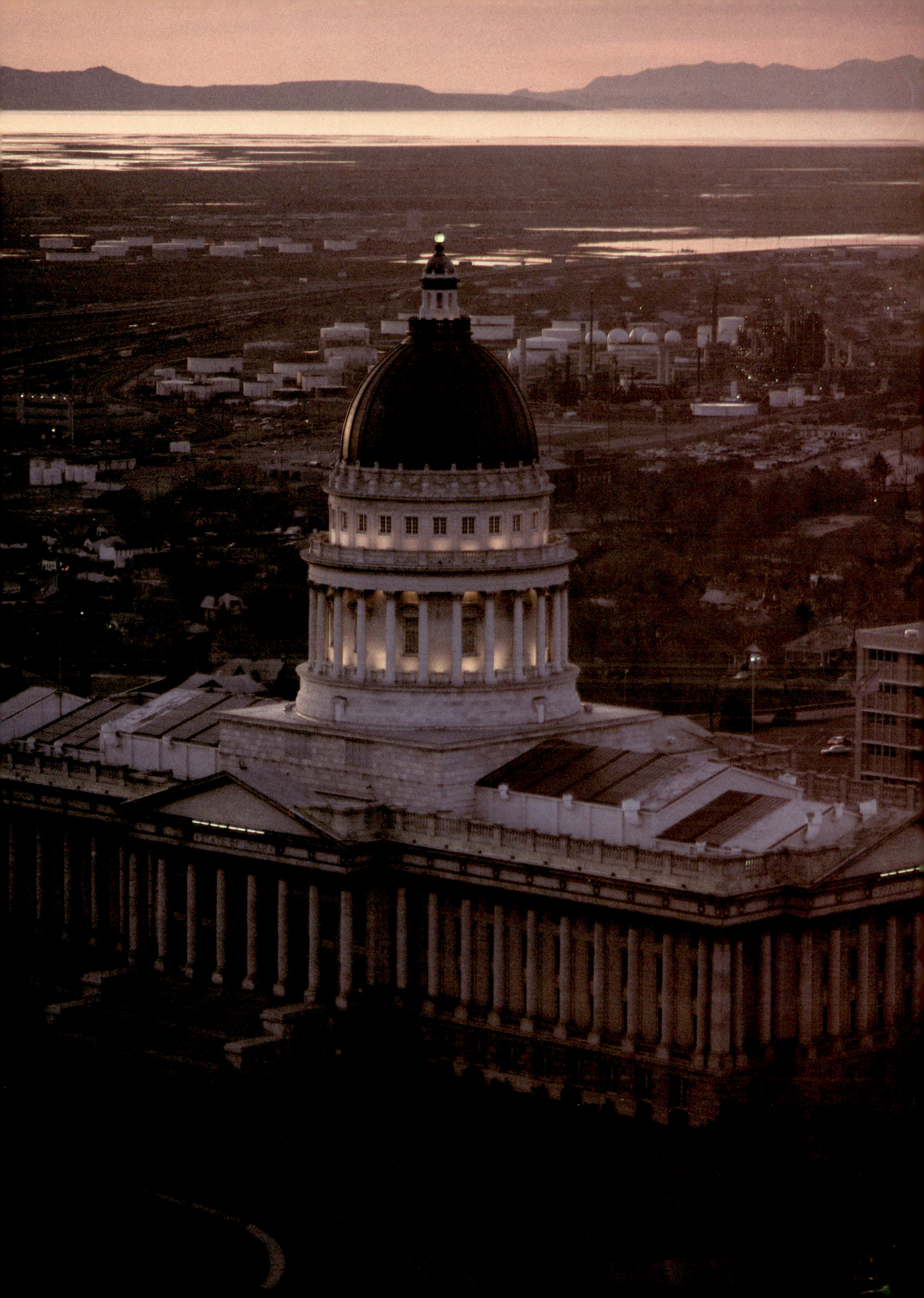

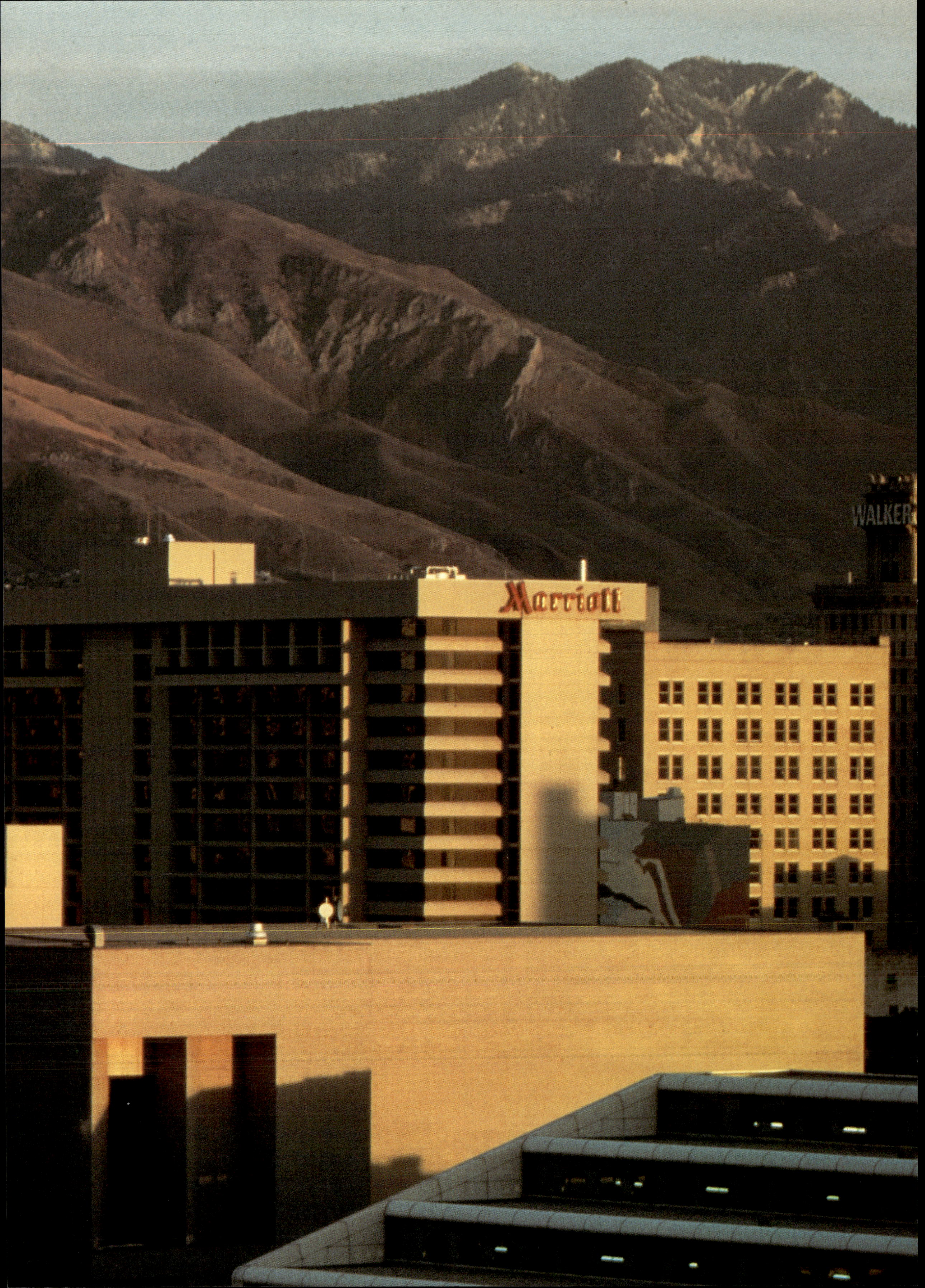
Marriott
WALKER

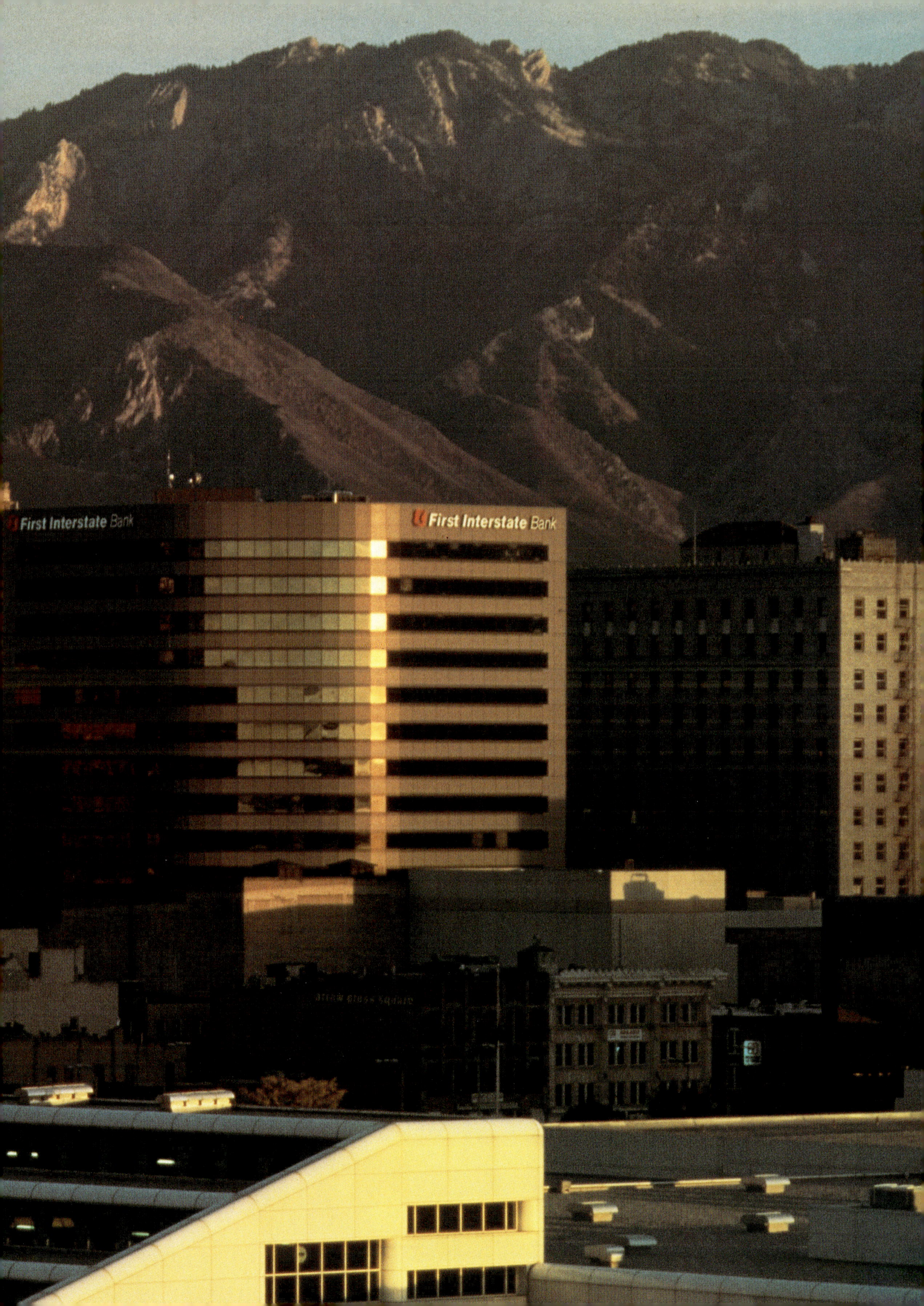

First Interstate Bank
First Interstate Bank

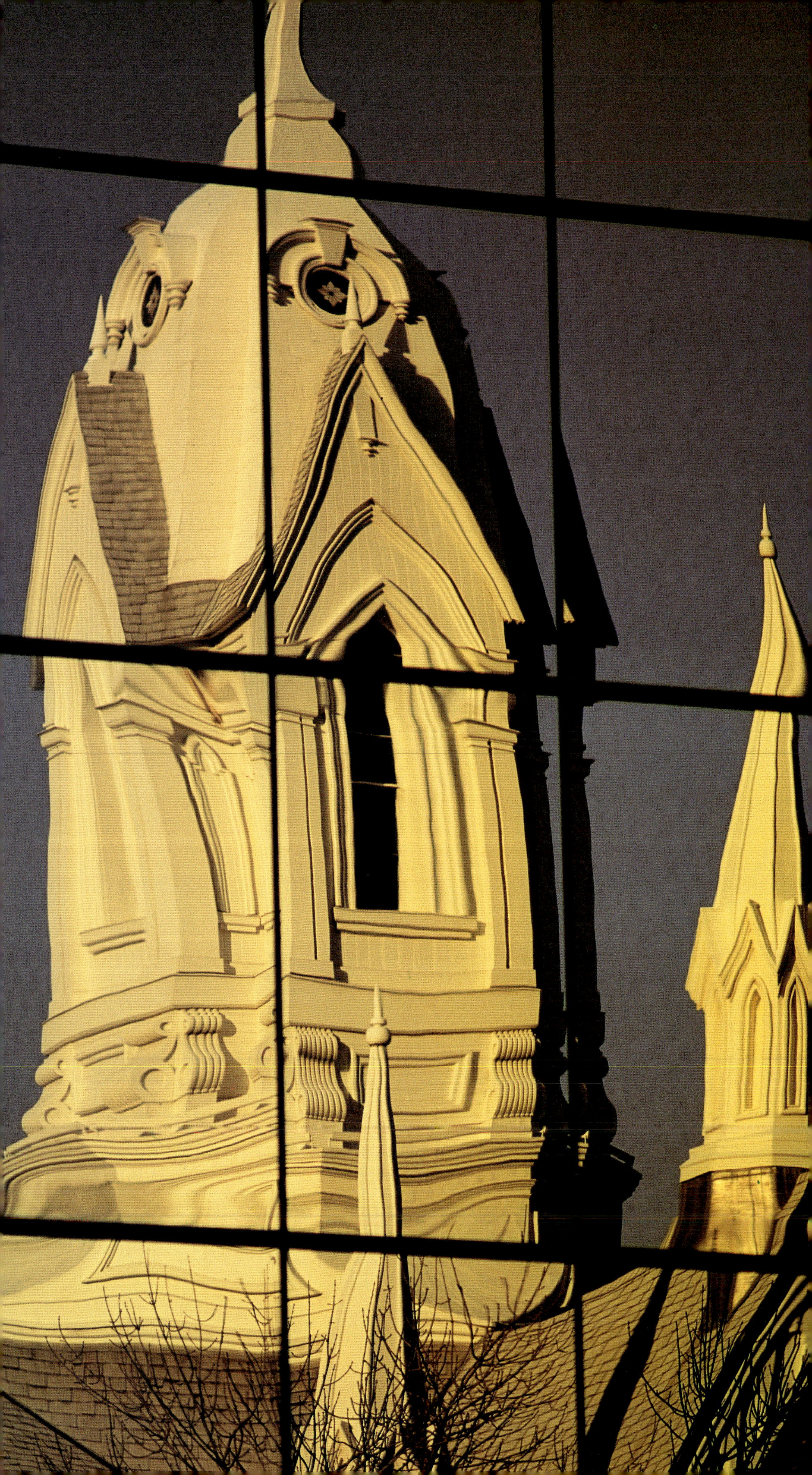

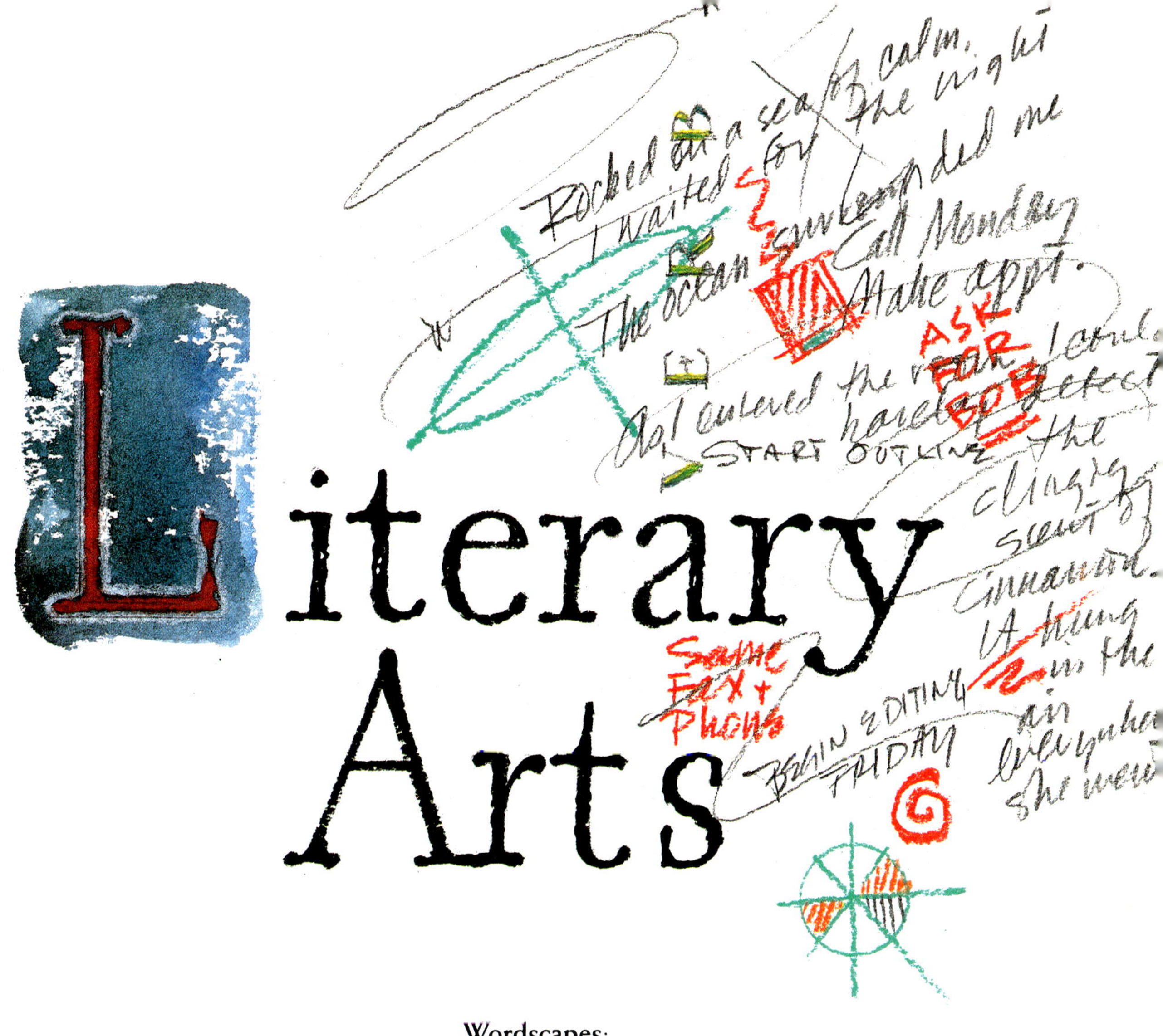

Literary Arts

Wordscapes:
The Literary
Scene

Edward Lueders

AT TIMES IT SEEMS TO ME that nearly everyone in the Beehive State is writing a story, a poem, a play, an article, a family history, a book—or at least thinking about it. Not surprisingly Utah's legacy of journals, poems, stories and personal accounts is

LITERARY OPPORTUNITIES

One way or another, we are alone when we read or write but most of us concerned with literature also enjoy and benefit from one another's company. Utah is rich in opportunities for such gathering. The state's high schools, colleges, and universities foster such groups through courses, clubs, publications, and readings. Writer's conferences, seminars, and workshops—a long-standing tradition in Utah—continue in many attractive locations. Among them are the Canyonlands Field Institute/Desert Writers' Workshops in Moab, the Southern Utah Creative Writing Conference in Cedar City, and Writers at Work, a week-long summer conference in Park City whose faculty includes publishers and literary agents. The Salt Lake Library System sponsors an editing and publishing conference each September that brings in professionals to meet with authors and others interested in the world of books. In the community at large, many literary organizations flourish.

continuous from the westering experience of the early pioneers to the present.

And few places on Earth offer such poetics of place. Utah's wild landscapes, its soaring mountains, broad valleys, high deserts and colorful canyonlands beg for literary description. The state's fabulous settings live on in the pages of prime Western authors of the past, from Zane Grey, whose *Riders of the Purple Sage* remains the quintessential popular Western novel, to the late Edward Abbey, whose *Desert Solitaire* memorialized his "Season in the Wilderness" as a ranger in then-remote Arches National Monument.

Friends in Bluff, Utah, have pointed out to me the rude wood cabin where, early in this century, Zane Grey lived and wrote. And I could show you the spot where, in the 1950's, Ed Abbey's Park Service house trailer stood. I could also take you to the slickrock prominence just outside the park boundary north of Moab where at dawn one luminous spring morning after his death in 1989 a hundred or so of us gathered to hear fellow authors Barry Lopez, Wendell Berry, Terry Tempest Williams, Dave Foreman, Doug Peacock, Chip Rawlins, Ann Zwinger, Ken Sleight, John DePuy and other friends memorialize *him*.

Nationally

known

AUTHORS

live and work

in Utah.

That vital literary connection with Utah landscapes and the Intermountain West continues in the work of our poets and fiction writers. It figures even more prominently in the environmentally concerned essays and prize-winning novels of Wallace Stegner, and the vivifying work of nature writers Stephen Trimble, Thomas J. Lyon and Terry Tempest Williams. Peregrine Smith Books in Layton, Utah, and the University of Utah Press in Salt Lake City feature in their lists books of local and regional natural history. *Petroglyph*, a journal devoted to personal observations of the world of nature, is published by students at Utah State University in Logan. *Weber Studies*, published for the general reader by Weber State University in Ogden, often carries writing sensitive to the ecosystems and natural beauty of the region.

Utah is especially hospitable to writers of children's literature and books for adolescent readers. Gloria Skurzinski, Barbara Williams, Ann Edwards Cannon, Dean Hughes, Margaret Rostkowski and Ivy Ruckman are among the nationally known young people's authors who live and work here. Maybe Utah's cultural emphasis on home and family accounts for this. It is also attributable to the attention given to reading, writing and literary activity in the schools. These same authors, and many others, frequently hold readings and workshops for students and teachers under the auspices of the Utah Arts Council's artists-in-the-schools programs and those of individual schools themselves. The presence of so many successful authors of young people's books reflects Utah's concern for the youth of the state, who are still open to growth and fresh imagination.

The imagination also gets full play in the work of Utah's science fiction writers. Heading that list is Orson Scott Card, winner of both the Nebula and Hugo awards, science fiction's highest accolades. Others have also been prize winners. M. Shayne Bell and Virginia Ellen Baker have won first place awards at the national L. Ron Hubbard Writers of the Future Competition. Dave Wolverton was Grand Champion in the Hubbard contest. Elizabeth Boyer of Copperton and Michaelene Pendleton of Moab are favorites of science fiction readers nationwide. These are thoughtful, polished, politically conscious writers, serious in their use of modern science as well as sophisticated in their writing skills. They have helped advance the field of science fiction well beyond the early stereotypes of bug-eyed monsters and little green men.

At Provo, Brigham Young University professor Marion K. Smith teaches a course in science fiction writing and is faculty sponsor for the student-edited *Leading Edge, The Magazine of Science Fiction and Fantasy*. BYU also hosts an annual sci-fi/fantasy symposium with the audacious title, "Life, the Universe, and Everything."

Other periodicals throughout the state invite the work of amateur and professional authors of all kinds. Community newspapers and the metropolitan dailies, *The Salt Lake Tribune*, the *Deseret News*, and Ogden's *Standard-Examiner*, carry freelance articles and features. *Salt Lake City Magazine* invites topical articles by local writers. Well into its second decade, *network* is the nation's oldest regional publication devoted to women's news and views. *Quarterly West* and *Western Humanities Review* are nationally established literary journals devoted to contemporary fiction, poetry, and criticism.

Popular notions of writing as a lonely, solitary business can be literally true in remote Utah settings. Karen Chamberlain, a 1993 winner of the Writers' Exchange Award given by New York-based Poets & Writers, Inc., is a good example. She lives and writes in a cabin at the end of some twenty miles of primitive dirt road beyond Dead Horse Point. Her computer runs off solar-generator power.

Indeed, there is an unmistakable strain of Western individualism in Utah's literary roster. I believe it has a great deal to do with Western space and the possibilities of solitude in its landscapes. The literary legacy of highly individual Utah authors is thus linked through both history and geography. I think of

The League of Utah Writers, with twenty-one chapters variously located, brings together writers from beginning to advanced levels. The National League of Pen Women has active chapters in Logan, Ogden, Provo and Salt Lake City. The Romance Writers of America Utah Chapter meets in Brigham City. The Utah State Poetry Society holds regular meetings and special programs throughout the state. In the Utah Arts Council's recently launched Tumblewords program (co-sponsored by an interstate consortium of arts organizations), Utah writers are reading in "underserved" rural communities. After the shakedown year, authors from Idaho and Wyoming will join in a much larger three-state circuit. In addition, it's traditional in Utah for private study groups to spring up among friends and neighbors for the discussion of books of common interest.

Salt Lake City nature writer Terry Tempest Williams, storyteller and ardent student of natural history of The Great Basin, won a Southwest Book Award for *Pieces of White Shell, A Journey to Navajoland.* The widespread admiration and gratitude that followed publication of her *Refuge: An Unnatural History of Family and Place* is reflected in the National Conservation Achievement Award from the National Wildlife Federation. The citation noted that "Terry Tempest Williams' eloquent and provocative writer's voice has given readers an important new understanding of the vulnerability of the natural environment in the West."

poets as different as Phyllis McGinley and May Swenson, yet both with a kind of Western wit at work in their wordplay; novelists as diverse as Virginia Sorenson, Vardis Fisher, and Richard Scowcroft, or historians Juanita Brooks, Bernard DeVoto, Dale Morgan, and Fawn Brodie—all dealing with native Utah material. It's always interesting to watch the expression of East Coast friends when they learn that Harold Ross, the unexampled early editor of *The New Yorker*, who set the distinctive, sophisticated, archly humorous style of that magazine, came from Utah.

The Creative Writing Program at the University of Utah begun by Brewster Ghiselin, the poet and authority on the creative process, has offered graduate work for master's and doctoral degrees in creative writing since the 1940's. For decades, the only universities where writers could pursue the Ph.D. through literary studies keyed to a creative dissertation were Utah, Iowa and Stanford.

This legacy has been passed on through a succession of notable faculty members, highlighted by U.S. Poet Laureate Mark Strand, Pulitzer Prize-winner Henry Taylor, Robert Mezey, Dave Smith, E.L. Doctorow, David Kranes, Edward Abbey, Judith Hemschemeyer, Hal Moore, François Camoin, Richard Howard, Francine Prose, Jacqueline Osherow and Larry Levis.

In its early years the Utah program pioneered the Summer Writers Conference. Professor Ghiselin brought the major authors of the day to work with Utah writers during what they affectionately referred to as "Brewster's Conference."

The life of literature depends on devoted readers as well as skillful writers. The number and quality of Utah's bookstores indicates literary vitality at both ends. National chain bookstores and a dozen or more independently owned booksellers supply a responsive, serious literature book-buying public that by national per capita standards outshines New York, Chicago, and Los Angeles. In downtown Salt Lake, Sam Weller Books is renowned for its voluminous stock of new, used and rare books. A Woman's Place Bookstore, emphasizing the literary aspects of feminism, has expanded to four locations. Fifth World Books and Gifts is a rare-and-used bookshop specializing in poetry, literature, and philosophy. Highbrow Books, "hiding up the alley at 9th & 9th," features all the fine arts. A Children's Hour Book Store doubles as a toy shop. The King's English is loaded in all literary genres and specializes in mystery and children's books. Waking

The life of literature
depends on devoted
R E A D E R S
as well as skillful writers.

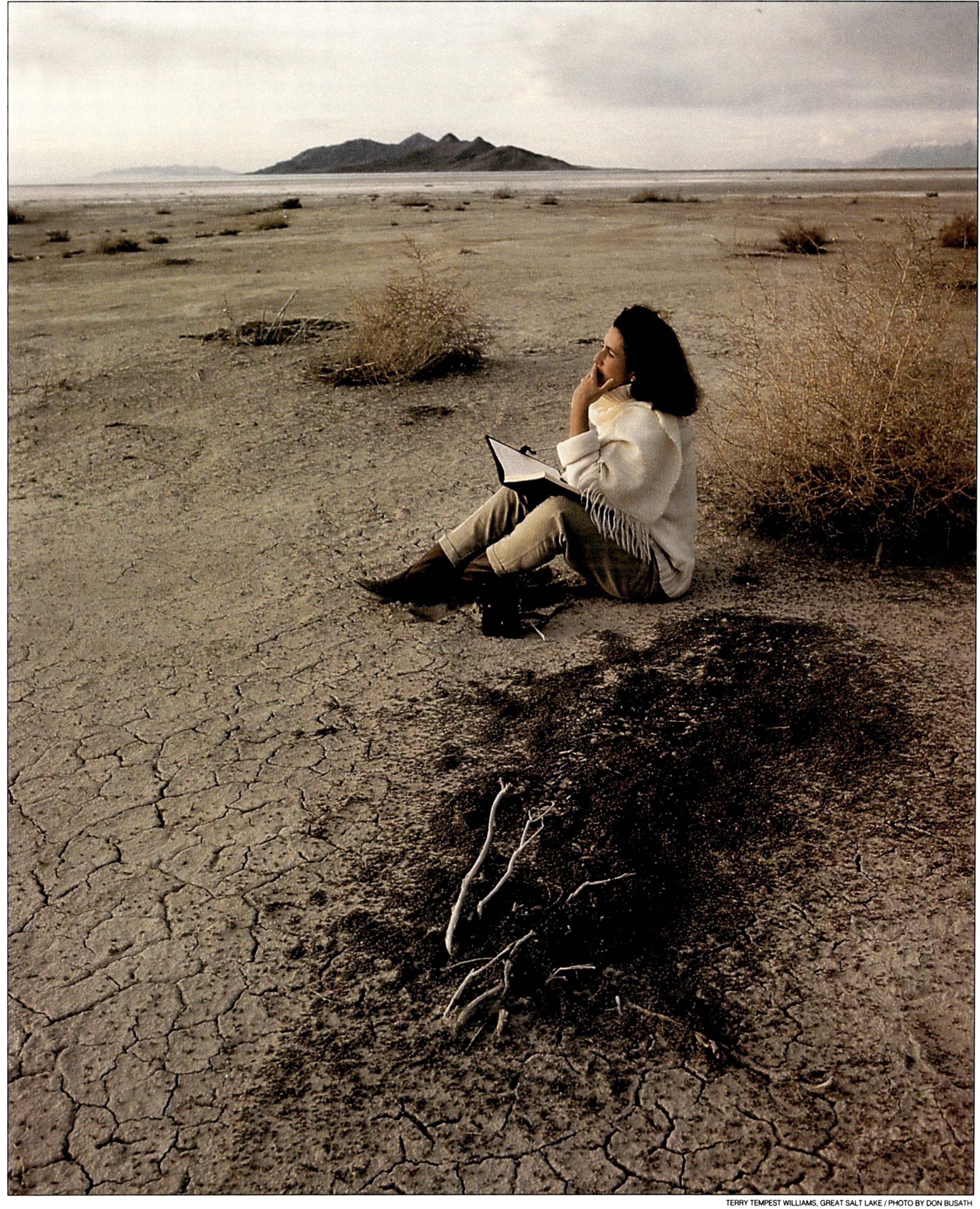

TERRY TEMPEST WILLIAMS, GREAT SALT LAKE / PHOTO BY DON BUSATH

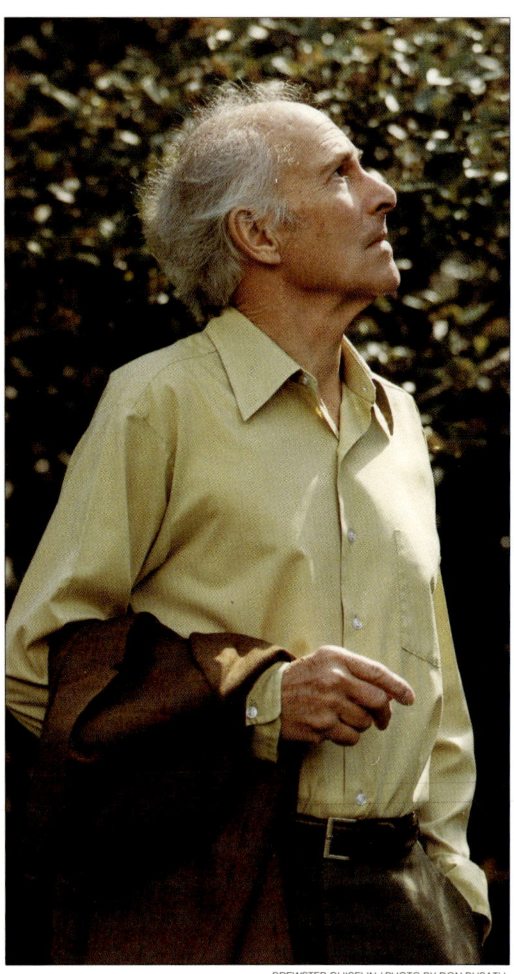

BREWSTER GHISELIN / PHOTO BY DON BUSATH

The book and author scene grows livelier every year. Westminster College of Salt Lake City has initiated an annual series of poetry readings by the nation's leading poets. City Art, also in Salt Lake, schedules weekly poetry readings combined with music and visual art by local artists. The College of Eastern Utah in Price has a Readers' Series directed by resident poets Jan Minich and Nancy Takacs. The Art Barn in Salt Lake City hosts monthly readings, free, as are all of these programs, and open to the public.

Backing statewide literary activities at both community and individual levels is the Utah Arts Council, a state agency, one of only a dozen or so in the country with a full-time literary coordinator on its staff. In that position, G. Barnes, himself a poet and folk musician, keeps touch with all facets of the state's literary arts. The council administers an annual Literary Prize Competition that awards $15,000 to Utah authors in a wide range of categories, including non-fiction and children's literature. Another annual writing contest is run by Junior Creative Writing Program, open to all Utah students, grades seven to twelve. It is co-sponsored by *The Salt Lake Tribune*, Utah State Poetry Society and a grant from the Utah Arts Council.

Contests, readings, workshops, institutions, organizations—there is plenty to encourage and assist the literary life in Utah. But moment to moment, day

Owl Books caters to university readers and often brings authors and readers together, as do all the independent bookstores, for authors' readings and book-signings.

In Logan the gathering place is A Book Store. In Orem it's Atticus Books and Coffee House. Ogden has the Wisebird Bookery and the Book Shelf. In Moab, José Knighton's Back of Beyond Books focuses on natural history, Native American, and Western authors. The town of Bluff, on the fringe of Navajoland, has the Desert Country Bookstore.

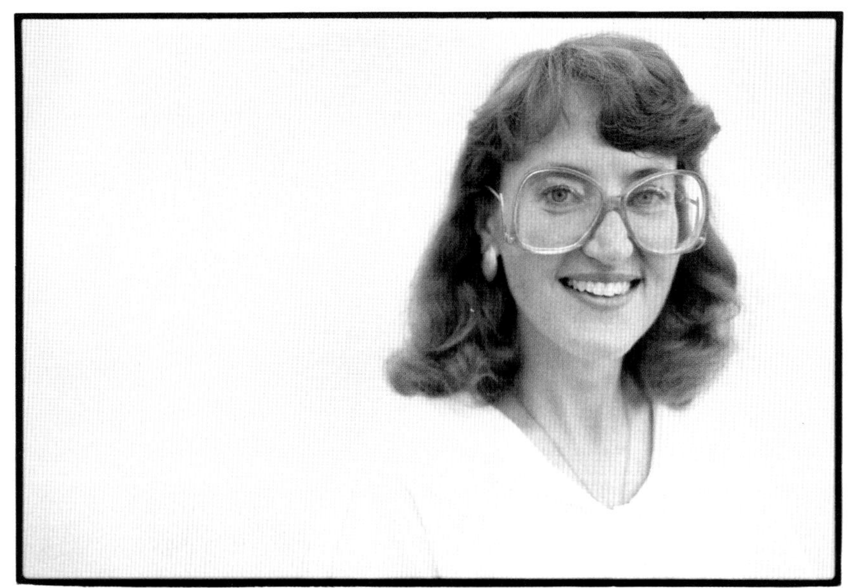

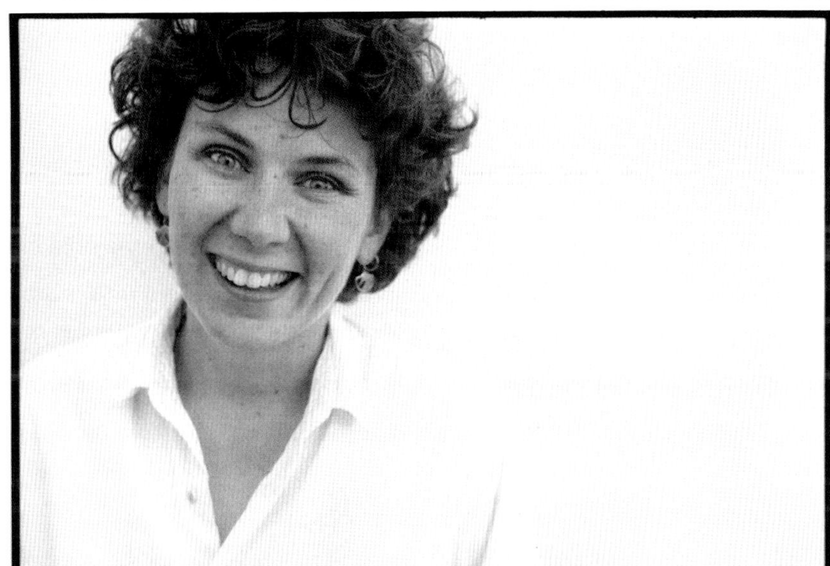

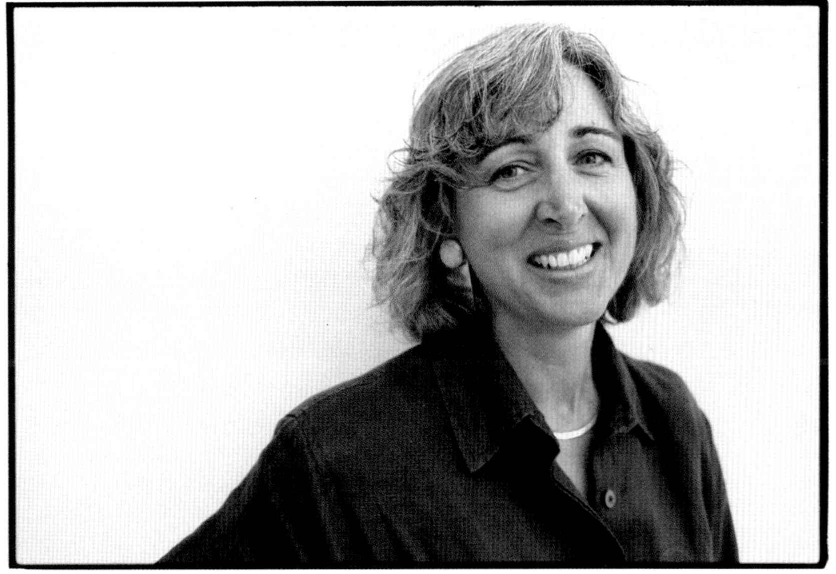

MERRY MELISSA ADAMS, LISA C. ORME BICKMORE AND PHYLLIS BARBER/ PHOTOS UTAH ARTS COUNCIL ARCHIVES

Literary
activities
include contests,
readings,
W O R K S H O P S
and organizations.

MARK STRAND

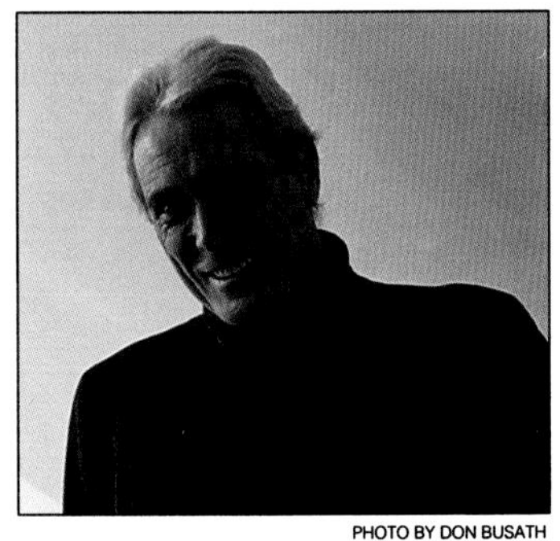

PHOTO BY DON BUSATH

Since Mark Strand moved to Utah to join the faculty of the University of Utah's Creative Writing Program in 1981, his distinguished writing career has been recognized with a succession of the country's most prestigious honors. Among them are a MacArthur Fellowship (sometimes called "the genius award"), the Bollingen Prize for Poetry and his appointment in 1990 as Poet Laureate of the United States. In addition to his stature as a poet, Strand is the versatile author of art criticism, distinctive fiction, and books for children.

after day, the literary activity throughout the state depends on the skills and energies of individuals: Betsy Burton of The King's English telephones American Indian novelist and former Utahn Thomas King to arrange a reading at the store. Katharine Coles finishes a draft of a new poem, then drives to Westminster College for editorial work with the staff of its literary magazine, *Ellipsis.*

Jerry Johnston of the *Deseret News* interviews a newly published Utah author, the subject of his next feature article. At perhaps the same moment, Paul Swenson drops by the editorial offices of *The Salt Lake Tribune* to turn in a pair of his deft reviews for the Sunday *Arts* section. In his upstairs study, Mark Strand checks proof on one of his recent poems before returning it for publication to *The New Yorker.* At Lamb's Restaurant, Sam Weller entertains visiting writers at lunch with stories of books and authors he's known through the years. Terry Tempest Williams jots down field notes as she observes bird life on the western shores of the Great Salt Lake. Pat Russell, faculty advisor for *Runes*, the literary magazine of Brighton High School, meets with her student editorial staff for an hour before school begins. In Logan, Professor Kenneth Brewer convenes fellow Utah State University writers to discuss one another's current manuscripts. Cedar City poet David Lee tries out his lines aloud as he composes one of his sly rural Utah verses. Novelist

Franklin Fisher and poet-musician Sandy Anderson shuffle through their manuscripts for selections they'll read at their upcoming City Art program. The Association for Mormon Letters meets to hear scholar-author William Mulder's historical overview of books by and about Latter-day Saints—editors, publishers, and authors from *Sunstone* magazine, *Dialogue, A Journal of Mormon Thought*, and Signature Books take notes. Poet Emma Lou Thayne returns from her morning walk with the germ of an idea for an essay in *network.* In his Layton office, publisher Gibbs M. Smith checks jacket copy for the latest in Peregrine Smith collections of cowboy poetry. Leslie Norris, the internationally renowned Welsh poet on the English staff at BYU, crafts a new poem specifically for Salt Lake City's Cathedral of the Madeleine, to be read at the cathedral's Festival of the Arts and Humanities. Levi Peterson revises the opening sentence of a just-completed short story of contemporary life in Ogden. At his word processor, Ed Lueders considers, shrugs and adds this sentence to conclude his piece on the literary arts in Utah...

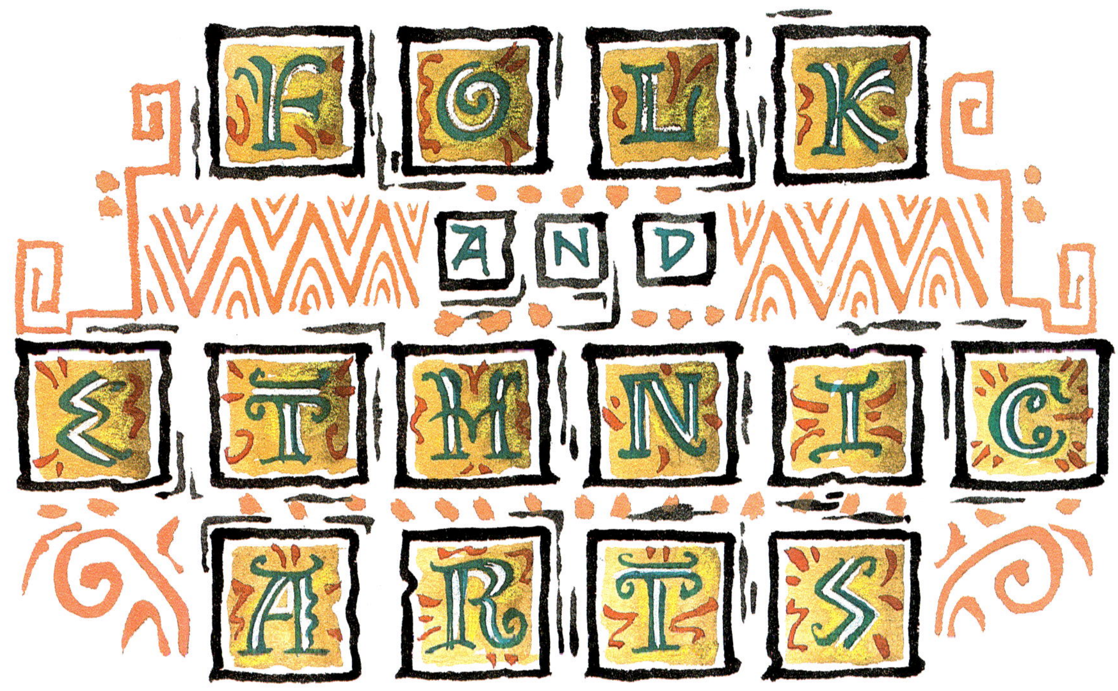

Indian Baskets, Pioneer Quilts
and Hispanic Music

Carol Edison

U TAH'S CULTURAL HERITAGE, like all of American society, is as diverse as the nations of the world, including American Indians and pioneer settlers from Britain, Scandinavia and the Yankee melting pot in the East. Immigration and the international influence of the Church of Jesus Christ of Latter-day Saints (LDS) have added Asian, European, Middle Eastern, African-American, Polynesian, and Central and South American cultures to the mix. How this diverse heritage influences Utahns' artistic expressions is demonstrated in the wide array of folk and ethnic arts practiced here today.

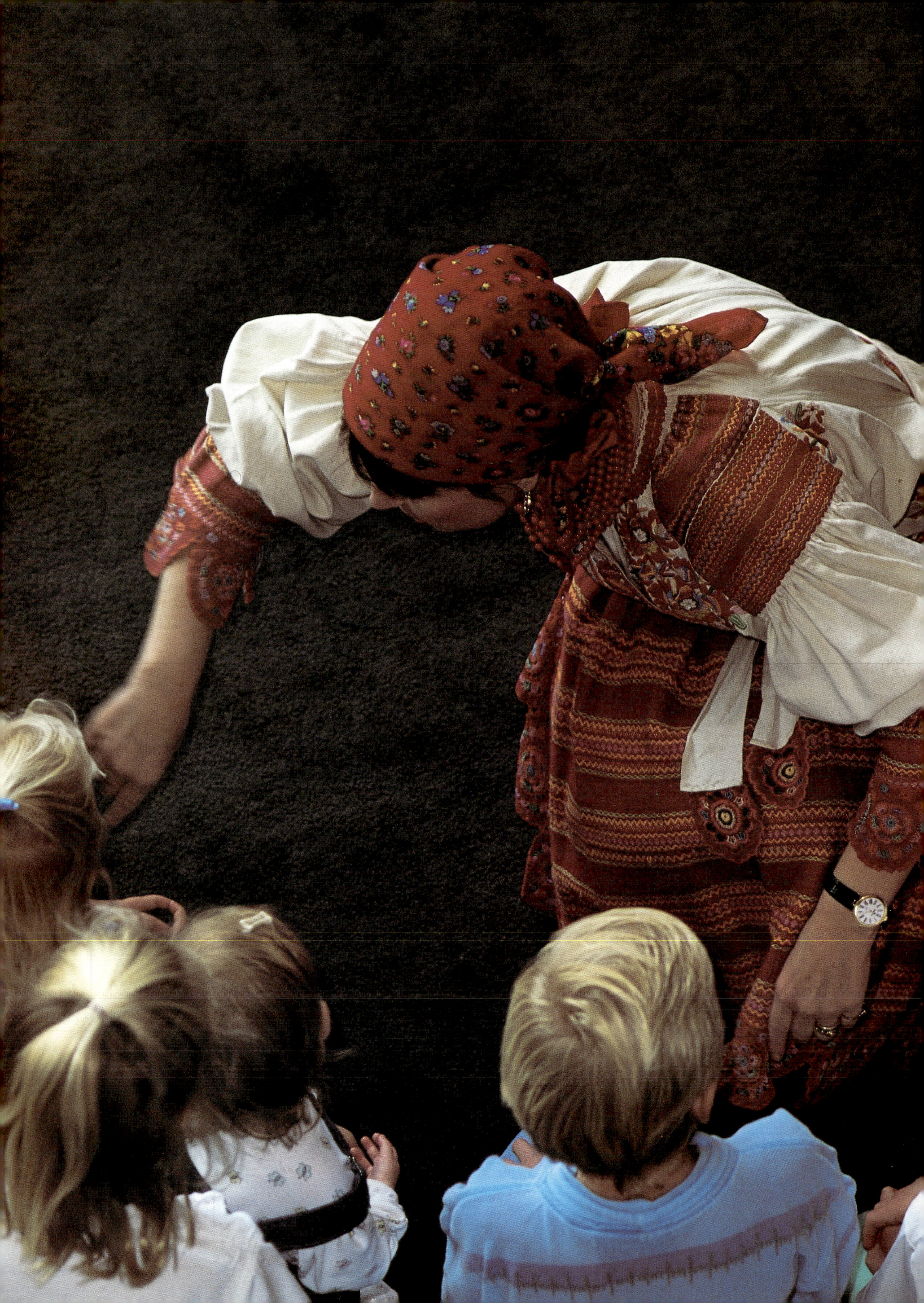

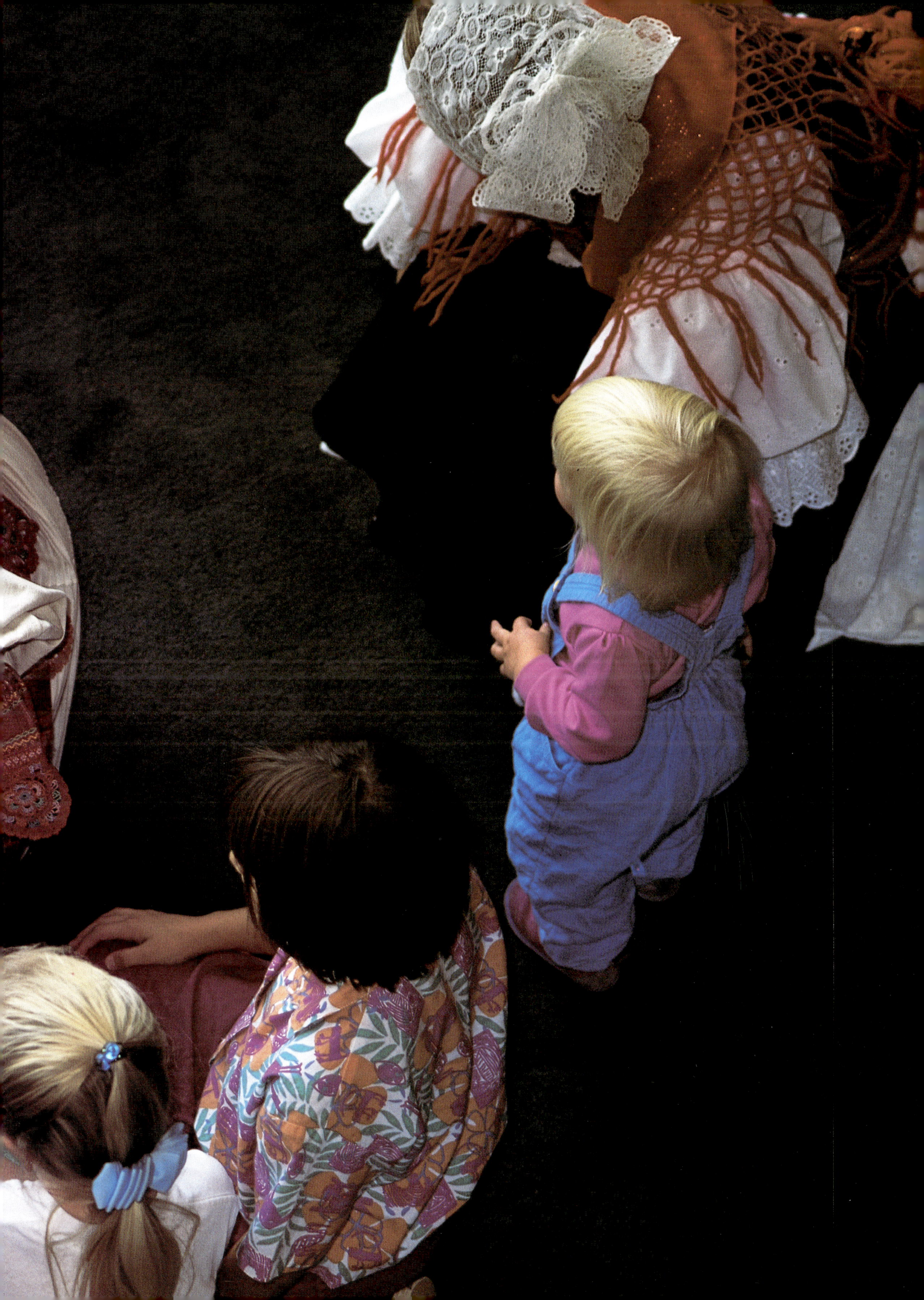

HISPANIC BANDS

Utah's estimated 100,000 Hispanics come from various cultural traditions and music, particularly dance music, which helps define each community. Waltzes from the Spanish colonial towns of the New Mexico-Colorado border, ballads and *corridos* of old Mexico and Latino *cumbias, salsas and merengues* from the Caribbean and South America are all regularly heard in Utah dance halls and bars. Styles range from the very traditional to original compositions that border on jazz or rock 'n' roll. Latin bands like Salsa Brava; Mexican bands, including Los Mercenarios and Fuego Tropical; and New-Mexican style bands like James Romero y los Amigos contribute to this vibrant music scene with performances for both local and regional audiences.

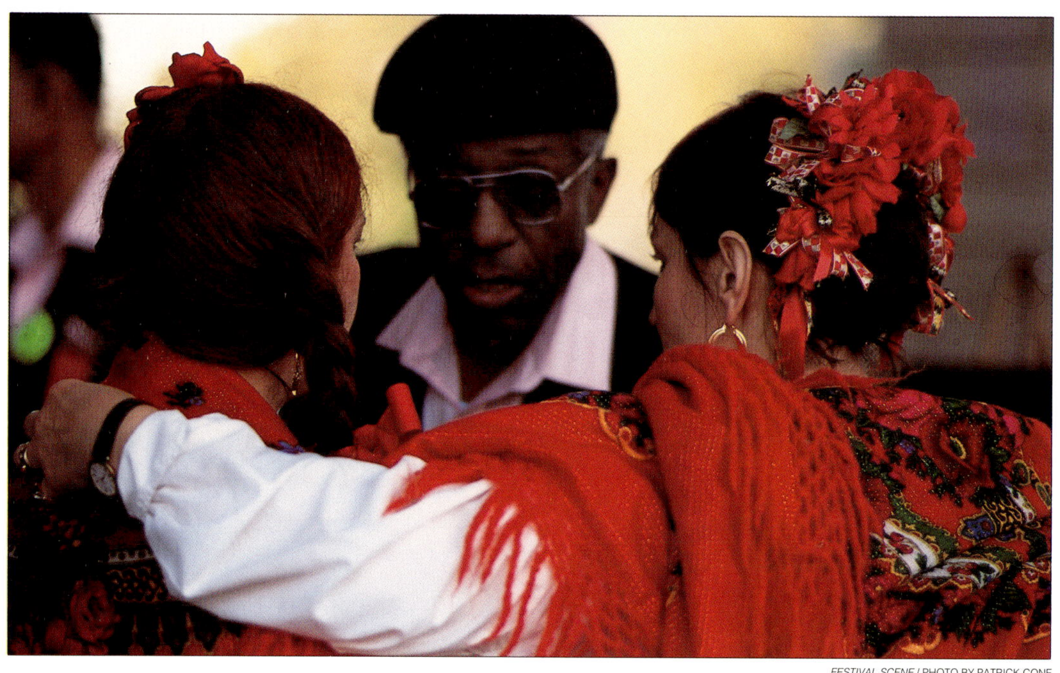

FESTIVAL SCENE / PHOTO BY PATRICK CONE

Folk arts are not those forms adopted through formal education or training. They encompass many forms of artistic expression and typically originate within groups whose members share ethnicity or national origin, occupation, religion, geography, or sometimes simply a way of life. Whether defined as folk or ethnic arts, all of these art forms are grounded in tradition—in information that has been handed down, adapted and refined over generations.

Some folk arts have flourished over time as part of continuous, community-based activities pursued as part of traditional community life. Many home-taught needleworkers, Indian crafts workers and musicians who learned to play "by ear" are part of this group. Other folk arts are learned and practiced as part of a conscious revival of traditional skills with the goal of re-creating a historical performance or artifact. Many talented craftspeople and performers are fascinated by the tools, techniques and products of the past, and they reproduce pioneer-style furniture or revive old-time music to regain and keep alive the knowledge and repertory of earlier times.

Yet other traditional art forms—especially ethnic arts—are embraced and mastered by artists who are members of the ethnic culture and by those who simply have great appreciation for the traditions. The art forms perpetuated by Utah's many folkloric dance troupes and ethnic bands symbolize ethnic heritage and identity and through their performance these groups reinforce and validate the values of the traditional culture.

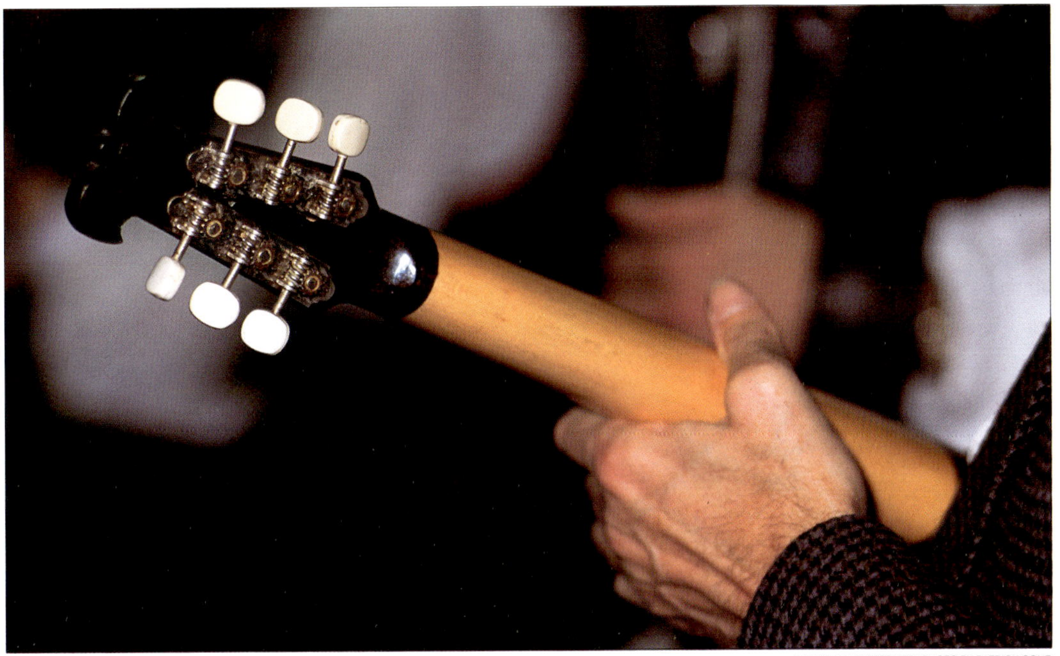
INDIVIDUAL PERFORMER / PHOTO BY PATRICK CONE

Folk arts
T H R I V E
in all of
Utah's Native
American
communities.

Six Native American tribes are resident within Utah's borders. The largest group—the Navajos—have lands in the southeastern corner of Utah, while the culturally and linguistically related Goshute, Northern Ute, Northwestern Shoshone, Paiute and Ute Mountain Ute are concentrated in both reservation and non-reservation lands in several areas of the state. A number of Indians also live in Utah's urban areas where the Native population includes many from non-Utah tribes.

The folk arts thrive in all of Utah's Indian communities because traditional ways are of extreme importance to Native groups. Baskets woven from locally gathered squaw bush or willow are made by the Goshute in Ibapah, the Ute Mountain Ute in White Mesa just south of Blanding and, more recently, by Navajo weavers living on the reservation. A few weavers still know how to make the traditional gathering and winnowing baskets that have been used for centuries to harvest and prepare berries, choke cherries and pine nuts or the jug-shaped storage baskets that are covered with pine pitch to keep water sweet and cool. And a few craftswomen still weave distinctive willow sunshades for the baby carriers, known as cradleboards, that have been used for centuries to carry and protect infants. But most weavers specialize in coiled baskets shaped like shallow bowls with either the well-known red-and-black design of the Navajo wedding basket or geometric and pictorial shapes and designs crafted from willow that has been split and dyed in various colors.

Among Utah's Navajo population another form of weaving—rug weaving—is a very significant art form. While traditional designs like Two Grey Hills are still very common, newer techniques such as Raised Outline also characterize this dynamic, ever-growing tradition.

Although only a few Indian artists in Utah still produce their own brain-tanned deer hide, many use the hides to make buckskin clothing and accessories that are then decorated with exquisite beadwork. Among the Paiute, the Shoshone and especially the Northern Ute groups, beadwork is a vibrant part

QUILTING

Quilting is probably practiced by more Utahns than any other form of art. Patchwork quilts, pieced from leftover scraps of fabric, or camp quilts, made from worn-out work clothes and tied together with wool yarn, were common styles a century ago. Today most functional quilts are made from new fabric, pieced or unpieced, with a color-coordinated design that is quilted or tied. With the possible exception of plain tricot quilts that display a quilted Mormon temple in the center, there is not a distinctively Mormon quilt style. Some contemporary quilters specialize in original pictorial and abstract designs and their quilts are often used as wall hangings rather than bed coverings.

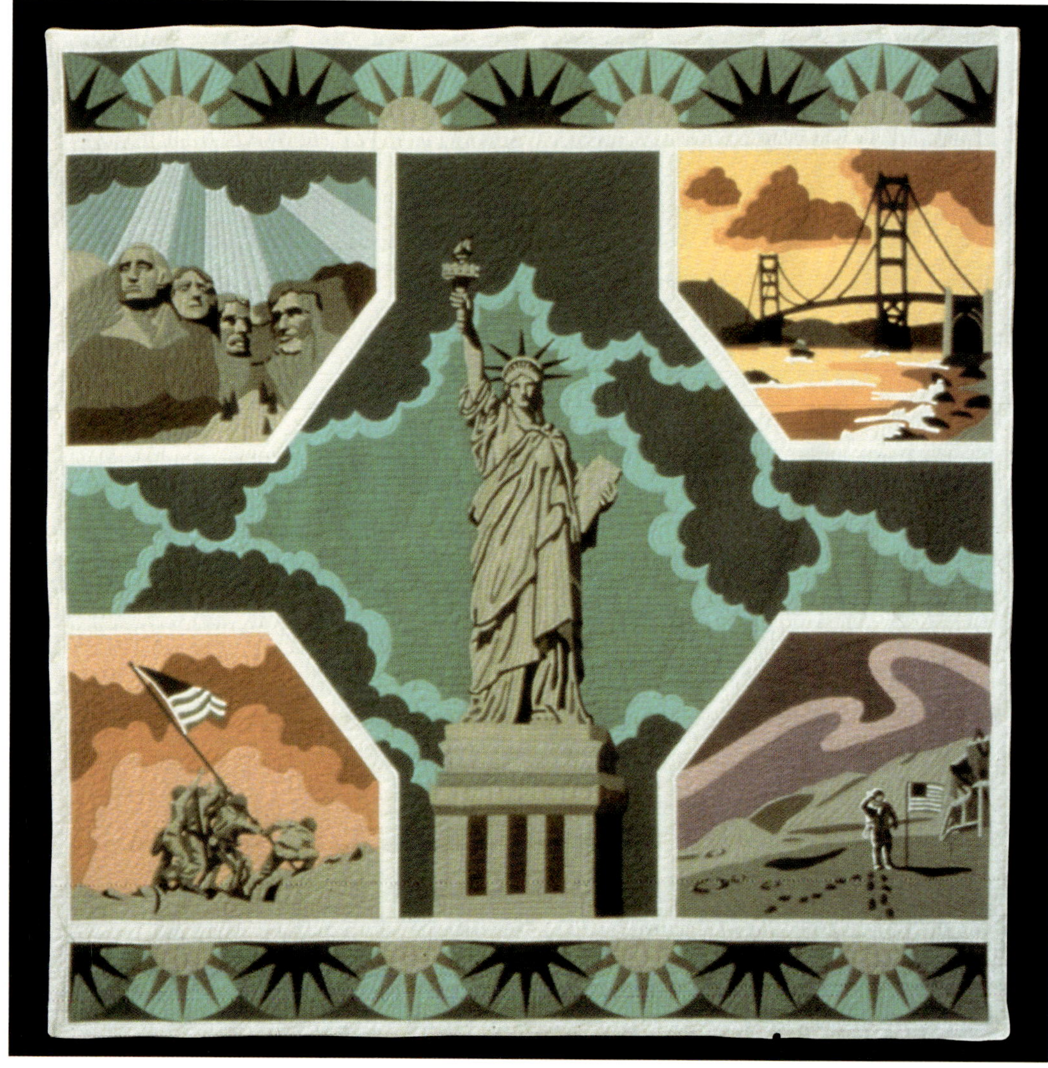

SPACIOUS SKIES / QUILT BY CHARLOTTE WARR ANDERSEN

CROATION FOLK DANCER / PHOTO BY PATRICK CONE

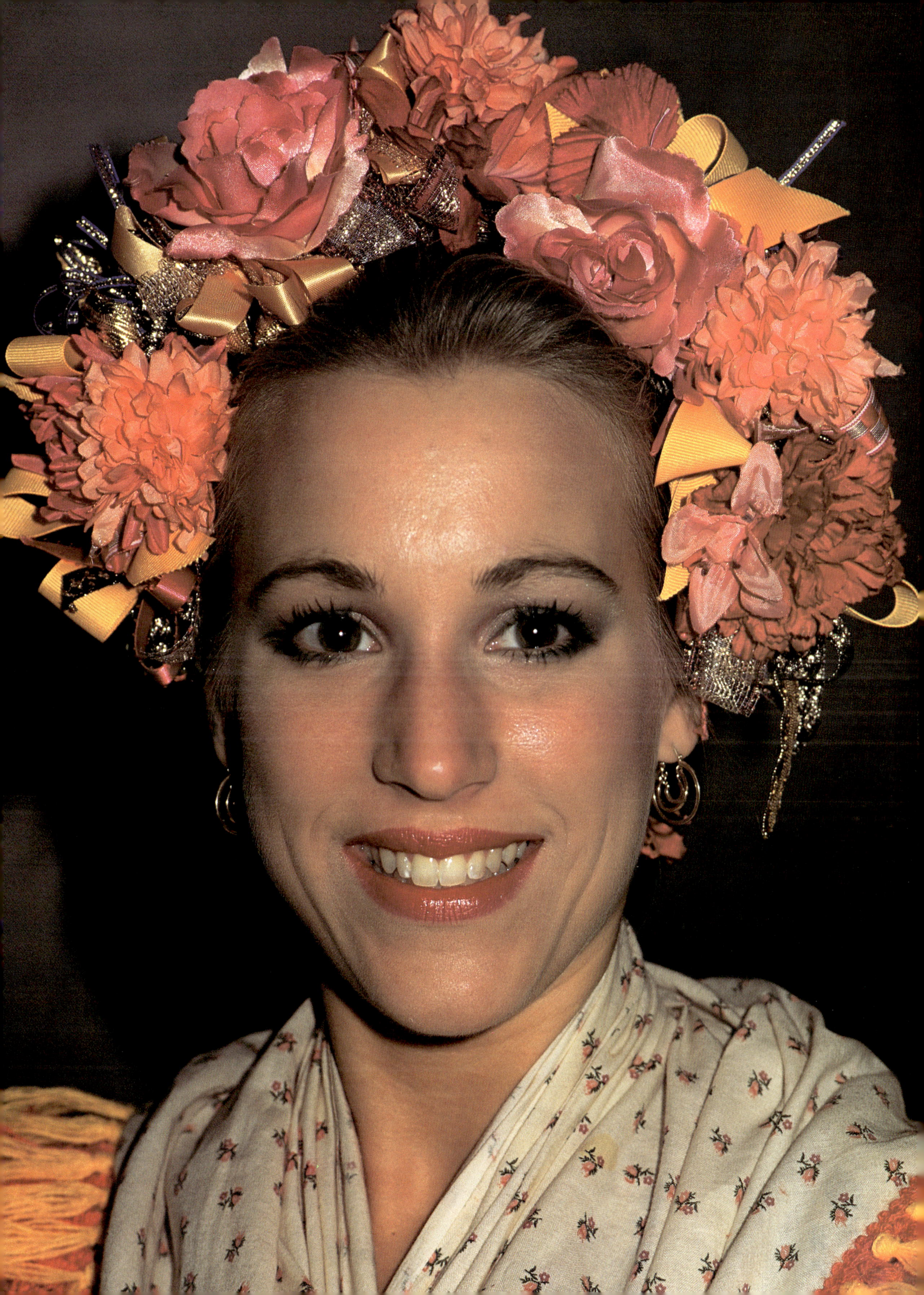

of cultural expression. Everything from dresses, leggings, moccasins and belts to jewelry, wallets, pens and even their pageant queens' crowns are typically covered with hundreds of colorful beads arranged in bright geometric and floral patterns. Drums, bustles, head coverings and other dancing regalia used for ceremonial events and powwows are lovingly and carefully made.

Powwows are community celebrations with music and dance contests, crafts and food sales and sometimes handgame (team gambling) competitions; in the last decade the number of these gatherings has grown dramatically. Although this tradition originated with the Plains tribes, powwows are now held in many regions, including Utah, and they attract participants from other tribes. Events like the Northern Ute Sun Dance and the Ute Mountain Bear Dance are either religious in nature or primarily for the Indian community.

Like the arts of their ancestors, the expressions of today's folk artists range throughout the domestic, occupational, decorative and recreational realms, from quilting and saddlemaking to yard decorations and old-time music and dance. And also like their pioneer forebears, contemporary folk artists have learned to create beauty in their everyday lives by pairing group-held values and personal ingenuity with the materials and tools at hand.

Utah has always been known as a state of quilters, a reputation that is as accurate today as it was a century ago. Then quilts were necessary for survival on cold winter nights. Now, though they still keep us warm, their popularity is based on other attributes that reflect Utah's pioneer heritage: the opportunity for individual creativity, the camaraderie of the quilting circle, the challenge of crafting beauty from scraps. The many fabric and quilt stores around the state, the quilting classes, competitions and quilt shows and the Utah Quilt Guild, with its network of active quilting circles, all testify to the pervasiveness of this traditional art form.

Rugmaking, like quilting, is a folk art passed down from pioneer times in which leftover materials are recycled into something useful and beautiful. Today's rugs are made from both rags and new materials and are woven or twined on looms, braided, hooked, or crocheted.

Like many who make rugs and quilts, needleworkers typically developed their skills in the traditional way, without formal instruction, learning from family or community. Doilies, tablecloths and runners, lace collars and trim, pillow slips, baby clothing and afghans are among the many items that are tatted, netted, embroidered, knitted and crocheted by needle artists across the state. Through the work of their hands, they remind us of the labor and the creativity that for generations have gone into making our homes places of comfort and joy.

Occupations that rely on the hand skills used during frontier times, such as those associated with ranching culture, have resulted in folk arts passed down through generations. A number of Utahns still craft saddle trees, saddles, boots and ropes and make various kinds of tack—reins, hack-amores and hobbles—from rawhide and even horsehair. Their arts supply the needs of our state's ranching culture and Utah's large population of horses—one of the highest per capita in the country.

Stonework, woodwork and other hand-powered building skills are also among the occupational folk arts practiced in Utah today. Though a few who make a living carving stone with hand chisels and wooden mallets learned from fathers and uncles in the traditional way, most are revival artists who began with an interest in learning to replicate the handmade furniture, wagons or buildings of a century ago. Such artists often have skills in wood-working, blacksmithing or marbeling and graining (painting wooden surfaces to look like more expensive materials) and they make fine reproductions of pioneer furniture or restore historic buildings and sites.

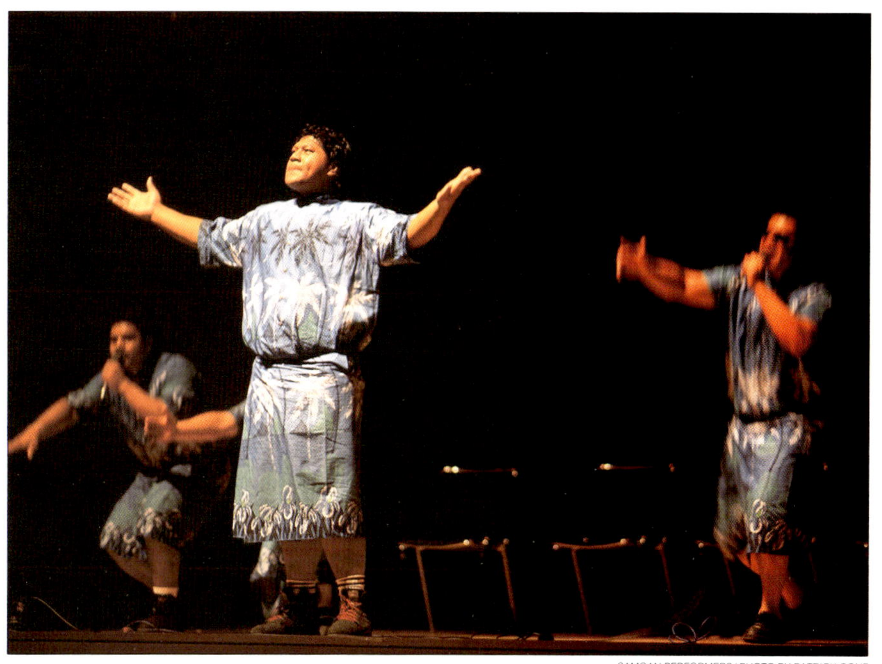

SAMOAN PERFORMERS / PHOTO BY PATRICK CONE

Many kinds of traditional art are created for purely decora-tive reasons. Carved or whit-tled wooden chains, puzzles or fans pro-vide examples of arts pursued for the pleasure creation brings. Miniature wagons or farm machinery, crafted in painstaking detail from wood or metal, are often a way for artists to preserve their own past.

A great many Utahns also enjoy decorating their homes and yards with items that symbolize their own cultural

Wood,
stone and
needlework are
P O P U L A R
Utah folk-art
forms.

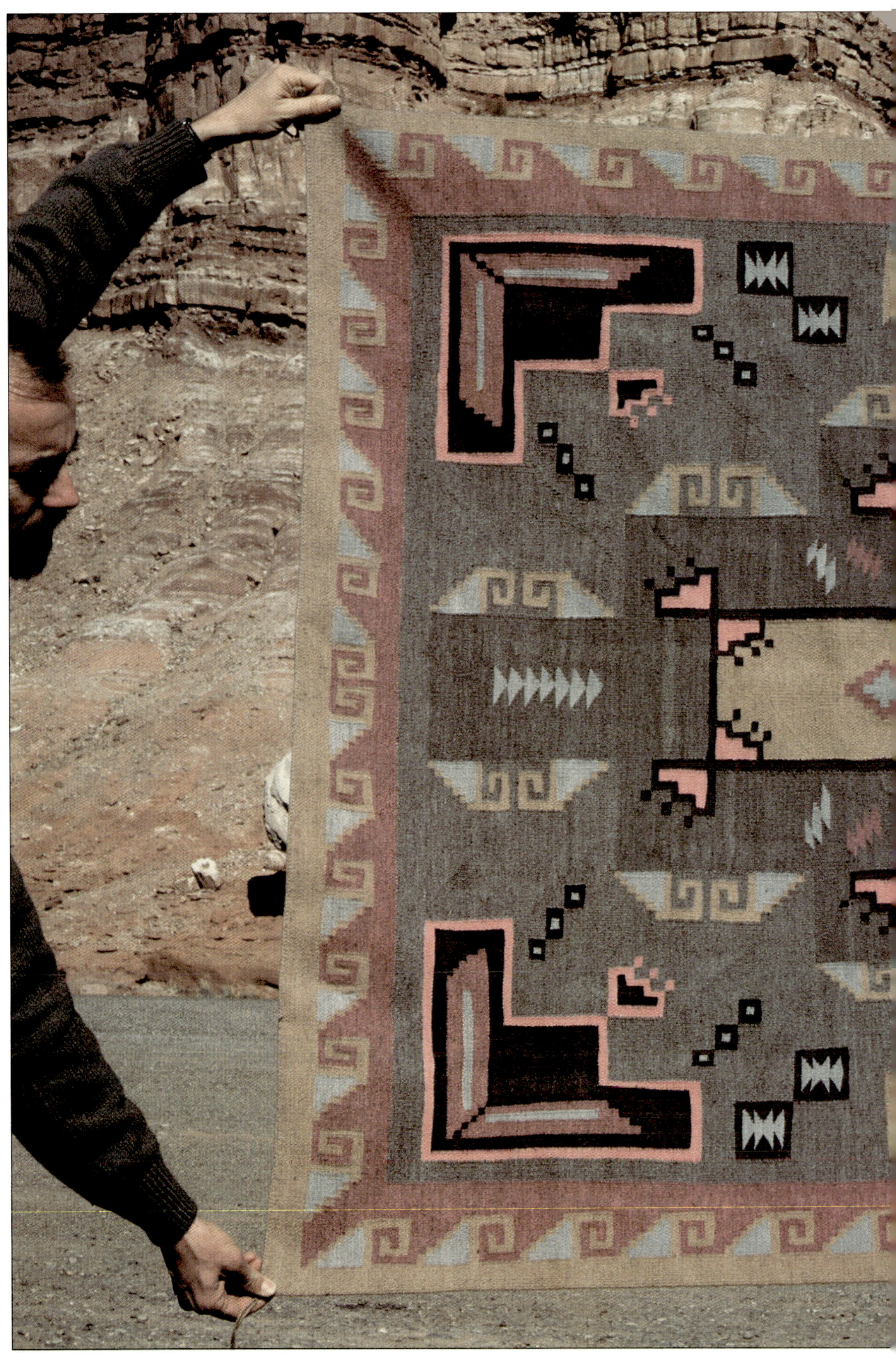

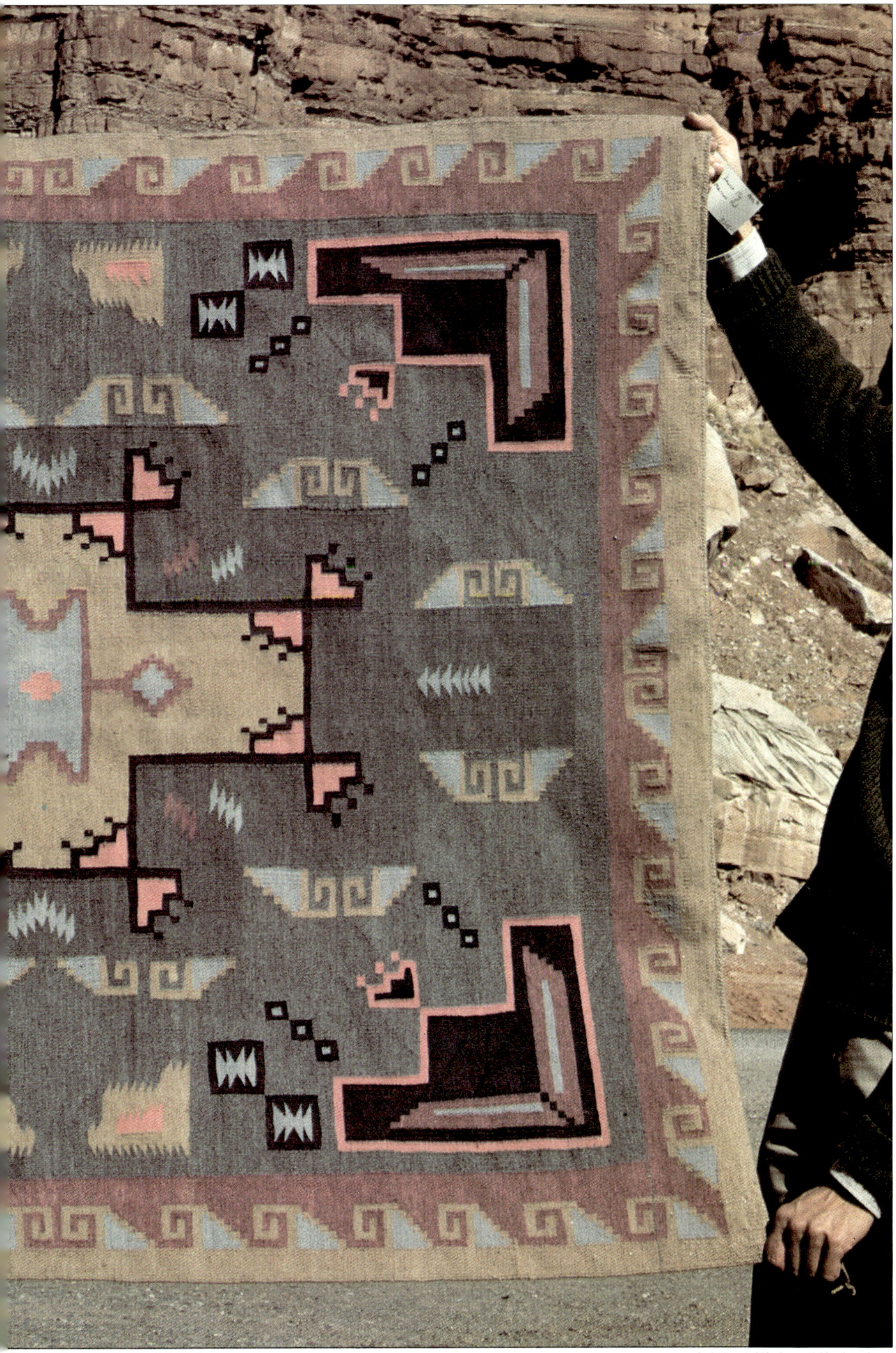

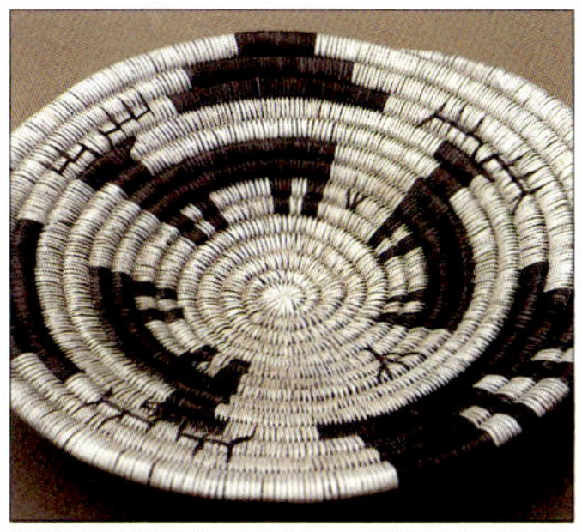

BASKET BY KEE BITSINNI / PHOTO UTAH ARTS COUNCIL ARCHIVES

NATIVE AMERICAN BASKETMAKERS

Goshute weaver Molley McCurdy still makes prehistoric-style gathering and winnowing baskets, while her neighbor Mollie Bonamont makes smaller, lidded baskets. They both weave willow frames and sunshades for baby cradleboards. South of Blanding, a number of Ute basketmakers still gather the squaw bush, split it with their teeth, and weave baskets with the black-and-red Navajo wedding design or with silhouettes of animals or human beings. And, recently, among Utah Navajos basketry is becoming an important art form as several families, including the Blacks, the Rocks and the Whites, participate in an unprecedented expansion of pictorial designs and styles that may signal the beginning of a new basketry tradition. The basketmaking community—and many others who respect the tradition—were gratified when Mary H. Black received a 1993 Governor's Award in the Arts.

NAVAJO RUG WEAVING BY LOUISE CLY / PHOTO UTAH ARTS COUNCIL ARCHIVES

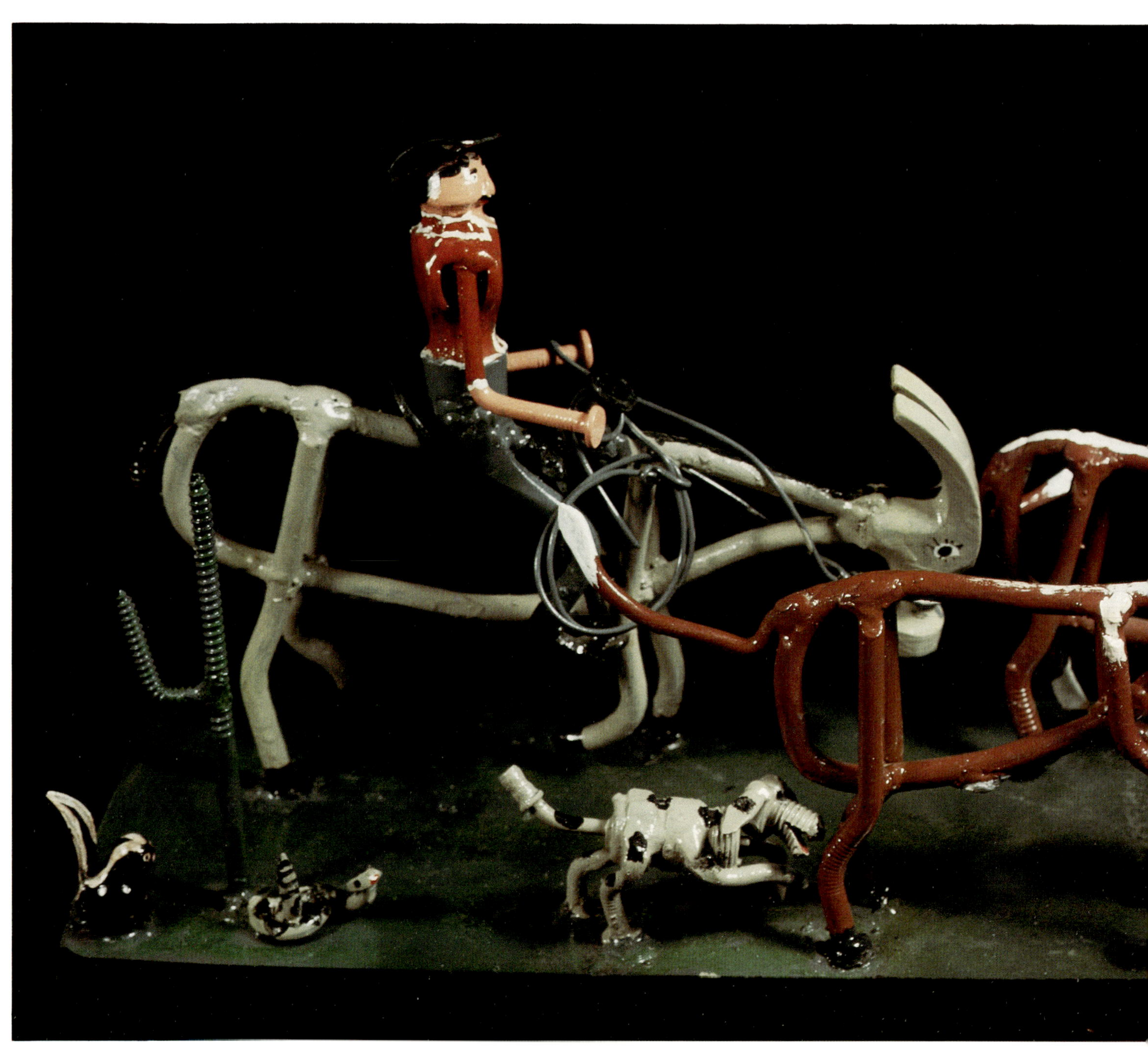

Common

hardware is

T R A N S F O R M E D

into sculpture

by M.J. Alldredge.

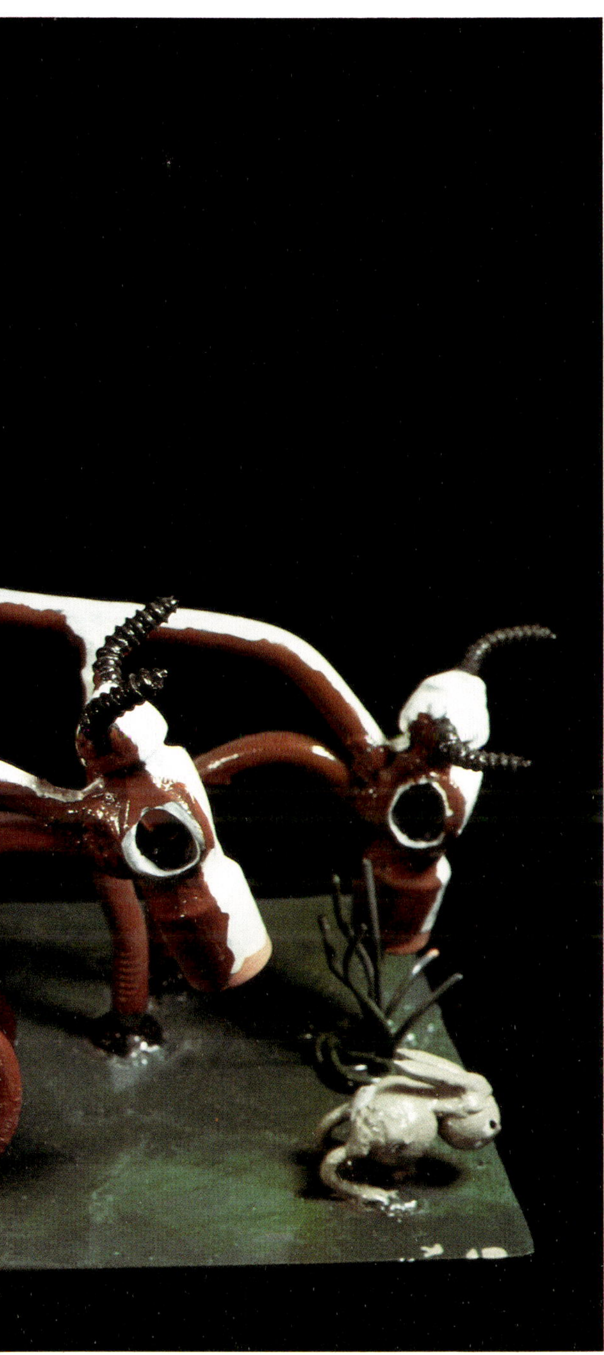

heritage. Mailboxes, fences and other yard art assembled using old wagon wheels, plows, or other farm implements eloquently express regional identity. Outdoor barbecues, rock fences, rock gardens and colorful fireplaces are fashioned with stones gathered from our mountains and deserts.

Utahns are also known for their strong tradition of flower gardens—a legacy from pioneer times when every home had a family orchard, vegetable garden and flower garden. Many gardens still abound in old-time varieties of bush roses, peonies, flags and lilacs.

Yard art assemblages and flower gardens COLOR the Utah landscape.

Although not as pervasive as the crafts, the traditional music and dance of Utah's Anglo-pioneer heritage are still alive, especially in rural Utah. In a number of small towns, community orchestras and bands still provide music for dances and other special occasions. Musicians who learned to play by ear, and who have often inherited their places in the town bands or orchestras from their parents, play a repertory of old-time dance tunes that date back at least fifty years. Though the number of dances has declined since the 1930's and forties, when outdoor dance halls were very popular in towns

FOLLOWING PAGE: *NATIVE AMERICAN POWWOW* / PHOTO UTAH ARTS COUNCIL ARCHIVES

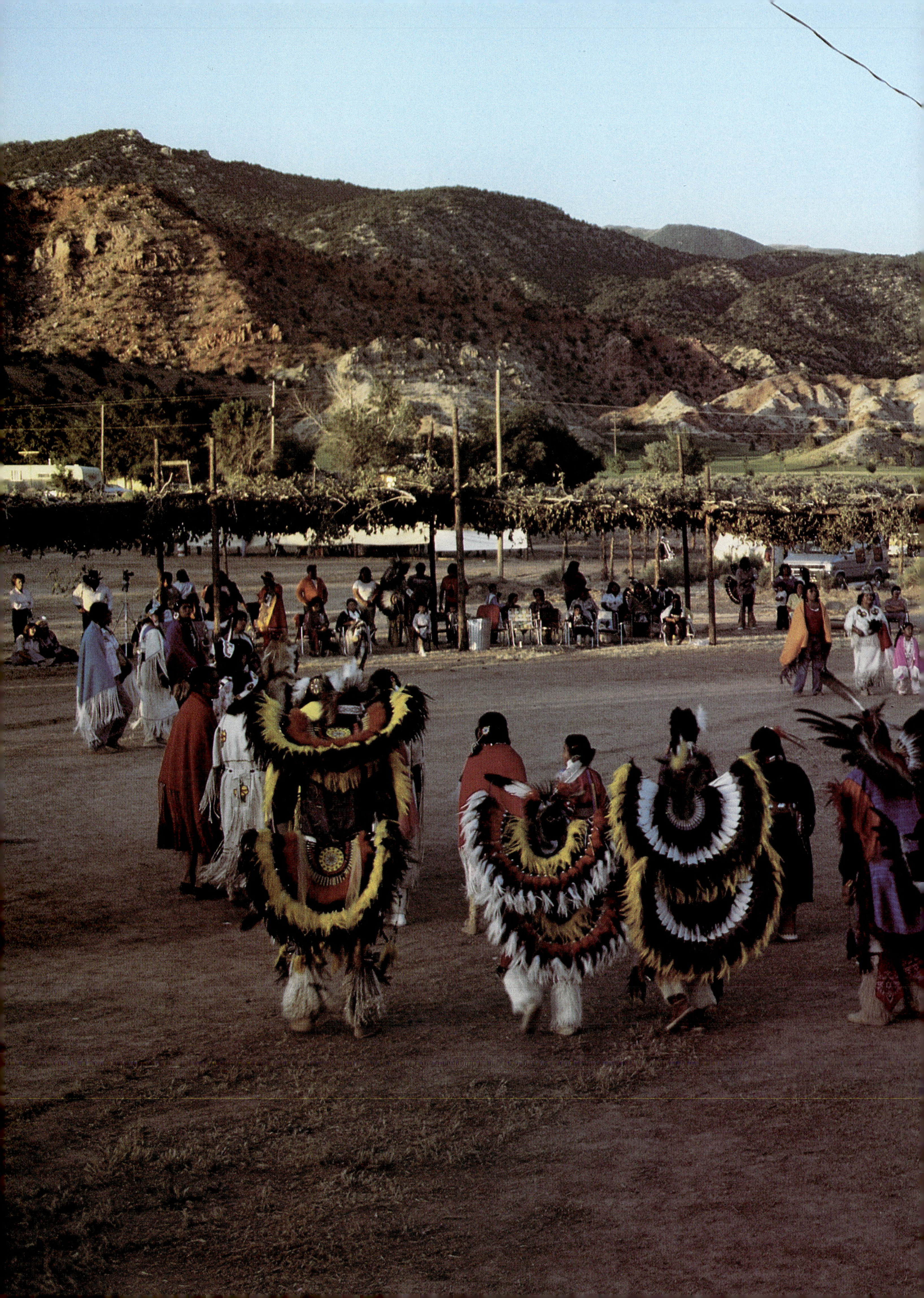

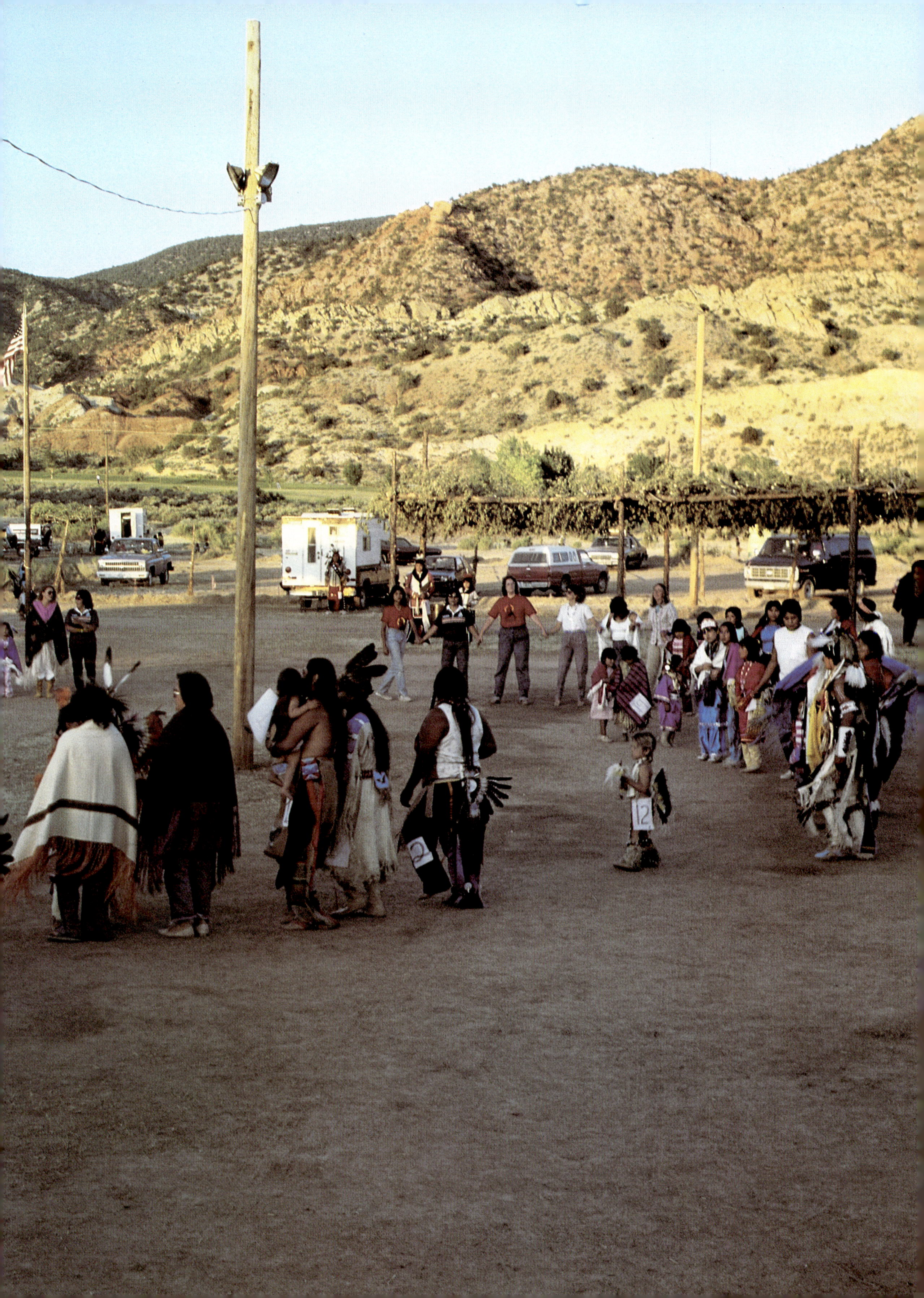

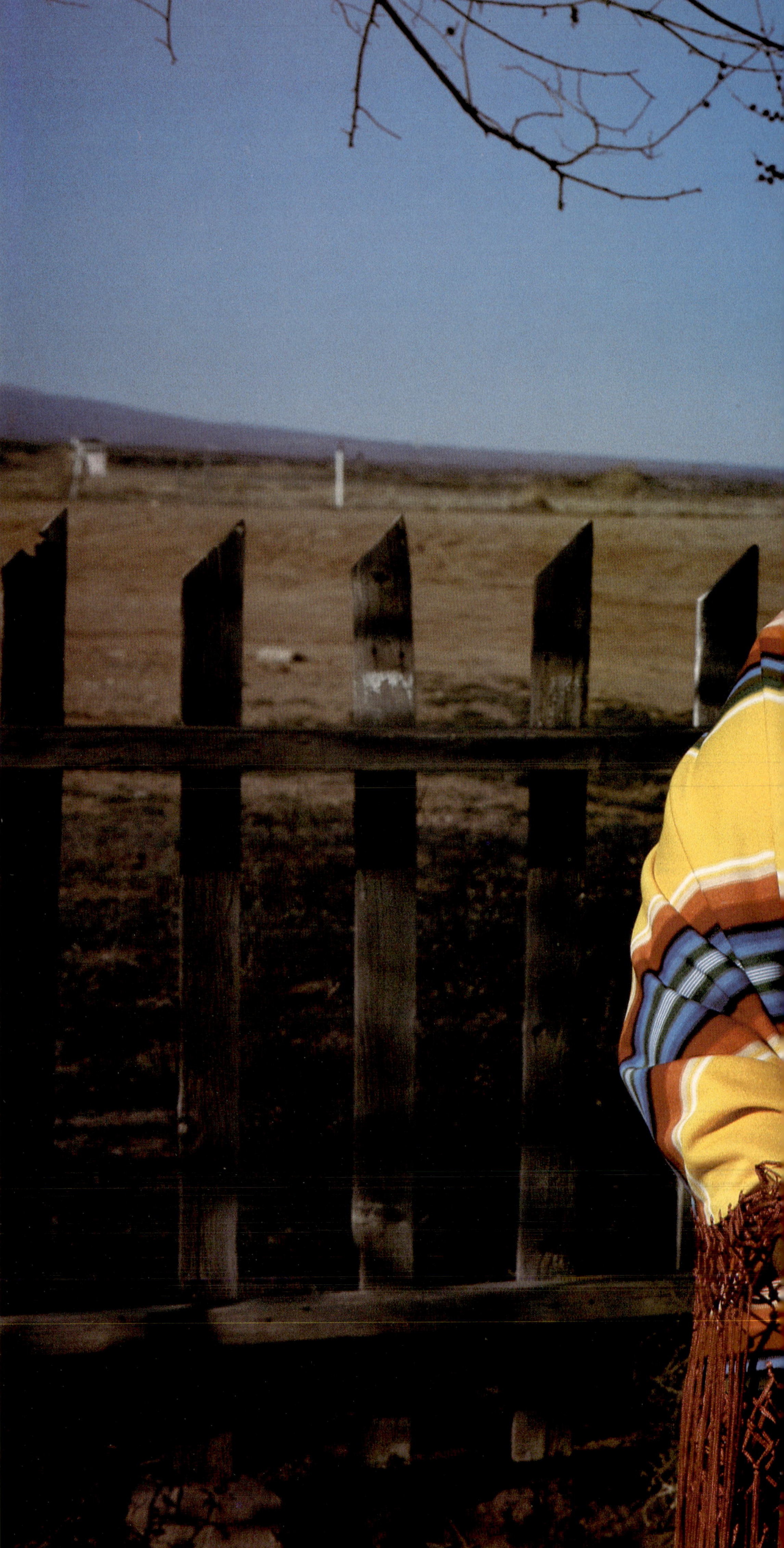

Cradleboard
making by
artisans like
Patty Dutchie
is an important
Native American

C R A F T

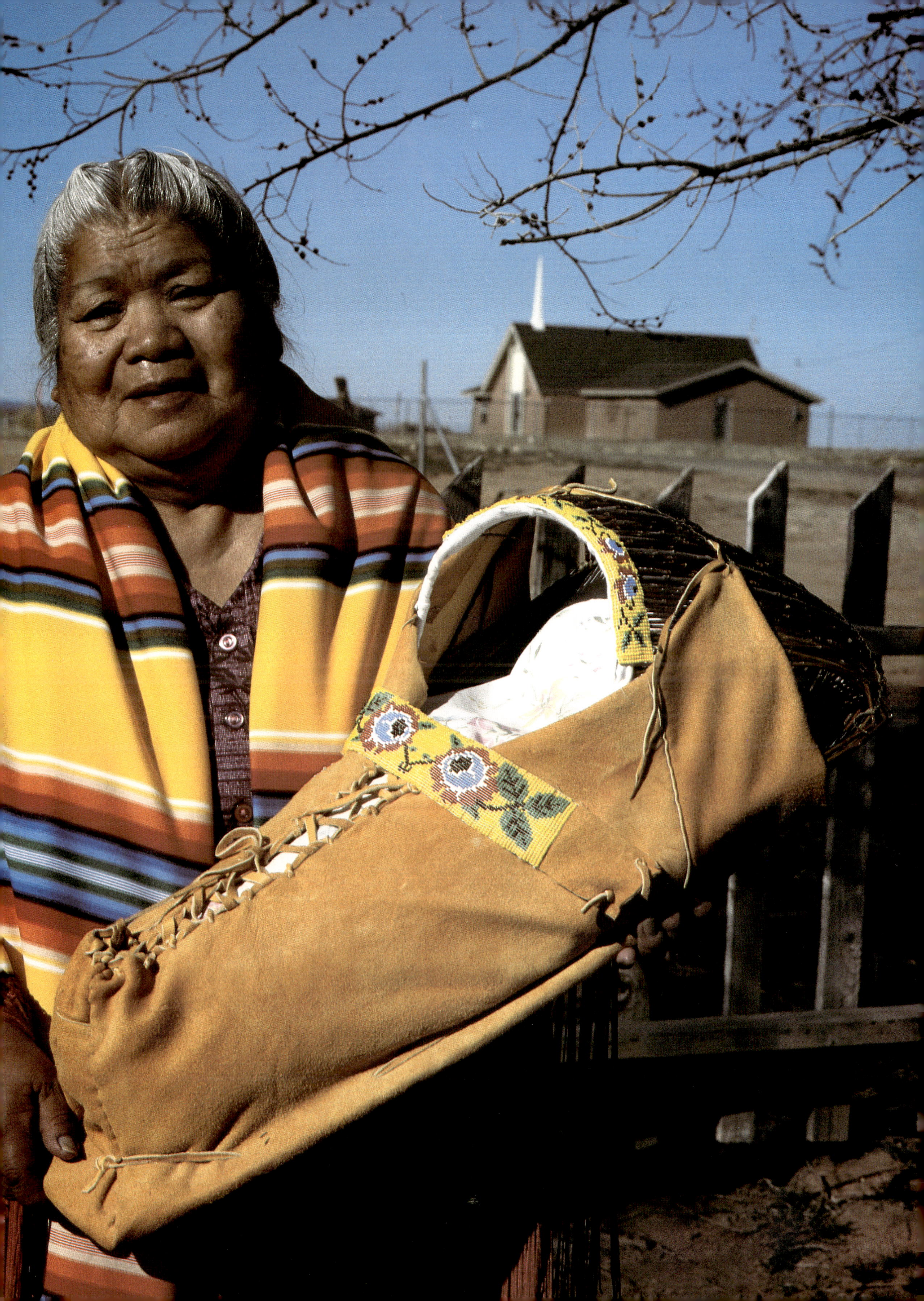

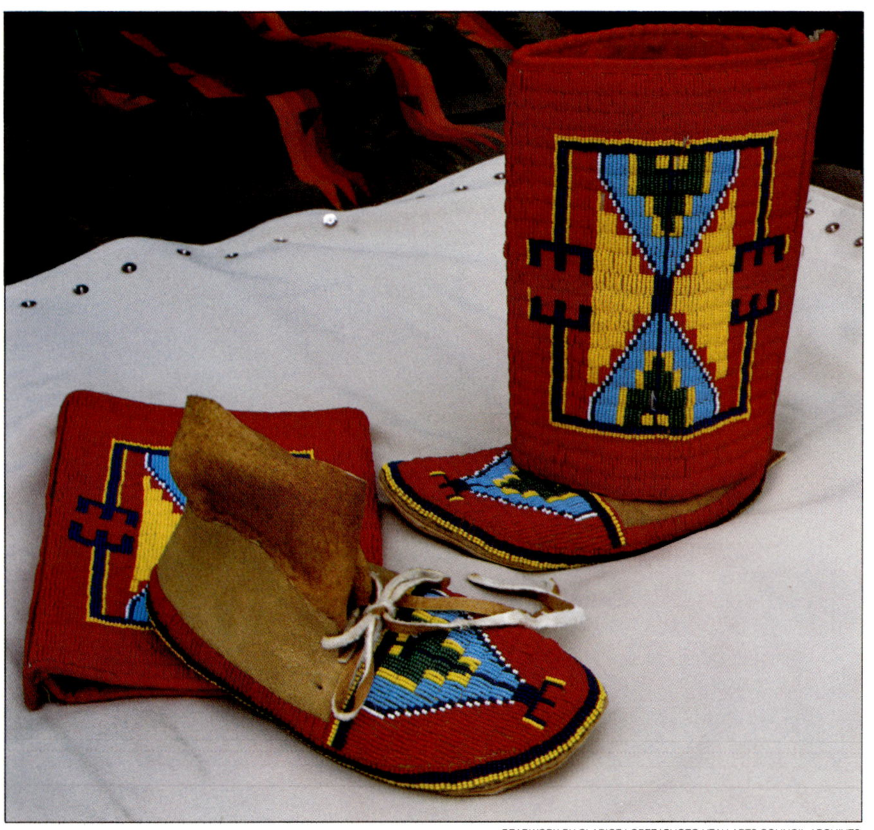

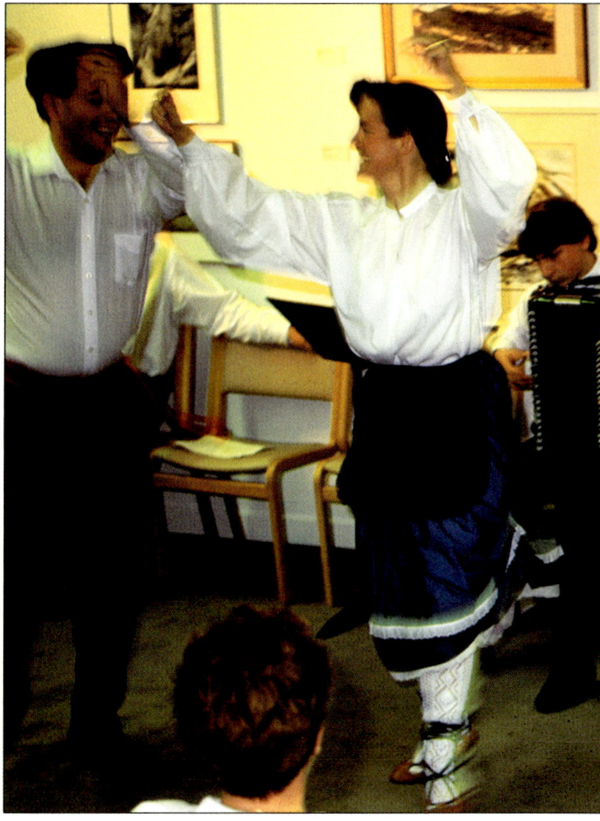

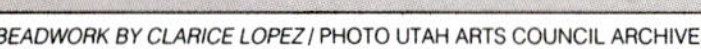
BEADWORK BY CLARICE LOPEZ / PHOTO UTAH ARTS COUNCIL ARCHIVES

like Hurricane and Koosharem, Hilldale and Bluffdale, social dancing is an important recreational and artistic activity. An even older musical repertory that dates from pioneer times is played by a number of talented revival musicians who re-create old-time tunes and performance styles.

Literary art forms, presented in performance, represent another aspect of Utah's folk heritage. Informal storytelling is a folk art we all share at family reunions, on camping trips, or during dinnertime conversation. Stories about pioneer-era hardships or frontier adventures with Indians are common, as are faith-promoting stories featuring encounters with the Three Nephites—heavenly beings who appear to help those in need. Especially widespread are stories about folk heros like Butch Cassidy or the unruly yet beloved Mormon apostle J. Golden Kimball.

Although poetry is usually thought of as a fine art, in the context of a folk community, writing and reciting poetry can also be folk art. A folk poet is typically the person in a community who is known for writing and/or reciting original or memorized verse to celebrate birthdays, anniversaries and other special occasions. Cowboy poetry, a

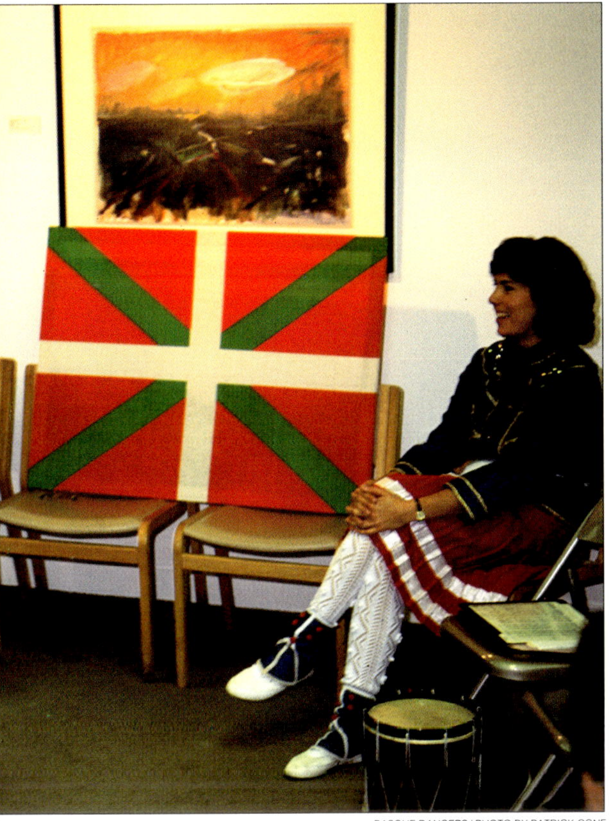

BASQUE DANCERS / PHOTO BY PATRICK CONE

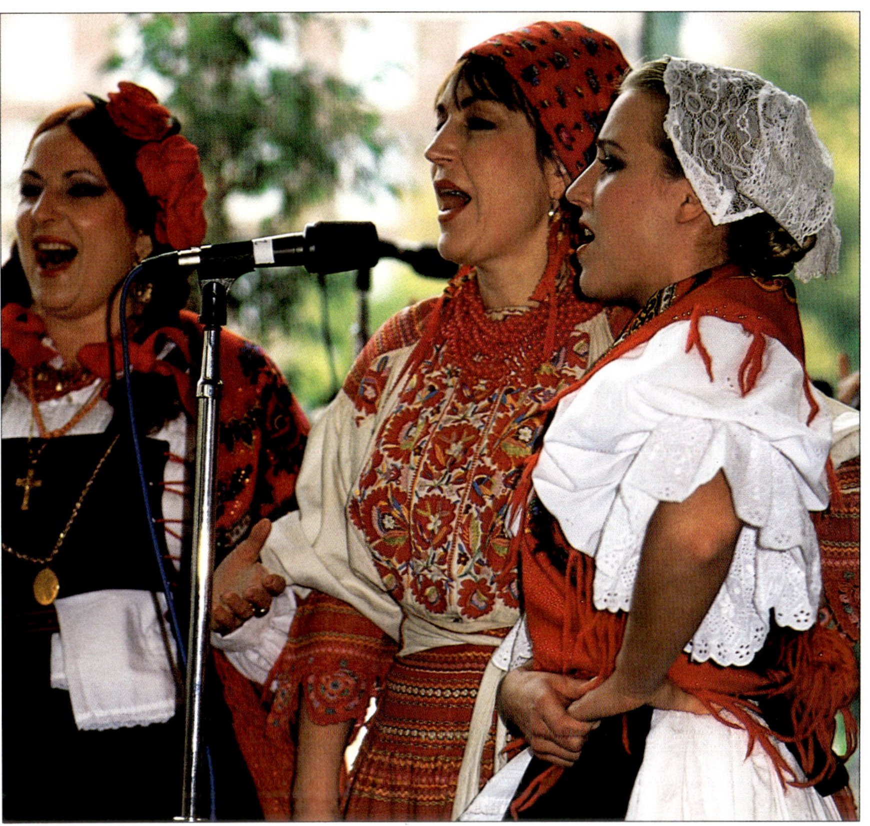

CROATIAN FESTIVAL / PHOTO BY PATRICK CONE

tradition in ranching communities, is perhaps the best-known form of folk poetry. Today Utah's cowboy poets share their work with a wider audience than ever before at poetry gatherings (festivals) in Parowan, Lehi, Ogden and throughout the Western region.

Decorative and
performing arts
interweave
compelling
C O N T R A S T S
in Utah's
folk scene.

Given the many foreign traditions that are represented in Utah's population, it is not surprising that Swedish weaving, Japanese origami, Armenian rugweaving and lacemaking, Chinese painting, Mexican piñata-making, Afghani embroidery, Russian toymaking, Polynesian quilting and European decorative painting are practiced in Utah. Even more activity revolves around performance traditions—perhaps because music and dance stimulate group participation.

CELEBRATIONS AND FESTIVALS

Community celebrations abound throughout Utah— nearly every rural town has a special event. Folk and ethnic arts are often featured and some celebrations spotlight local products: for example, Peach Days in Brigham City, Watermelon Days in Green River and Lamb Days in Fountain Green. Most include parades, talent shows, quilt auctions and craft displays; picnics, softball games, rodeos and outdoor dances.

In urban areas, ethnic festivals like Juneteenth (an African-American celebration) or Utah Slavia are becoming more common. During the last fifteen years folklife festivals designed specifically to celebrate local culture and traditions have been added to this calendar of annual events. *Asian Festival:* Utah's Asian community includes third- and fourth-generation Japanese and Chinese residents as well as newly arrived immigrants from Polynesia and refugees from Laos, Vietnam and, most recently, Tibet. On the first Saturday of May, the groups join together and present an exquisite festival featuring performances of music and dance from their respective traditions and food from the various cuisines.

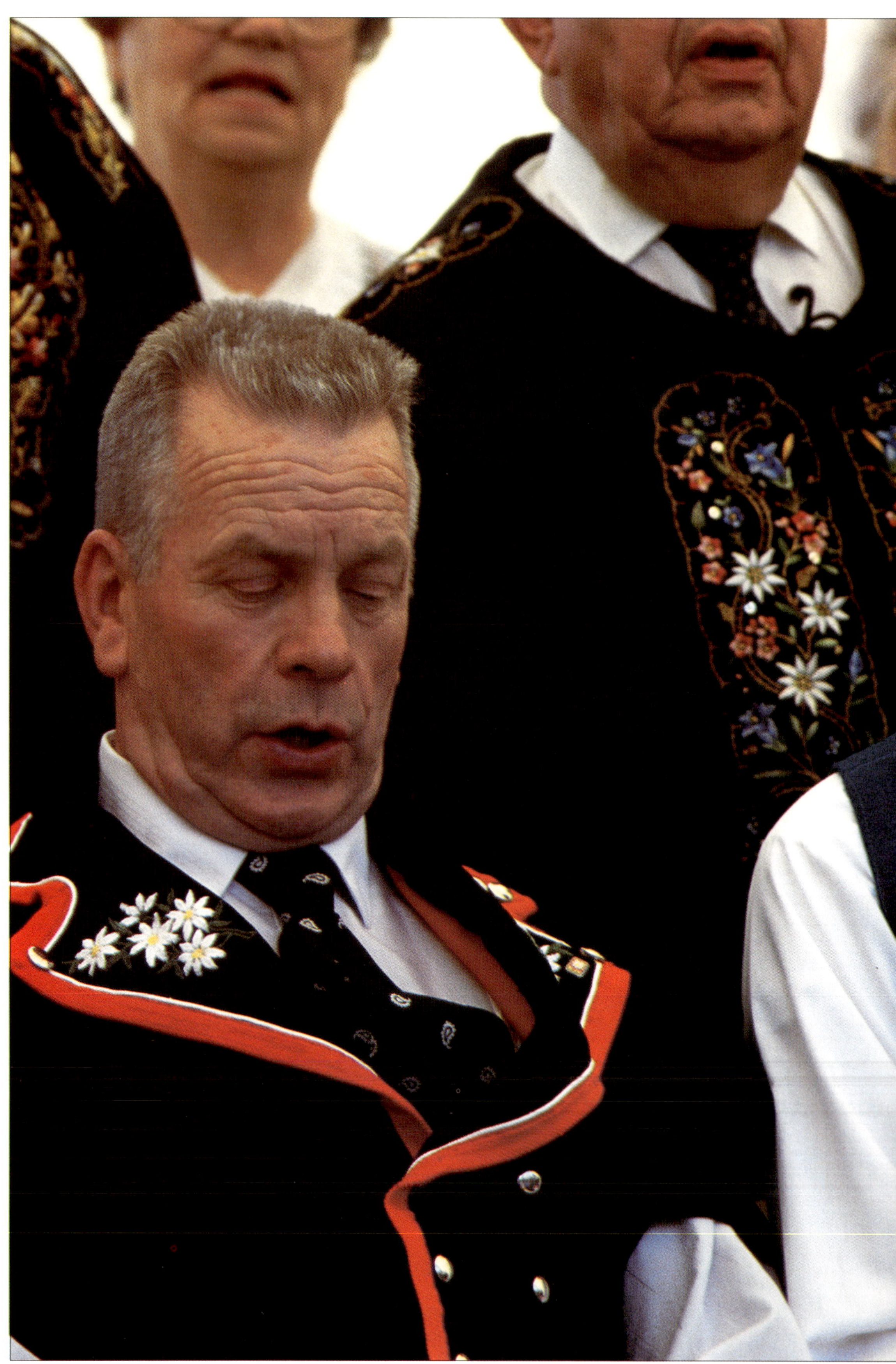

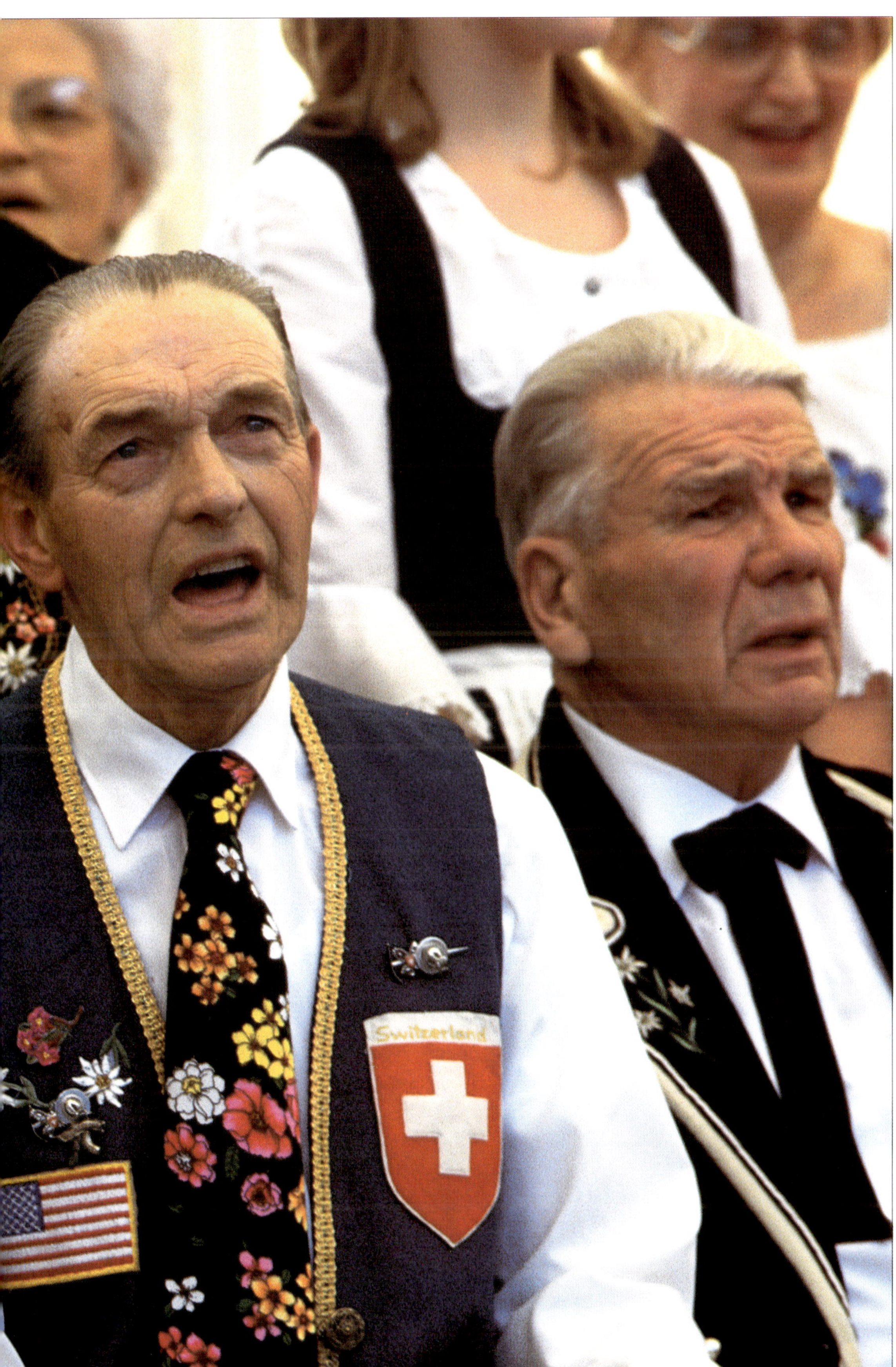

SWISS CHORUS / PHOTO UTAH ARTS COUNCIL ARCHIVES

Living Traditions Festival: Celebrating the cultural diversity of Salt Lake's population with performers, craftspeople and cooks from more than forty local ethnic communities, this event is a week before Memorial Day weekend.

Festival of the American West: A ten-day festival at Utah State University in Logan begins the last weekend in July. Native American, Hispanic and Anglo-pioneer art forms are presented by craftspeople and performers from throughout the West. Living history demonstrations and a very popular Dutch-oven cooking competition re-create the frontier arts.

Greek Festival: Utah's Greek community, one of the oldest and most active ethnic groups in the state, shares music, dance and glorious food with eager non-Greeks the weekend after Labor Day.

Harvest Homecoming Celebration: Little Fruita, now in the middle of Capitol Reef National Park, has always been known for its fruit trees. On the last weekend of September, local folk artists celebrate the harvest by demonstrating the traditional domestic and occupational skills that have always defined rural life and culture in Utah. Visitors may harvest their own winter supply of apples.

Within the Hispanic population, Utah's largest ethnic group, music and social dancing are thriving. On weekends, it is not unusual for there to be three or four dances with live music. Similarly, on Sunday mornings there are at least a dozen services at African-American churches featuring fine gospel music. Whether singing up front with the choir or singing and responding as part of the congregation, those who attend these services renew their group membership and celebrate their ethnicity through traditional arts.

In Utah's Tongan community, music and dance are part of all family and religious celebrations. But at important community events, such as a visit from the king or queen of Tonga, group members perform the most traditional works composed by their local masters—standing and sitting songs featuring group singing with choreographed hand and foot movements.

Likewise, the Japanese Buddhist congregations of Salt Lake and Odgen come together each spring to prepare for an ancient religious holiday, the Obon. People of all ages rehearse folk dances for street celebrations held in July. Both communities are strengthened through group participation in traditional arts.

Utah's Basque, Greek, Hispanic and Filipino communities are among those with active programs for teaching and performing folkloric dance. The Scots and the Tongans both have marching bands—the Scots play bagpipes, of course, while the Tongans have brass bands, a reflection of British influence in Tonga. And in some of Utah's ethnic communities—the East Indian, Laotian, Thai and Chinese—both the classical and folk dance traditions symbolize ethnic identity.

Ethnic music and dance are also enjoyed and performed by many Utahns who are not part of a continuous tradition within an ethnic community. As in other forms of revivalism, these musicians and dancers are very dedicated and have achieved great skill. Musicians who specialize in Irish or Scottish music or dance and dancers who have learned the steps to long-forgotten village dances from Eastern Europe frequently take part in ethnic community celebrations. Their performances are valued for their beauty, the atmosphere they provide and the symbolic statement they make about the importance of art in maintaining cultural heritage.

Utah's folk and ethnic arts bring the values and ideals of the past into the present. Whether part of a continuous community tradition, a revival of skills and repertory from earlier times or a symbolic expression of ethnic identity, they add beauty, excitement, and purpose to our everyday lives.

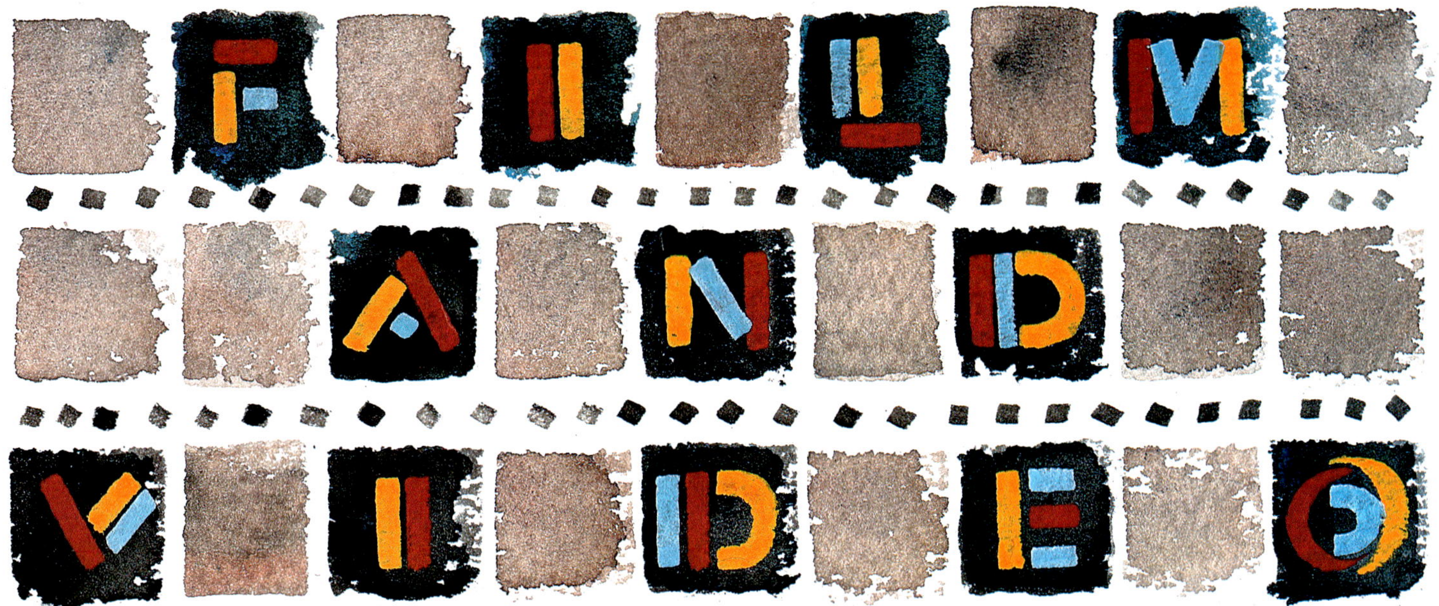

Oh, Shoot!
Filmmaking
in Utah

Sharon Lee Swenson

FILM IS A culture's collective dream. We sit together in the dark, focused on a silver screen on which our most intimate desires and fears are enacted. Immobile, we share visions of what we most yearn for and dread.

Film is alchemical—its reality encompassing the gritty hours of work that produce ephemeral celluloid fantasies and revealing to us the beauty of the physical world which daily life often obscures. The impact of Utah's land-

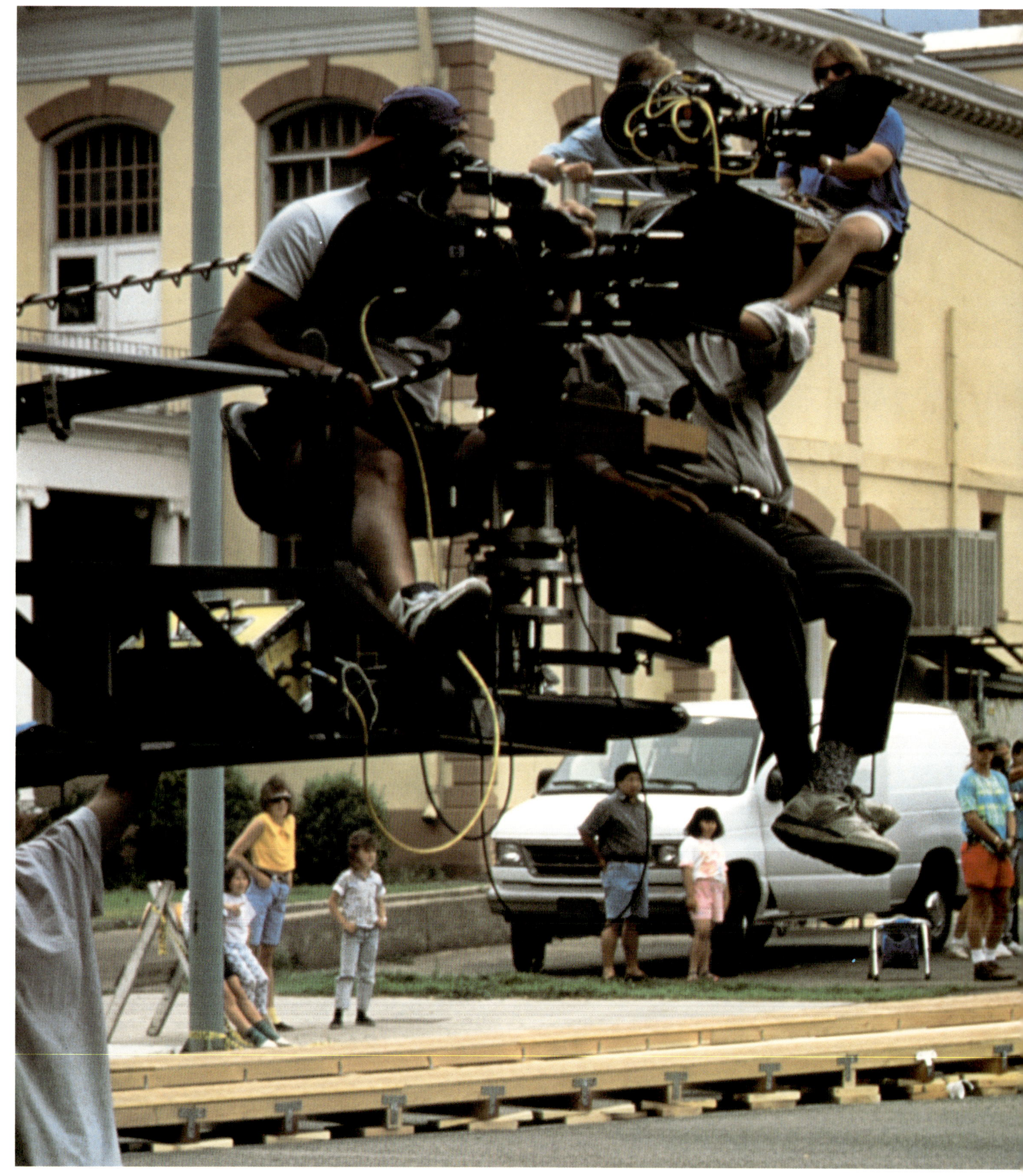

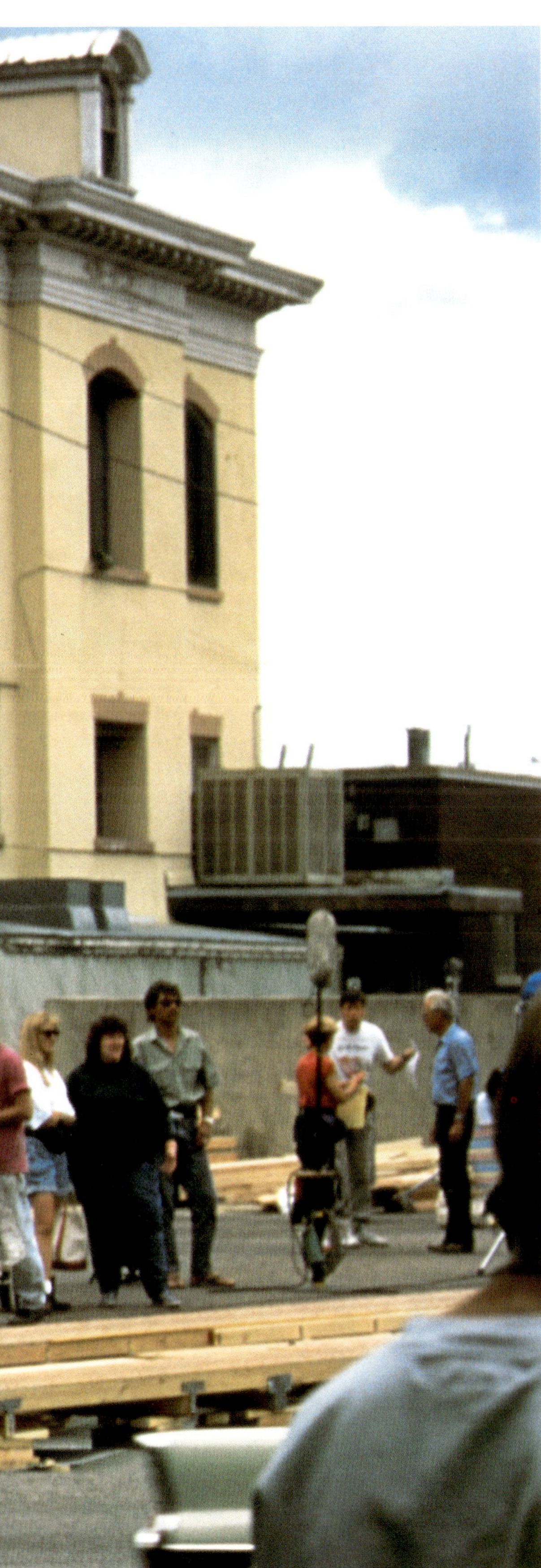

scapes is sometimes more visible on film than in our everyday experience. Utah's vistas have chameleon-like qualities: the land encompasses stark, twisted stumps in arid deserts, massed pines and aspens, lakes and wetlands, high plains and mountain meadows—all transformed by the play of clouds and shafts of sunlight as well as the framing of the camera's lens.

This "redemption of physical reality"—this play on the way the fantasy of film renders the world's reality visible—has been vivid in Utah-made films since the 1920's. The state's geographical diversity means a production can capture cosmopolitan urban or classic redrock or 1930's rural or 1950's suburban settings. Utah is also a right-to-work state, which means that only one and a half hours by air from Los Angeles, hardworking, well-qualified, nonunionized film crews are available. The diverse population also includes highly trained professionals who are members of such industry unions as the Screen Actors Guild.

Rich financial bounties have been harvested from the state's character: In fiscal 1992-93, according to the Utah Film Commission, a record 87 million film production dollars were spent here.

The first film made in Utah was the 1922 silent epic *Covered Wagon*, according to James D'Arc, curator of the

ROBERT REDFORD

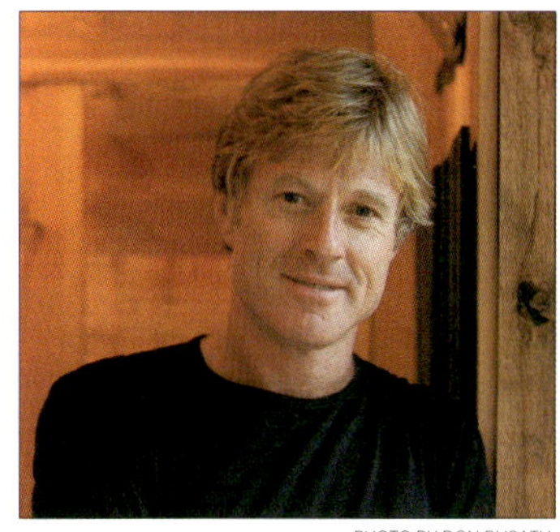

PHOTO BY DON BUSATH

Though he's a native of Santa Monica, California, who works extensively in Hollywood and New York, Robert Redford centers much of his energy on the 7,000 acres he owns in Provo Canyon. Sundance houses a ski resort, a world-class restaurant and the Sundance Institute.

Redford is committed to the history and traditional values of his adopted home. He has written about Utah's past (*The Outlaw Trail*), devoted energy to environmental issues and cultivated opportunities for independent artists of every age at Sundance.

Redford's accomplishments in Hollywood demonstrate his ability to develop thoughtful and thought-provoking films. Who can forget his charming early performance with Jane Fonda in *Barefoot in the Park* (1967)? Less visible but more significant is his work as executive producer, beginning with *Downhill Racer* in 1969. Redford's first directorial effort (*Ordinary People*, 1980) won him an Oscar. He has directed *Milagro Bean Field War* (1988) and *A River Runs Through It* (1992) which garnered an Oscar for cinematography.

JAN ANDREWS

Educated as an anthropologist and cultural ecologist, Utahn Jan Andrew's films speak to issues key to Utah culture. She is at work on *Geography of the Imagination*, a meditation on landscape as metaphor which is also a self-referential look at a woman "at a certain age." Andrews is as ingenious at developing funding as she is at making films. Grants from the Utah Humanities Council helped fund *Exiles: Between Two Worlds* (1989), concerning Southeast Asian immigrants in Utah, and *Cold Moon at the Center of the World* (1991), about the 1955 termination of federal support of the Southern Paiute Indian Tribe. An American Film Institute/ National Endowment for the Arts grant assisted production of Lysistrata, *Lysistrata: A Mystery in the Making* (1990), filmed with an all-woman cast and crew.

Andrews' film work was stimulated by a Federal Health Planning Agency grant to study Bedouin culture in Egypt and her first film, *Seduction*, made in 1985, a cross-cultural examination of women and adornment. *Anasazi* (1985), is an experimental film about vandalism of Southern Utah Anasazi sites.

Arts and Communications Archives at Brigham Young University's Harold B. Lee Library. Directed by Five Points, Utah, native James Cruze, it was filmed in the tiny town of Garrison on the Utah/Nevada state line.

While films have been made here ever since, the state has enjoyed two significant periods of filmmaking ferment. The first began in the late thirties, launched by Hollywood filmmaker John Ford's first visit to George White's ranch near Moab and to Gouldings' Trading Post just outside Monument Valley.

Ford's Utah-made films helped make him a legendary *auteur*, belying his modest self-description: "I make Westerns." Visitors can still eat a Navajo taco in the rugged cavalry dining hall Ford built at Gouldings' for *She Wore a Yellow Ribbon* (1949) before venturing out onto John Ford Point to view the red stone "mittens" he made American icons in *Stagecoach* (1939) and *The Searchers* (1956). Today peacocks peck the dirt around a ramshackle wood cabin built at White's Ranch for Ford's *Cheyenne Autumn* (1964). Nearby in the Fisher Towers area, the mica-streaked sand of the Wagon Wheel escarpment looks just as it did when Ford shot *Wagonmaster* there in 1950. The films and the places where they were made still vibrate with spiritual energy—this is holy ground.

Ford also ventured into Cedar Meadows, just east of Cedar Breaks, to make his first technicolor film, *Drums Along the Mohawk*, with Henry Fonda and Claudette Colbert, released in 1939. Here the high mountain valley portrayed New York State at the time of the Revolutionary War. In 1943, the versatile meadow played a Montana ranch in *My Friend Flicka*, starring Fred MacMurray and Roddy McDowall. The filmmaking boom triggered by Ford continued beyond the fifties with Frank Sinatra's "Rat Pack" joining the filmmaking gang in Kanab in 1963 for *Sergeants Three*, a remake of *Gunga Din*.

It's an odd sensation to see places you know intimately from films but have never before visited in person. But if you stop in Kanab today, you can still stay in the Dean Martin Room of Parry Lodge, established in the early thirties by the Parry Brothers (Chance, Whit, and Gronway) who helped initiate filmmaking in Southern Utah. If you eat in the right cafe there, you may still hear locals talk about the time Sinatra wanted a certain deli-style sandwich unobtainable in town, so he had it delivered in his private plane. To show his gratitude for the city's willingness to let his jet overrun the community's prop-only runway, he donated playground equipment for area kids.

A traditional Western main street haunted by gunslingers and solid citizens survives a few miles south of Kanab, and northwest of town you can explore the canyon where Clint Eastwood filmed parts of *The Outlaw Josey Wales* in 1975.

St. George was part of this boom, too. The area's most notorious film is probably *The Conquerer* (1956). Here the deserts of southwestern Utah became the steppes of Eurasia and John Wayne the leader of a Mongol horde. Years after the filming, tabloids buzzed about the startlingly high percentage of the film's cast and crew who had suffered or died from cancer—could it be linked to the radioactive sand of the Utah location, downwind from the Nevada A-bomb test site? This collision of movie-reality and ordinary human experience was frightening: Could the beautiful landscapes have become toxic?

The second wave of feature film-making, which began in the late seventies, was more regionally focused, fostering a variety of films different from the Hollywood product of the earlier period.

The ferment in Utah film was trig-gered by several catalytic personalities. In 1976 John Earle, working with the Utah Arts Council and assisted by Sterling VanWagenen, coordinated an ambitious Bicentennial Film Festival. Earle became head of the state's Film Development Office, where he ener-gized production not only by those out-side the state but by talented local film-makers as well.

A strong interest in independent filmmaking, film study and exhi-bition made Salt Lake City a flashpoint for film. Utilizing state resources and mobilizing local business-es, VanWagenen and Earle inaugurated the Utah/U.S. Film Festival in 1977 with a dual focus on independent regional filmmaking and work in the humanistic tradition of John Ford. The festival has survived, changed and thrived. Today it is the Sundance Film Festival in Park City, where audiences pack theaters to view independent films from interna-tional venues, and hot new talents prac-tice dealmaking with representatives of a more established power base.

The synergy included dynamic interest in filmmaking and film study, an inventive and extensive exhibition pro-gram coordinated by Ranae Pierce at the Salt Lake City Public Library, and devel-opment of local commercial filmmaking.

At the University of Utah, Tom and Vivian Sobchack taught film history and theory. Independent filmmaker Mort Rosenfeld taught film production there, too, while pursuing his own experimen-tal projects (*Down in the Valley* and *Circle Game*), drawing in local acting talent including Linda C. Smith, David Kranes and Shelly Osterloh. The university was a base for a vibrant group that included filmmakers Trent Harris, Ren Weiss, Mike Cassidy, Judy Hallet and Larry Roberts; producers Sterling VanWagenen and Jack Vetterli; film programmers Ranae Pierce, Barbara Bannon, and Dale Christensen; and *Utah Holiday* editor/film critic Paul Swenson. The diverse talents of the period are suggested by the careers of four of those filmmakers.

Trent Harris completed his degree in film at the University of Utah and worked in local television on experimental documentaries like "Atomic Television" for KUTV's *Take-2*, as well as more traditional news pieces. Then he attended the American Film Institute (AFI) in Los Angeles, where he met Crispin Glover, Sean Penn and Warren Beatty. After freelancing scripts in Los Angeles and crewing internationally for National Geographic Films, he procured funding for his own independent feature *Reuben and Ed* (1991), starring Glover, which he shot in Salt Lake City and Hanksville. In 1993 Harris returned to Salt Lake to work on *Plan 10 from Outer Space*, his second feature with local roots.

Ren Weiss completed only two experimental narratives before his early

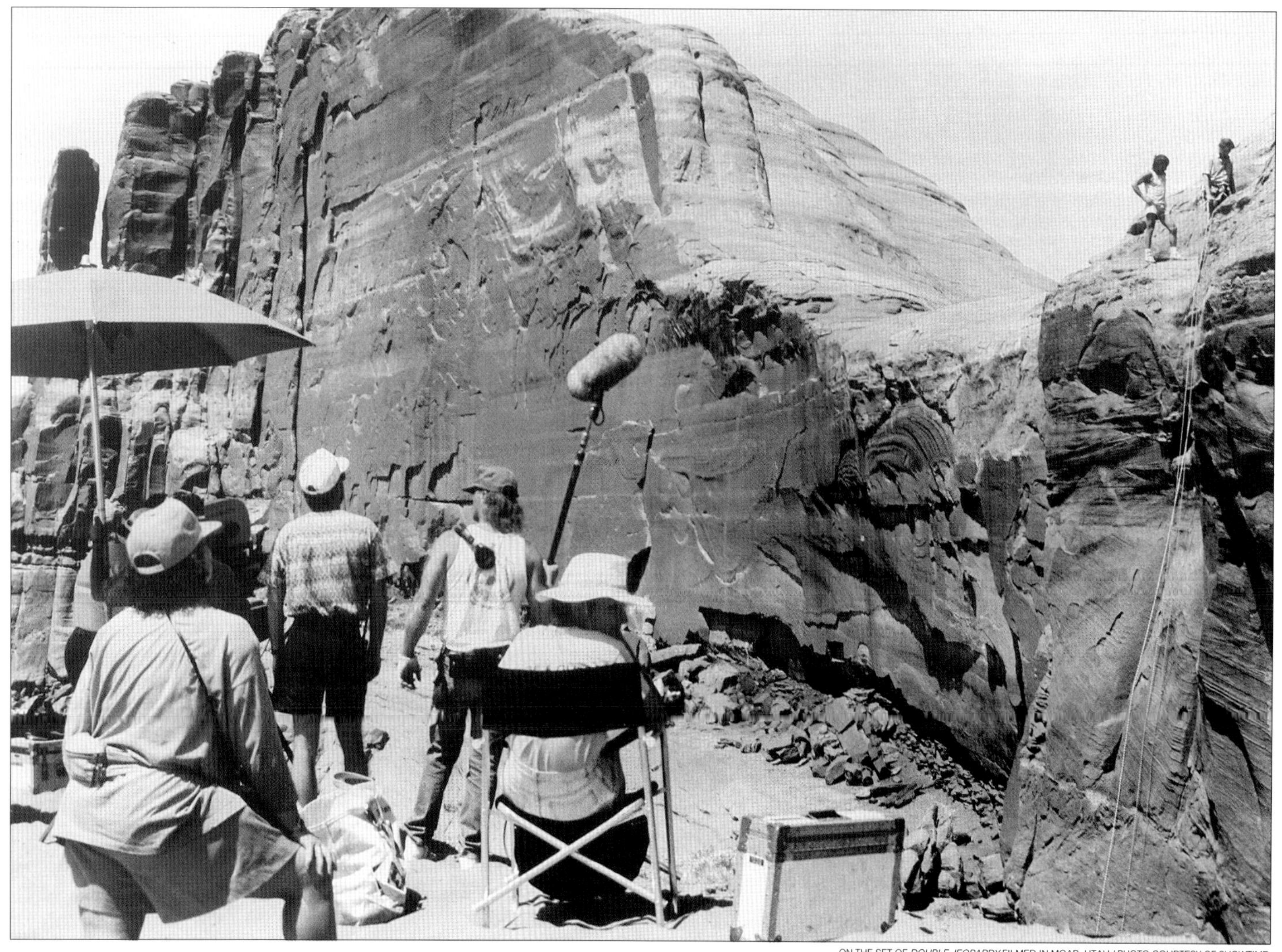

ON THE SET OF *DOUBLE JEOPARDY* FILMED IN MOAB, UTAH / PHOTO COURTESY OF SHOWTIME

death; one—*The Big Nickel*—showed great promise.

Judy Hallet, who had worked on films in Afghanistan with her architect husband Stan before coming to Utah, created solid documentaries for KUTV Channel 2 during her time here. Now based in Washington, D.C., she continues her work with National Geographic Films.

Larry Roberts created both experimental films (*Patty in Kansas, Strong Willed Women Subdue and Subjugate Reptiles*) and documentaries (such as *S-L One*, about the country's first nuclear power accident). He and co-director Diane Orr made the award-winning *The Plan*, a stark study of a Utah Young Mother of the Year. At the time of Roberts' death in 1989, he and Orr were working on a feature based on the life of environmentalist Everett Ruess.

In addition to vigorous experimental work, the period was marked by more commercial independent filmmaking. Charles Sellier of Sunn Classics developed effective demographic marketing and distribution strategies. Rather than making films and then identifying a market for distribution in more traditional ways, Sellier conducted extensive surveys to identify viewer

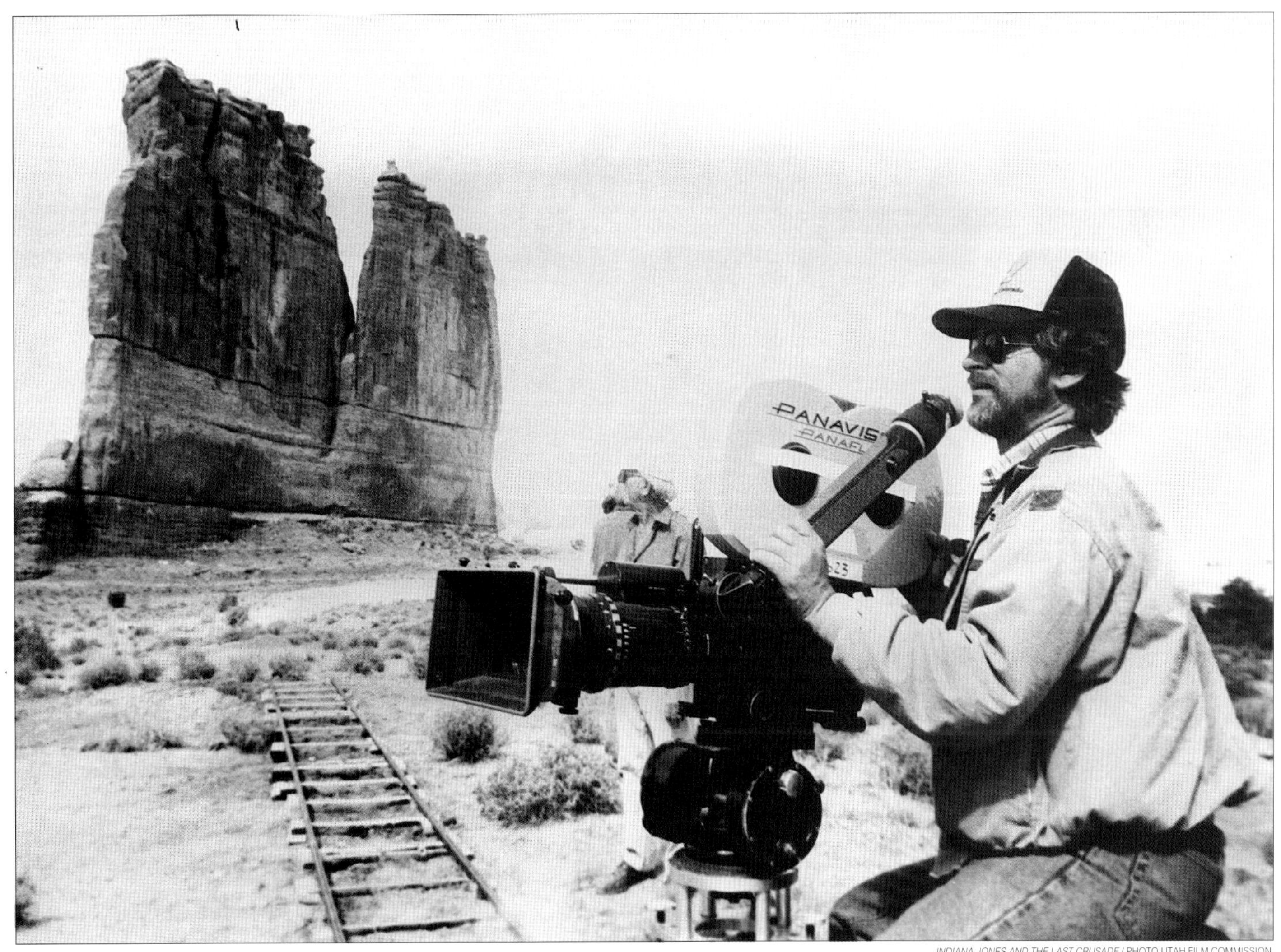

INDIANA JONES AND THE LAST CRUSADE / PHOTO UTAH FILM COMMISSION

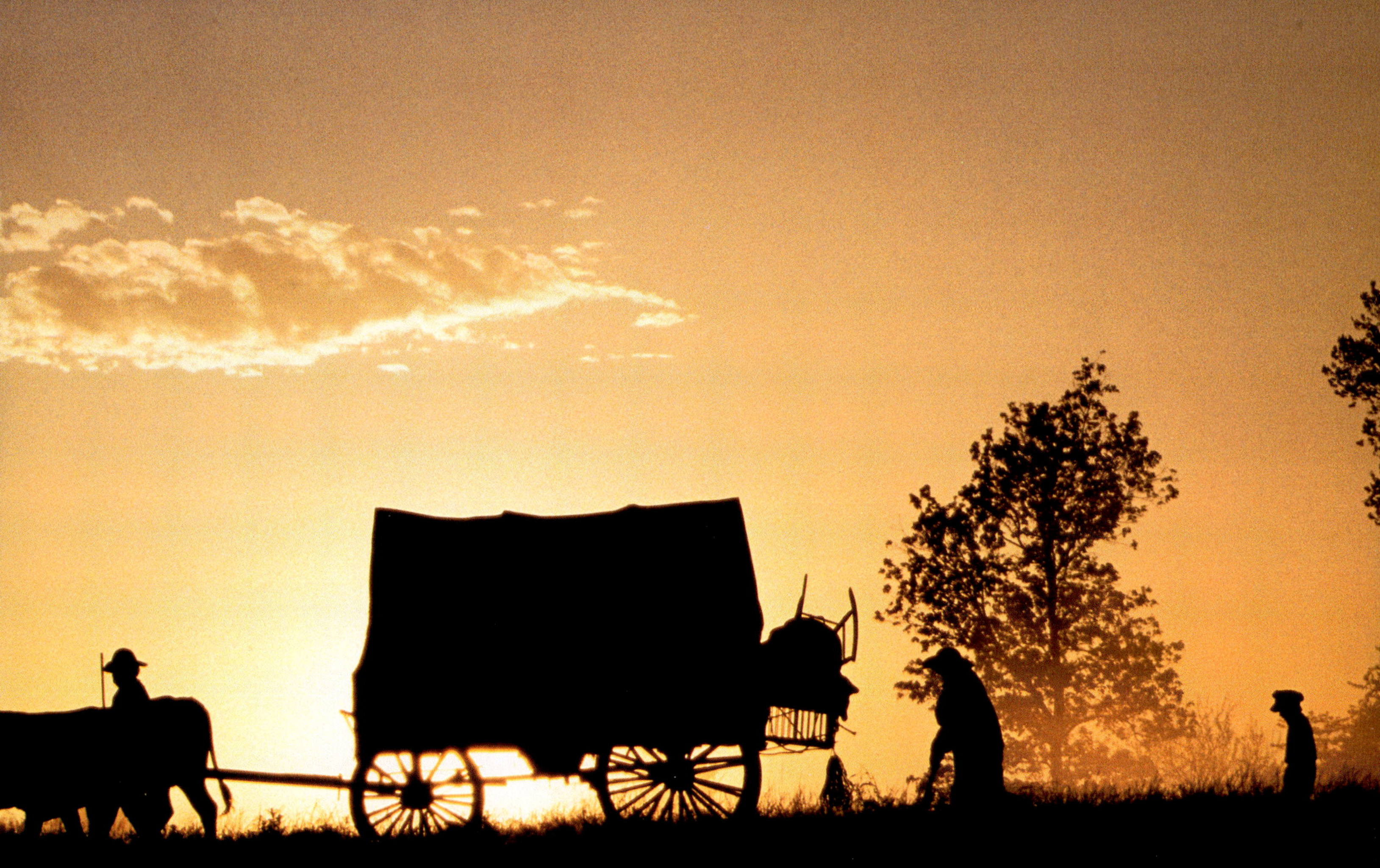

interests and tailored films to fit them. He also made extensive use of a "four-wall" distribution plan in which his company would rent a movie theater for a flat fee for a certain number of days and then generate publicity to maximize audiences for a limited number of screenings. During the late seventies and early eighties, Sellier was extremely successful financially, producing *In Search of Noah's Ark* and *Hangar 57*, as well as the *Grizzly Adams* television series. Sellier supported the Utah/U.S. Film Festival in its first four years and functioned as a Roger Corman-esque trainer for young filmmakers.

Ironically, the name most identified with Utah film is that of California-born Robert Redford, who fell in love with the Wasatch Mountains as a child traveling cross-country with his family. His affection for the land and traditions of Utah led him to buy a piece of property in Provo Canyon that included a small ski operation called Timp Haven Resort. He renamed the resort to honor the character he played in *Butch Cassidy and the Sundance Kid*, the 1969 film that catapulted him to national celebrity.

Redford's development of Sundance included a utopian vision of an arts community. He served as an advisory board member to the first Utah/U.S. Film Festival, where he was particularly interested in the focus on independent film. He invited Sterling VanWagenen to join him in planning the Sundance Institute, which was established in 1981 to help independent filmmakers learn the skills and obtain the resources necessary for making films.

The Institute has supported development and production of varied independent works, including *Belizaire the Cajun, Desert Bloom, Promised Land, A Dry White Season, Waiting for the Moon, El Norte,* and *Poison,* and has sponsored screenings of independent films in Russia and Japan. Today, the Institute continues the Filmmakers' Lab and also sponsors the Sundance Film Festival in Park City, a Children's Theatre and a series of popular theatrical productions in a new Sundance facility.

Redford stimulates film in Utah indirectly as well. His desire to make a film in his own backyard helped convince Sydney Pollack to film *Jeremiah Johnson* along the Wasatch Range in 1972 and to make *The Electric Horseman* (1979) in the St. George and Zion Park areas. *Horseman,* incidentally, helped develop the career of a rancher/horse wrangler/character actor named Wilford Brimley.

Redford's presence in Utah attracted other California film people who built homes in the Sundance area. One, producer Dan Melnick, made most of

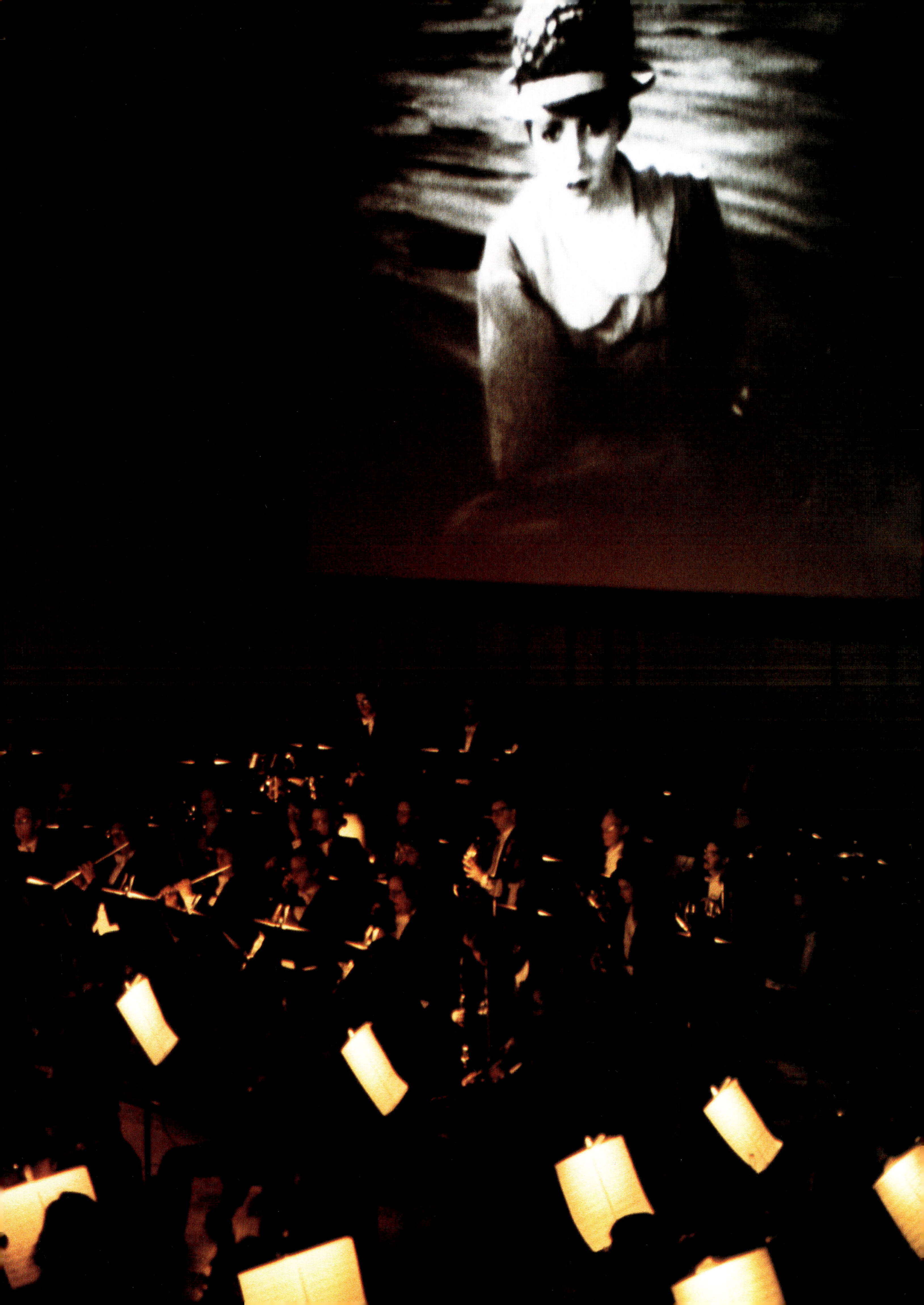

STERLING VAN WAGENEN

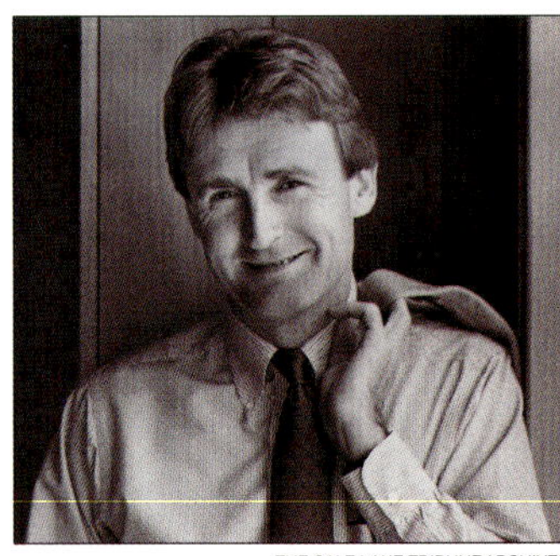

THE SALT LAKE TRIBUNE ARCHIVES

In October 1992, Sterling VanWagenen was recognized as a visionary with the Crystal Heart Award of the newly established Heartland Film Festival in Indiana for his direction of *Alan and Naomi* (1991). In June 1993, he spent two weeks working with artists developing new works in Heartland's play and script workshop.

Utah native VanWagenen has long been committed to the independent film movement, being involved in some way with virtually every significant development in Utah filmmaking since 1976. He was instrumental in organizing the Utah/U.S. Film Festival (now the Sundance Film Festival) in 1978, the Utah Cinema Council, the Utah Media Center (now the Utah Film and Video Center), and with Robert Redford cofounded the Sundance Institute.

Footloose (1984) in Utah Valley, particularly at the Lehi Roller Mills, because reportedly he wanted to be able to sleep in his own bed during the production. In a different but very effective way, Leigh von der Esch has also been instrumental in putting Utah on the filmmaking map. After some demanding dues-paying work for Sunn Classics in the early eighties, she polished her organizational skills working in the Salt Lake mayor's office. As head of the Utah Film Commission, she has forged excellent connections between local crews and outside producers. Her skilled staff does good location scouting and facilitates connections in a way that makes Utah's sometimes remote locations more reachable. Since the late eighties, Utah has experienced an amazing amount of film activity for a state with such a small population. Significant productions by outside companies have included Michael Cimino's meticulously detailed remake of *Desperate Hours* (1992), utilizing the Salt Lake Avenues area, the Westminster College campus and sound stages in Orem; Ridley Scott's *Thelma and Louise* (1991), in which Dead Horse Point stood in for the Grand Canyon; and Stephen King's *The Stand*, a television mini-series for which greenhouses around the state were filled with sheaves of corn.

Another variety of filmmaking by several local independent companies focuses on creative development and marketing of product for general family

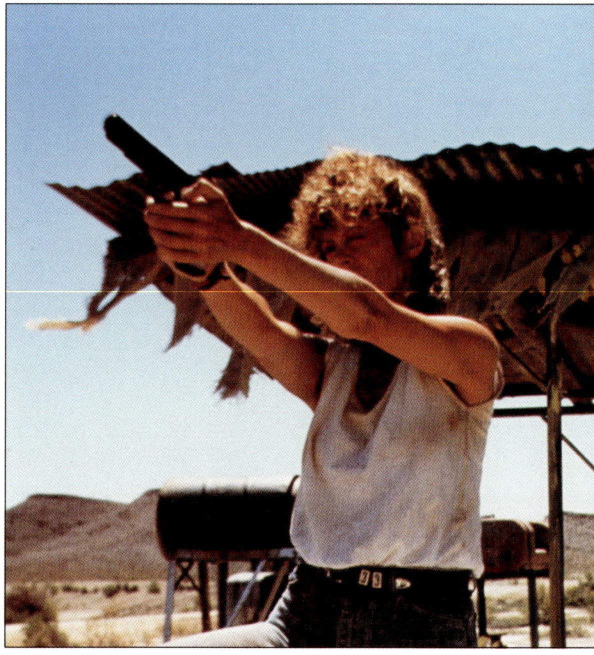

audiences. Leucadia Film Corporation is concentrating on high-quality independent films with a primary release on home video. Ian Cumming, chairman of Leucadia National, is the founder and David Anderson the head of Leucadia Film Corporation. *The Witching of Ben Wagner* (produced in conjunction with Disney Studios) was the first project Leucadia distributed. *Alan and Naomi* (1991), another early Leucadia production, won a number of national and international prizes, including a jury prize at Austria's Kinderfilmfest, the Gran Premio Città Bellinzona Silver at Italy's Festival Ragazzi Bellinzona, and Best Film at the French Festival International du Cinéma Jeune Public. By the end of 1993, Leucadia will have *The Good-bye Bird* in limited distribution, to be followed by *Windrunner* in 1994 (both films directed by William Clark).

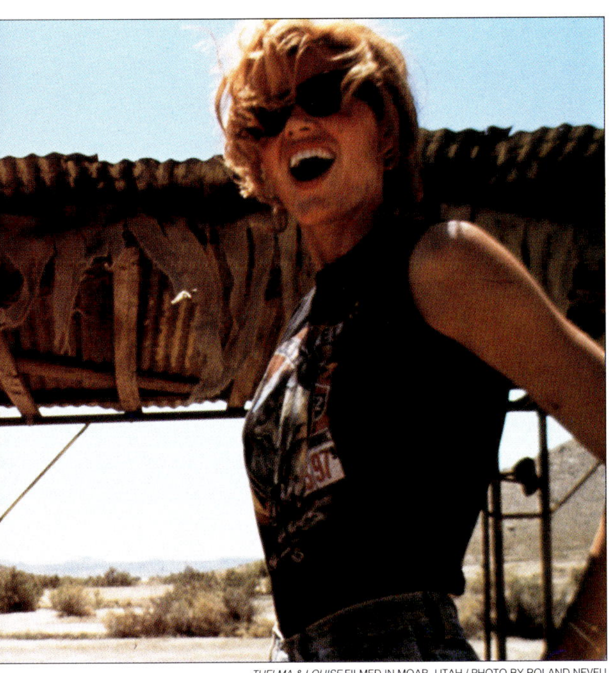

Feature Films for Families, headed by Forrest Baker, developed a tele-marketing network for mail-order sales of family films on video. The company now distributes twenty-six film titles, four of which it produced. The first project, *In Your Wildest Dreams* (1990), was directed by Bruce Neibaur. The second, *The Buttercream Gang* (1991), inspired copycat "gangs" of children who help people in their neighborhoods, as well as a 1993 sequel, *Secret of Treasure Mountain* (directed by Scott Swofford). *Split Infinity* was directed by Stan Ferguson, *Seasons of the Heart* by T. C. Christiansen, and *Rigoletto* by Leo Paur. With Pannonia Studios of Budapest, the company distributes the animated feature *Willy the Sparrow*, and a new film, *The Seventh Brother*, is in production.

Craig Clyde and Bryce Fillmore of Majestic Entertainment filmed and dis-tributed *Little Heroes* on a shoestring budget in 1991. Its success on cable and home video led to *The Legend of Wolf Mountain* (1992) with *Wind Dancer* following in 1993. The company formed a relationship with Sunset Hill Productions of New York City in 1992 and plans a fourth feature, *Walking Thunder*, in 1994.

Combinations of novel land-scapes, human drama, and high-tech cinematography/projection mark the work of another independent filmmaker with strong Utah ties. Writer/director/producer Kieth Merrill's first film was an Oscar-winning documentary, *The Great American Cowboy* (1974). He followed with other documentaries (*Wheels of Fire, Indian,* and *Matter of Winning*) and several feature films shot in Utah (*Windwalker, Harry's War, Take Down,* and *Three Warriors*). Merrill and partner Douglas Memmott developed "destination cinema," employing huge visual images (65 or 70mm) to create films of key vacation spots. Merrill's destination film projects include documentaries on such tourist attractions as the Alamo, the Grand Canyon, Niagara Falls and the Church of Jesus Christ of Latter-day Saints (LDS) Polynesian Cultural Center in Hawaii. Most recently, he completed *Legacy*, a large-format film on Mormon pioneers and is moving forward on controversial large-screen films for West Yellowstone and Zion Canyon.

VanWagenen directed the Emmy award-winning *Christmas Snows, Christmas Winds* for public television. In 1985 he produced the Academy award-winning feature film *The Trip to Bountiful*, written by Horton Foote. In 1988 he co-produced, with Redford, the documentary *Yosemite: The Fate of Heaven*. In 1989 he collaborated with Horton Foote in producing *Convicts*, starring Robert Duvall and James Earl Jones.

He is currently developing a remake of the French thriller *Eyes Without a Face* for Touchstone Pictures and *Ancestors*, a thirteen-part series for national public television. He is also an adjunct professor of film and creative director of the Media Arts Development Lab at BYU.

These two projects involve a key point of controversy. Tensions deepen and divide those who love Utah's landscapes. Some feel that the very process of recording and projecting the beauties of Utah's vistas may destroy them. Others believe this is a healthy way to strengthen the state economically and share its beauty. Debate over permits to shoot movies and television commercials on public lands reveals the tip of a huge iceberg of dispute about multiple use of Utah's diverse terrain.

The energy of film in Utah in the nineties is not restricted to production and distribution. Creativity and scholarship thrive at local universities and at the Utah Film and Video Center. Tom Sobchack was joined in the eighties by scholar/screenwriter Bill Siska and filmmaker/teacher Brian Patrick, and together they have created an interdisciplinary film program at the University of Utah which involves the departments of English and theater and the school of architecture. The program's graduates maintain a strong tradition of independent documentary/experimental filmmaking.

At Brigham Young University, the critical studies and filmmaking staff (including Dean Duncan, Tom Lefler, Charles Metten, David Scheerer and Sharon Swenson) is backed up by strong support from the nearby LDS Motion Picture Studio and the Communication Archives of the Harold B. Lee Library. The archives, directed by the encyclopedic James D'Arc, house original papers of diverse filmmaking personalities, including director Howard Hawks, composer Max Steiner and producer-director Cecil B. DeMille.

At the Utah Film and Video Center, housed adjacent to Abravanel Hall in the Salt Lake Art Center, Mary Cranney and Casey Williams support production by independent film and video artists and screen films for audiences interested in non-traditional viewing experiences.

An eclectic group of independent Utah filmmakers support themselves with other kinds of work while they pursue their art. These diversely talented film artists include Claudia Sisemore (noted for her documentaries on leading Utah artists such as Maurice Abravanel and Alvin Gittins), Steve Olpin (who earned the Heartland Film Festival's Crystal Heart for his 1992 documentary on Utah potter Joe Bennion), Casey Williams, Rhea Gavry, Russ Johnson, Verna Huiskamp, Kevin Hanson, Luis Ruiz, Anne Kocherhans, Kent Maxwell, Lorette Bayle, Kent Gumbert and Jan Andrews.

Filmmaking in Utah is as dramatically varied as our scenery. The state's culture and landscape have generated some of the most compelling—and some of the schlockiest—work ever seen on movie screens.

Technological developments and the nature of the people working in the medium promise that films shot here in the future will project realities only dreamed of now.

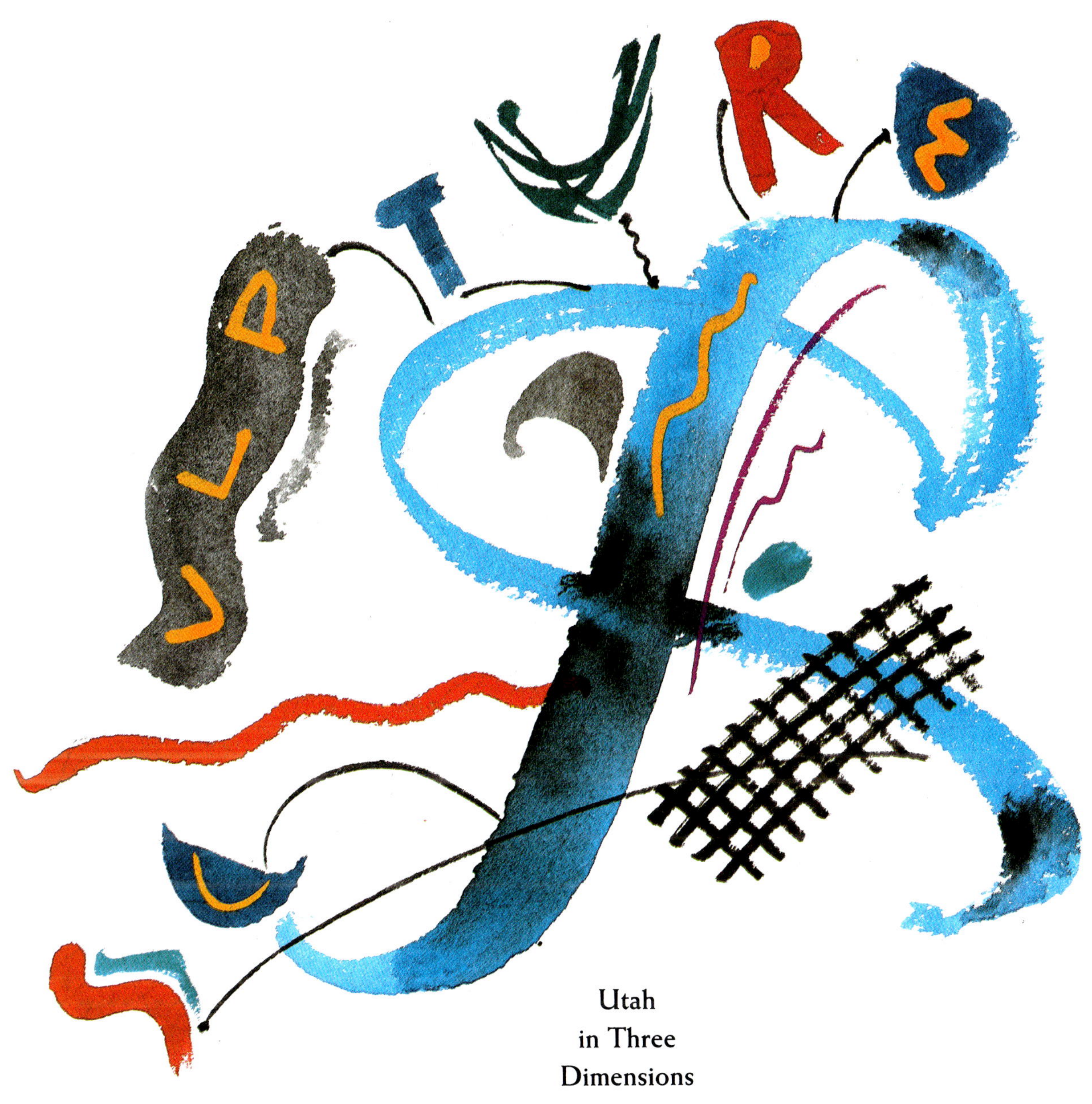

Utah
in Three
Dimensions

Steven W. Rosen

THE EARLIEST MANIFESTATIONS OF sculpture in Utah are small, hand-held effigy figures probably created as objects of worship or veneration by the prehistoric peoples of the southeastern part of the state. These objects, made of clay and decorated with geometric designs, date back nearly a thousand years. Their precise use and function are mysterious to us today, but as archaeologists and anthropologists continue to work, more light may be shed on these three-dimensional kachina ancestors. The kachina format of succeeding centuries is still followed,

JANET SHAPERO

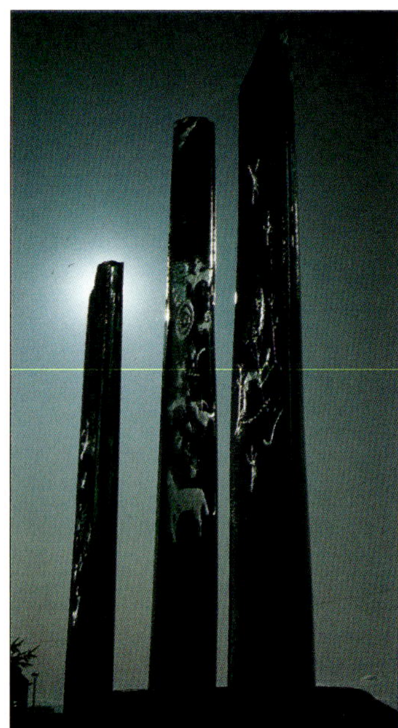

THE SEASONS OF OUR STORY BY JANET SHAPERO

Janet Shapero teaches sculpture at Utah State University. She spent a decade studying and working in Italy as a sculptor and before that had a career as a filmmaker. She began making figurative sculpture as a youngster in Boston. Her current sculpture is designed to relate to its surroundings and combines materials such as sandstone monoliths with glass, creating a structured contrast between man-made circumstances and the natural world. She was awarded a commission by the board of the Utah Arts Festival. She has exhibited her work in exhibitions in the United States and Italy.

most noticeably among the Hopi peoples of Northern Arizona. The trappers and early Anglo explorers carved bone and antler into toys and good-luck charms. Precious few survive, but they do provide evidence that sculptured objects were being made in the region.

Utah, then, has a thousand-year-long tradition of sculpture, and current work is being avidly collected by individuals, corporations and art museums around the world. The state boasts a great number of works located out-of-doors as well as in more formal settings such as museums, private homes and commercial buildings. Sculpture, perhaps more than other art objects, has a visual and tactile appeal that makes it readily accessible. A three-dimensional work in bronze, wood, clay, or metal can be walked around and examined from many points of view. Sculpture can look like an old friend or the neighbor down the street, or it can tease the eye with geometric shapes or contorted angles. It can be painted upon, shiny or dull, minuscule or massive in proportion. A work of sculpture can rely solely on manmade materials or incorporate "found objects" discovered in the world of nature or the salvage yard. It can be commemorative in nature or narrative in function, such as portraits, figures, or ornamentation on a headstone, a wall memorial, or a church façade.

With the entry of the Mormons in 1847, a firm foundation for the arts was established. But because church

members were busy building an agricultural society that took nearly all their effort, little time could be devoted to the visual arts. There is, however, a rich three-dimensional legacy in the pine furniture produced by craftsmen from Europe, who had entered the Salt Lake Valley as converts to the Church of Jesus Christ of Latter-day Saints (LDS). By the 1870's, church members were traveling throughout America and to Europe, bringing back ideas and concepts about painting and sculpture as well as the other visual arts.

Church authorities, including the patriarchal head, Brigham Young, encouraged members with artistic talent and sent artists to the East and to Europe to sharpen their skills and broaden their outlook. From 1900 onward, all the arts were flourishing in Utah, and sculpture took precedence as sculptors such as Cyrus E. Dallin (1861-1944); the Borglum brothers, Gutzon (1867-1941) and Solon (1868-1922); Mahonri McIntosh Young (1877-1957) and the younger Fairbanks brothers, J. Leo (1878-1946) and Avard (1897-1987) began to attain stature as truly American sculptors. Dallin, who had gone to Paris to study in 1888, is best known for his treatment of Native Americans who, through his hands, were sculpted with great respect and characterized as vibrant and dignified

FOLLOWING PAGE: *BLOCK 57 INTERIM LANDSCAPE IMPROVEMENTS GLASS BLOCK WALL* / PHOTO BY JAMES McBETH

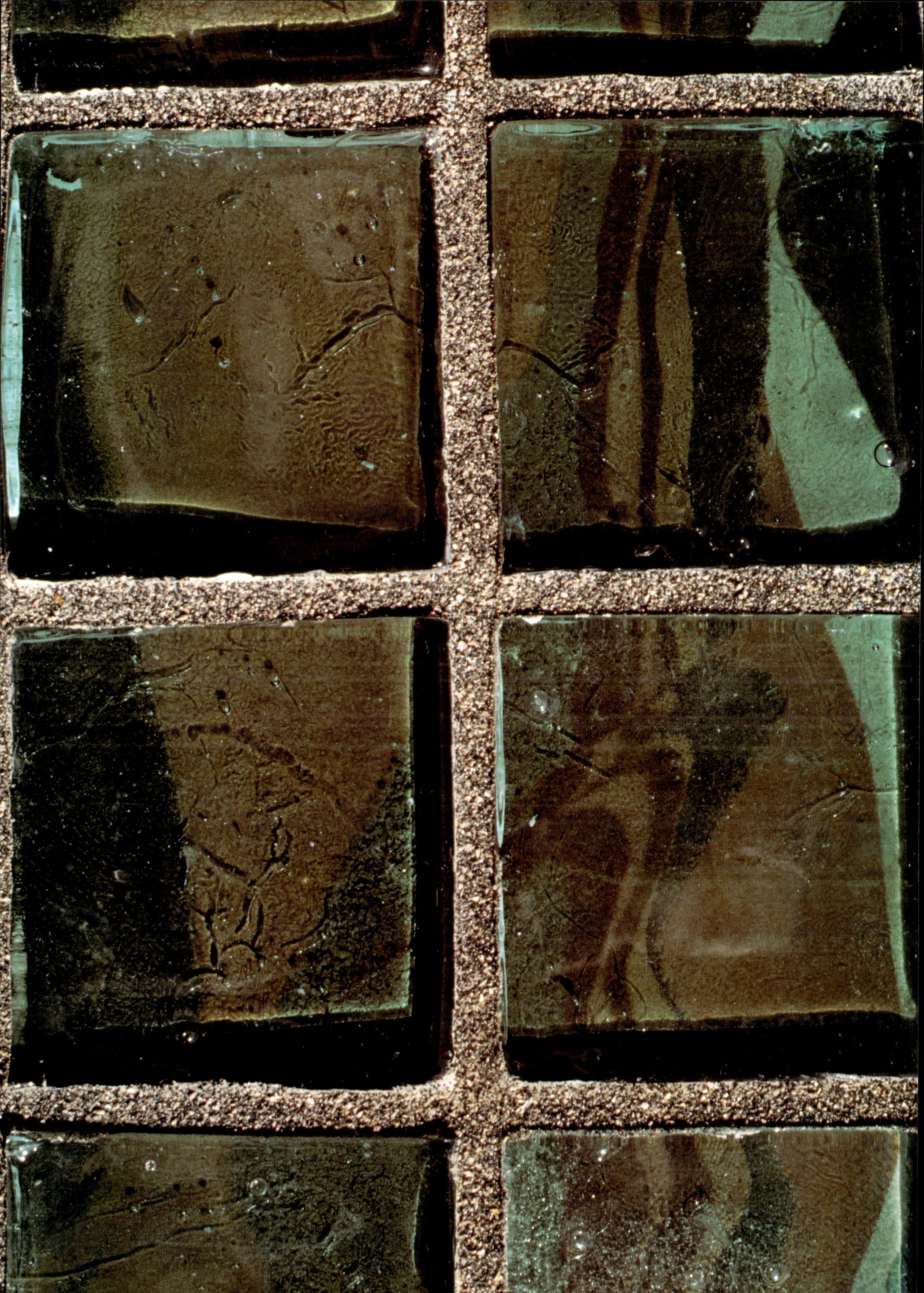

individuals. Additionally, he was the designer and a sculptor for the *Brigham Young Monument* at the intersections of Main and South Temple Streets. The Borglums each attained national status, with Gutzon receiving accolades for the *Mount Rushmore Monument* in the Black Hills of South Dakota, while Solon created realistic sculpture of humans and animals that, regardless of their size, brought to the viewer a real sense of activity.

Of the Utah Six, Young was to become the most widely acknowledged sculptor. His career saw the completion of major works, such as the *This Is the Place Monument* at the entry to Emigration Canyon and the *Seagull Monument* on Temple Square. He was an accomplished portrait sculptor and made a successful transition from realist to modernist.

In addition to their sculpture projects, the Fairbanks brothers distinguished themselves as teachers and academicians. Their collective works, found in many of the state's museums, rely on narrative prescriptions using traditional forms that represent the best and brightest among Utah's early sculptors.

Through the Depression and into the post-War period, innovative sculpture in the state tapered off, but large-scale ensembles such as the façade sculpture on the recently renovated Cathedral of the Madeleine by Maurice and Millard Brooks, the *Monument to the Handcart Pioneers* on Temple Square by Torleif Knaphus (1881-1985), as well as Young's *This Is the Place Monument*, continued to keep sculpture alive. By the mid-fifties, however, the visual conservatism of the earlier generation had begun to wear thin and a new generation of sculptors began to set sail. College and university art departments began to expand, and sculpture offerings across the state became more plentiful and varied. Angelo Caravaglia (University of Utah) and Larry Elsner (Utah State University) began to make objects that would help set the qualitative tone for sculpture for many years. Their contributions to the civic landscape, plazas and gardens led to the profusion of outdoor sculpture projects completed or in process around the state.

Caravaglia's sculpture brought modern and contemporary styles to the forefront. Trained in one of the nation's most innovative art schools, The Cranbrook Academy, he became a "three-dimensional designer" at the University of Utah in 1956. Even though he worked with traditional materials, he gained the enmity of Avard Fairbanks, continuing the eternal battle between traditional visual values and the pioneering innovative spirit. A decade after Caravaglia's arrival, sculptors in the state began to reflect his enthusiastically modern temperament and sculpture in Utah began the assault on convention.

Traditional visual values are being TRANSFORMED with pioneering spirit.

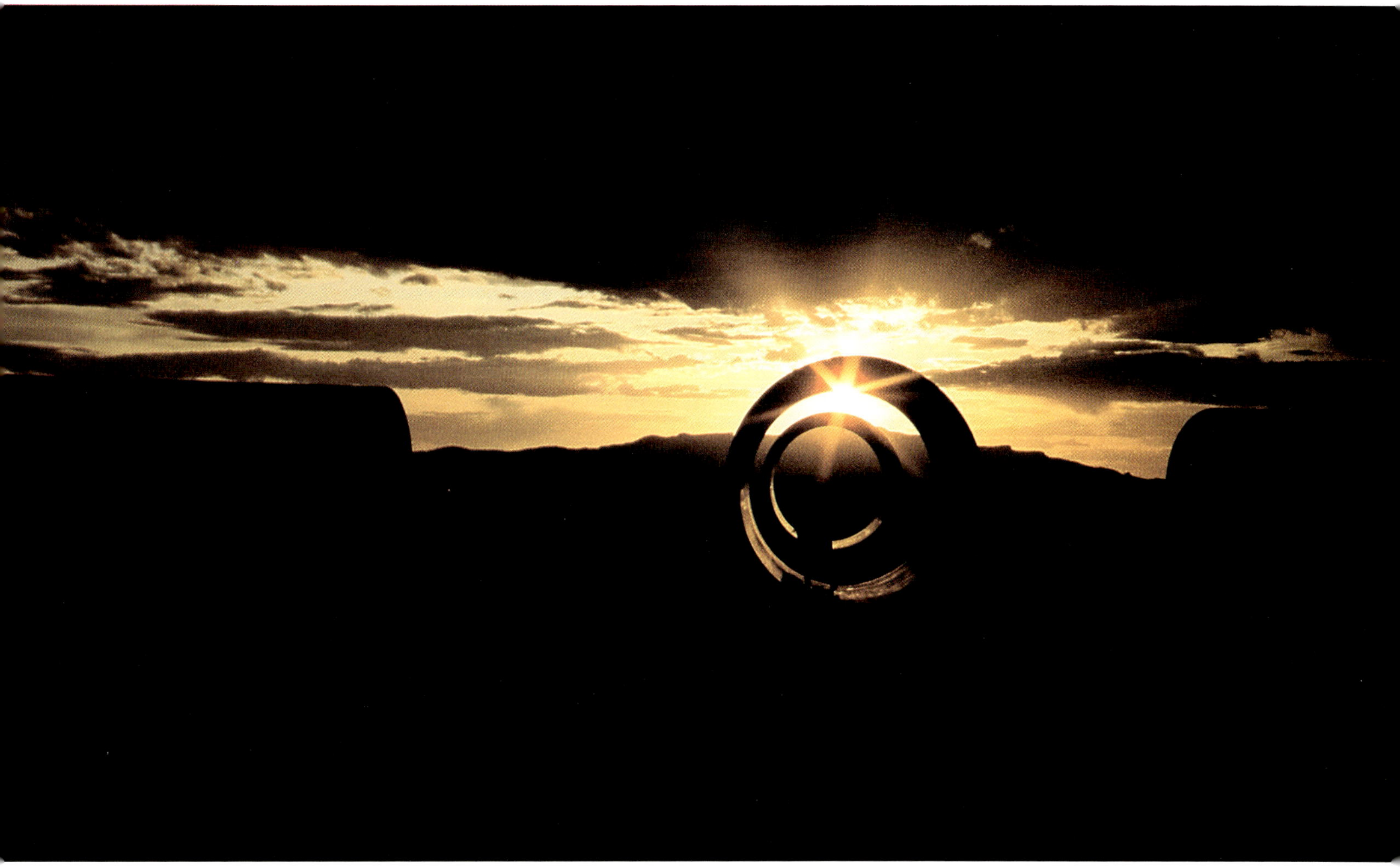

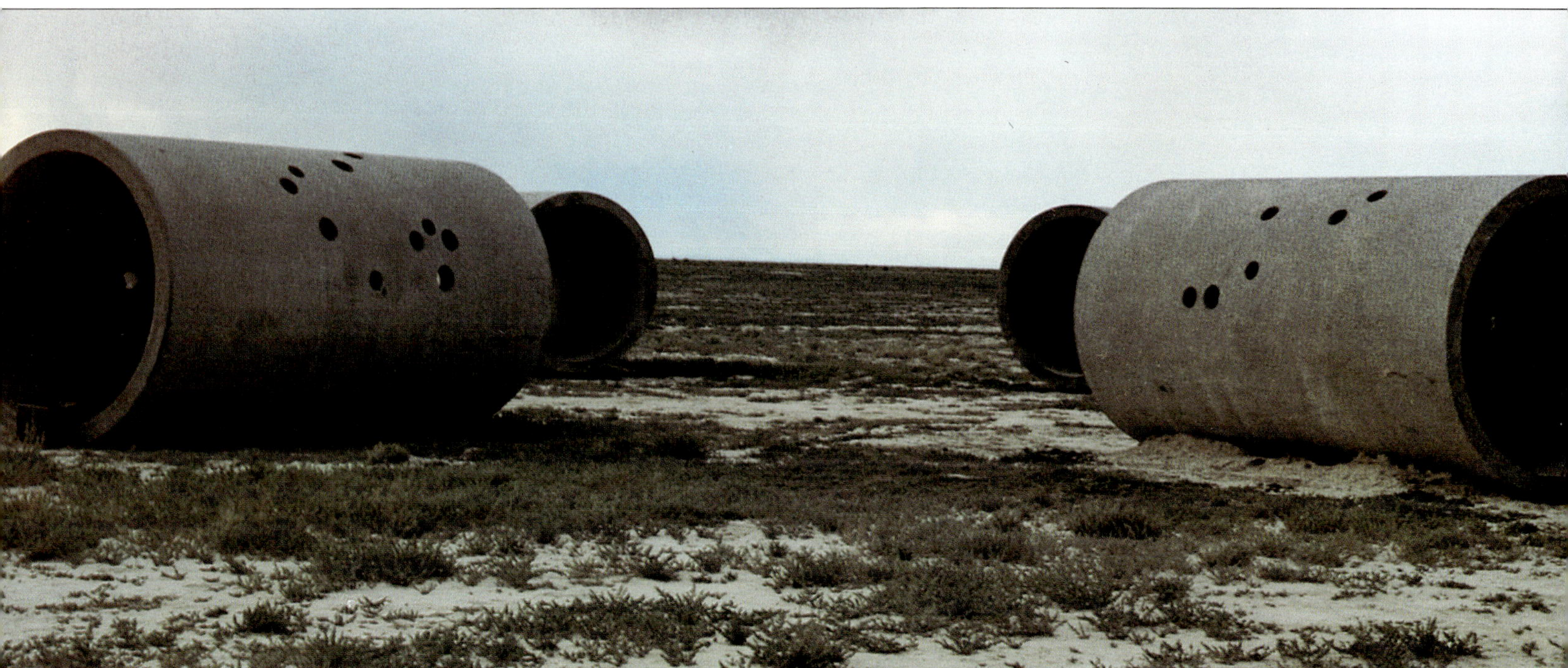

SUN TUNNELS SCULPTURE BY NANCY HOLT AT DESERT SITE NEAR LUCIN, UTAH / PHOTOS BY JANE MARTIN

Three sculptors of the next generation set out to blend old and
new ideas. Jim Young, educated
at Utah State University, began teaching at the College of Eastern Utah
(Price) and received commissions for
commemorative sculpture and portrai-
ture. His earliest three-dimensional
expressions were drawn from nature, but
he moved from naturalism to brightly
painted geometric shapes. James
McBeth completed his graduate work at
the University of Utah in 1965 and
began teaching at Weber State
University. His portrait and figurative
work relies on classical Greek and
Roman ideas and includes thematic concepts borrowed from ancient myths,
which in his hands are always energized
and active. In the 1970's McBeth began
to experiment with nontraditional materials such as Plexiglas to work through
his ideas, which convey a sense of tranquility. He has received numerous commissions for liturgical sculpture which
now adorn churches throughout the
area. Dennis Smith, educated at
Brigham Young University (BYU)
enjoys a reputation as a creator of

Outdoor

sculpture

is often

E N E R G I Z E D

and active.

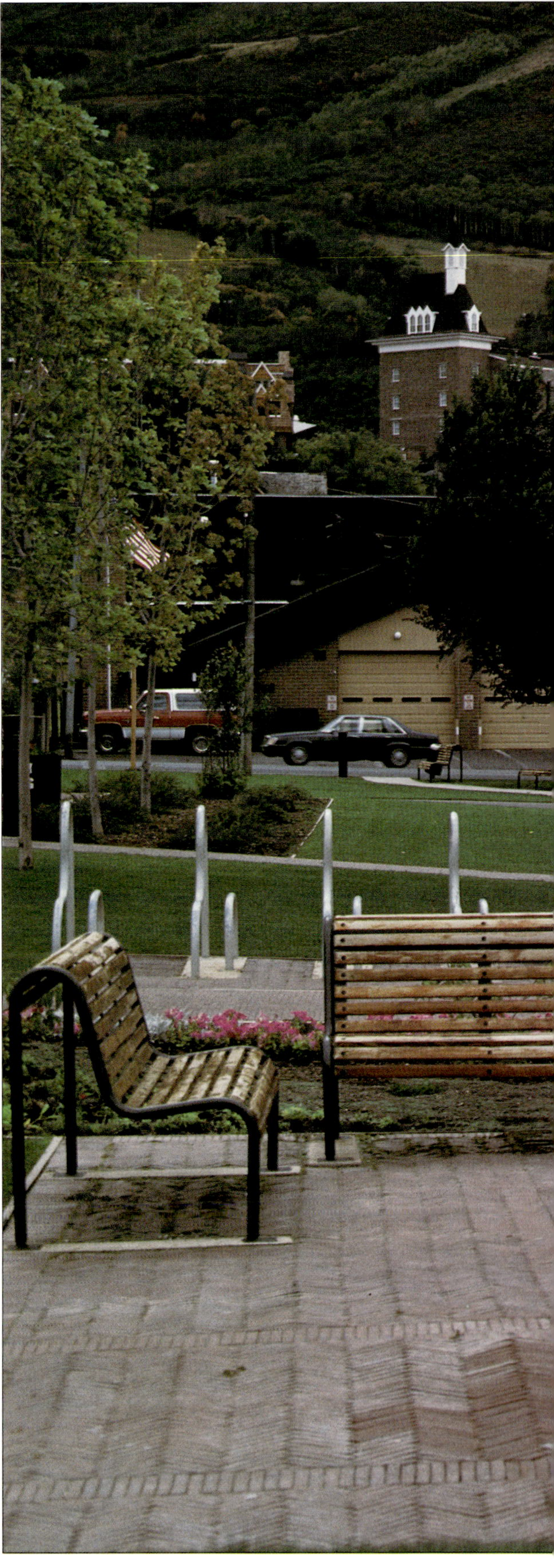

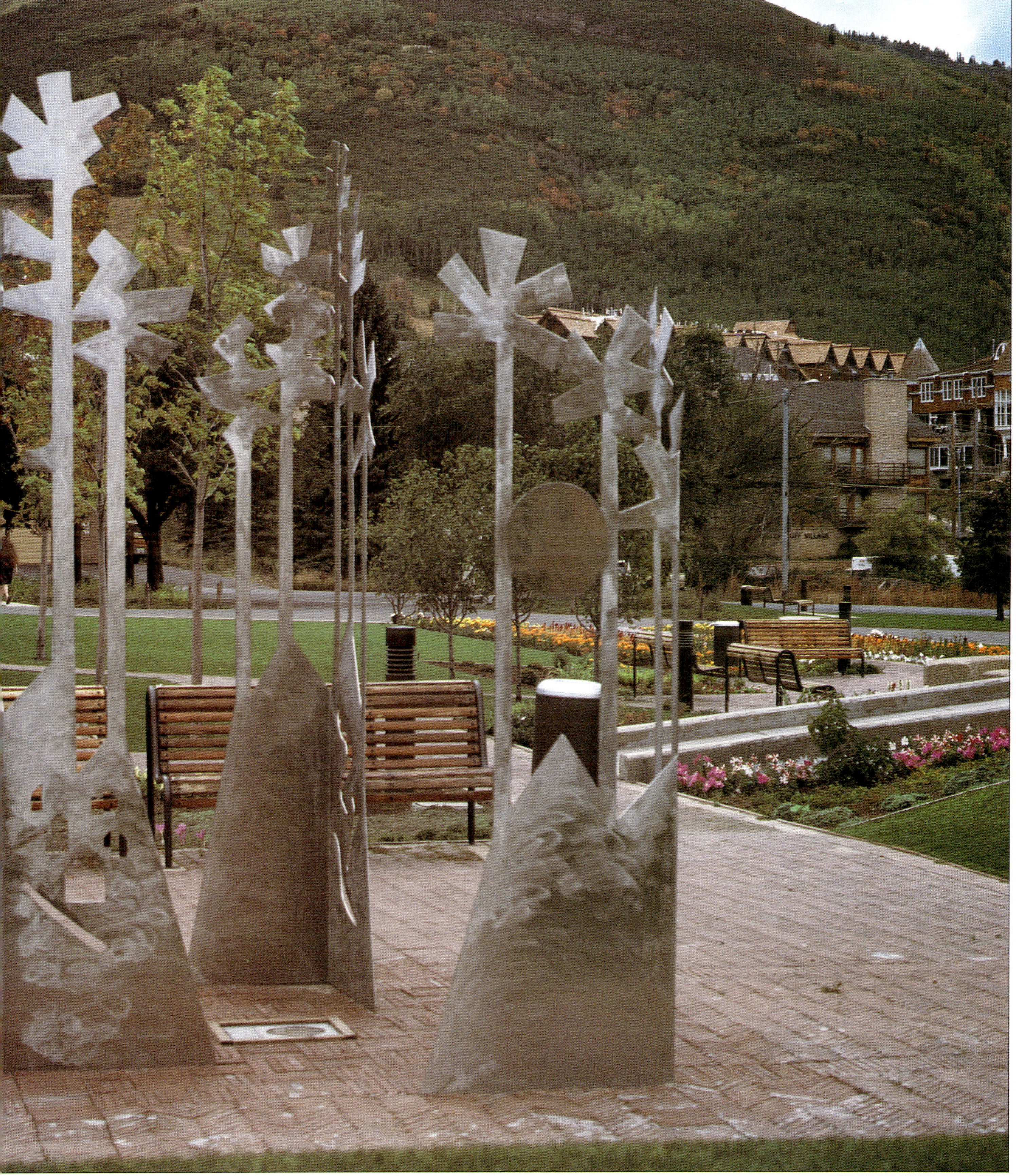

JAMES McBETH *PARK CITY SCAPE* IN STAINLESS STEEL

fanciful figures and machines constructed from metal sheets and rods. He has written a number of works for the LDS Church and has completed bronze sculptural ensembles in Salt Lake City and Provo.

The continuation of a figurative tradition, whether abstractly conceived, geometrically projected or as recognizable shapes, has always engaged Utah's sculptors. James Avati's figures with their controlled emotional content and impressionistic sensibility are visually engaging and thought-provoking. Life sculptors such as Jerry Anderson, John B. Mortenson, Clark Bronson, Clayton Robbins and Edward Fraughton have achieved considerable status, having successfully captured classical Western themes in metal and stone. The proud Indian, the lone horseman and the iconic cowboy come to life at the hands of those committed to visually preserving America's Western spirit. Blair Buswell has sought a wider venue for his figurative productions by casting portraits of sports figures such as Bear Bryant and O. J. Simpson. Finally Ursula Brodauf Craig creates highly stylized full-length figures in wood and metal that are provocative in their deliberate lack of detail.

The last quarter of the twentieth century—with its vast social dissonance, shifting demographics and narcissistic entrenchment—has produced a veritable explosion of sculpture. And not only do sculptors seek new and different ways to define space, they have themselves also become participants in the creation of three-dimensional form through dance and theater performance. Sculpture has moved from the pedestal and the commemorative marker to objects in virtually every known substance, and the sculptor is often thought of as the architect, landscape designer and construction engineer all in one package.

The new sculptors have gained acknowledgment through public exposure of their work. Since Angelo Caravaglia's Federal Plaza sculpture was dedicated in 1965, dozens of works are to be found in myriad settings throughout Utah which, incidentally, leads the region in the number of sites occupied by sculpture. Each artist seems to compose his or her own "ism" and abstract, geometric, assembled expressive and conceptual pieces assail our senses.

There is a rich
three-dimensional
L   E   G   A   C   Y
in Utah.

Figurative
traditions have
E   N   G   A   G   E   D
Utah's sculptors.

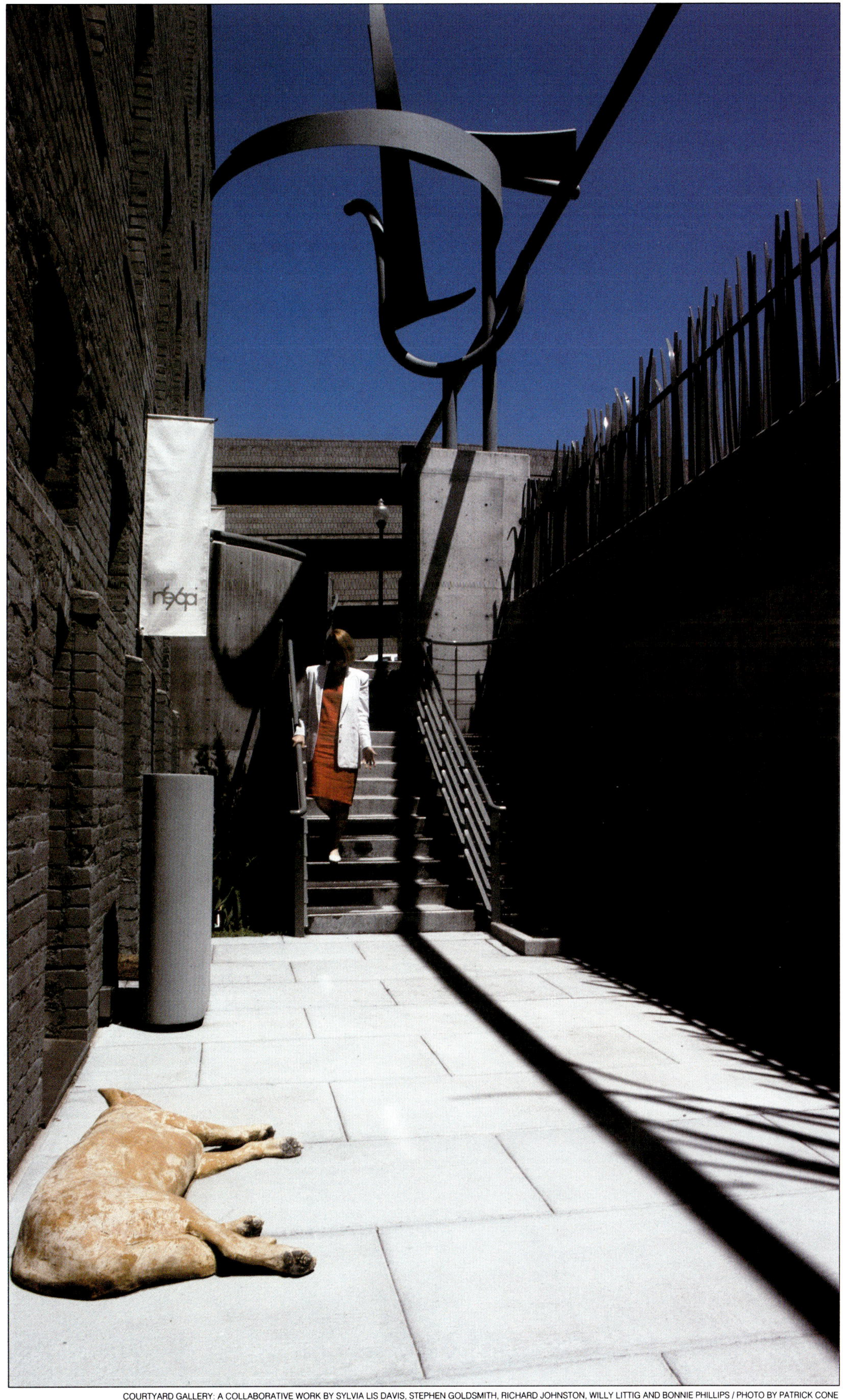

COURTYARD GALLERY: A COLLABORATIVE WORK BY SYLVIA LIS DAVIS, STEPHEN GOLDSMITH, RICHARD JOHNSTON, WILLY LITTIG AND BONNIE PHILLIPS / PHOTO BY PATRICK CONE

W. NEIL HADLOCK

W. Neil Hadlock has worked in bronze, steel and aluminum. He was a founding member of the North Mountain Artists Cooperative in Alpine, Utah, and currently serves as chair of the Department of Sculpture at Brigham Young University. The rationality and studied orderings of his geometric forms have given way to a more lyrical transformation of content and expression. Works by Hadlock can be seen at the Delta Center in Salt Lake City and on the campus of Brigham Young University, as well as in museum and private collections statewide.

STEPHEN GOLDSMITH

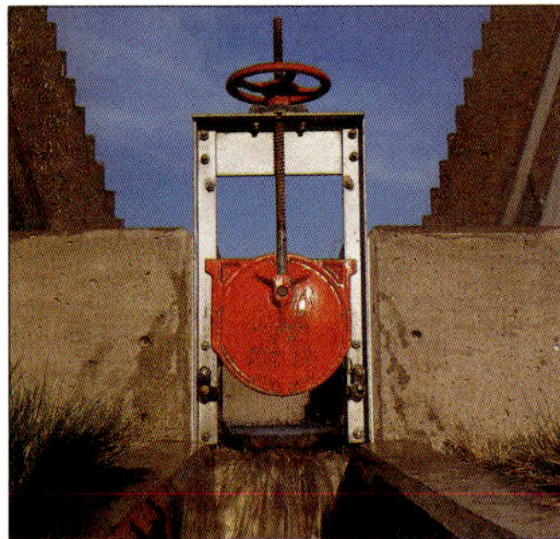

DETAIL OF *HEAD GATES* SALT LAKE CITY COMMUNITY COLLEGE CAMPUS / PHOTO BY ANDRÉ RAMJOUÉ

Stephen Goldsmith has received an array of commissioned projects, including the stone and water sculpture at the entrance to the Primary Children's Medical Center and the concrete watercourse project at the eastside entrance of the Salt Lake Community College on State Street near 1700 South. In addition to work in private collections, Goldsmith's sculpture is exhibited extensively in galleries and art centers as part of one-person and group shows. He currently holds the position of Founding Executive Director for Artspace, an innovative studio and housing project for artists and craftspeople. In 1992 he was named Salt Lake Artist of the Year.

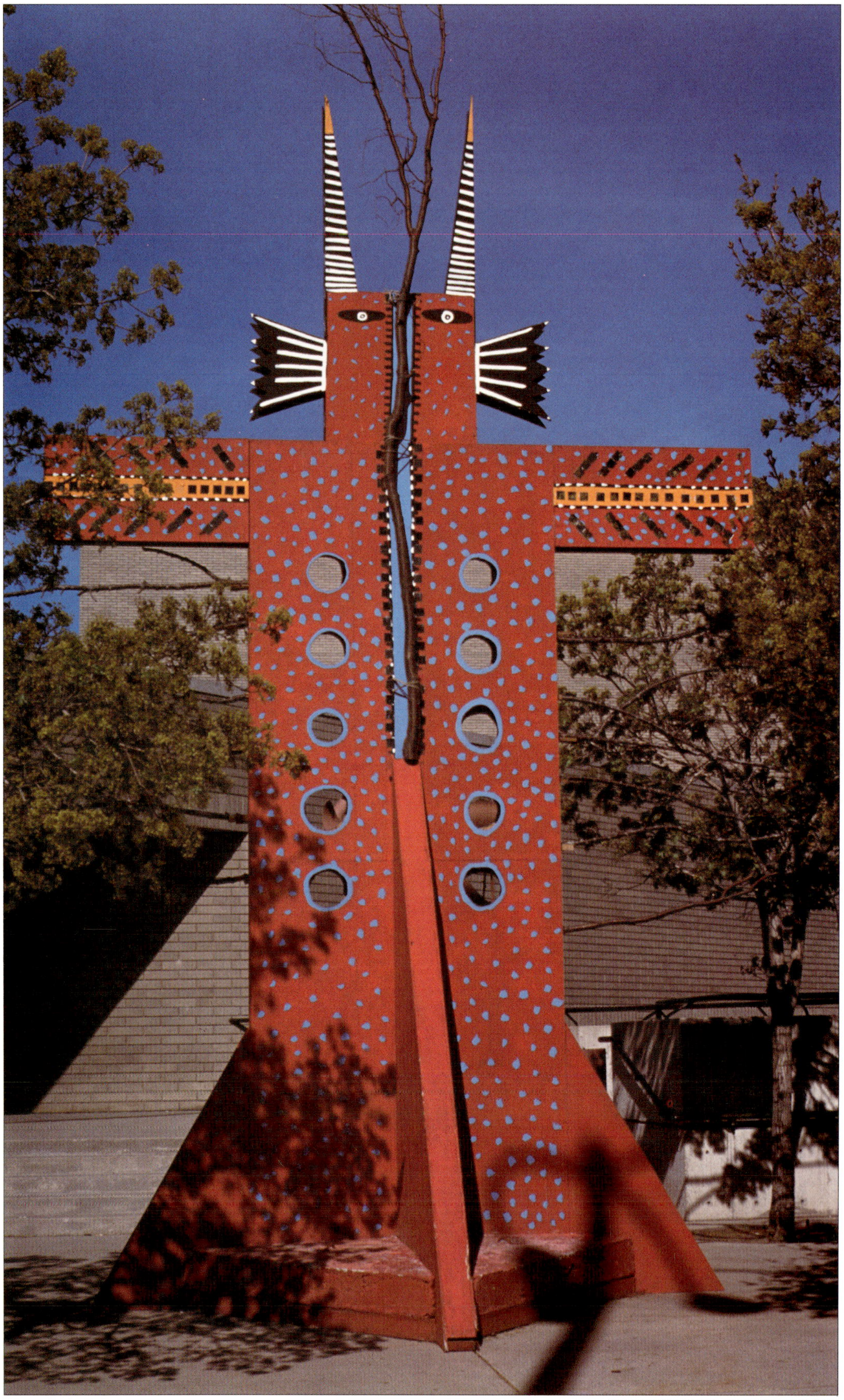

BONNIE SUCEC'S *MYTHICAL FIGURE*, ACRYLIC ON WOOD

Sculptors who have a history of relating abstract form to a surrounding space include Von Allen, who teaches at Brigham Young University, and Michael Hullet and Richard Johnston, who, after teaching at the University of Utah, moved to California. Each has received numerous commissions for works in all media. Allen was recently commissioned to create a sixteen-foot-high ceramic piece for the plaza of the new art museum at BYU. Hullet is best known for brightly colored, large-scale surrealistic images that convey a sense of fantasy and whimsy. Johnston incorporates mechanical traditions and elusive shapes into his works which float in space despite their monumentality.

Geometric works of art continue to hold our interest. Crisply designed spaces produced by Italian Renaissance painters and symmetrical full-length sculptures by their colleagues drew legions of admirers even in their own time. Geometric decoration and the horizontal and vertical lines of architecture have entranced populations with their orderliness and appeal to rationality. Likewise, sculptors who manipulate geometric shapes seek to order the world around them. Frank Nokas combines like geometric forms into ascending composite monuments that with their painted surfaces intrude on the landscape and contrast vividly with the cityscape in which they are found. Frank Riggs has consistently worked in a large scale, using aluminum sheets folded into a variety of shapes that echo Utah's landscape.

David Adams also works in a geometric tradition with his multi-pastel-colored free-standing groups of triangles and pieces that attach to walls, enlivening otherwise drab surfaces. W. Neil Hadlock, who currently teaches at BYU, is another whose work has undergone various transformations, including a passage from square and rectangular shapes fabricated from weathering steel to highly polished curvilinear pieces that, with their brightly painted surfaces, help to define the space they occupy. Hadlock's more recent works combine the hardness of geometry with the curvilinear grace of fragmentary figures.

Sculptors continually seek new expressive modes in which their ideas may find a comfortable home. Imitation and reinterpretation of the figure and the landscape have provided pathways for the sculptor and the conceptual artist to follow. These same paths have opened up to broad vistas that incorporate modes of perception, psychology and social responsibilities that have become important subject-matter concerns.

Day Christensen represents a strain of conceptual thinking that transcribes and modifies objects from the natural world by taking them from their original setting and rearranging them in a new

> Surrealistic images convey a sense of
>
> F A N T A S Y and
> W H I M S Y .

location, thereby promoting a contextual change. David Holz likewise manipulates materials to alter the observer's perception of a natural setting by intrusively interjecting objects into unlikely sites. Frank McEntire works from the point of view of an assemblage artist who blends and creates images from found objects that, more often than not, carry ecumenical religious messages. With each—Christensen, Holz and McEntire—the object conveys a circumstance that may be either readily apparent or entirely internalized and artist-centered.

Stephen Goldsmith and Janet Shapero come to their conceptualized approaches from literature and a real concern for the world around them. Shapero, who was trained as a carver, has sought expression of her thinking by using mesh screens and glass that act as foils or masks to a world that is easily seen but not entirely penetrable or understood. Goldsmith, conversely, embraces the world around him and delights in creating sculpture that enhances and delimits its surroundings.

As Utah approaches its centennial of statehood, the development of the world's sculpture can be traced from prehistory to yesterday through the hands of Utah's sculptors. For modern times, the last three generations have produced a veritable history book of American sculpture that evokes the mood and temperament of the time in which it was created. Joining with "Utah's own" have been sculptors Robert Smithson (*Spiral Jetty*, 1970) and Nancy Holt (*Sun Tunnels*, 1973-76). Their respective works, sited in the isolation and quietude at the edge of the Great Basin, continue to be an inspiration for the state's artists.

Utah enjoys the luxury of a highly motivated population, a constituency that avidly supports serious artistic endeavors and a commitment to the three-dimensional ideas that have proliferated in the state's parks and plazas. Credit for our vast visual wealth belongs to the universities and colleges that provide a Renaissance-like relationship of patron and artist and to the state's public and private corporations that have subsidized sculpture programs.

The Utah Arts Council has been a leader in helping to secure funds for outdoor sculpture, and the state has realized a proliferation of projects, including sculpture created under the sponsorship of a 1% for Arts Program that has seen to the placement of work in state buildings and on university campuses. Likewise, Salt Lake City's Arts Council has promoted the introduction of sculpture into the urban environment and, aided by many of the state's corporations and foundations, has provided a comfortable and enthusiastic home for the sculptor. Across the state, other centers have also contributed to the visual litany of sculpture, making Utah's bounty much more than a series of commemorative markers.

The object
C O N V E Y S
a circumstance.

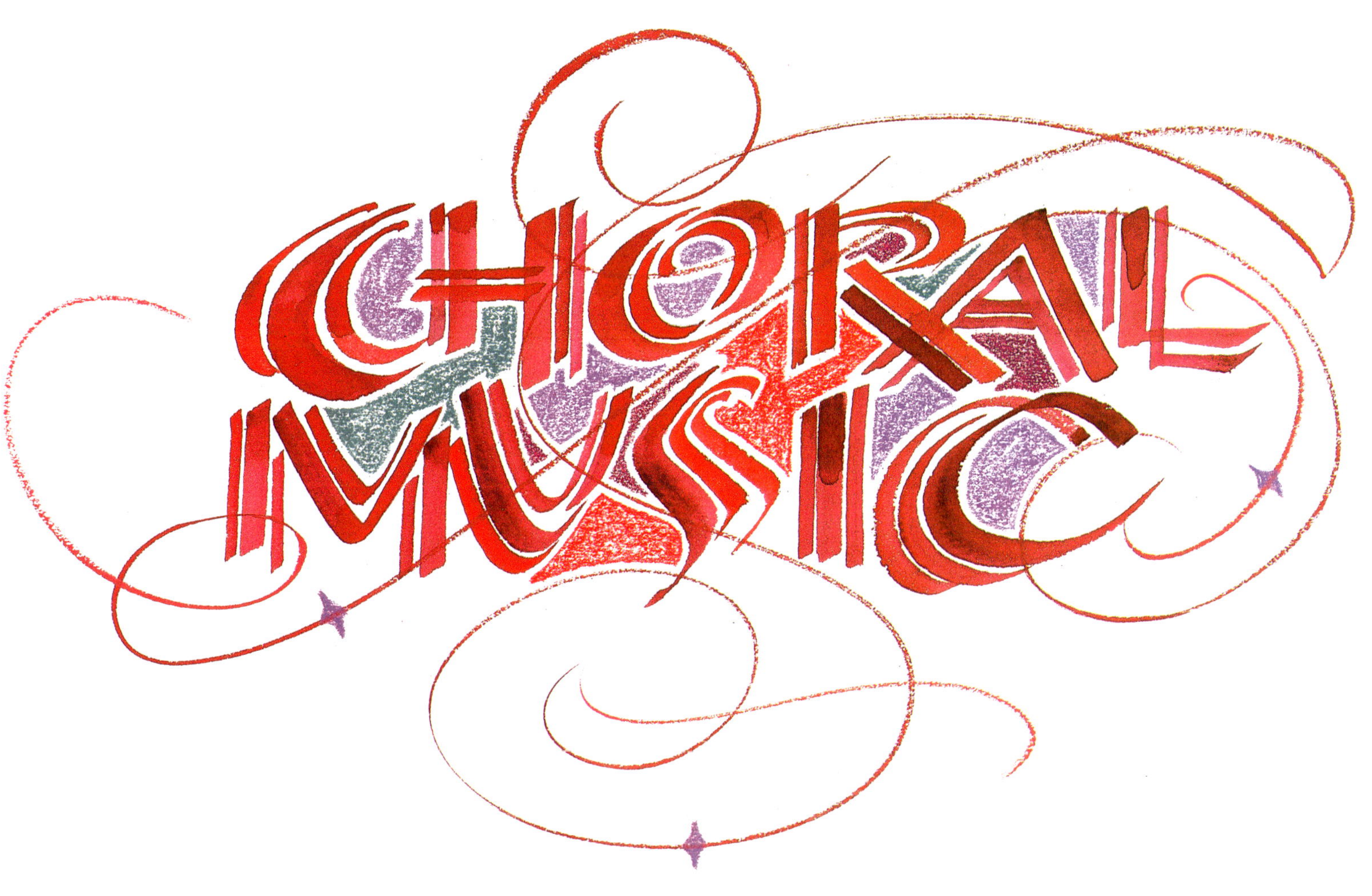

Break Forth

Into

Song

Edgar J. Thompson

"Let the Valley Sing . . ."
from "Let the Mountains Shout for Joy," an
anthem by Utah composer Evan Stephens.

ON A BRISK WINTER EVENING in late November, Salt Lake City's magnificent Abravanel Hall is filled to overflowing with an audience unlike any other. Young and old, families, friends, sweethearts, members of church, community and

NEWELL B. WEIGHT

Newell B. Weight received B.A. and M.A. degrees from Brigham Young University and the D.M.A. degree from the University of Southern California. In addition to teaching in the public schools, he taught for twelve years at Brigham Young University, where he founded and conducted the A Cappella Choir.

In 1962 Dr. Weight joined the University of Utah faculty, where he established the University of Utah A Cappella Choir and raised that ensemble to an exceptional level of virtuosity, creating an oft-imitated style of choral performance.

Dr. Weight's influence in the field of unaccompanied singing has been far-reaching as his numerous students have themselves become outstanding practitioners of the choral art. Dr. Weight became music director of the Utah Chorale, the forerunner of the Utah Symphony Chorus, in 1975, holding that post until 1982. He retired from the University of Utah in 1984.

school choirs—singers of all kinds and from all walks of life—have come this evening to celebrate a Salt Lake City musical tradition. Tonight they are not just an audience, but part of a mighty chorus, joining their voices with the Utah Symphony Chorus, Orchestra and soloists in the annual *Messiah* Sing-In heralding the beginning of the music-filled holiday season.

Some three weeks later in the historic Mormon Tabernacle, the Oratorio Society of Utah presents its annual performance of the same great musical work, *Messiah*, renewing a tradition dating back to 1915.

Between these two signal events, Salt Lake City and the entire state are witness to a kaleidoscopic procession of musical events, ranging from concerts by the famed Mormon Tabernacle Choir and other community choirs to university, high school, junior high, church and cathedral choirs. All these are latter-day symbols of the rich tradition of choral singing that has been a part of Utah since the settling of the valley of the Great Salt Lake.

> *"Let them all break forth into song . . . "*
> —Evan Stephens, Let the Mountains Shout for Joy

Singing, the most fundamental of all musical acts, figures importantly in the lore of all civilizations, real or imagined. Biblical accounts abound with human and heavenly choirs; and in the

Silmarillion, J. R.R. Tolkien's gods literally sing the universe into existence. Since unrecorded time, song has guided, inspired and comforted humankind. Perhaps, then, it is only natural that in a society which would find refuge in the harsh Western wilderness, having endured unimaginable hardships and tragedy, this most uniquely human of expressions would find fertile soil and flourish. And so it has—the valley has truly "broken forth into song."

Just what accounts for the popularity of choral singing? While a symphony orchestra is limited by the skill of its weakest player, under a skilled leader a chorus can become greater than the sum of its individual parts. Singers with quite ordinary vocal skills can blend together to produce a choral sound of extreme loveliness and develop into an ensemble of uncommon virtuosity and artistry.

Another factor is the repertoire itself—a vast and varied literature with more than four hundred years of tradition. Choruses are often categorized according to the type of literature they perform, which may range from large choral/orchestral works to unaccompanied Renaissance motets, from sacred music to Broadway, jazz, or barbershop tunes.

Finally, choral singing is a social act which draws people together.

Friendships formed between choral singers are often lifelong, and many married couples have met their spouses while singing in choirs. Indeed, the associations among people in a chorus engaged in the deeply affecting experience of making music are an integral part of the *choral experience*, and the sense of loyalty and devotion which chorus members develop toward "their choir" is seldom fully understood by those who have never experienced or shared in it.

The Wellspring
"Come, come ye Saints, no toil nor labor fear . . . "

—William Clayton, Mormon pioneer hymn

Accounts of the trek across the Plains and the early settling of the Salt Lake Valley speak of the importance of music, singing and dancing to the morale of the Mormon pioneers. Hardly had they settled into the task of building their Zion than they turned their attention to the matter of recreation and culture. With the active encouragement of Brigham Young, the Social Hall and Salt Lake Theatre were constructed and the cultural foundations of the community established.

On August 22, 1847, the choir that would become the Mormon Tabernacle Choir sang at the first General Conference of the Church of Jesus Christ of Later-day Saints (LDS) held in Utah. Since that time, the choir has grown steadily in stature as well as function and is today a model for numerous other choirs in the way it must serve so many different musical constituencies.

While the Tabernacle Choir may be seen as a large and expert church choir whose role is to provide musical inspiration for its congregation, it also maintains a continually growing international reputation. Fame began with the choir winning second prize at the 1893 Chicago World's Fair, followed by the establishment of a national broadcasting tradition in 1929. It captured the prestigious Grammy award in 1959, and continues today through local concerts such as the Tanner Gift of Music with the Utah Symphony, numerous recordings, and frequent worldwide concert tours. Thus, in addition to ecclesiastical duties, the choir must maintain credibility in the professional music world as well, a role requiring proficiency in the entire gamut of choral literature, both sacred and secular.

The Community Chorus in Utah
" . . . a permanent oratorio society is worthy of every consideration."

—The Salt Lake Tribune, May 17, 1914

Many of the Mormon pioneers came from the British Isles, bringing with them a strong tradition of choral singing. Historians have noted that the new community loved dancing, the theater and music of all kinds, and as early as 1855 the Deseret Musical Society

SALT LAKE SYMPHONIC CHOIR

The Salt Lake Symphonic Choir was formed in 1949 by a group of graduating students from South High School who had found great pride in singing in the school's a cappella choir and wanted to continue their singing experience. Thus began one of the state's most successful and long-lived choruses. Under their founder Armont Willardsen and, since 1975, George Welch, the eighty-voice choir has expanded its local reputation and gained international recognition through its numerous concert tours. The Symphonic Choir is under professional concert management and is today the largest independent touring choir in America. Since its founding, the choir has toured biennially throughout the United States, Canada and Mexico.

advertised to prospective émigrés in England that they were "much in want of Oratorios of Handel, Haydn, Mendelssohn, &c.; the Masses of Mozart, Haydn, Beethoven &c., and new works of merit . . ."

The modern era of Salt Lake City's musical life essentially began in 1869 with the appointment of George Careless, a recent émigré from England, as director of the Tabernacle Choir and the Salt Lake Theatre Orchestra. A graduate of the prestigious Royal Academy of Music in London, Careless enjoyed a long and distinguished career in the Salt Lake Valley as a conductor and music educator, marked with distinction not only by service to his church but also by his numerous programs for the community at large. In 1875 his Philharmonic Society orchestra and Handel and Haydn Society chorus presented the first performance of Handel's *Messiah* between Chicago and San Francisco.

After Careless, the most influential musician on the scene was Evan Stephens, who, as organizer, conductor, composer, music educator and, later, conductor of the Tabernacle Choir, had a profound effect on the musical life of the entire state. Stephens had earned a reputation as an organizer and conductor of concerts with children's choirs in Logan and Salt Lake and organized the Salt Lake Choral Society for presentation of a grand festival in the Salt Lake Mormon Tabernacle.

The two main requirements of this organization, which drew its membership from all faiths, was "no discussion of politics and no talking about religion." Among other offerings, the society presented Haydn's *The Creation* in 1893, but disbanded soon afterward, partly because the concert audience in Salt Lake City seemed more interested in light opera than in oratorio. In the intervening years, singing societies in Utah have come and gone, but many, including those listed below, have endured and become major factors in the musical life of the state.

The Oratorio Society of Utah (Morris Lee, conductor), the oldest continuing musical organization in Utah outside the Tabernacle Choir, was founded in 1915 by Squire Coop, who had been a professor of music at the University of Utah. The Utah Symphony Chorus (Ed Thompson, conductor) is descended from the University of Utah combined choirs, and the Salt Lake Symphonic Choir (George Welch, conductor) was founded in 1949 by South High School choral educator Armont Willardsen. The chamber choir Pro-Musica (Bryce Rytting, conductor) was formed by former University of Utah professor John Marlowe Nielson, who also figured prominently in the histories of both the Oratorio Society of Utah and Utah Symphony Chorus.

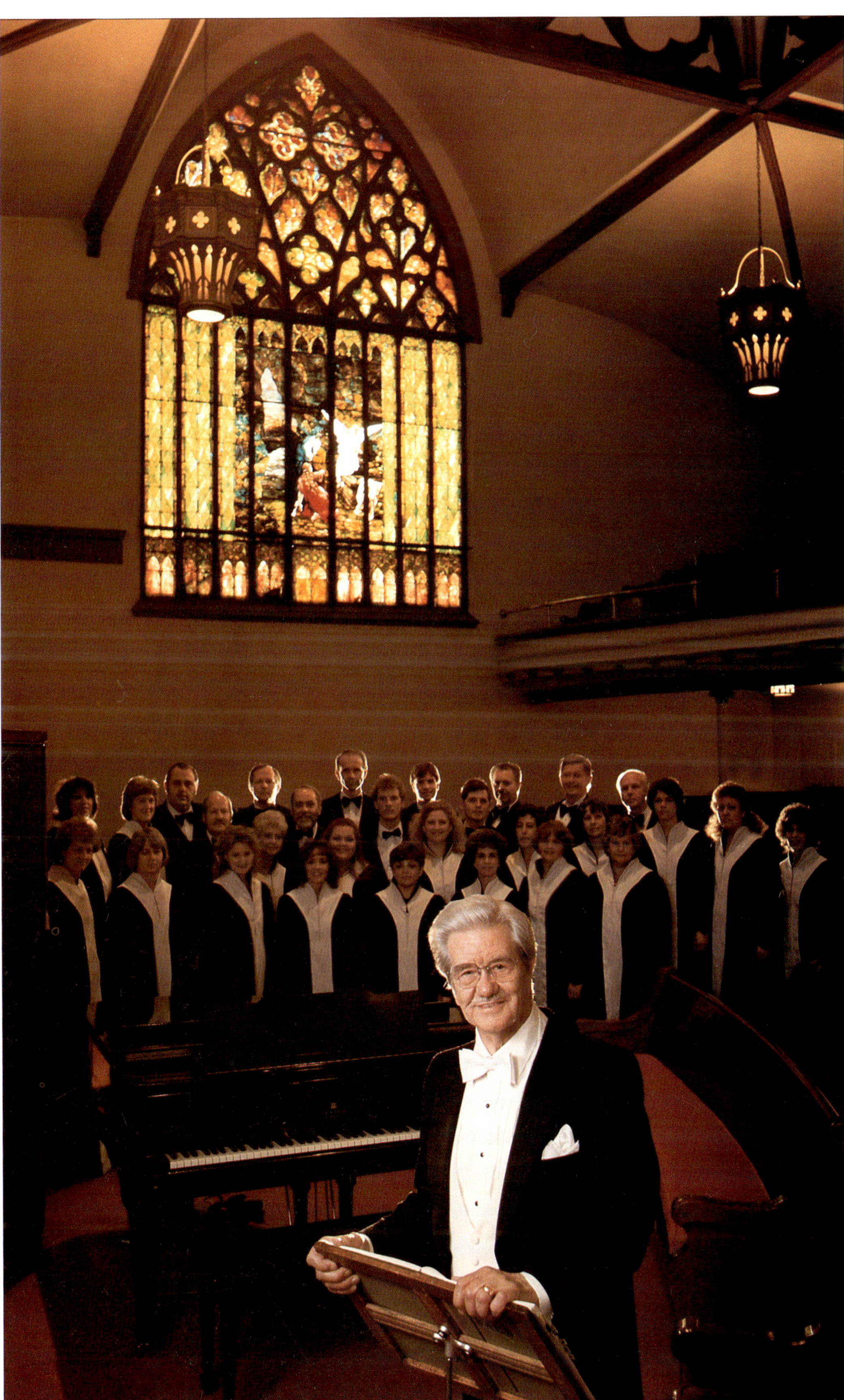

PHOTO BY DON BUSATH

JOHN MARLOWE NIELSON

John Marlowe Nielson has been, in a word, ubiquitous. Few people have been so deeply involved and contributed so much to the vocal and choral activity of any community.

Having attended the Juilliard School of Music and Columbia Teachers College in New York City, Nielson served on the U of U faculty for thirty-one years, as a vocal instructor and choir director. He directed the University Men's Chorus from 1941 to 1973 and in 1950 founded the University Civic Chorale, which later became the Utah Symphony Chorus. He served as director or co-director until 1973. In 1976 Nielson founded and is the permanent conductor of the Pro-Musica choir specializing in literature especially suited for a small virtuoso ensemble.

In 1961 Nielson was appointed Music Director of the Oratorio Society of Utah, a post he held until 1987. During his tenure with the society, he trained the choir for its traditional presentations of *Messiah*, and conducted the ensemble on tours to Israel in 1983 and 1987.

In May 1984, Nielson received the Honors in the Arts award of the Salt Lake Chamber of Commerce.

Brigham Young University (BYU) professor Ralph Woodward founded the Valley Chorale, now known as the Ralph Woodward Chorale; and in Utah County, the Utah Valley Choral Society (Lois Johnson, conductor) was formed in 1974 by BYU professor Jacob Bos. In Ephraim, Snow College professor Harry Dean established a tradition, now in its sixty-fifth year, which brought together community and college choirs to form the Snow College Community Choir and Orchestra (Judy Morgan, conductor).

Ogden has been host to several oratorio choruses and directors, including the Ogden Chorale (Edward Sandgren),

Ralph Woodward was the first recipient of the Doctor of Musical Arts degree in choral music to be awarded by the University of Illinois. He taught music at Drake University in Des Moines, Iowa, and at BYU for some twenty-nine years, serving primarily as director of choral activities and conductor of the A Cappella Choir.

Choirs under his direction have been featured in many national and international music conventions and festivals winning honors, including first place in the International Eisteddfod in Wales and the International Choral Festival in Spittal, Austria. Dr. Woodward has received many professional honors, including the Karl G. Maeser Excellence in Teaching and Distinguished Teaching Awards from BYU, the Utah Music Educator of the Year Award, the Utah County Arts Council Award, and the State of Utah Total Citizen Award. He is the founder and conductor of the Valley Chorale, renamed the Ralph Woodward Chorale. Dr. Woodward retired from BYU in 1985.

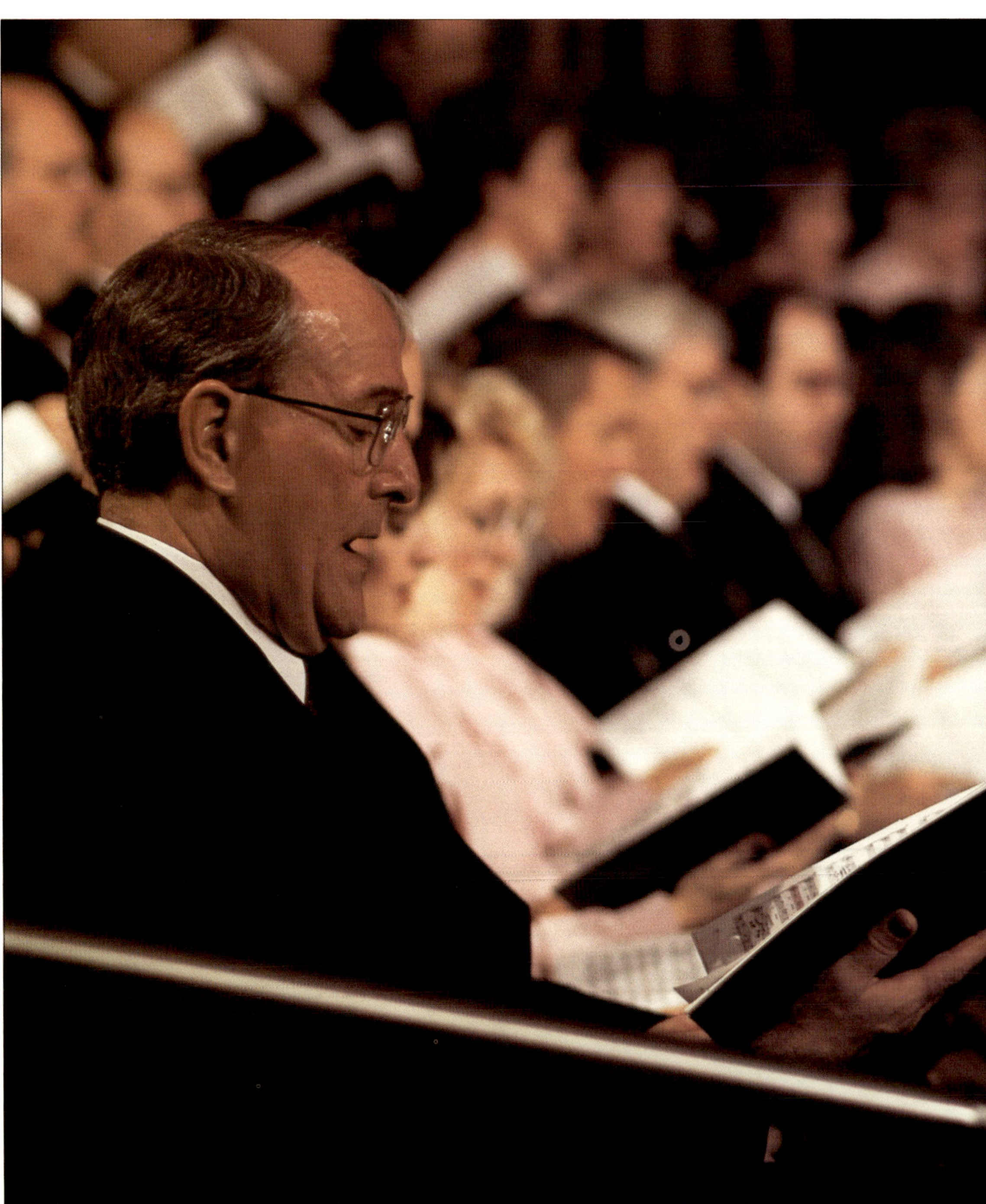

Ogden Tabernacle Choir (Lester Hinchcliff), and Weber College (now University) Community Choir (Glenn Hanson, Ronald Wooden and Evelyn Harris).

In Cedar City, the Choir of Southern Utah (Floyd Rigby, conductor) enjoys a colorful history as well as a fine reputation dating from its primary founders William Manning and Blaine Johnson and, more recently, James Dunaway and Mark Mecham. Cache County's Northern Utah Choral Society (founded by William Ramsey) is conducted by Utah State University professor Will Kesling.

In recent years, choirs founded

JEROLD D. OTTLEY

Jerold D. Ottley has been conductor of the Mormon Tabernacle Choir since April 1975, following a brief period as assistant conductor. He is generally credited with having raised the overall musical standards of the choir by imposing new requirements for membership, including restricting the length of a singer's tenure and imposing rigorous standards of musicianship in addition to outstanding vocal skills.

Dr. Ottley is a native of Salt Lake City with degrees from Brigham Young University, the University of Utah and the University of Oregon. In addition, in 1968 he studied conducting, voice and choral performance practice at the Academy of Music in Cologne, West Germany, as a Fulbright scholar.

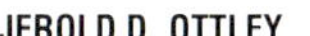

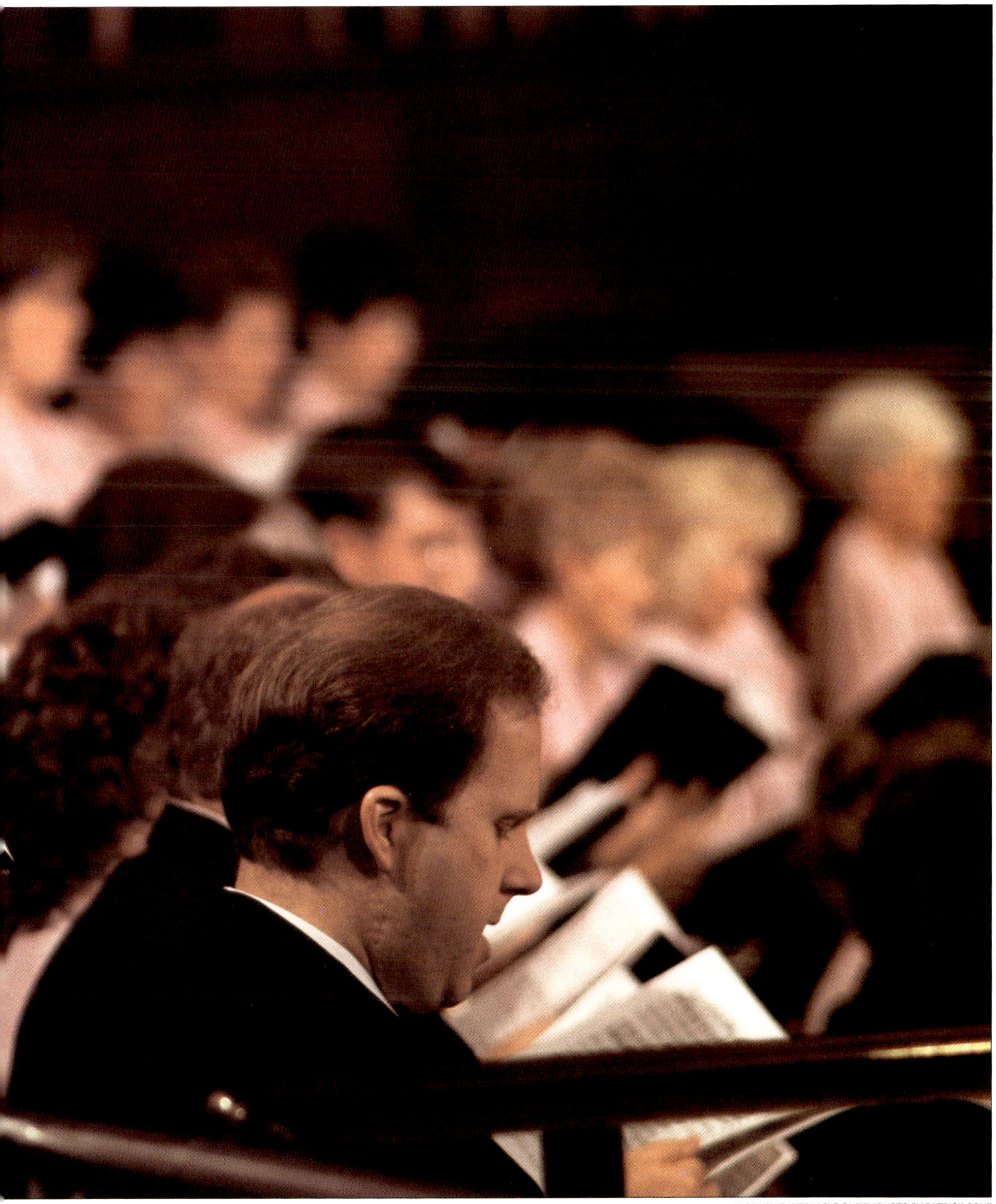

MORMON TABERNACLE CHOIR / PHOTO BY PATRICK CONE

ORATORIO SOCIETY OF UTAH

The Oratorio Society of Utah was organized in 1915 by the gifted and noted music educator Squire Coop and other community leaders and musicians as the Salt Lake Oratorio Society. For the next twenty-five years, Coop was the driving force of the Society, even after leaving Salt Lake City in 1922 to join the faculty of the University of California at Los Angeles. The Society's primary offerings in oratorio were Handel's *Messiah* and Haydn's *The Creation*. Over the years the society has presented no fewer than seventy-seven performances of *Messiah*, twelve of *The Creation*, nine of Mendelssohn's *Elijah*, and four of Beethoven's *Christ on the Mount of Olives*. All the Society's performances have featured an array of both local and imported conductors and soloists.

Since Coop's tenure as both chorusmaster and performance conductor, the society has featured nationally prominent conductors with the chorus being prepared by the society's music director. The music directors have been prominent in Salt Lake's musical scene, including two who were destined also to become directors of the Mormon Tabernacle Choir (J. Spencer Cornwall and Jay E. Welch), and David Shand, who became associate conductor of the Utah Symphony. But none has had the longevity and lasting overall influence of John Marlowe Nielson, who has played an important role in the choral music of Salt Lake City during his very lengthy career.

Today, the Oratorio Society looks back on a heritage as the oldest continuing musical organization in Utah outside of the Tabernacle Choir. The Society's present music director is Dr. Morris Lee.

Concert-level

V E R T U O S I T Y

is achieved

by both adult and

childrens' choirs.

and/or conducted by a new generation of musicians are earning high critical praise and making an important contribution to choral performance in the state. The Salt Lake Vocal Ensemble, under Mark Pearce, is a true chamber ensemble devoted to the art of unaccompanied singing; the South Davis Community Choir, conducted by Michael D. Huff, presents a literature primarily centered in oratorio; and Utah Chamber Artists, under founder/conductor Barlow Bradford, is uniquely chartered as both a choral and instrumental ensemble, performing either as a combined group or separately.

There are also outstanding choirs devoted to specific repertoire, including the Salt Lake Men's Chorus (Robert Mensel, conductor), Schubert Singers women's chorus (Gordon Quigley, conductor) and Treble Clef Women's Chorus (Mark Howarth, conductor); barbershop choruses, such as the Beehive Statesmen (Milton Christensen, conductor) and Mt. Jubilee Chorus, formerly Sweet Adelines (Victoria Postma, conductor).

Several children's choirs have achieved concert-level virtuosity: the Salt Lake Children's Choir (Ralph Woodward, Jr., conductor), the Utah Children's Choir of American Fork (Kay Asay, conductor), the Utah Valley Children's Choir (Beverly Thomas, conductor), and the Cache Children's Choir (Bonnie Slade, conductor).

Choral Music Education in Utah
*"Here should be an efficient choral organization
capable of interpreting the masterpieces of
oratorio and opera . . . "*

—Squire Coop, address to the students and faculty

of the University of Utah, October 1905.

To their credit, the pioneers recognized the importance of education and early on established public schools. Singing was always an important part of the school curriculum, and most of the choirs discussed here have been founded and/or conducted by one or another of the state's gifted music educators. Evan Stephens remained active as an educator throughout his life, and virtually all succeeding directors of the Tabernacle Choir, including J. Spencer Cornwall, Richard P. Condie, Jay Welch and Jerold Ottley, were schoolteachers prior to their calling to conduct the Choir.

Lasting traditions of excellence were established in many of the state's high schools—traditions that in many instances endure to this day. In Box Elder County, educator Earl Johnston was influential at Box Elder High, while Gene Jorgensen and his successor Carl Ashby established a virtual choral dynasty at Bear River High School. Jorgensen's sister, Dorothy Brown, performed a similar feat at Carbon High School in Price, while in Weber County superb programs were established by Glenn Hanson and Dale Blackburn at

Ogden High School and by Joseph Graves at Weber High. In Iron County, Shirley Roper and James Dunaway forged a strong program at Cedar High School. Finally, in Salt Lake County, Leo Dean (Hillcrest High), James Maher (West High), Paul Christensen (Highland High), Armont Willardsen (South High), Lisle Bradford and Lorraine Bowman (East High) and Donald Ripplinger (Skyline High) were also among the leaders in the state's music education programs.

Utah's colleges and universities have always exerted a powerful influence on choral music education. Many of the conductors in today's strongest high school, college and community choral programs were students of Newell B. Weight and Bernell W. Hales (U of U), John R. Halliday and Ralph Woodward (BYU), Blaine Johnson (Southern Utah University), William Ramsey (USU) and Ronald Wooden and Lyneer Smith (Weber State University).

Presently a new generation of conductors at these schools is exerting an influence on choral music performance and future educators. These include Ronald Staheli and Mack Wilberg (BYU), John M. Cooksey and Edgar J. Thompson (U of U), Will Kesling (USU), Mark Henderson (Weber State University), Bart Shanklin (Southern Utah University), Russell

BERNELL W. HALES

Bernell W. Hales, native of Salt Lake City, holds degrees from the U of U, Columbia University and the University of Oregon.

Dr. Hales' teaching experience spanned nearly forty years beginning in 1948 at Uintah High. He joined the music faculty at the U of U in 1965, where he taught until 1988.

At the university, Dr. Hales' Chamber Choir established a standard of virtuosity and ensemble that remains today virtually unparalleled. The choir earned fame and influence as they toured through-out the western United States, Hawaii and Mexico and appeared at the Music Educators National Conference.

Wilson (College of Eastern Utah), Judy
Morgan (Snow College), and Jeffrey
Haagenson (Dixie College).

All of these people and institutions
have formed the collective base of an
extraordinarily strong music education
program that is the force which drives
the mighty choral engine that has
become such an integral and important
part of the musical fabric of the state.

> *"Let the Mountains shout for joy,*
> *Let the valley sing and the hills rejoice . . . "*

Ringing true as any prophecy, these
words from Evan Stephens' anthem
are an appropriate summation of
Utah's tradition of choral singing.
Descended from a pioneer heritage,
it streams into the present, spreading
ever outward like the expanding arms
of a great spiral galaxy. What is the state
of the choral art in Utah? Flourishing—
from border to border. From church
or school choirs to numerous community singing societies, there is
something here for everyone.

> *"Let them all break forth into song!*
> *Let them shout, and sing, and be glad . . .! "*

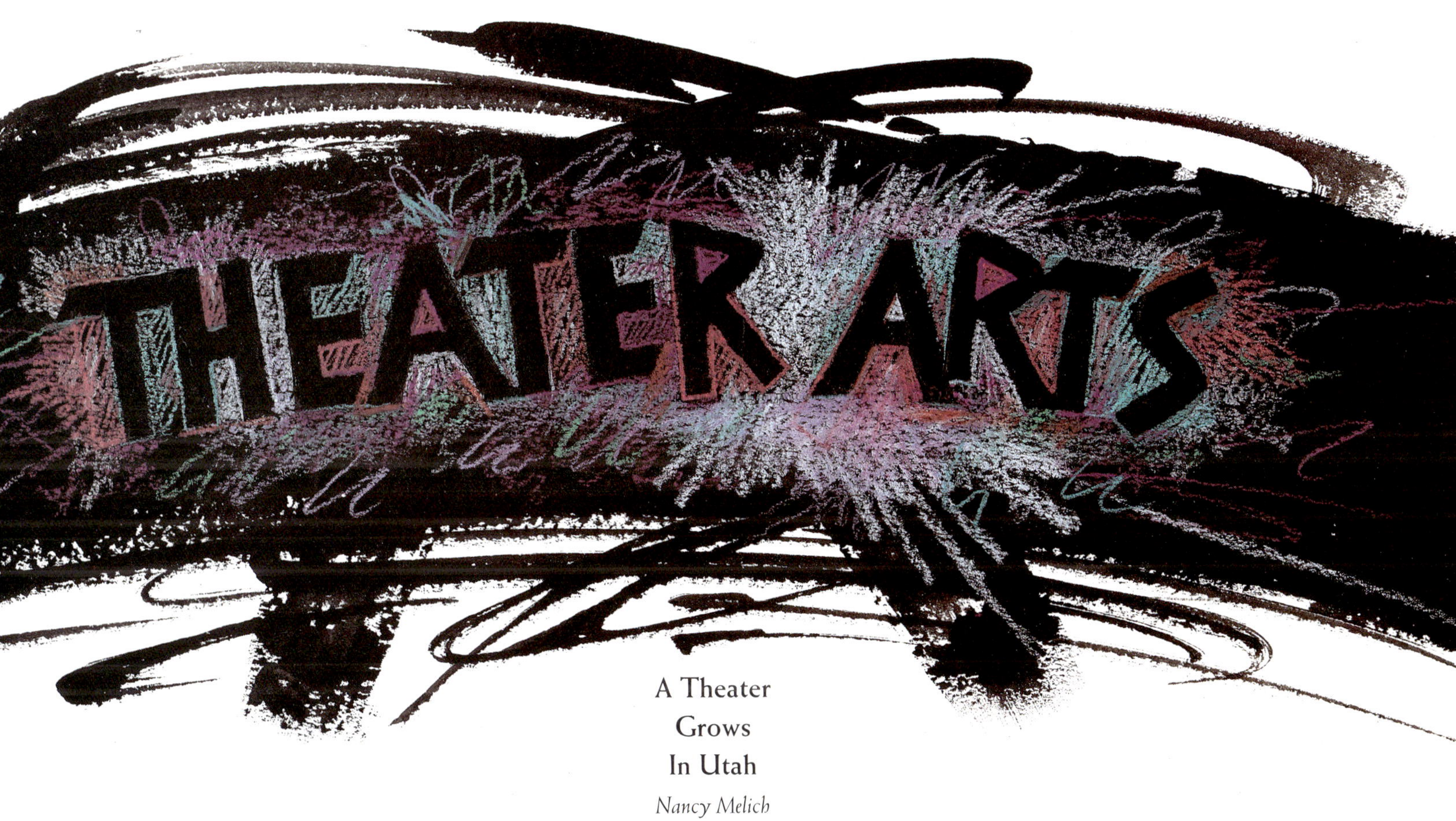

**A Theater
Grows
In Utah**

Nancy Melich

T HE STORY GOES LIKE THIS. A visitor standing in line at a Broadway theater is approached by an usher who asks, "Where you from?"

"Salt Lake City," answers the tourist.

"Ah, no wonder you're here. Guess there isn't much theater out your way."

Credit the erroneous conclusion to the provincialism of New Yorkers.

Or better still, invite the usher to Utah for a winter "play." There would not be enough hours in the stay to attend the weekly offering of twenty-five productions—give or take a stage. Remain for the summer and the choices will double.

Whether drawing from works by Neil Simon or William Shakespeare, Andrew Lloyd Webber or Richard Rodgers, August Wilson, Emily Mann, Wendy Wasserstein or David Henry Hwang, productions in Utah reflect those found in metropolitan areas twice the size.

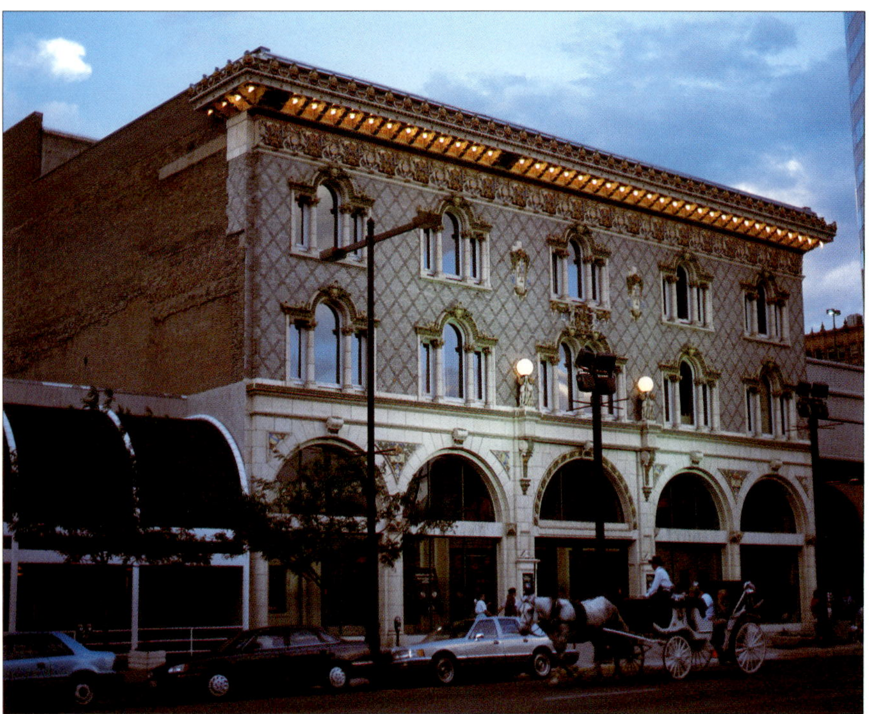

CAPITOL THEATRE, SALT LAKE CITY / PHOTO BY STEVE GREENWOOD

Old chestnuts, musical classics, plays in progress, proven dramas—they are all here. Magical cats, red-headed orphans, revolutionaries on barricades and chorus lines with singular sensations are box-office regulars. Hamlet has been seen on roller skates; Guenevere impersonating a harlot; Charlotte and Emily Brontë playing war games.

National tours of *Jesus Christ Superstar* have wowed audiences on three occasions and community groups have staged the rock opera in the capital city's Christian churches.

Over the years, the bare-it-all comedy *Oh! Calcutta!* found receptive patrons in the Beehive State, as did the rock musical *Hair*. A tired production of *The Best Little Whorehouse in Texas* didn't fare as well in 1983, but Salt Lake Acting Company's rousing *La Cage aux Folles* was an instant success when it opened six years later.

No other theatrical production in the history of the state has caused such a box-office stampede as the mega-hit *Les Miserables* in 1991. When tickets went on sale for the return appearance in '92, phone lines were jammed in a four-state area and buyers lined up for hours in subzero weather. British producer Cameron Mackintosh was so taken by the Utah response, he ran a full-page ad in *Variety* thanking the "Les Miz" fans. The national tour was back again in the summer of '93, playing once again to standing-room-only crowds.

Yes, Utahns have a penchant for live theater, both in front of and behind the footlights. The relationship began around 1850, when Utah pioneers offered the first community theater productions in the Old Bowery (now the Tabernacle on Temple Square) and at the University of Deseret (known today as the University of Utah).

Sensing the importance dramatic productions were having in the cultural lives of these new Utahns, Brigham Young decided to give them a home of their own. The Salt Lake Theatre, a majestic building two blocks southeast of Temple Square, opened in 1862, the first such facility west of the Mississippi. A resident stock company enjoyed immediate success with performances five nights a week, sometimes featuring traveling artists on their way from Chicago to San Francisco.

When the Golden Spike was driven at Promontory, Utah, in 1869, who would have guessed its impact on Utah theater? But with the emergence of a transcontinental railroad, full-scale national tours began putting the Salt Lake Theatre on their itineraries, and local companies had to look elsewhere for a place to perform.

Maud May Babcock had more in mind than her responsibilities as physical-education teacher when she arrived at the University of Deseret in 1890. Elocution was a passion. For forty-four years, "Mrs. B.," as her students called her, worked to put theater in the classroom and on the stage. When she retired from the University of Utah, she had founded two departments, one college, a university-community theater and the Varsity Players, the first professional American company sponsored by a university.

Kingsbury Hall, a 2,000-seat performance space on the University of Utah campus, was dedicated in 1930. In 1943 C. Lowell Lees moved to Utah to head the Department of Speech. His vision included strengthening the school's theater program by establishing connections with national theater organizations and adding ballet to the curriculum. He also wanted to build a replica of the old Salt Lake Theatre (which had been demolished in 1928) and establish a company with a nucleus of professional actors.

In the span of one season, "Doc Lees" brought to Kingsbury Hall such acting luminaries as Orson Welles, Katharine Cornell, Jeanette Nolan, Dan O'Herlihy, Roddy McDowall, John McIntyre and Judith Evelyn.

In addition to bringing professional actors to the university on a regular basis, Lees directed the University-Community Theatre and was the driving force behind the establishment of Pioneer Memorial Theatre.

This memorial to the old Salt Lake Theatre and the pioneers who had built it was dedicated in 1962, and a new era in Utah theater began. Under the

Capitol Theatre

M E M O I R S

would run the gamut of opera pop and theatre.

twenty-year guidance of Keith Engar, the theater offered a six-show season supported by a full-time professional staff of designers and business managers. When musicals were offered, a professional orchestra was hired.

Under his tenure, Engar built the largest season-subscription audience of any Utah arts organization and, in 1984, after a nationwide search, appointed New Yorker Charles Morey as the theater's first artistic director.

Two years later, Pioneer Theatre Company (PTC) signed a League of Regional Theatres contract with Actors' Equity Association, becoming the first and only fully professional theater in the Intermountain West. Under Morey's guidance, the theater company has grown artistically, gaining a national reputation for quality and setting a standard for Utah acting companies to emulate.

Though the company operates with a $2 million budget and draws its actors, designers and directors from auditions in New York, Los Angeles and Utah, it still struggles with name identification.

There are those who confuse PTC with Salt Lake City's Promised Valley Playhouse, a restored downtown theater owned by the Church of Jesus Christ of Latter-day Saints (LDS) and reserved for church-sponsored productions. Others erroneously believe that because

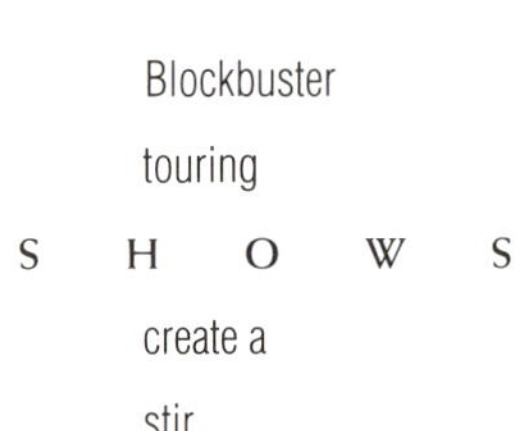

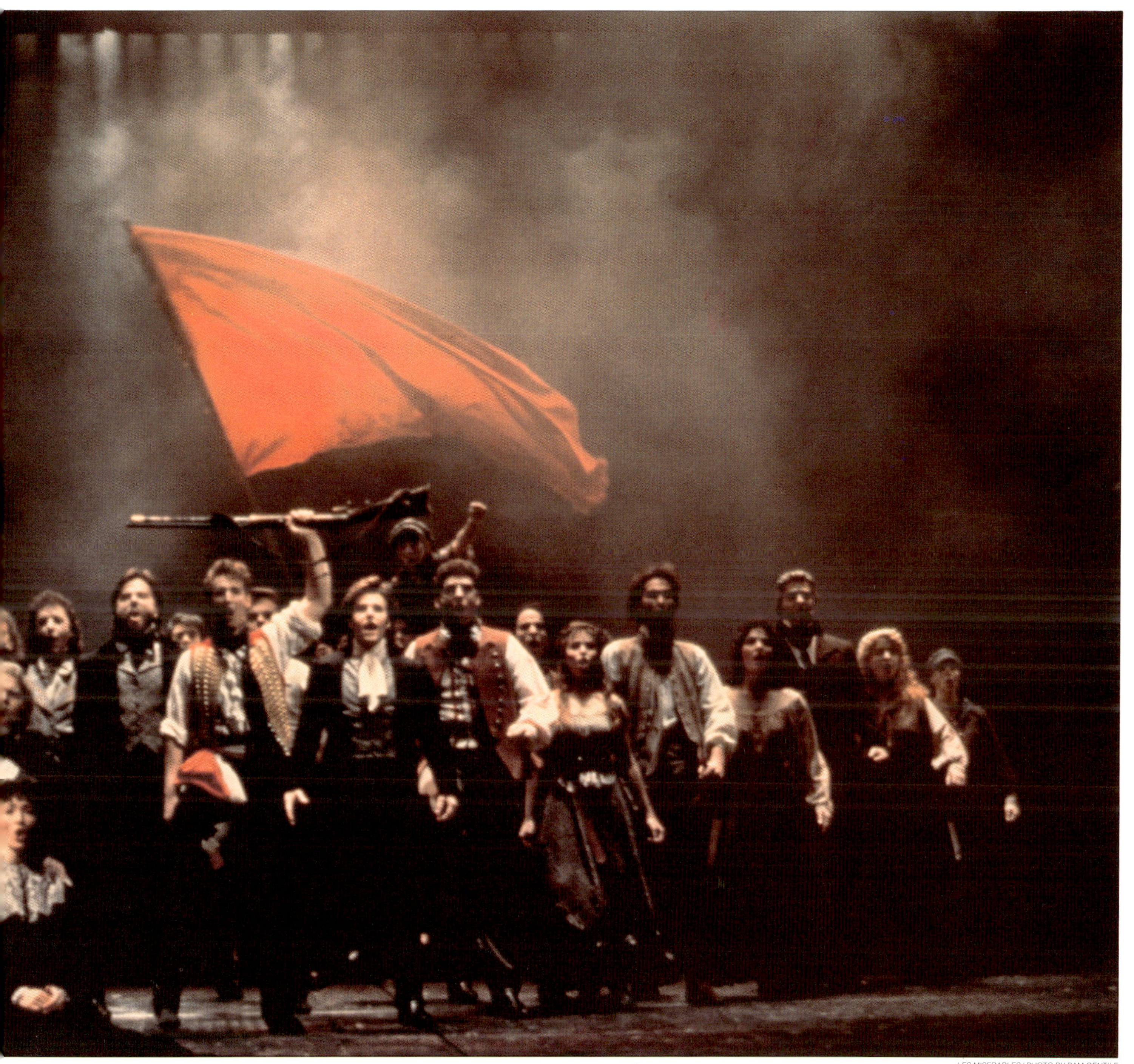

LES MISERABLES / PHOTO BY PAM GENTILE

FOLLOWING PAGE: *CYRANO DE BERGERAC*, UTAH SHAKESPEAREAN FESTIVAL ARCHIVES

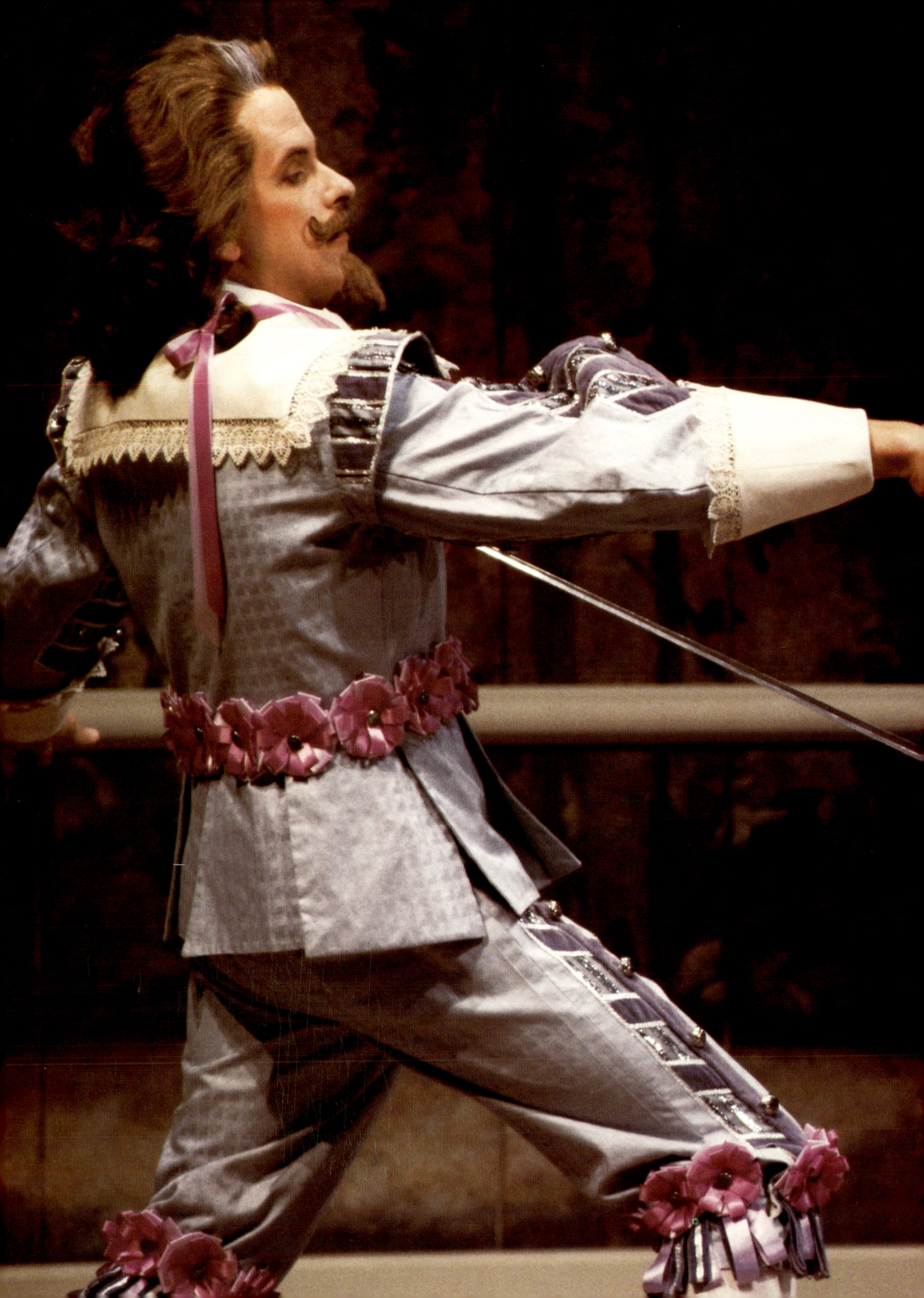

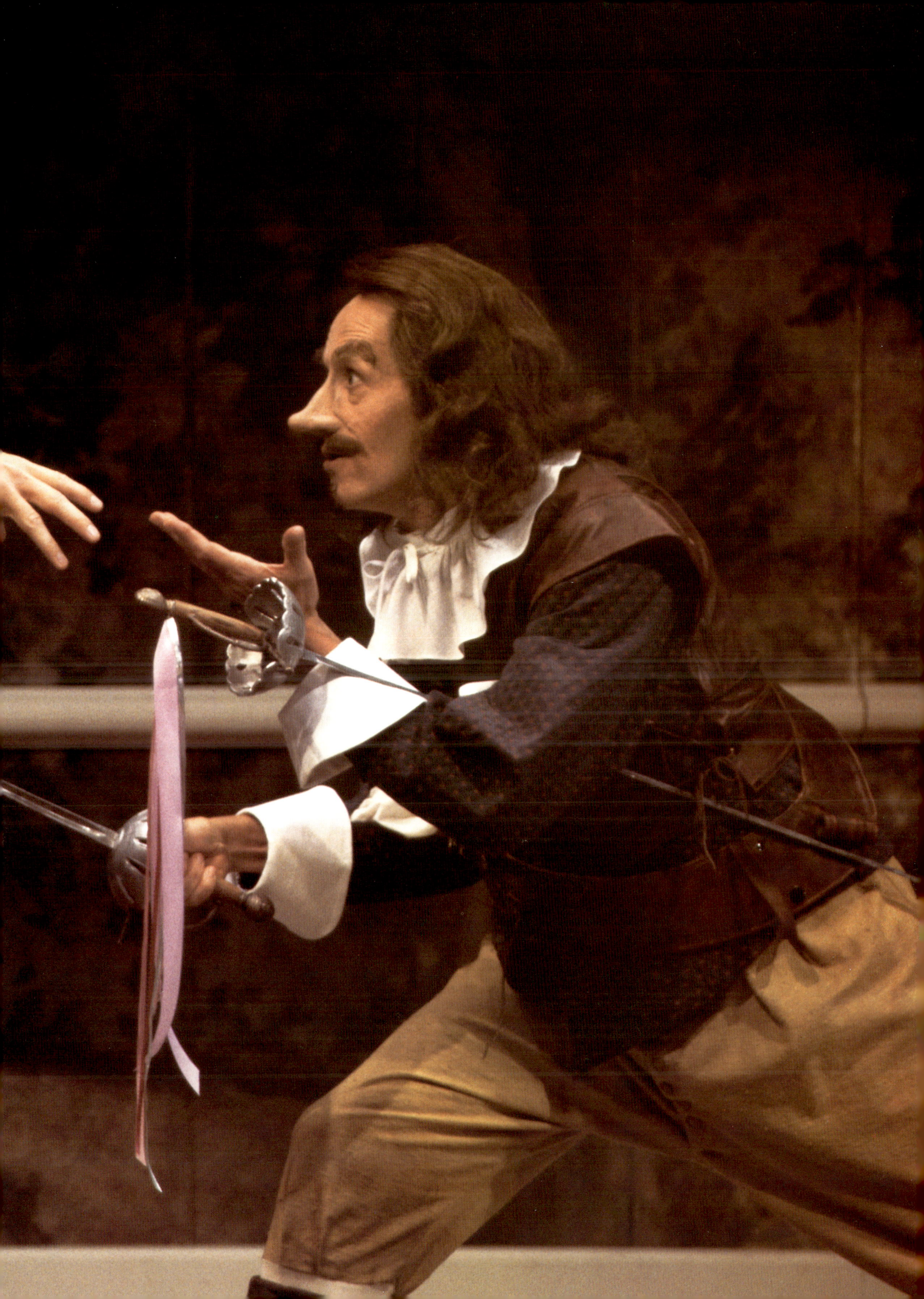

Pioneer Memorial Theatre is housed on the University of Utah campus, the theater must surely feature only student performances. Wrong on both counts.

Pioneer Theatre is one of approximately fifteen professional theaters in the country affiliated with universities. Among the other notables are the Yale Repertory Theatre (Yale), McCarter Theatre (Princeton), Syracuse Stage (Syracuse) and American Repertory Theatre (Harvard).

As with most theaters, whether on Broadway or in Salt Lake City, audiences are drawn to musicals. The most financially successful shows in recent

Traditional and

O R I G I N A L

dramatic scripts

flourish on

Utah's stages.

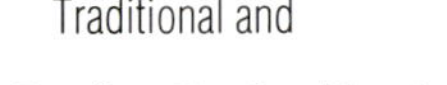

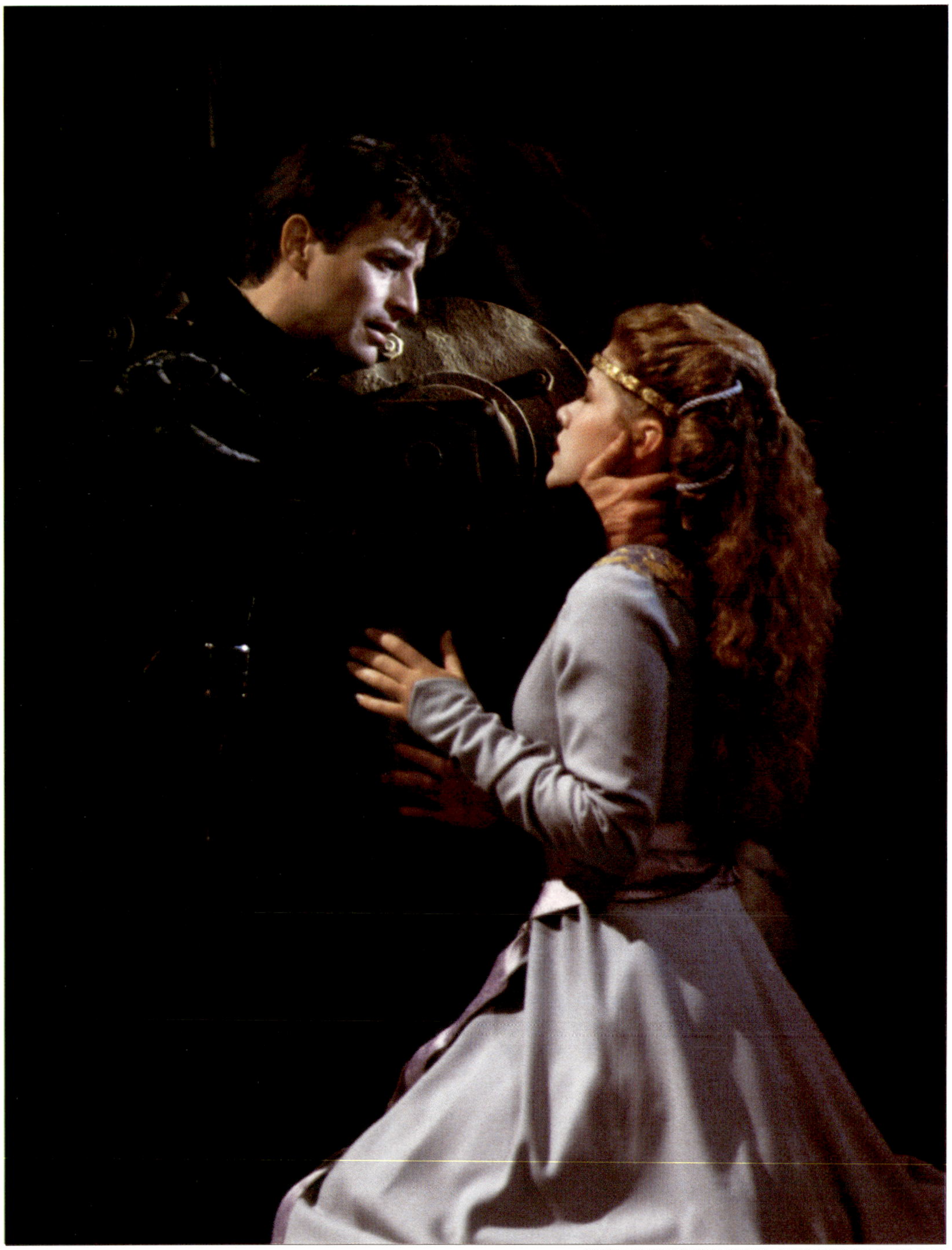

years for PTC have been *My Fair Lady* and the 1992-93 season finale *Evita*, which broke all existing box-office records. The Tim Rice-Andrew Lloyd Webber collaboration was 60 percent sold out before the curtain went up.

The PTC season is a mixture of musicals, classics and recent Broadway dramas, such as August Wilson's *Fences* and Herb Gardner's *Conversations with My Father*. Nontraditional casting is rarely employed and plays dealing with AIDS or premieres of original works have yet to be tried at the 1,000-seat house. For anyone accustomed to paying $40 to $60 for professional theater, ticket prices at PTC remain a bargain, from $8 to $28.

The Salt Lake Acting Company (SLAC), now in its twenty-third season, is the city's main alternative theater, though the designation is misleading. SLAC does not produce cutting-edge theater. In recent years the company, under the guidance of founder and former artistic director Edward Gryska, has moved to middle-of-the-road fare. Still, the intimate 150-seat theater, housed in a historic LDS church known as the Marmalade Hill Ward, has earned the loyalty of Salt Lake City's "in" crowd, looking for what it perceives as the *avant garde.*

SLAC has the distinction of being the first to present a nude actor on a Utah stage (*Hair*) and first to offer plays on a continuing basis dealing with

homosexual themes: *La Cage aux Folles, The Lisbon Traviata, M. Butterfly*. In 1984, the company was selected from 120 leading theaters by the Foundation of the Dramatists Guild/Columbia Broadcast System to receive one of five Fund for New American Play awards.

SLAC, the sixth-largest performing-arts company in Utah, also has premiered new works by Utah authors David Kranes, Aden Ross and former Utahn Wendy Hammond, as well as by other writers from around the country. Twice a year the company offers a series of free staged readings of new plays and during the holidays it presents a musical satire on life in *Salt Lake, Salt Lake*.

Mr. Gryska, a Chicago native, believes the quality of Utah theater has climbed steadily in the past twenty years, more specifically the past decade. He cites the now-defunct Theatre 138 and Lagoon Opera House as having been trailblazers for the continued growth of today's small theaters.

TheatreWorks West (TWW), the resident theater company of Westminster College of Salt Lake City, comes the closest of any established group in Utah to offering untried works as part of its season. Under the artistic direction of Fran Pruyn, TWW has presented first looks at works by unknown Utah authors as well as modern stagings of old classics.

In 1992, TheatreWorks West premiered *Ballad of the Mountain Meadows*, based on a tragic incident from Utah's history in 1857. The intriguing play

FRED ADAMS

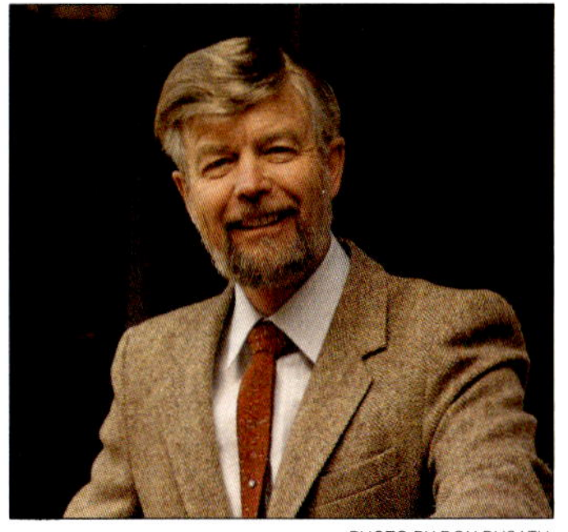

Most people know Fred Adams as the force behind the Utah Shakespearean Festival. What they may not know is that the force first struck him in 1961 while he was sitting at the Fluffy Bundle Laundromat in Cedar City, Utah.

As the clothes took their time drying, Adams and his wife, Barbara, wrote down their dreams on the back of an envelope. Their love was theater. Their home was Utah. The Oregon Shakespeare Festival was their role model.

Under the tireless leadership of founder and producing director Adams, the Utah Shakespearean Festival has become one of the premier offerings of its kind in the country. Puck-like in spirit, Adams has a penchant for flamboyant clothes and gracious, albeit effusive, speech. Whether speaking to a group of dignitaries in Tel Aviv or sharing french fries with an aspiring student, the Adams style is contagious—the stuff of which dreams are made.

with original music is noteworthy because of its attempt to relate dramatically, and without sugar-coating, a fascinating part of the state's past. Productions concerning Utah's heritage are usually well-intended but not thought-provoking.

Now in its ninth year, the Hale Center Theater has found a niche in the community that is unparalleled. Catering to the strictly-for-family-entertainment-only crowd, the 350-seat house is open year-round and is generally filled to capacity.

The annual version of *A Christmas Carol* at the Hale sells out weeks before the curtain rises. This community theater features double casting for all productions, taped music for its musicals and the most personable audiences west of the Mississippi. Everyone seems to know everyone else and intermissions resemble happy family reunions.

The acting company includes veteran performers and schoolchildren; the seasons boast comedies penned by "Grandmother Hale," who at 84 not only writes but continues to perform in her own comedies. The South Salt Lake theater was founded by Mrs. Hale and her husband Nathan and is now operated by their grandchildren, as are the other successful Hale playhouses in Orem, Grover and Panguitch.

There are dozens of light-appetite theaters in Utah, including City Rep and the knee-slapping style found at the

Desert Star Playhouse. In a laid-back atmosphere, this Murray theater is filled with formula entertainment that has proven popular with family audiences: original musical-comedy spoofs in the tradition of melodramas.

Ice cream, soft drinks, and pizza are served while audiences boo stage villains and cheer heroines. Seating is at small tables, and sing-alongs accompanied by a player piano begin each performance. Evenings end with an *olio*, a themed musical revue.

The Salt Lake Community College's season of six standard musicals at the Grand Theatre is a showcase for Utah talent providing affordable entertainment as well as an opportunity for young performers to step onstage. The college has also formed an alliance with Whittier Elementary School as part of their mission to build theater audiences of the future.

The productions, under the guidance of managing director Pat Davis, utilize students and professionals in a variety of positions—as actors, musicians, and stage and set technicians. Large casts of varying ages, sizes, abilities and ethnic backgrounds are trademarks of this viable enterprise. Since the "Grand" opening of the renovated theater in 1990, audiences in the 1,200-seat theater have continued to grow and season-ticket holders are on the rise.

Park City Performances operates year-round in the historic Egyptian

SHAKESPEARE lives in Cedar City.

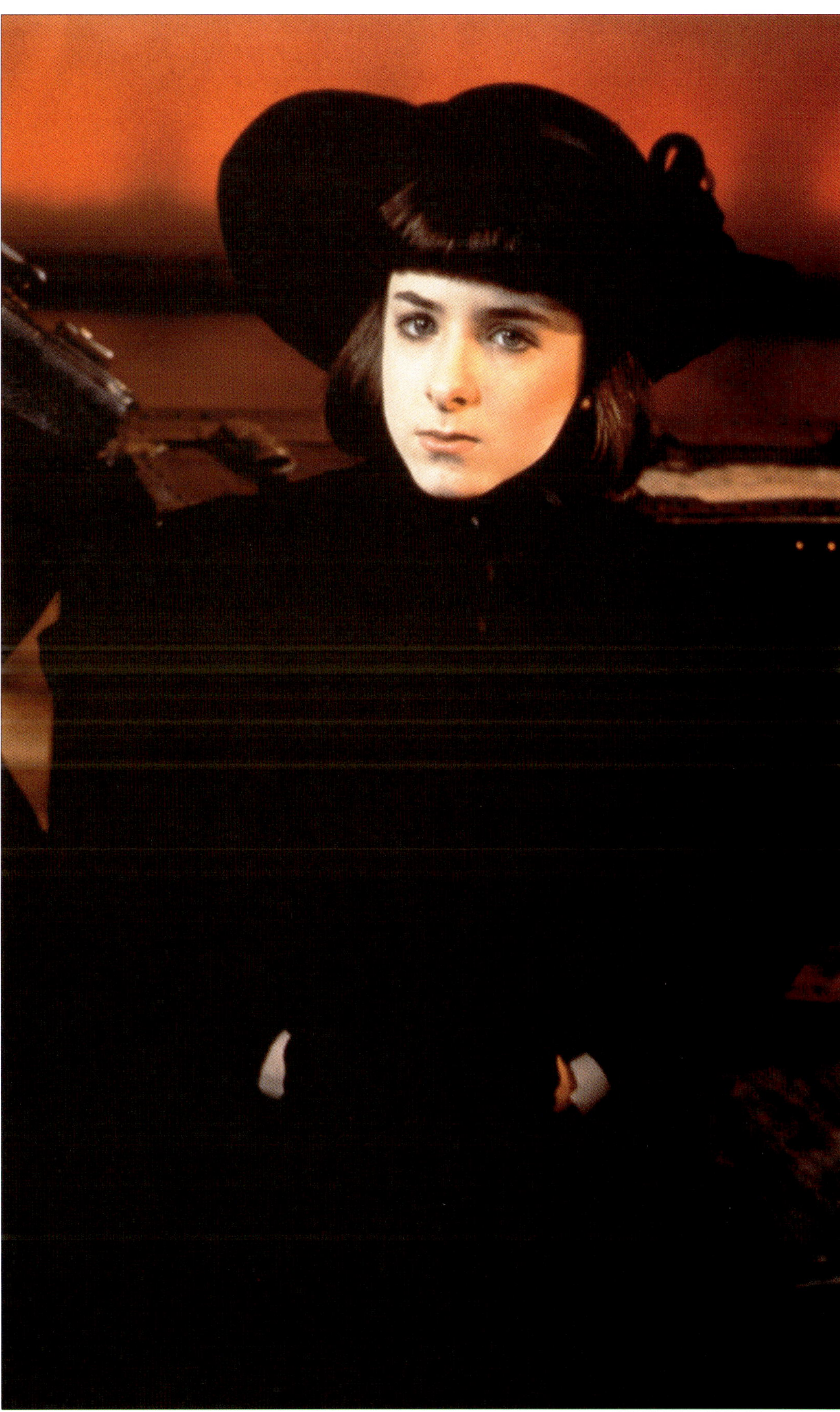

THE SECRET GARDEN / PHOTO COURTESY OF SPACE AGENCY

Opening night is

M A G I C A L

whether in school,
community or
professional theaters.

Theatre and in recent years has moved toward semi-professional status under the guidance of former artistic director Rafael Colón Castanera. The Old Lyric Repertory Company in Logan, founded and guided by W. Vosco Call for twenty-seven years, presents a four- or five-production summer season in the historic Lyric Theatre.

The outdoor Sundance Summer Theatre, operating since 1970, is a mainstay for musical entertainment in the mountains of Provo Canyon. Artistic director Jayne Luke had a dream fulfilled in 1992 when the new million-dollar, two-stage outdoor Eccles Theatre was dedicated.

Ogden's Utah Musical Theatre has enjoyed tremendous growth in its five-year history. Artistic-managing director James Christian presents a four-show summer season. Most productions are presented before standing-room-only houses. Future plans call for the company to leave its home at Weber State University and become the anchor performing-arts group for Ogden's refurbished historic Egyptian Theatre. The casts for all summer productions include professional and nonprofessional actors and directors, some from out of state.

The granddaddy of all summer drama events, however, is the critically acclaimed and highly successful Utah Shakespearean Festival in Cedar City.

Founded in 1961 by Utah native Fred Adams, the festival operates deficit-free with a budget exceeding $2.5 million. The June-to-September season features six plays in two theaters: the outdoor Adams Theatre, used by the BBC in 1981 to film part of its *All the World's a Stage* series starring Jeremy Irons, and the new indoor 750-seat Randall Theatre.

Attendance continues to climb annually with more than 148,000 people expected for the 1994 season. Auditions are conducted in major cities around the country and the company, including designers and directors, is selected from Equity and non-Equity talent.

Recognizing that the plays are the festival's major drawing card, management has made it possible for patrons to attend six plays in three days. Tickets are $10 to $24. Literary seminars, nightly green shows in the courtyard, backstage tours, and "royal feastes" where visitors dine without utensils are among the numerous events offered. A new play component was added in '93, featuring staged readings of original works, often with the playwright present.

The state's newest venture into the world of plays is the Sundance Children's Theatre, which began operation in the summer of '91 under the auspices of Robert Redford's Sundance Institute. The program is an outgrowth of the nationally recognized Playwrights Lab at Sundance, founded in 1980. The lab shifted gears in 1991 to the development of works specifically for young audiences. Future plans include projects from both genres.

The adult Lab, one of the state's best-kept secrets, was guided by Utah playwright David Kranes. Authors from around the country spent two weeks in the Wasatch Mountains taking risks with their craft. Using a pool of state and national actors and directors, the playwrights were free to explore ideas without the pressure of full-scale productions.

Pulitzer Prize-winning playwrights Robert Schenkkan (*The Kentucky Cycle*, 1992) and Tony Kushner (*Angels in America: Millennium Approaches*, which received the Pulitzer as well as the Tony Award in '93) worked on their celebrated epics during Sundance summers. In fact, of the five finalists for the 1992 Pulitzer Prize, three of the dramas are by Sundance Lab alums: *Kentucky Cycle*, *Sight Unseen* by Donald Margulies and *Miss Evers' Boys* by David Feldshuh.

The intention of the newly formed children's-theater lab is to encourage American playwrights to write works of intelligence for young audiences, creating a new body of literature for children. Authors come to Sundance in July to work on their projects. Children's productions of original works are staged during the daylight hours in the newly constructed King Outdoor Theater at the resort.

There is little question, however, that the blockbuster touring shows such

as *Les Miserables* and *Cats* cause the greatest stir in Utah. People, who ordinarily would never set foot inside a theater, line up for hours to attend these events at less than bargain prices. Though fly-by-night Phantoms have slithered into town, Andrew Lloyd Webber's superhit

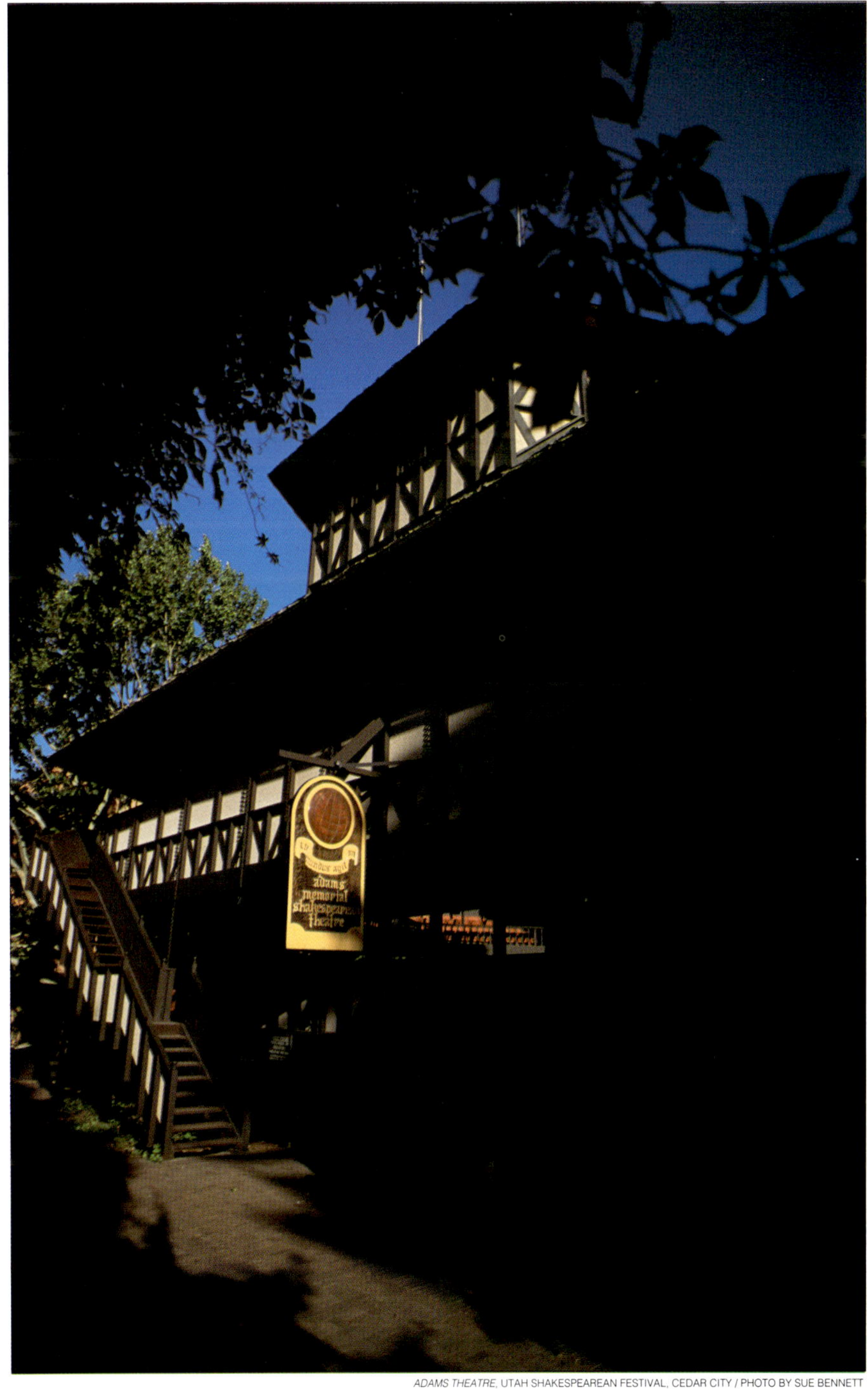

ADAMS THEATRE, UTAH SHAKESPEAREAN FESTIVAL, CEDAR CITY / PHOTO BY SUE BENNETT

The Phantom of the Opera has yet to make an appearance. Surely the "real" masked tenor—with falling chandelier in tow—will darken a Salt Lake City stage before the year 2000 arrives.

Credit the Theatre League of Utah (TLU), established in 1990, for bringing national tours back to the city on a regular basis. Granted, the TLU season lineups are predominantly musicals—*Love Letters* the lone exception—but that is what sells. When acclaimed British actor Lynn Redgrave brought her one-woman show *Shakespeare for My Father* to Salt Lake City in the spring of '93, ticket response was dismal. *Les Miserables*, on the other hand, returned for a third time that same summer and tickets were snapped up months in advance.

David Kranes has viewed Utah's theater patterns from several perspectives—University of Utah theater professor, playwright, patron and artistic director—for more than two decades. Though pleased with the growth of professionalism in Utah theater, he is disturbed at the lack of risks companies are willing to take.

The passion to produce "new, untried, serious, probing work" has declined in the past ten years, Kranes says. He misses theater that brought people together and "made them feel like they were in the presence of something happening. The deep passion that theater can evoke—as opposed to entertainment only—is rarely found." He says the official response as to why companies are playing it safe is always "the economy."

"That is the great catch-all phrase—'we have to present light entertainment or audiences won't come.'" Kranes does not subscribe to the economy excuse, saying it is more a failure of vision and nerve, a condition that exists nationwide.

"I still believe that theater dedicated to probing the author's intent and produced with passion will thrive."

Stay tuned.

And until then, call your friends in New York and invite them to an evening at the theater—in Utah.

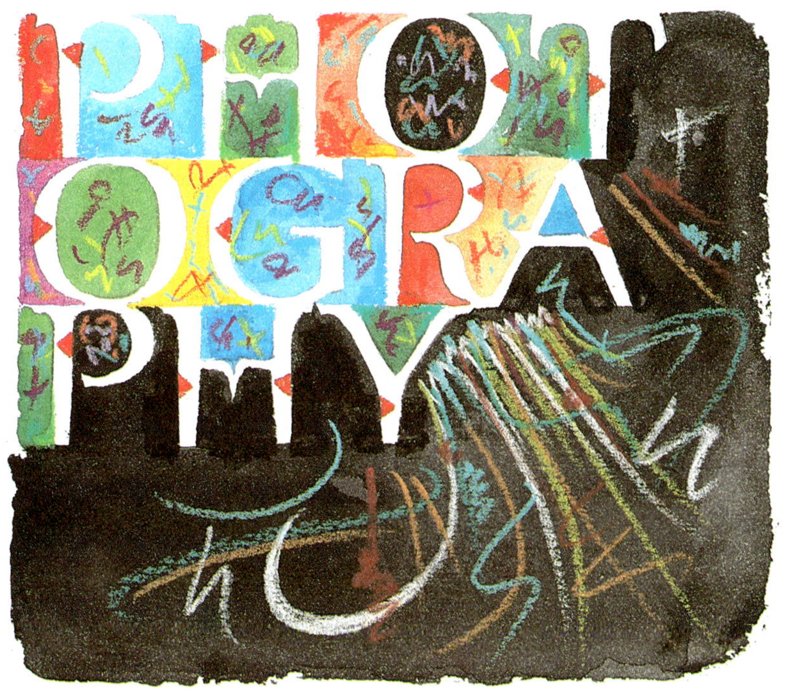

**Utah Photography
State of the Art**

John Telford

L ESS THAN A DECADE before Utah became a state in 1896, George Eastman introduced the Kodak, a hand-held amateur camera, with the slogan "You press the button and we do the rest." The $25 camera with a hundred-exposure roll of film turned photography over to the general public and,

according to photographic historians Helmut and Alison Gernsheim, was responsible for "the evils from which photography is suffering today" and marked the end of serious photography. Sometime in 1894, prominent Utah photographer Charles R. Savage wrote a discouraging diary entry: "Not doing

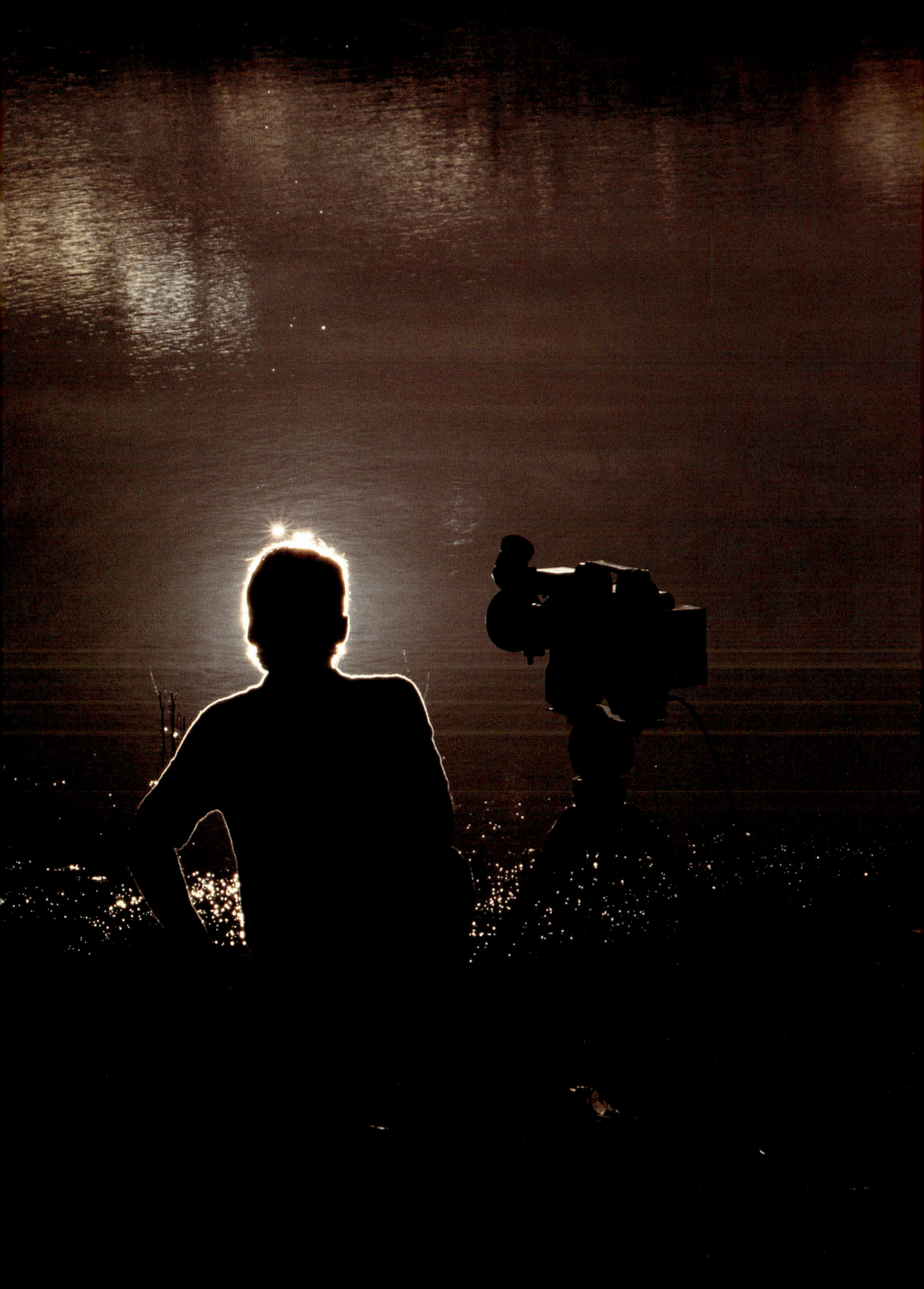

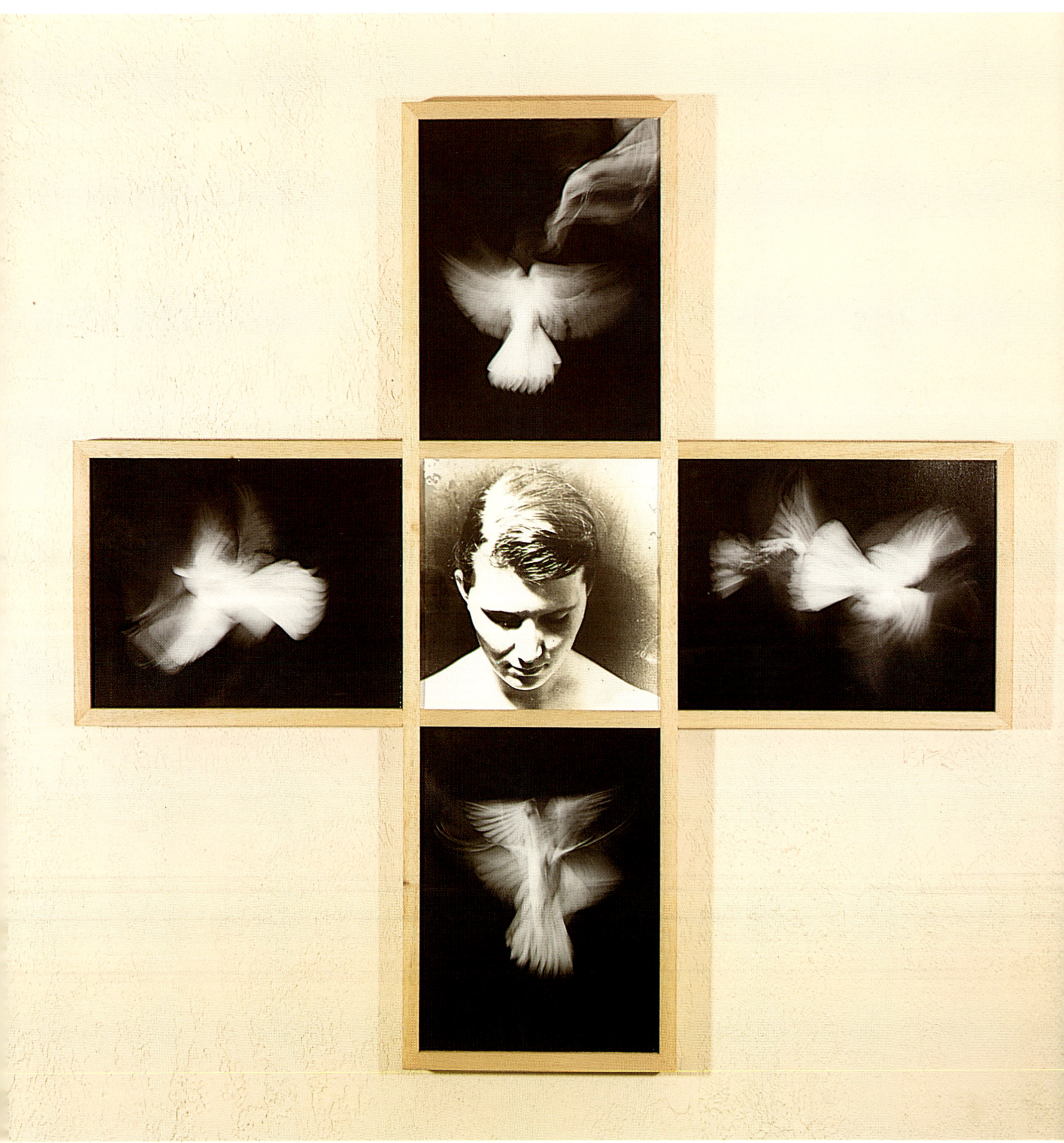

PREVIOUS PAGE: SUNRISE OVER A POND, HWY 89 IN GARFIELD COUNTY, UTAH / PHOTO BY STEPHEN SMITH

THINGS I'VE SAID TO GOD / PHOTO BY JOHN REES

much viewing [photographing] lately . . . . Nearly everybody is becoming a photographer. Business is changing to developing and finishing views for amateurs. Most of the magazines now published are illustrated by photo engravings—the demand for views is gradually falling off."

The great Utah photographer, lamenting his changing role, had made hundreds of "views" of Utah and the West, including the photograph of the driving of the Golden Spike at Promontory Point in 1869 that was the predominant image of that event, reproduced as a woodcut and wood-engraving in newspapers and magazines. From its invention in 1839, photography had been the domain of an elite group of *magicians*—viewmakers who revealed the world to a stationary population. The photographs were of monumental places and events—cathedrals, pyramids, natural wonders, wars and the like—made exclusively by professionals.

Photographers enjoyed celebrity status and earned large sums of money selling views and stereo cards to a visually starved public. George Eastman's invention changed that, forever. The ubiquitous audience for photography suddenly became the makers of photography. As amateurs began making pictures for themselves, they changed not only the role of the photographer, but also the aesthetics of the medium.

The first generation of amateur picture makers made very intimate views of their surroundings and experiences with no obligatory commitment to describing universally important facts or events. They were largely untrained in art or composition, which shows in their vast personal archives that record friends and relatives and personal, private events. Ignorant of any pictorial conventions, they most often blundered but occasionally showed real brilliance. A term borrowed from hunting, describing a hurried shot taken without deliberation at a fast-moving animal, was applied to this new generation of photography—the snapshot.

The first large-scale movement in worldwide photography was under way as Utah became a state. Trying to recapture the status of art in photography, and their importance as photographers, professionals had created the Pictorial school. Processes that were difficult, if not impossible, for the "Sunday Snapshooters" were espoused by the Pictorialists. Strict guidelines for picture content, subject matter, and style were adopted, even demanded, by the photographic artists. The processes included platinum, gum-bichromate, bromoil, carbon and various toning combinations. The subject matter was atmospheric landscapes, evocative portraits and impressionistic structures. Sharp detail was deplored, but feelings and suggestion were celebrated. Literal, sharply articulated descriptions gave

BARBARA RICHARDS

In a recent survey of some of Utah's most important photographers which sought their opinions on their most significant and influential colleagues, Barbara Richards appeared on every list. She came to Utah from northern Minnesota in the mid-1970s and has stayed to photograph. "My photographic education," she says, "consists of two basic photo classes." But her photographs show maturity and sensitivity that indicate she has learned a great deal from many other sources.

Until recently, Richards photographed in black and white with "a philosophy of photography and equipment [that] is extremely simple." Simple, maybe, but certainly not ordinary. Her black-and-white photographs of soft, quiet landscapes are silvery in light and emotion and expressively revealing about their maker.

Currently, Richards is working in color and utilizing the computer for further exploration in visual manipulation. The photographs are still soft, but the digitized colors are bold and vibrant. She can be seen frequently on KULC Channel 9, where she teaches a television course for the University of Utah called Photographic Seeing.

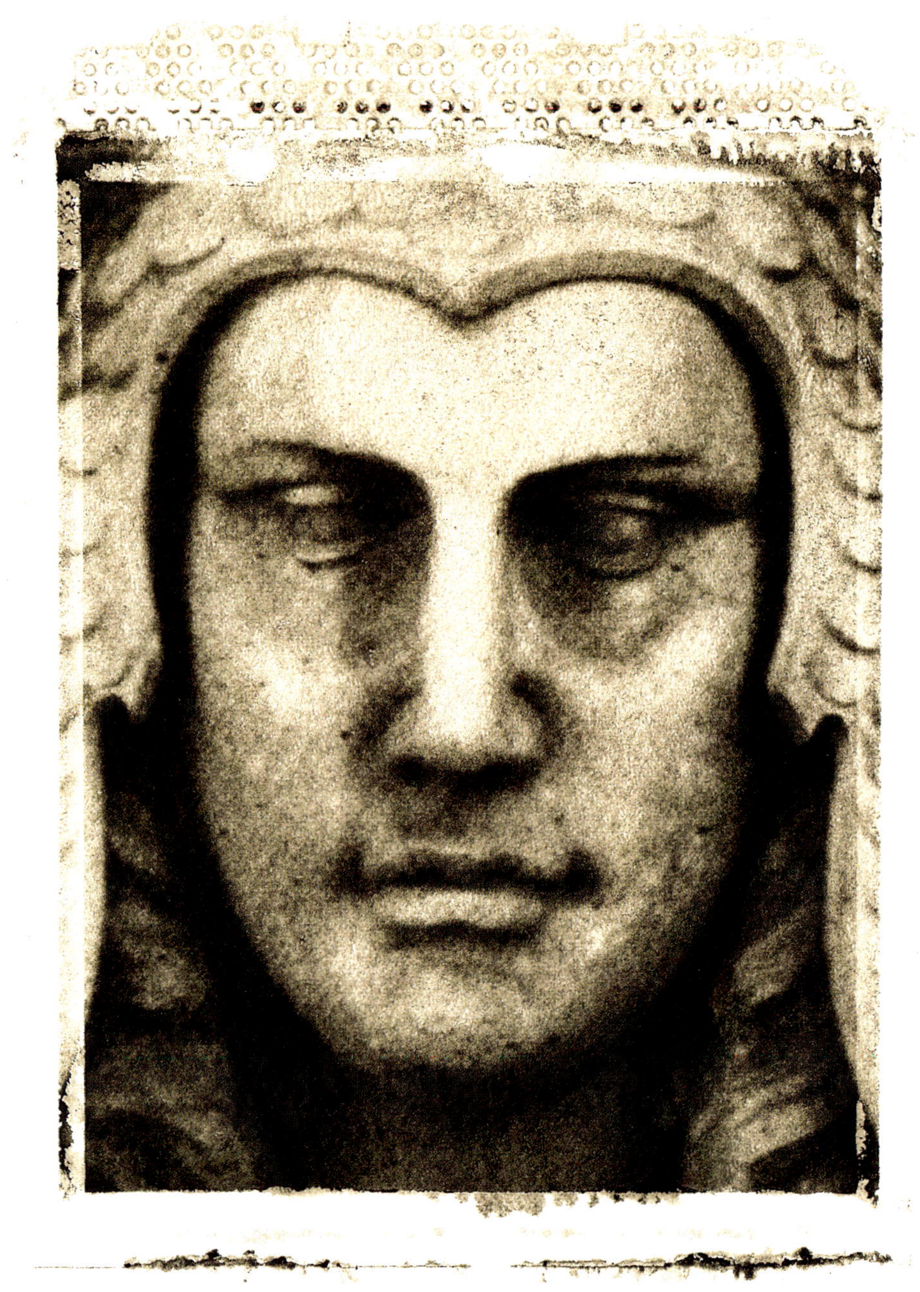

SALT LAKE CITY AND COUNTY BUILDING DETAILS / PHOTO TRANSFERS BY MICHAEL ROBERTS

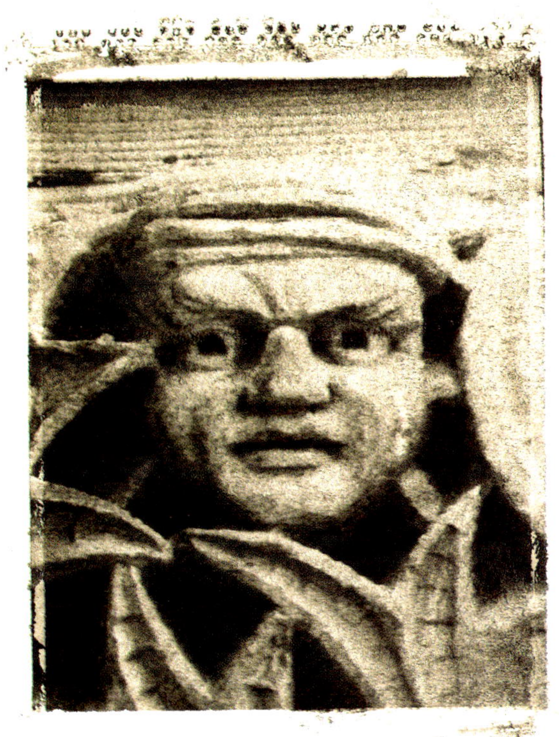

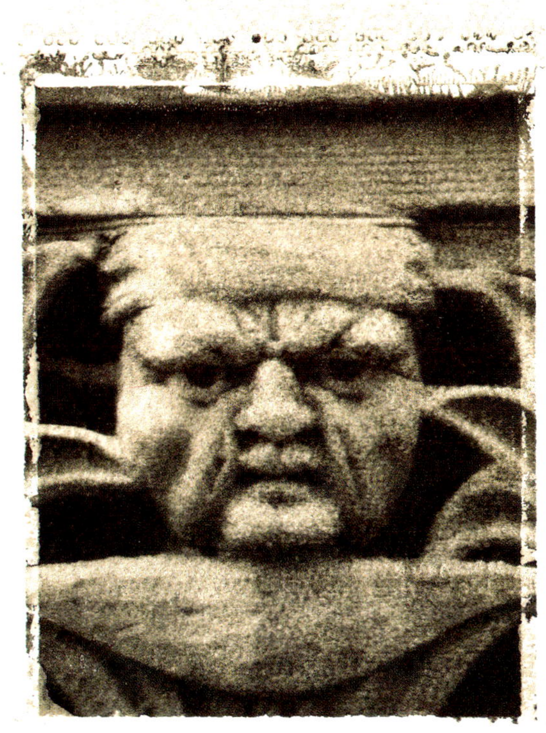

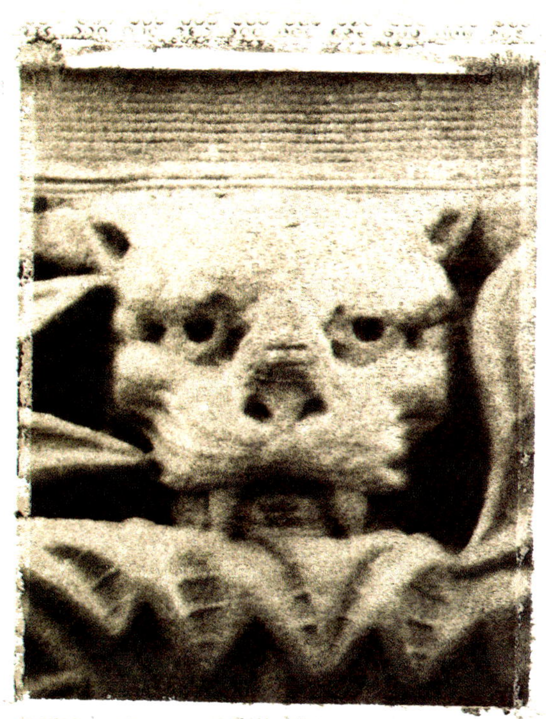

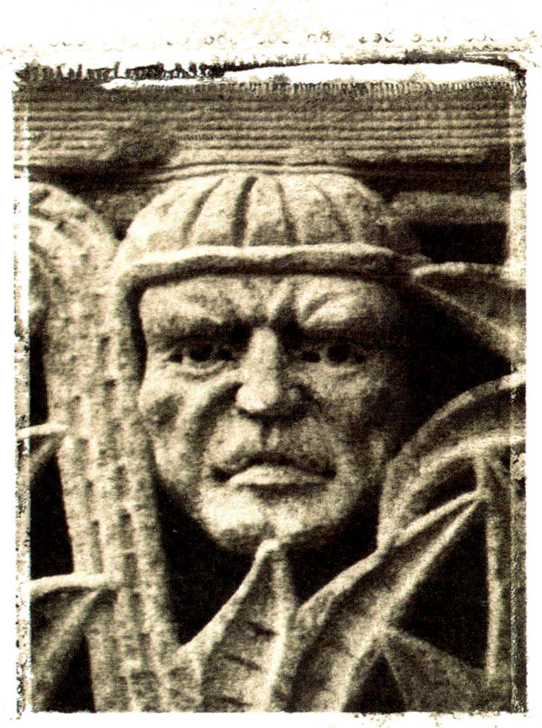

FOLLOWING PAGE: *RITE: SUBDUCTION* / PHOTO BY FRED WRIGHT

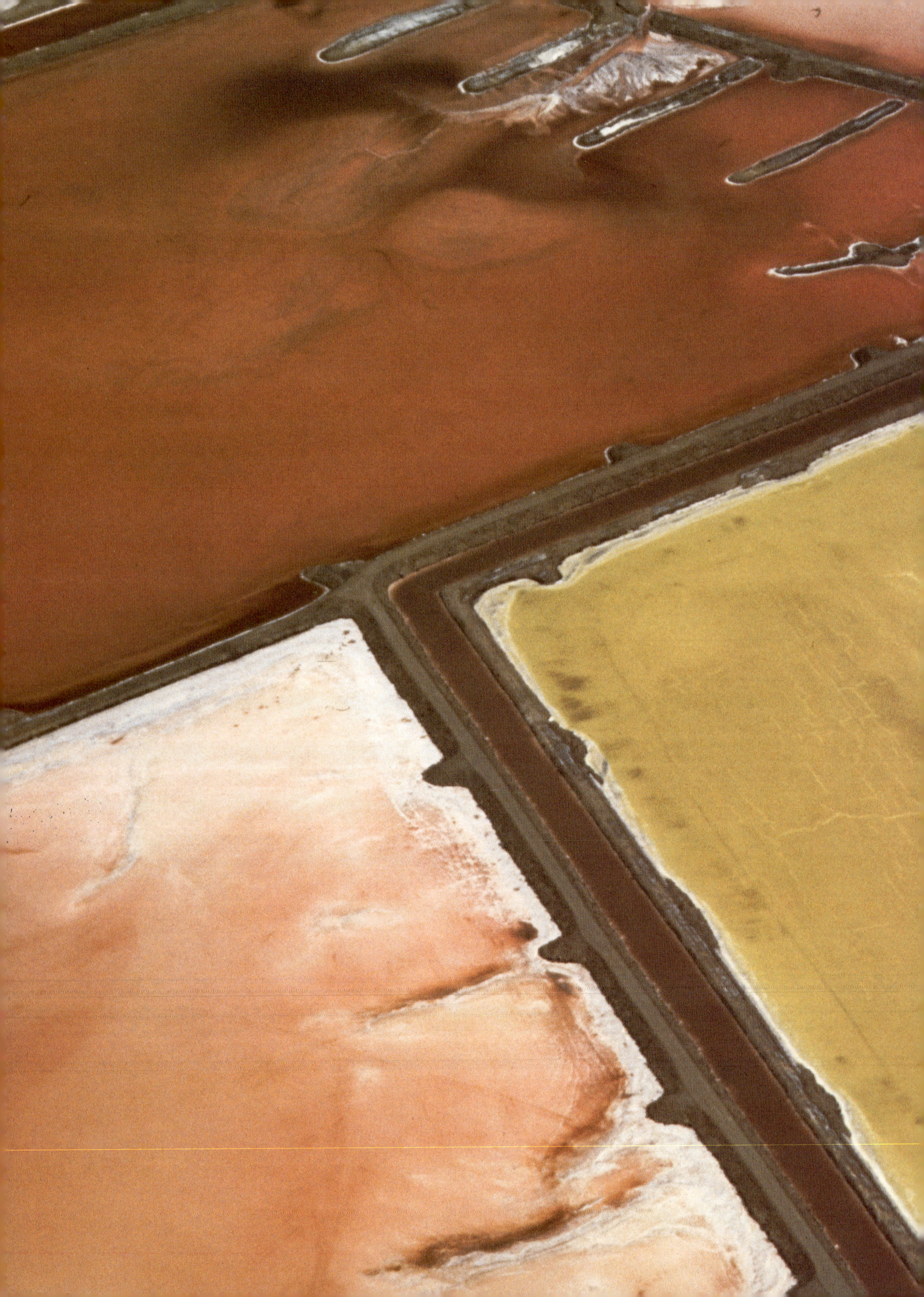

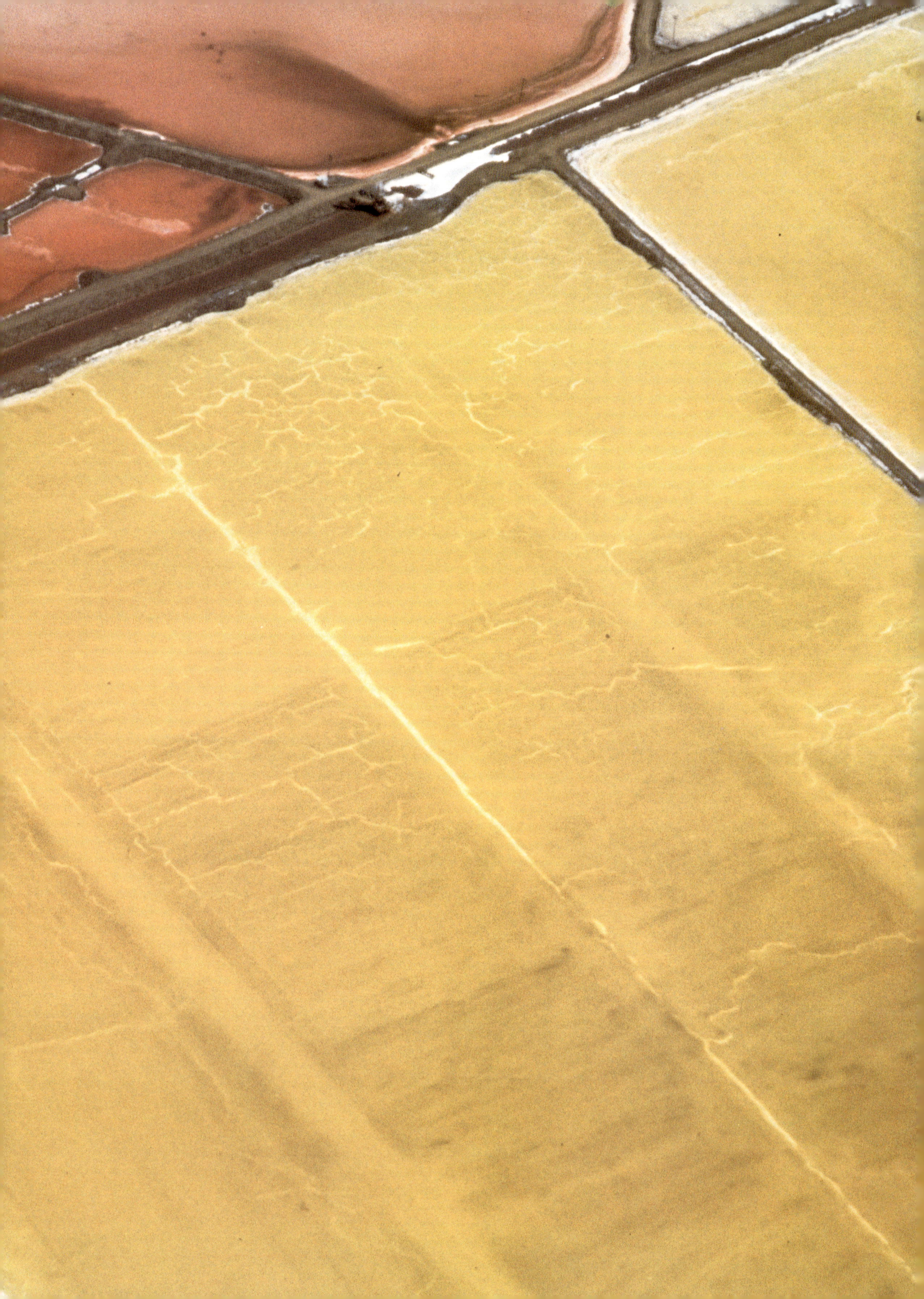

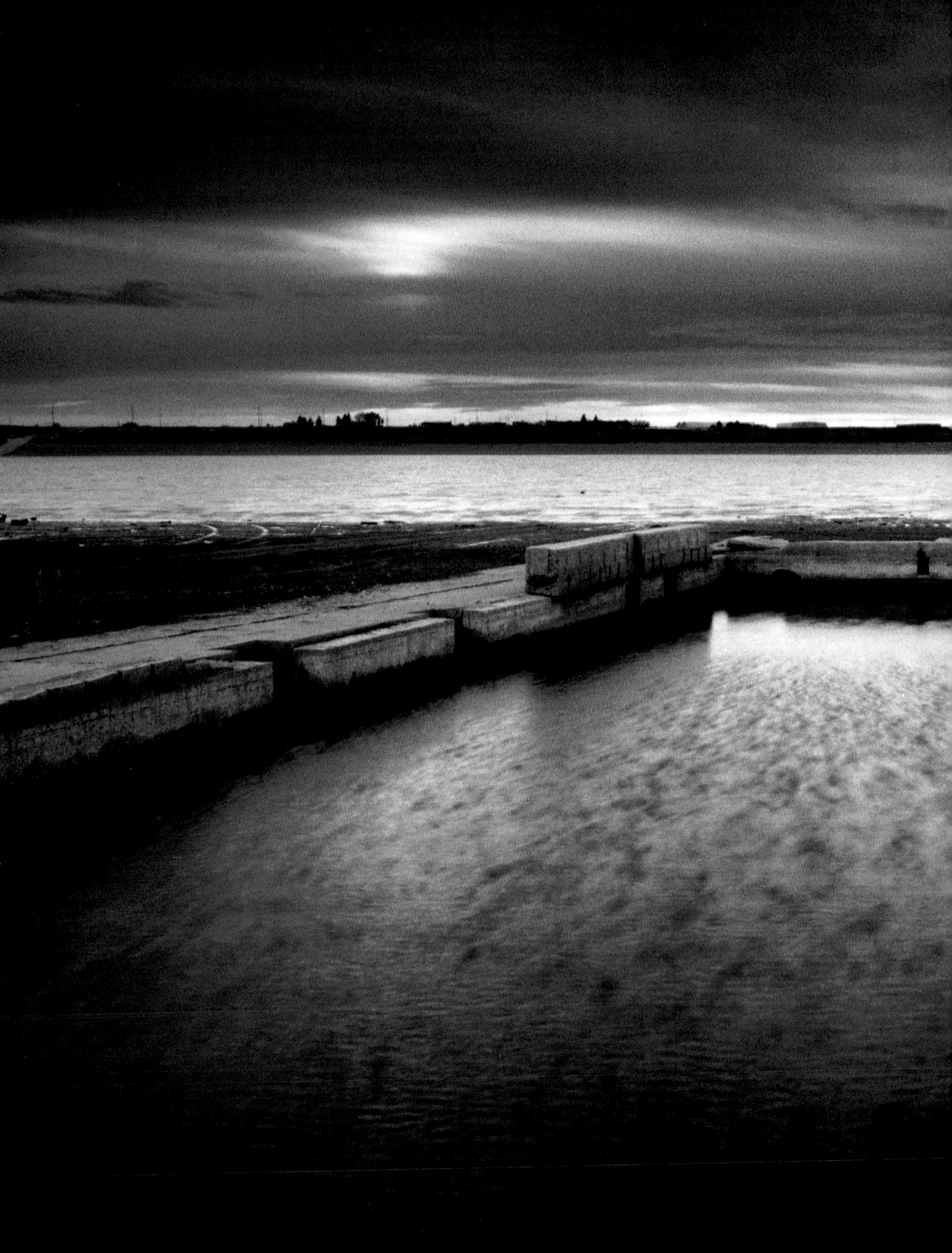

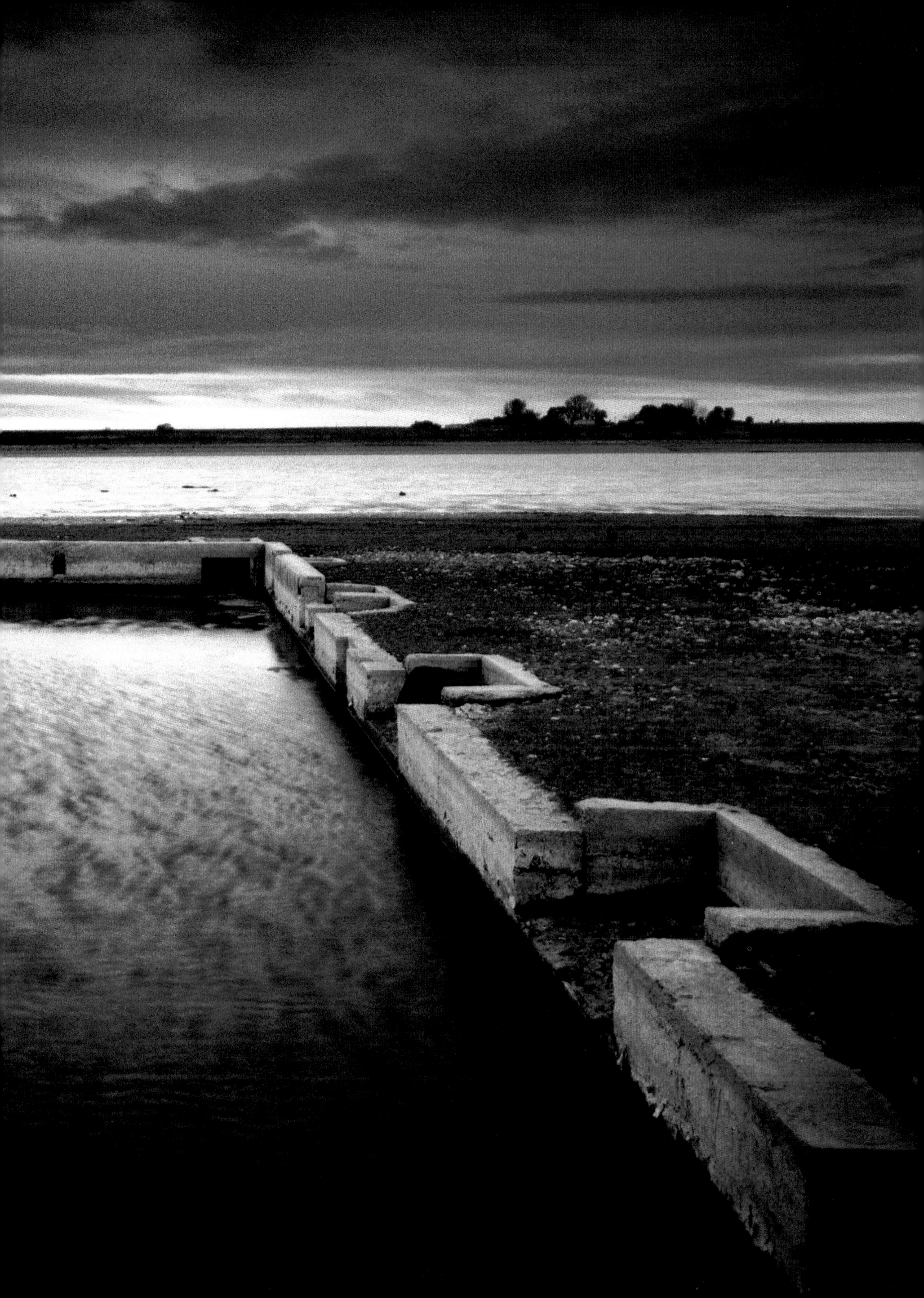

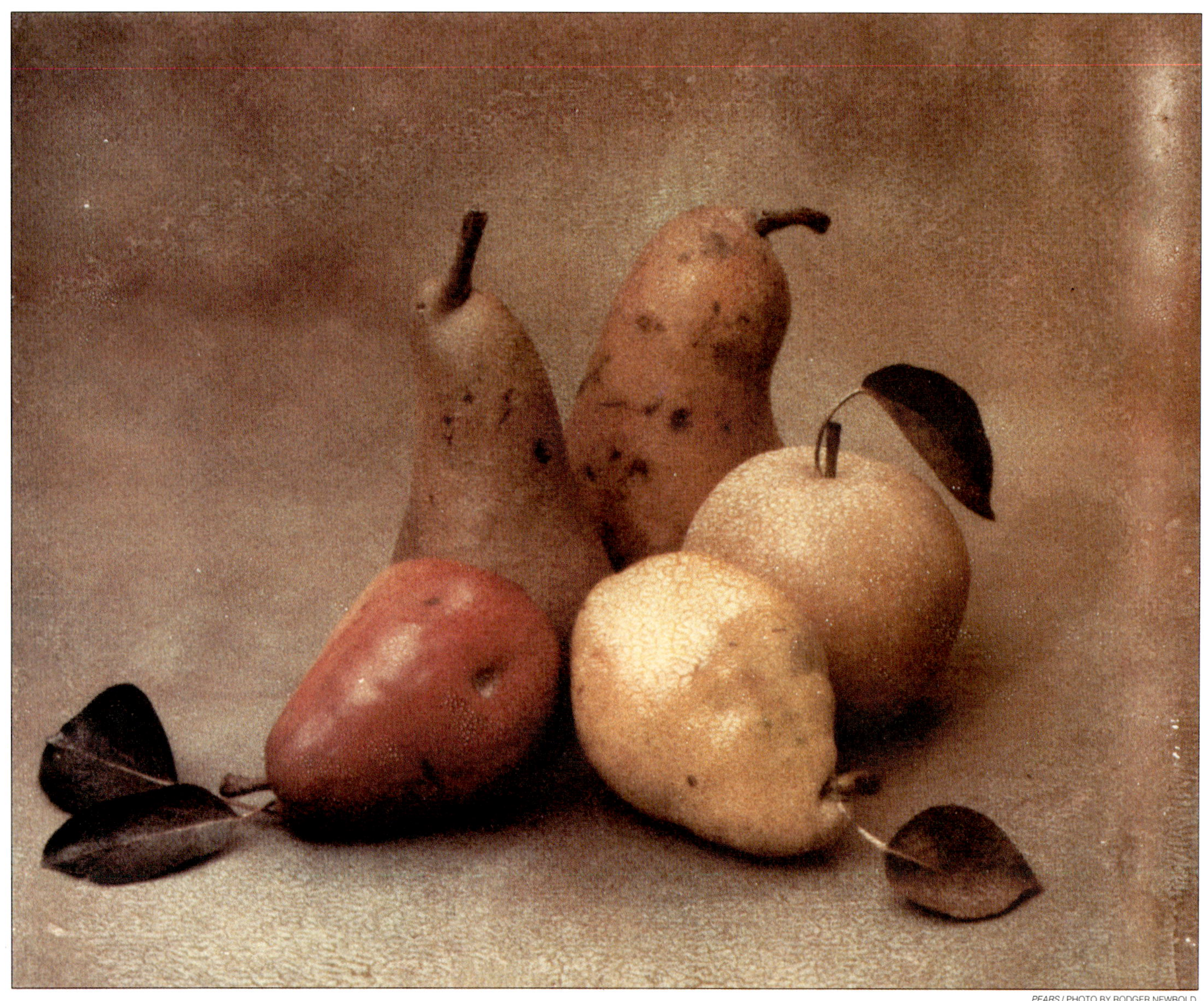

PEARS / PHOTO BY RODGER NEWBOLD

way to soft, impressionistic, imaginative prints that could not be duplicated by the army of hand-camera Sunday snapshooters.

All of this is important as we look at the current state of the art in Utah photography, because in a loose definition, contemporary photography follows criteria established by this rift between *serious* formal photographers and loosely structured *snapshot* photographers. To agree with the Gernsheims that the hand-held camera put an end to serious photography would be to disregard the vast body of spontaneous photographs produced by the 35mm camera, the contemporary version of Eastman's invention. All of the work inspired by photographers from Jacque-Henri Lartique and Henri Cartier-Bresson to Robert Frank, Lee Friedlander, and others of the street photographers would have to be labeled as insignificant and be summarily dismissed. Unthinkable!

More important is the under-standing of precedents and criteria that define the different styles of contemporary photography. The well-founded, easily accessible landscape photographs of Ansel Adams follow the tradition established by the *view* makers, serious art Pictorialists, and the large-format Group f.64 photographers, including Edward Weston, Wynn Bullock, Minor White and Paul Caponigro. The less formal Conceptualist, Postmodernist, spontaneous photographers follow a tradition established by the so-called amateur snapshooters. For many, their work is harder to understand and appreciate. On one hand, the photographs are emotionally felt; on the other, they are cerebrally deciphered.

Naturally, a great deal of cross-fertilization has taken place between these two extremes. For example, Alfred Stieglitz, the renowned leader of the Photo Secession, used a hand-held camera for much of the work he did in New York. But the criteria and philosophy established by these two opposite camera camps are still evident in photography, including Utah photography.

William Mortenson, a leading spokesman for the Pictorialists, taught at East High School in Salt Lake City for a short time before moving to San Francisco, where he engaged in a colorful editorial word battle with Ansel Adams in *Camera Craft Magazine* over the divergent philosophies of the dying Pictorial and growing f.64 movements (f.64 referred to the smallest aperture in the camera lens and was associated with extreme sharpness, articulated detail, and maximum depth of field).

The influence and philosophy of William Mortenson and the Pictorialists can easily be seen in the work of Utah photographers George Midgley (1882-1979) and Ray and Marie Kirkland of Bountiful. The beautifully crafted bromoil transfers made by these master printers represent not only the aesthetic philosophy of the Pictorialist movement but also a nearly impossible, and nearly extinct, printing process. Having won hundreds of awards for his bromoils, ninety-one-year-old Ray Kirkland is now one of the last living bromoil photographers in the world. "I'm working harder than ever now," he says, as he prints from more than fifty years of negatives for an upcoming exhibition. "I'm learning a lot and getting better all the time."

Twenty years ago, art photography was nearly unknown in Utah. Only minimal programs were available in college curricula, and then only photojournalism or hobby-type courses were taught. Serious photography was rarely exhibited, and collecting photographs as art was unheard of. The Edison Street Gallery in Salt Lake City was the first gallery exclusively devoted to exhibiting photographs. From 1972 to 1976, many young

CRAIG LAW

Craig Law, one of Utah's most prolific and accomplished photographers, is well recognized in many parts of the country. Born and reared in Cache Valley, he has distinguished himself since 1978 as a member of Utah State University's faculty.

His photographic accomplishments include more than eighty exhibits (from Taipei to Paris, and Utah, too) with jurors' and purchase awards in twenty of those. He is included in fifteen permanent collections. His photographs are exclusively black and white: gelatin silver, platinum, gravure and carbon, for which he is recognized as one of the nation's leading practitioners.

Law's extensive body of eloquent and sensitive human figure work is augmented with his large-format landscape photographs, full of light and the essence of the precious metals with which he prints.

From the landforms of the *City of Rocks* to the *Waterways of the Arid West*, Law exhibits a gentle sensitivity to the land and concern of its use. *Waterways of the Arid West* and *Indian Rock Art* are current projects.

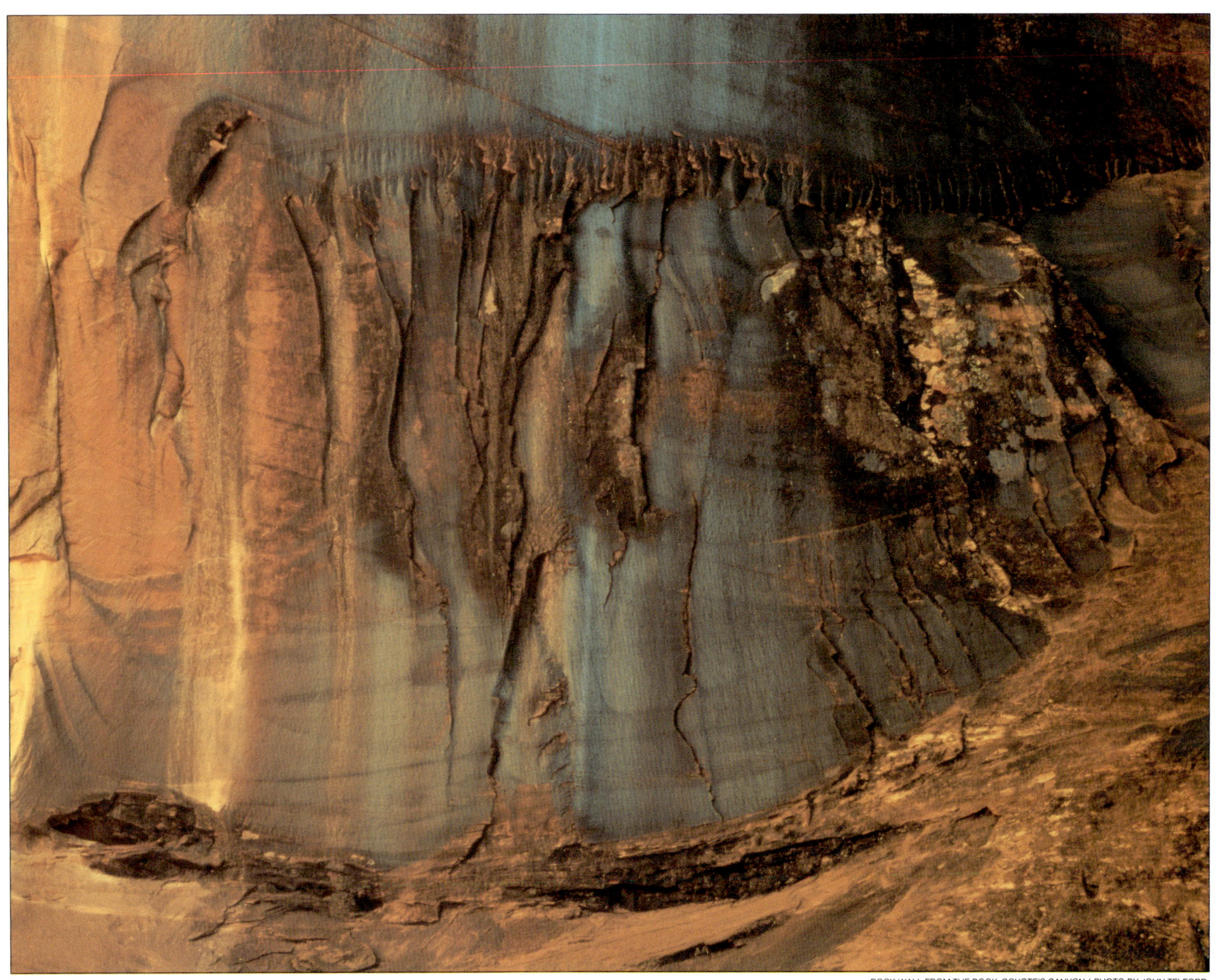

ROCK WALL FROM THE BOOK *COYOTE'S CANYON* / PHOTO BY JOHN TELFORD

photographers saw their first original Ansel Adams, Edward Weston, Imogen Cunningham and Eliot Porter prints on the walls of this small two-room gallery. The first juried photographic competition in Utah, with Wynn Bullock as juror, was sponsored by the Edison Street Gallery. The first photography workshops in Utah were also sponsored by the gallery, and many of today's top Utah photographers were first exhibited there.

It is easy to see that a state dominated by its landscape is dominated by landscape photography. Ansel Adams, Minor White, Eliot Porter and many others found inspiration in Utah.

And now the best contemporary landscape photographers from all over the country—all over the world—come to Utah to photograph. Judy Dater, in writing a juror's statement to Utah '86 Photography, said, "The landscape was the major theme, not surprising in an environment so rich in visual beauty." In his 1990 juror's statement, Gary Faye echoed those feelings: "Words like beautiful are truly inadequate." Even in 1992, juror John Pfahl wrote, "I would venture a guess that regular infusion of the renowned Utah landscape would bring even the most torpid photographer to attention. It was certainly a pleasure to see the framed evidence of such a fertile environment."

However, the overpowering landscape has also been the grounds for criticism of Utah photography. Bill Jay, Utah '88's juror, wrote, "In Utah photography, there is . . . a heavy emphasis on work that is emotional, instinctive and, yes, blatantly pictorial." He also pointed out a lack of "intellectual lines of photographic inquiry," noting that "Marxism, racism, etc.; street photography dealing with the human condition, its foibles and failings; or even many works which explore the areas which overlap ink painting, printmaking, and the other visual arts" were missing. He also observed that, "On the map of international photography, Utah is still labeled terra incognita. Even with the fine-mesh network of contemporary American photography, Utah remains a black hole on the grid." Judy Dater noted the "conspicuous absence of Post-modernism, appropriation, and deconstruction" in Utah photography. John Pfahl complained that Utah photographers ". . . left out a vast range of responses to life, culture, and events in today's world. Such intense and ever-present issues as homelessness, environmental pollution and AIDS seem not to have entered the collective conscience of these photographers at all. It was as if they couldn't see the forest for the (aspen) trees. The political theories and arguments that give such energy to the work of photographers in other parts of the country seem barely to have rippled the surfaces of this beautiful work."

Each nationally recognized juror from the last four Utah Photography exhibitions recognized, however, that photography is "alive and well in Utah." The high quality of craft was applauded, and the diversity of processes as well as the broad range of ideas, vision, and trends was noted. Bill Jay concluded his 1988 statement with: "Fortunately, for me, I can indeed state with all honesty that there is no paucity of photographic talent in Utah and that the standard of work is, in truth, of high caliber. You have known it for some time. Now I know it. How about letting the rest of the country know it."

Included in this well-kept secret of highly recognized Utah talent are con-

UTAH PHOTOGRAPHY

Utah photography is more visible today than ever before. Photography is frequently shown at the Salt Lake Art Center, Utah Museum of Fine Art, BYU's new Museum of Fine Art and other public and private galleries. Many of Utah's photographers are represented by the leading and most progressive galleries.

All of the major universities in the state offer degrees in photography, and workshops and seminars on numerous photographic topics and techniques are offered by several public and private organizations.

These photographers hold the Professional Photographers of America master's degree and are recognized nationally and/or internationally for the craft of portrait photography: Don Blair, D. Gary Blair, Linda Boyd, Don Busath, Drake Busath, Bill Duncan, Alan Gibby and David Newman. Ken Miles' fine documentary style defies classification.

SUSAN MAKOV

Like many Utahns, Susan Makov came here by choice, from Long Island, New York. She is a full professor at Weber State University, where she has been teaching photography and printmaking for the past fifteen years. Makov's mixed-media prints, in which she paints on either black-and-white or color photographs, are her most recognized work. Photographing ordinary indoor scenes from "unordinary" vantage points, with lenses that distort and exaggerate perspective, she then applies vibrant color with a myriad media to complete the energetic pieces.

Recently, Makov has been creating two-dimensional photographs which she incorporates into three-dimensional pieces inspired by New Mexican Santeros (saint makers). "While dealing with the form of these artists," Makov says, "I have invented my own saints. .... St. Agatha's breasts were cut off because she would not marry. I have used this motif as a saint against breast cancer."

Makov is working on a guidebook of Southwest trading posts due for publication in 1994.

temporary photographers Craig Law, who Bill Jay pointed out as being "as accomplished as any [photographer] of the genre which I have seen anywhere in the world;" Susan Makov, whose mixed-media photographs challenge the viewer with creative exploration of subject matter as well as presentation; and Barbara Richards, whose silvery landscapes glow with sensitivity and who more recently has included the computer to further explore and manipulate her vision. With reluctance and repidation, but at the insistence of other photographers and curators, the author includes his own name on this list of Utah photographers. David Pursley, Salt Lake Art Center curator of education, writes: "John Telford is one of a small handful of Utah's premier landscape photographers."

The list of contemporary Utah photographers would not be complete without Richard Burton, whose black-and-white photographs of the Great Salt Lake and color photographs of Utah's Highway 89 show a contemporary insight into the social landscape; John Schaefer, recent recipient of the Mayor's Award and director and co-founder of The Children's Photographic Workshop; Erica Wangsgard, whose distinctive style of applied color photographic prints reveals vivid color patterns derived from unlikely natural subject matter; Roger Newbold, landscape photographer and teacher, who

has recently turned his attention to computer-assisted prints from aerial photographs which are then further altered with Prismacolor pencils; Brent Herridge, the prominent portrait photographer who organized and curated the highly visible photography exhibits in the Salt Lake City Airport; Ed Rosenberger, who was featured in Polaroid's *Test* magazine for his large Polaroid transfer collage prints; John Rees, recent BYU graduate, whose mixed-media pieces have explored and challenged the cultural icons that have shaped his life; and no fewer than thirty additional photographers altogether. The styles of these photographers are what really describes the current "State of the Art" in Utah photography— eclectic and diverse: from the large-format black-and-white and color landscape work to the photograph as a point of departure with applied color, transferred, or digitized; from politically charged work that confronts social issues to mixed-media pieces that explore cultural issues and icons.

The diversity of processes is also strong. Traditional gelatin silver black-and-white prints of very high quality are current in Utah photography, as well as non-silver prints of platinum, carbon and iron salts. Color photographs ranging from Cibachrome and traditional chromogenic prints are frequently seen,

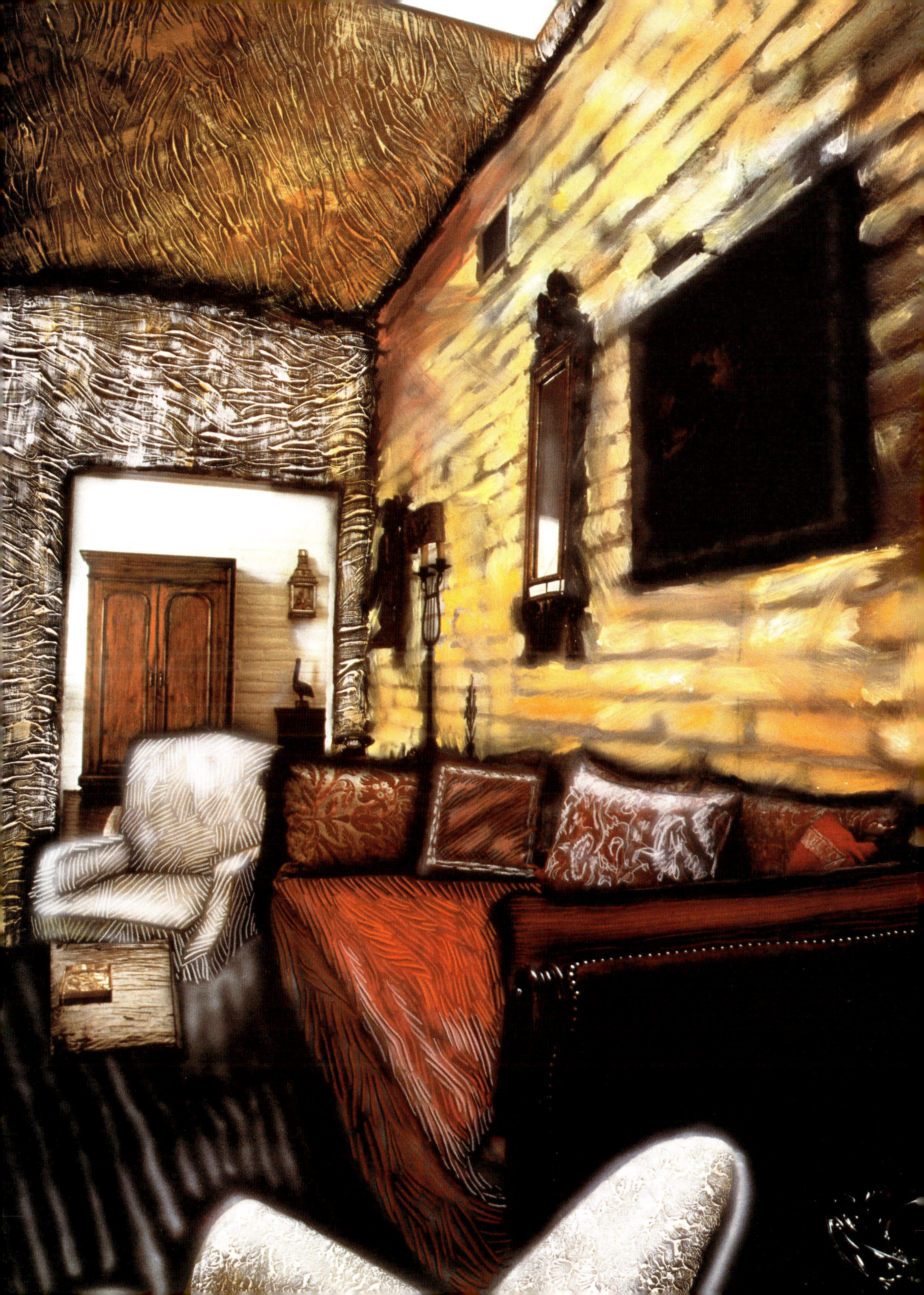

as well as Polaroid transfers and other manipulated and cross-processed prints.

In writing about Utah photography, David Pursley of the Salt Lake Art Center says:

Utah photographic art has grown significantly since the early years of C. R. Savage and George Edward Anderson. Our heritage has been the unique character of our population and our even more unique environment. Our land has been our identity and, consequently, the photographic imagery produced here has been very connected to it. However, in recent years we have seen a significant divergence of subject matter, style, and content entering the work of contemporary artists. There are several factors for this; one being the proliferation of national photographic publications offered which will include a variety of photographic styles, the abundance of photographic programs offered on the college and community level, and finally the change in creative sensibilities towards the photographic milieu of our times. This coupled with the number of opportunities for the photographic education with a variety of artists has expanded the perceptions and possibilities of photographic use. Lastly, artists are seeing photography as one more method in communicating their ideas. Therefore, photographs are being included in paintings and sculptural works as well as taking on, less and less, a monocular view of the world. This is a very exciting time for art and especially photography in Utah.

Digital photography represents the first major change in photography almost since its inception. Certainly not since the invention of color photography has so much excitement over change and potential in the medium been evident. The marriage of the camera and the computer presents to photographers a freedom of expression that has hitherto been very difficult if not impossible. Barbara Richards is but one of many Utah photographers exploring this new method of visual expression.

As talented new photographers continue to mature, Utah photography will continue to grow in its eclectic diversity. In some areas of the country, photography is accused of being exhausted, consumed, and used up. All that can be done, according to some critics, has been done, as evidenced by some photographers turning to historic themes and processes. The nice thing about living in "terra incognita" is that Utah photographers don't know it yet and continue to produce high-quality, expressive, and explorative images with their cameras.

Our land
has been our
I D E N T I T Y
and we experience
it with our images.

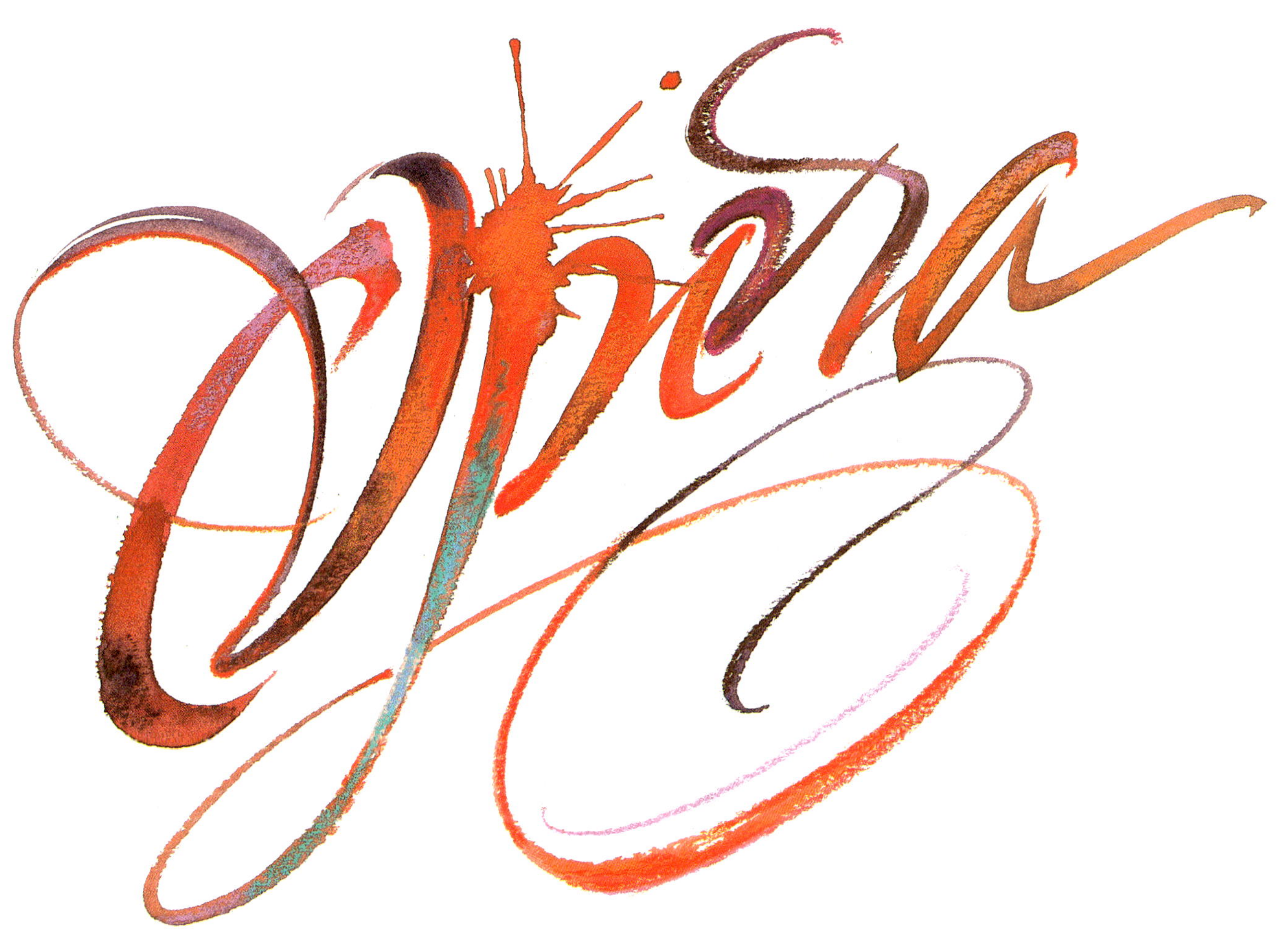

**Opera Scales
the Heights
in Utah**

Dorothy Stowe

NESTLED AT THE foot of the towering Wasatch Mountains, Salt Lake City enjoys its own operatic setting, worthy of Puccini's *Girl of the Golden West* or Moore's *Ballad of Baby Doe.*

And the city has opera to match its mountains, produced by the thriving Utah Opera Company, which offered its first performances in 1977. Since 1978 the company has been resident in the Capitol Theatre, a spacious permanent home seating nearly 1,900, which opened in the 1920's as an elaborate venue of the Orpheum vaudeville circuit. The Capitol was restored to its original beauty with funding by a Bicentennial bond issued in 1975.

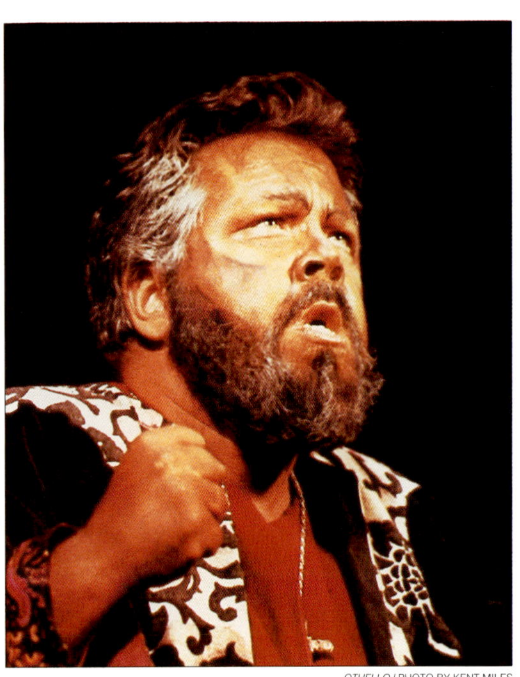
OTHELLO / PHOTO BY KENT MILES

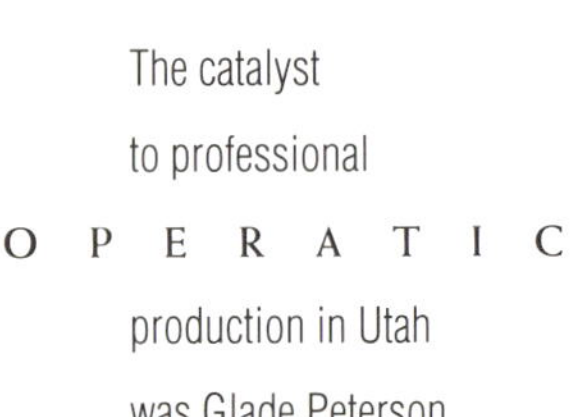

A member of OPERA America, the company is among the fastest growing in the country. Indeed, Utah Opera is a regional treasure, with three productions a year, a thriving subscription base, enthusiastic audiences from throughout Utah and neighboring states, and firm financial support.

In October 1992, Verdi's *Un Ballo in Maschera* sold out all five performances, a not-uncommon occurrence for the company; and in January 1993, all tickets for Puccini's *Madama Butterfly* were gone two weeks before it opened!

The catalyst to professional operatic production in Utah was Glade Peterson, who returned to his native state with a burning desire to produce big-time opera. Born a farm boy in Fairfield, he left Utah to become leading tenor with the Zurich (Switzerland) Opera for twelve years and guest at many other European houses.

Peterson's experiences and executive savvy, coupled with a good measure of old-style Western grit, proved sufficient to launch Utah Opera. Never much of a diplomat, he antagonized many. But with heartfelt dedication and tireless effort, he made friends and devotees who respected what he was attempting and threw in their moral and financial support.

Besides singing tenor leads in several early company productions, Peterson became widely recognized as Mr. Utah Opera, particularly at Salt Lake City's Days of '47 Pioneer Day, where he rode a handsome Arabian with silver saddle and trappings in the parade and sang the national anthem to open the rodeo.

Opera first appeared in Utah more than a century ago, in the old Salt Lake Theatre—a unique ornament of the Old West which early demonstrated the Mormon pioneers' dedication to culture. Begun in 1861 and finished in 1862, with Grecian façade and seating for 1,500 in parquet and four circles, the theater was declared by many visitors to be the equal of opera houses in the country's populous eastern cities. All this in a raw frontier settlement of 20,000 souls.

With the coming of the transcontinental railroad in 1869, the theater became a regular stop for touring dramatic and musical attractions; these and frequent presentations by local talent kept the house lighted some twenty nights a month.

A listing of late nineteenth-century programs at the Salt Lake Theatre mentions several opera companies—almost all, surprisingly enough, run by women. The Martha Stephens Grand Opera, Emma Jack's Grand English Opera, Frances Wilson Opera of New York, W. T. Carleton Opera, Della Fox Comic Opera Company and Lydia Thompson and Her English Company performed many light operas. Nor did they blanch at bringing such heavyweights as *Mignon*, *Il Trovatore*, *Faust* and even Wagner's *Tannhäuser*.

With the sale of the theater and lot to Mountain States Telephone and Telegraph in 1928, an era closed. But talented Utahns continued to provide opera for themselves, often outside in the summer. During the 1920's the Salt Lake Civic Opera thrived on a diet of operettas by Herbert, Friml and Romberg. The stage was in Nibley Park, overhanging the pond, with Spencer Cornwall (later director of the Mormon Tabernacle Choir) conducting. In 1939 a now-legendary production of *Aida* took place on the Park Building steps, sponsored by the University of Utah music department.

In 1947 Maurice Abravanel arrived to shape and conduct the Utah Symphony. Among his accomplishments was an illustrious background in music theater conducting—on Broadway, in Europe and at the Metropolitan Opera. For twelve golden summers (1948-60), he led opera under the stars in the University of Utah stadium, with major national guest artists such as the fledgling Beverly Sills, Robert Rounseville, Charles Kullman, Ralph Herbert, Elaine Malbin and Dorothy Sarnoff.

With the demise of this series, opera moved indoors at the university under two auspices, both headed by Ardean Watts—the opera workshop and the University of Utah Opera Company. Each produced two or three operas a year, including popular standards and substantial modern works. The present Utah Opera, fully independent, is an outgrowth of this university program.

Utah Opera currently presents three operas in five performances each, including a Sunday matinee. The orchestra (members of the Utah Symphony) is led by well-known national conductors, while on stage are expert singers of the country's regional circuit—many of whom are about to break through to the top—and an occasional Metropolitan Opera star.

Utah Opera-goers have seen Aprile Millo, now a leading soprano of the Met, sing her first *Aida* (and her first full-length performance on any stage).

ARDEAN WATTS

Among his dozens of hats, from 1965 to 1978 Ardean Watts wore those of founder, artistic director, producer and conductor of the University of Utah Opera Company. Based in Kingsbury Hall, the company staged three productions a year, moments that remain magical in memory.

A Renaissance man of boundless energy, Watts had his own jazz band before joining the University of Utah music faculty, where he taught: opera workshop, chorus, orchestra, theory, computer composition. He chaired the dance department, conducted Ballet West performances, worked on summer operas with Maurice Abravanel, and served as associate conductor of the Utah Symphony. Abravanel considered him "my right arm."

His interests include cooking and mushrooming, botany and bird watching, roller-skating adventures, his loving wife Elna, and eight diversely talented children. Retiring from the university in 1993, Watts took over chairmanship of the Utah Arts Council.

They have enjoyed Metropolitan Opera artists Kallen Esperian as Mimi and Donna Anna; Martina Arroyo as Butterfly; Roberta Peters as Lucia, Violetta, and the Merry Widow; Cynthia Munzer as Azucena and Amneris; Elizabeth Holleque as Tosca, Ariel Bybee as Dorabella; Natalia Rom as Desdemona; and Giorgio Tozzi as Gianni Schicchi.

Other guests of outstanding national note are Frances Ginsberg, Dan Bernardini, Greer Grimsley, Kay Paschal, George Gray, Hans Gregory Ashbaker (a native Idahoan), Rico Serbo, Jake Gardner, Cynthia Clarey and Pamela South.

With Glade Peterson's untimely death in April 1990, the opera board despaired of finding a man to take his place, so settled instead upon a woman—Anne Ewers, a prominent stage director of opera in the U.S. and Canada and former director of the Boston Lyric Opera. She now also serves on the board of OPERA America.

Ewers is in close touch with the national operatic scene, well aware of who's hot among singers, directors, conductors and stage designers. She continues her own directing career on a reduced scale and brings abundant enthusiasm to her adopted state. "I love it!" is among her favorite expressions.

Responsible for much magic at Utah Opera is costumer Susan Memmot-Allred, raised in tiny Scipio, who has been here since the company's inception. Again and again visiting artists applaud the beauty of her costumes and request to rent them for other performances. Allred has established a profitable costume rental sideline which enriches the opera coffers by $25,000 or more a year.

Coincidentally, Ewers has surrounded herself with a staff of women, including music director Lynn Jemison-Keisker; publicist Judith Frisbie-Goins; Darleen Merrihew, who has fund-raising responsibilities; and Leslie and Michelle Peterson, daughters of Glade Peterson. Now director of operations, Leslie Peterson assisted her father for years and was interim acting general manager between his death and Ewers' appointment. Michelle Peterson serves as production manager. Utah Opera is budgeted around $1.7 million annually and operates consistently in the black.

The early settlers of Utah survived rigors of the trail and hardscrabble homesteading to produce a progeny blessed with an abundance of healthy, beautiful voices. Good teachers and training also abound in the state, and local auditions of the Metropolitan Opera and San Francisco Opera locate many fine talents, some of whom move on to national prominence. Among these are Salt Lake-born tenor Stanford Olsen, who now stars at the Met, and soprano Linda Kelm, a Valkyrie at the Met, who has sung Brünnhilde in Seattle.

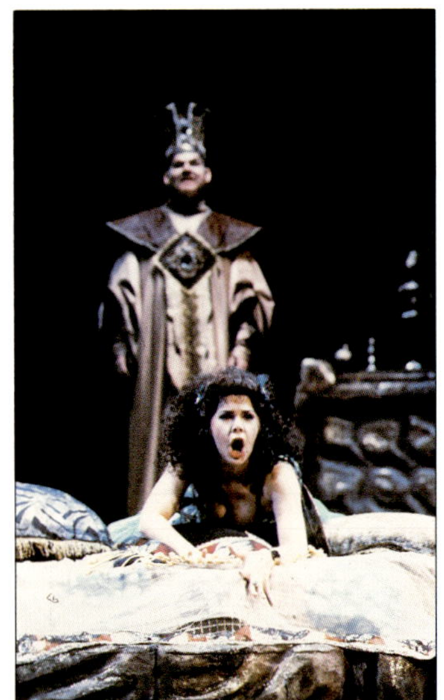

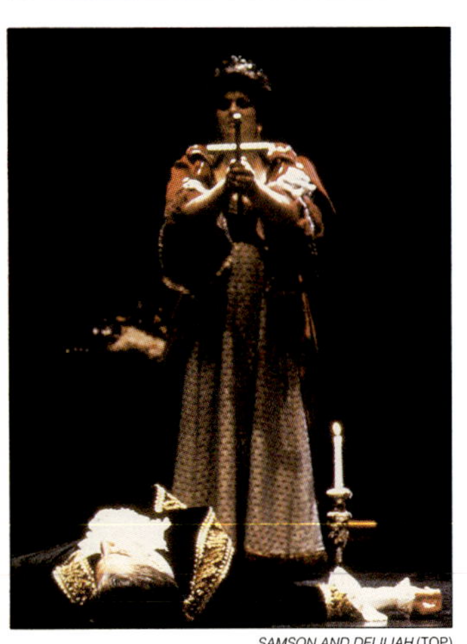

SAMSON AND DELILIAH (TOP)
TOSCA (BOTTOM) / PHOTOS BY ROBERT CLAYTON

ith aid from the National Endowment for the Arts, Utah Opera sponsors a young artists program, taking a contingent of five or six talented singers, in two sessions a year, for training in all aspects of the professional operatic art. These young singers regularly perform *comprimario* roles in mainstage productions, often working with such Utah professionals as nationally renowned JoAnn Ottley, who has thrilled local audiences as the Queen of the Night, Violetta, and Lucia.

Utah students get a sampling of opera's fun as well as its beauty through Utah Opera in the Schools, funded by the Utah State Legislature. Utah singers tour mini-productions to 80,000 students a year, performing for every child in the Utah school system from kindergarten through high school at least once in every four years.

This may involve two hours of travel over dirt roads to an outpost with ten children and a teaching principal. "They often urge us to stay longer, to invite the townspeople to come," says Darleen Merrihew, who has been with the company from the beginning. "We can go where the Symphony can't go, and they love us!"

The Opera also does as many as ten three-day residencies in Utah schools annually, tracing the making of an opera in all aspects, right up to its stage performance. Such grassroots exertions give a clue as to why the audience for Utah Opera is exceptionally young in comparison with supporters in most locales.

mong Utah universities, Brigham Young University consistently displays excellence in producing good student opera, with annual productions of such major works as Mozart's *Magic Flute*, Verdi's *Falstaff*, and the Puccini masterworks.

MICHAEL BALLAM

International tenor Michael Ballam, born and raised in River Heights near Logan, is a graduate of Utah State University with a doctorate in music from the University of Indiana (1976). Ballam went on to sing with more than seventy opera companies, including the likes of Chicago Lyric, San Francisco, Santa Fe, Philadelphia, Washington, St. Louis, Kentucky and Michigan operas, among many others. As a recitalist singing a mix of musical comedy, opera arias and religious music, charismatic Ballam generates magic nationally and locally.

Since joining Utah State's music faculty in 1988, Ballam has earned the University's Excellence in Teaching Award (1992). He was also the catalyst for the restoration of the Ellen Eccles Theatre in downtown Logan.

Ballam is now helping to fill that theater, with performances by the Utah Festival Opera Company, of which he is artistic director. Following a successful 1993 season, he projects three productions each summer with emphasis on attracting the many seasonal residents drawn to northern Utah's cool mountains, canyons and lakes.

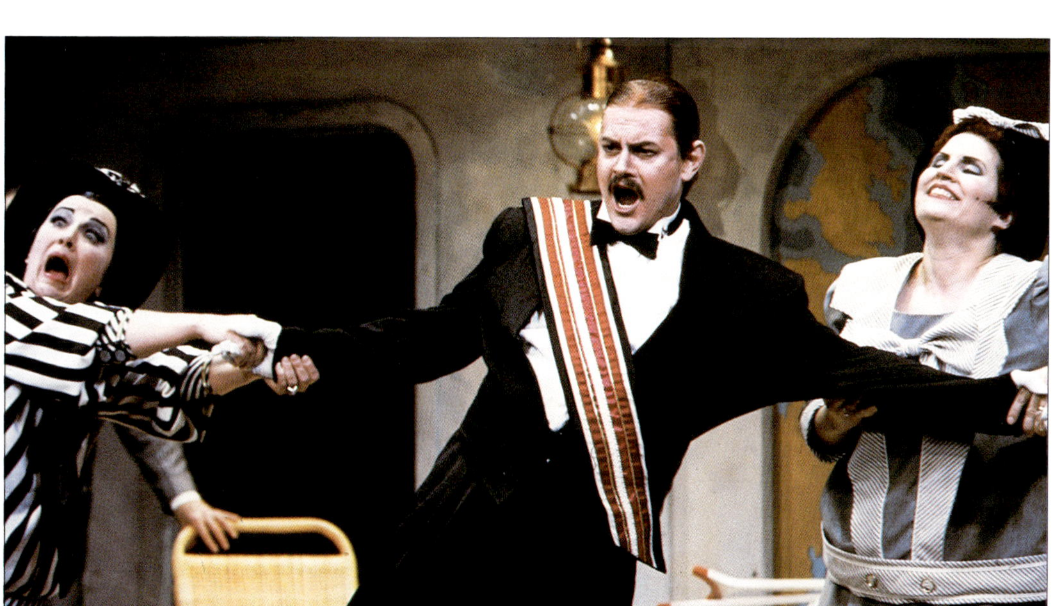

CINDERELLA / PHOTO BY ROBERT CLAYTON

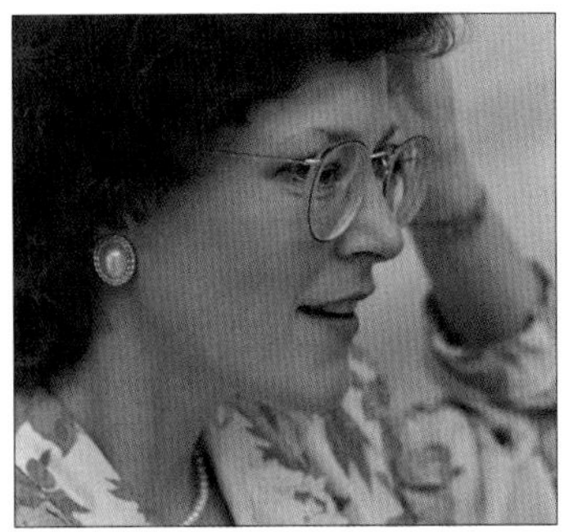

Anne Ewers and Utah Opera make a perfect fit. Raised in Illinois, a graduate of the University of Texas at Austin, she worked for a time at San Francisco Opera and lived nine years in Boston, staging opera throughout the United States and Canada. From 1984 to 1989, she was general director of Boston Lyric Opera.

With the death of Glade Peterson, Ewers was on the short list for personal interviews. It was love at first sight. "The minute I got off the plane, saw those mountains, and met the people, I knew this was the place for me," she says.

A slight, dynamic young woman who exudes almost palpable enthusiasm, Ewers aims to present the standard works as well as operas of the central repertory not seen here before. She's proud of her work with the hearing impaired and of the Utah Opera's Young Artists Training Program, subsidized by the National Endowment for the Arts. Ewers stages for other opera companies as time permits. She serves on the executive committee of OPERA America's board of directors.

Those who wish to sing a little themselves might try the Salt Lake Opera Theatre, with dedicated Bob Zabriskie as artistic director and conductor of talented amateurs who produce sometimes erratic, sometimes brilliant homegrown opera.

The small city of Logan, located in Utah's scenic Cache Valley, shows promise of emerging as a summer opera center under the aegis of the recently restored Ellen Eccles Theater. There the Utah Festival Opera Company produced three opera programs in the summer of 1993, with an impressive subscription ticket sale, including many out-of-state patrons.

Behind this ambitious project is Utah tenor Michael Ballam, a veteran of the regional scene in America, who has come home to teach at Utah State University in Logan while still concertizing and singing opera nationally.

Ballam has quickly tuned in to the potential for artistic growth provided by thousands of summer visitors from California and elsewhere, who descend *en force* to spend the hot months in cool, beautiful Cache Valley. "We can have culture here and now which we couldn't have dreamed of five years ago," says Ballam. His support comes from private donors, a strong board of directors, Utah State University and investors.

Ballam's plan is dependent upon summer production, when he can line up major singers and conductors of his acquaintance to come for reduced fees, with the added attraction of a free vacation in Cache Valley. Fred Adams of the Utah Shakespearean Festival, a member of Utah Festival Opera's board, joins Ballam in supporting the concept of enticing visitors to the state for a week, not just a weekend.

Opera in Utah came into existence and continues its robust growth thanks to a few giants—Maurice Abravanel, Ardean Watts, Glade Peterson, Anne Ewers—but, even more, thanks to an enlightened citizenry who love and support this most all-inclusive of the arts.

Growing demand for professional opera tickets, proliferation of community productions, development of Utah's fine natural talent, the sound of a recorded aria drifting on the evening air—all these signs betoken a state that gives more than lip service to its love of opera.

The people, events and works identified here are those which appear in the text of this book and which, for a period of time however brief have called Utah their home. Authors, as authorities in their respective fields, compiled their material to support the focus they identified as pertinent to the discipline they were invited to discuss by the arts advisory committee.

Meridian International, Inc. and the Salt Lake Area Chamber of Commerce recognize that many vital people and activities serving to enrich the Utah arts scene were not included by the selected authors. They are no less important for not having been included in *Utah, State of the Arts.*

Caroll Shreeve

INDEX